YĀMUNA'S VEDĀNTA AND PĀÑCARĀTRA: INTEGRATING THE CLASSICAL AND THE POPULAR

HARVARD THEOLOGICAL REVIEW
HARVARD DISSERTATIONS IN RELIGION

edited by
Caroline Bynum
and
George Rupp

Number 10

YĀMUNA'S VEDĀNTA AND PĀÑCARĀTRA: INTEGRATING THE CLASSICAL AND THE POPULAR

by
Walter G. Neevel, Jr.

SCHOLARS PRESS
Missoula, Montana

YĀMUNA'S VEDĀNTA AND PĀÑCARĀTRA: INTEGRATING THE CLASSICAL AND THE POPULAR

by

Walter G. Neevel, Jr.

Published by
SCHOLARS PRESS
for
Harvard Theological Review

Distributed by

SCHOLARS PRESS
University of Montana
Missoula, Montana 59812

YĀMUNA'S VEDĀNTA AND PĀÑCARĀTRA: INTEGRATING THE CLASSICAL AND THE POPULAR

by
Walter G. Neevel, Jr.
University of Wisconsin—Milwaukee
Milwaukee, Wisconsin 53201

Library of Congress Cataloging in Publication Data

Neevel, Walter G., Jr.
Yāmuna's Vedānta and Pāñcarātra.

(Harvard dissertations in religion ; no. 10)
Bibliography: p.
1. Vedanta. 2. Yāmunācārya. 3. Pāñcarātra.
4. Philosophy, Hindu.
I. Title. II. Series.
B132.V3N4 181'.48 77-4048
ISBN 0-89130-136-4

Printed in the United States of America
1 2 3 4 5
Printing Department
University of Montana
Missoula, Montana 59812

TABLE OF CONTENTS

Preface ix

Abbreviations xv

PART ONE: THE INTEGRATION OF VEDĀNTA AND PĀÑCARĀTRA WITHIN THE ŚRĪ VAIṢṆAVA TRADITION

Chapter I. Introduction 3

Chapter II. The Relation of the Classical Vedānta and the Popular Pāñcarātra 17

Chapter III. The Āgama-Prāmāṇya: Yāmuna's Defense of the Pañcarātra Revelation 29

Chapter IV. Yāmuna and His Vedāntic Sources 55

A. In the Āgama-Prāmāṇya 56

B. In the Ātma-Siddhi: 66

The "Commentator" and the Bhagavān Śrīvatsāṅka Miśra

Chapter V. Nāthamuni and Yāmuna: The Early Śrī Vaiṣṇava Teachers as Integrators of the Classical and the Popular 77

PART TWO: YĀMUNA'S VEDĀNTA

Chapter VI. The Ātma-Siddhi: Breaking the Code

A. Introduction: Critical Problems in the Analysis of the Extant Text 97

B. The Recovery of the Structure and Argument of the Extant Text 105

Chapter VII. The Siddhāntas or Conclusions of Yāmuna's Vedānta: 149

The Introduction to the Ātma-Siddhi (The Sanskrit Text and an Annotated Translation) 150

Chapter VIII. Yāmuna's Pāñcarātrika Vedānta: The Svarūpa/Svabhāva Distinction and Relation as an Integrating Principle 169

Appendix I. Nāthamuni as Reflected in Yāmuna's Works 195

Appendix II. Correlation of the Extant Text of the Ātma-Siddhi 203

Appendix III. Structure of the Pratijñā Series of the *Ātma-Siddhi* 207

Appendix IV. Concordance of the Editions of the *Āgama-Prāmāṇya* 211

Notes 215

Bibliography 291

For Mary Ann

and

For our Indian Friends

and Fellow Students

That our Separate Histories

might become

our Common Heritage

PREFACE

The Hindu tradition is one of the oldest continuous religious traditions; it is also one of the most varied, flexible and adaptable. This work is a study of the integrative process whereby the ancient classical Vedic tradition has maintained its continuity, viability and integrity while adapting itself to new eras through the incorporation of vibrant popular movements. As a study in intellectual history, it focuses upon the relation of the major Vedic or Brāhmanic intellectual tradition, Vedānta, to one of the most important of these popular Bhakti or devotional movements, the Pāñcarātra Tāntric tradition of theistic, temple-oriented religious practice or ritual, and, especially in Part One, upon the integration of Vedānta and Pāñcarātra within the Śrī Vaiṣṇava sectarian movement.

This study is based primarily upon the incompletely preserved literary corpus of Yāmuna, the "teacher's teacher" (paramācārya) of the more well known Rāmānuja and the first representative of the Śrī Vaiṣṇava Viśiṣṭādvaita school of Vedānta for whom we have extant texts. Yāmuna was a Poet-Philosopher who combined dialectical skill and epistemological sophistication with poetic sensitivity and a practical concern for basic human and religious problems. His preserved literary corpus is a rich and varied one, including two devotional hymns (the Stotra-ratna and the Catuśślokī or Śrī-stuti) and the brief but exceedingly influential verse summary of the Bhagavad Gītā entitled the Gītārthasaṃgraha as well as four philosophical works, the Āgama-prāmāṇya, in which he defends the Pañcarātra Āgama or revelation, and his three fragmentarily preserved Vedāntic works, Ātma-siddhi, Īśvara-siddhi and Saṃvit-siddhi, which are usually grouped together as the Siddhi-traya. In this work, the major concentration will be upon his two most substantial systematic works, the Āgama-prāmāṇya and the Ātma-siddhi, and upon the relation of Vedānta and Pāñcarātra within them.

The major analytical accomplishments of this study are contained in Part Two and consist of the recovery of the structure and argument of the extant text of the Ātma-siddhi and the "breaking of the code" in which Yāmuna's Vedāntic Siddhāntas or "Established Conclusions" are presented in its introductory section (see Chapters VI and VII and Appendices II and III). On the basis of this analysis, it has been possible to recover four of Yāmuna's major and previously unrecognized Siddhāntas (see Chapter VII), to understand more fully certain key aspects of his Vedāntic system, and to demonstrate how these aspects are related to his attempt to resolve the fundamental theoretical problematic between Vedānta and Pāñcarātra (see Chapter VIII). It has also been possible to gain fresh insights into the manner in which Yāmuna's central theoretical position provided the seminal basis for the Viśiṣṭādvaita system of Vedānta (see Chapter VI, pp. 122-42; Chapter VII, especially notes 51-62 and 71-76; and Chapter VIII, pp. 182-93).

While the bulk of this study is devoted to Yāmuna's Vedānta, a distinctive characteristic of my approach in contrast to most previous work on Indian intellectual history is the degree to which I draw upon a wide range of literary and historical evidence, especially the traditional Maṇi-pravāḷam (Sanskritized Tamil) biographical accounts of the early Śrī Vaiṣṇava Teachers, in order to provide in Part One a fuller historical and social context for the intellectual developments. The most significant contribution made in this regard is the analysis of the roles of the four earliest Teachers, as representatives of distinct Brāhmanic social classes or communities, in the integration into the classical Vedic tradition of originally non-Vedic popular movements, not only Pāñcarātra but also the ecstatic devotional piety represented by the vernacular Tamil hymns of the Āḻvārs (see Chapter I; Chapter III, pp. 29-37; Chapter IV, pp. 69-75; and Chapter V, especially pp. 82-94).

Other contributions that should be highlighted include my proffered solution to the long-standing puzzle about the "original" meaning of the name "Pañcarātra" (see Chapter I, pp. 8-10) and my analysis of the adversary but ambiguous, and often surprisingly positive, relationship between the famous Vedāntin Śaṅkara on the one hand and Yāmuna and Pāñcarātra on the other (see Chapter II; Chapter VII, notes 48-52 and 55-59; and Chapter VIII).

The attempt to recover the contribution of a fascinating and significant but archaic and fragmentarily preserved author like Yāmuna is an arduous task that is made possible and endurable only by the assistance and kindness of many people. Professors John B. Carman and Daniel H. H. Ingalls of Harvard University guided me through the basic research and inspired me by the example of their precise but sensitive humanistic scholarship. Professor Carman, my formal thesis advisor and a specialist in Śrī Vaiṣṇava history and thought, has been helpful both as a teacher and as a friend and played a major role in seeing the original dissertation through to its completion. My study is most directly a continuation of the ground-breaking scholarship of Professor J. A. B. van Buitenen of the University of Chicago, to whom I am indebted not only for his allowing me early access to a manuscript of his translation of the Āgama-prāmāṇya but also for his continuing guidance and other personal acts of assistance.

I am also indebted to such Śrī Vaiṣṇava scholars as M. Narasimhachary, K. K. A. Venkatachari, R. Ramanujachari and U. T. Vīrarāghavācārya who have helped by opening the treasure-house of their tradition to the questioning, oft-times inordinately so, eyes of this historian of religion and by making me constantly aware of the continued significance of the Poet-Philosopher Yāmuna to the eyes of faith. Dr. Narasimhachary, now of Vivekananda College in Madras, generously allowed me early and full access to the fruits of his own thorough study of Yāmuna's works, especially his critical edition of the Āgama-prāmāṇya, and read with me Yāmuna's philosophical writings. Dr. K. K. A. Venkatachari, now Director of the Anantha-charya Research Institute in Bombay, read the traditional Maṇi-pravāḷam biographical accounts with me and assisted me in too many other ways for me to recount or ever repay. Professor Ramanujachari, the distinguished translator of Yāmuna's

Siddhi-traya, regularly discussed problematic points with me and especially showed his kindness by introducing me to Pandit U. T. Vīrarāghavācārya of Madras, perhaps the most learned Śrī Vaiṣṇava interpreter of Yāmuna's works. Pandit Vīrarāghavācārya did me the honor of receiving me and of giving me as a gift his personal copy of his exemplary Sanskrit commentary upon the Siddhi-traya, a work that has been of invaluable assistance at many points. Among the distinguished Indian scholars who guided and assisted my research was also Dr. V. Raghavan of the University of Madras; along with countless other students of Sanskrit literature, I am indebted to his vast knowledge, sage guidance and active personal concern.

Among the many other teachers to whom I am indebted, I would like to acknowledge explicitly one more who has contributed very little to the content of this work but has hopefully influenced its style and spirit, Wilfred Cantwell Smith, formerly Director of the Center for the Study of World Religions at Harvard University, who embodies in his teaching, research and writing an inspiring combination of precise and profound historical scholarship and warm respect for the persons about whom he is studying. As his student, I have tried always to keep in mind that Śrī Vaiṣṇava Hindus would be reading this work and to write in such a manner as to take seriously both the concerns of academic historians of religion and those of persons who view these matters through the eyes of faith.

I would also like to acknowledge gratefully the support which I have received from the following institutions: the Danforth Foundation whose long support of my graduate study reached its initial fruition in this work; the American Institute of Indian Studies whose Junior Fellowship for 1967-68 enabled me to conduct the basic research; the Rockefeller Foundation for its Doctoral Fellowship for 1968-69; the Center for the Study of World Religions at Harvard University for a fellowship during 1970-71 and for the long-term and continuing support of its world-wide scholarly community; the Harvard Theological Review for its invitation to publish this work in this series; the Department of Philosophy, University of Wisconsin-Milwaukee, for released time for research during

Semester II, 1975-76; and the Graduate School, UWM, for its Research Grant for 1976-77 that has supported the final preparation of this work for publication.

Unless otherwise indicated, the translations in this book are my own, although obviously indebted to the previous translators and interpreters of Yāmuna's writings. I have adopted the convention in these translations of using parentheses for Sanskrit terms and other matter explicitly a part of the text and brackets for additional explanatory material that I have felt it necessary to supply for an adequate understanding of the texts and their implicit background. In transliterating the Sanskrit texts, I have used liberally the hyphen (for separating the elements of compound words) and the double hyphen (for separating words joined by external euphonic combination) in the hope of making certain aspects of the Sanskrit terminology accessible to others than experts in the language.

Finally, I would like to express my gratitude to Ms. Deborah Kurimay and to Mary Ann Neevel for their efficiency and care in the typing and editing of the final manuscript. To say that Mary Ann has been long-suffering through these many years would be true but unfair; what she has primarily been long in are patience, interest and enthusiasm. In gratitude, this book is dedicated to her and to the many Indian friends that we have made together.

W.G.N.

Milwaukee, Wisconsin
January 5, 1977

ABBREVIATIONS

I. YĀMUNA'S EXTANT WORKS

AP	Āgama-prāmāṇyam, The Pandit edition
AP(CE)	The Āgamaprāmāṇya of Śrī Yāmunāchārya, critically edited by M. Narasimhachary, unpublished manuscript, 1966
AP(CE 1976)	Āgamaprāmāṇya of Yāmunācārya, critically edited by M. Narasimhachary, Gaekwad's Oriental Series, No. 160, 1976
AP(tr)	Yāmuna's Āgama Prāmāṇyam, English translation by J. A. B. van Buitenen
AtS	Ātma-siddhi in ST
AtS(A)	Ātma-siddhi in ST(A)
AtS(V)	Ātma-siddhi in ST(V)
AtS(1972)	Ātma-siddhi in ST(1972)
CŚl	Catuś-ślokī
GAS	Gītārthasaṃgraha
GPrak	Gūḍha-prakāśa, see ST(V)
GPrak(1972)	Gooda Prakasa, see ST(1972)
IśS	Īśvara-siddhi in ST
IśS(A)	Īśvara-siddhi in ST(A)
SR	Stotra-ratna
SS	Saṃvit-siddhi in ST
SS(A)	Saṃvit-siddhi in ST(A)
ST	Siddhi-traya by Yāmunācārya, Annamalai University edition and translation by R. Ramanujachari and K. Srinivasacharya, 1943
ST(A)	Siddhi-trayam, edited with Siddhāñjana-vyākhyā by P. B. Aṇṇaṅgarācārya, Bombay, 1954
ST(V)	Siddhi-trayam, edited with Gūḍha-prakāśa-ākhya-ṭippaṇa by U. T. Vīrarāghavācārya, Tirupati, 1942
ST(1972)	Sri Yamunacharya's Siddhi Trayam with a Sanskrit Commentary (Gooda Prakasa), edited by U. T. Viraraghavacharya, with an English Introduction and translation by R. Ramanujachari, Madras, 1972
SVy	Siddhāñjana-vyākhyā, see ST(A)

II. OTHER WORKS

ABORI	Annals of the Bhandarkar Oriental Research Institute
AhirS	Ahirbudhnya-saṃhitā
ALB	Adyar Library Bulletin
AOS	American Oriental Series
BBh	Bhāskara's Brahma Sūtra Bhāṣya, Chowkhamba Edition
BhGBh	Bhagavad Gītā Bhāṣya of Śaṅkara
BL	Buddhist Logic by Theodore Stcherbatsky
BSBCŚ	The Brahma-Sūtras of Bādarāyaṇa with the Comment of Śaṅkarācārya. See S. K. Belvalkar
BSBh(K)	Śaṅkara's Brahma Sūtra Bhāṣya, Kāśī Sanskrit Series
ChUp	Chāndogya Upaniṣad
GBh	Gītā-bhāṣya by Rāmānuja
GPP(3000)	Guruparamparā (Vaḍagalai), see Brahmatantra Svatantra Svāmi
GPP(6000)	Guruparamparā (Teṅgalai), see Pinbaṛagiya Perumāḷ Jīyar
GPrak	Gūḍha-prakāśa, see Siddhi-traya edited by U. T. Vīrarāghavācārya
HJAS	Harvard Journal of Asiatic Studies
HIP	A History of Indian Philosophy by S. Dasgupta
HR	History of Religions
IHQ	Indian Historical Quarterly
IIJ	Indo-Iranian Journal
ILA	Indian Logic and Atomism by A. B. Keith
ILM	Advanced Studies in Indian Logic and Metaphysics by S. Sanghvi
MBh	Mahābhārata
NyK	Nyāyakośa, see B. Jhaḷakīkar
NyT	Nāthamuni's Nyāyatattva
PrakP	Prakaraṇa-pañcikā by Śālikanātha Miśra
ŚBh	Rāmānuja's Śrī Bhāṣya
ŚBh(K)	Rāmānuja's Śrī Bhāṣya, edited by R. D. Karmarkar
ŚBh with Śruta-Prakāśikā	See Rāmānuja, Brahmasūtra-Śrībhaṣya with Śrutaprakāśikā

SVy — Siddhāñjana-vyākhyā, see Siddhi-traya edited by Aṇṇaṅgarācārya

TA — Tattvāloka in PrakP

TS — Tarka-saṅgraha, edited by Athalye

UA Adhik. — Utpatti-asaṃbhava-adhikaraṇa, Vedānta Sūtras II.ii.42-45, the Pāñcarātra section of the Tarka-pāda

VAS — Rāmānuja's Vedārthasaṃgraha, van Buitenen's edition and translation

VS — Vedānta Sutras

WZKS — Wiener Zeitschrift für die Kunde Südasiens

WZKSO — Wiener Zeitschrift für die Kunde Süd- und Ostasiens

YIB — Yāmunamunis Interpretation von Brahma-sūtram 2, 2, 42-45, by G. Oberhammer

PART ONE:

THE INTEGRATION OF VEDĀNTA AND PĀÑCARĀTRA WITHIN THE ŚRĪ VAIṢṆAVA TRADITION

CHAPTER I

INTRODUCTION

Yāmuna, who flourished in South India in the first half of the eleventh century C.E., is honored by Śrī Vaiṣṇava Hindus as their fourth Teacher or Ācārya and as the one who attracted to their tradition Rāmānuja (fl. twelfth century C.E.), their sixth and greatest Teacher who provided the classical expression of their school of Vedānta, Viśiṣṭādvaita.[1] Yāmuna was a seminal thinker of extraordinary integrative power and a transitional figure of significance not only in the development of the Śrī Vaiṣṇava tradition but in Indian intellectual and religious history in general. As the first Śrī Vaiṣṇava Teacher for whom we have preserved works, he provides an unusually fruitful focus for the study of an influential religious movement and school of thought in the process of formulation.

The Śrī Vaiṣṇavas, a Hindu tradition or sect (saṃpradāya) of devotees (bhaktās) to the Lord Viṣṇu in association with His consort, the Goddess Śrī, are of particular interest and significance in the religious and intellectual history of India because the period of their formation spanned one of the most momentous transitional epochs in Indian history and because the distinctive pattern of their development provided an influential model for many later Hindu Bhakti movements. Spanning the latter part of the first millenium C.E. and the first of the second, the formulation of the Śrī Vaiṣṇava tradition coincided with the transition from what can be called Classical India, which was dominated by the interaction between Vedic and Buddhist traditions, to Medieval India, in which Buddhist influence waned and which was characterized by Hindu-Muslim interaction and competition. This transitional period was also characterized by an ever increasing "popularization" of Indian life, as ancient classical traditions, which were dominated by an essentially elitist social or monastic leadership employing the Sanskrit language, became increasingly challenged, influenced and broadened by more egalitarian popular movements that promoted the use of vernacular languages as the primary medium of expression.[2]

The Śrī Vaiṣṇava was the first such classically based tradition to integrate fully such a popularly oriented religious movement, the Vaiṣṇava Bhakti or devotional piety based upon the ecstatic hymns that were composed in the Tamil language by the poet-saints called the Āḻvārs ("those who have plunged deep in the ocean of the love of the Blessed Lord") and that have been collected in the Divya-prabandha ("Divine Collect"), which has come to be another Veda or sacred revelation (the Tamil or Drāviḍa Veda) to Śrī Vaiṣṇavas.[3] Indeed, the Śrī Vaiṣṇava tradition derives its basic character and its enduring significance and influence precisely from its integration of classical Vedic elements (especially the Vedānta darśana) and popular, originally non-Vedic ones (not only the Tamil Bhakti of the Āḻvārs but also the Vaiṣṇava Tāntric temple tradition called Pāñcarātra) into a viable pattern that provided a model for a number of later Hindu sectarian movements during the Medieval period. The Śrī Vaiṣṇava school of Vedānta, the Viśiṣṭa-advaita or "Qualified Non-dualism," provided a theistic interpretation of the Upaniṣads that established a solid classical theological basis for popular devotional religion and that, in its essentials, has remained the theoretical undergirding of Hindu Bhakti religion up to the present day.[4]

The present work will not be a comprehensive treatment of the integration of classical and popular traditions within the Śrī Vaiṣṇava movement. As a Sanskritist and an intellectual historian, my emphasis will be upon the classical and intellectual aspects,[5] upon the role of the Vedic and Vedāntic Sanskritic tradition, along with its articulators, the Brāhmanic class, as the integrative agent that has been primarily responsible for the preservation of the continuity and integrity of Hindu culture and religion. In Yāmuna and the other early Śrī Vaiṣṇava Brāhmanic intellectual leaders or Teachers, we will see instructive examples of classes of Brāhmans who, throughout centuries and millenia, have insured the continued vitality of the classical Vedic tradition not through resistance to new developments but through the open embracing of vibrant popular movements.

In many respects, my study is a contribution, from a classical intellectual and textual perspective, to the continuing exploration of M. N. Srinivas' fruitful conception of "Sanskritization," which J. A. B. van Buitenen has defined as "a process in the Indian civilization in which a person or a group consciously relates himself or itself to an accepted notion of true and ancient ideology and conduct" as preserved through the Vedic and Sanskritic tradition.[6] My work has in large part been inspired by van Buitenen's seminal article ("On the Archaism of the Bhāgavata Purāṇa") in which, in dialogue with anthropologists and drawing heavily upon Śrī Vaiṣṇava developments and especially Yāmuna's defense of the Pāñcarātra tradition, he provides new perspectives upon and insights into this process of "Sanskritization."[7] However, the term "Sanskritization," as van Buitenen has pointed out,[8] has ambiguities that can be misleading, especially when dealing with a tradition such as Pāñcarātra whose texts are written in the Sanskrit language but which appears to be largely non-"Sanskritic" or non-Vedic in origin and character.

Therefore, I prefer the concepts of the Classical and the Popular, and their interaction and integration, as providing a model that is not only more balanced and adequate with regard to understanding the particularities of my study but also of more general applicability and relevance to the study of cultural and religious change. On the one hand, the process of the "classicization" (i.e., "Sanskritization," "Vedicization," "Brāhmanization") of new popular movements provides for continuity and stability through periods of transition as the new movements are endowed with increased authority, prestige and staying-power through their inclusion within the classical tradition and their accommodation to classical norms. On the other hand, the equally significant process of the "popularization" of classical traditions provides for change and revitalization of ancient norms and practices as they are made relevant to the flourishing movements of the day. The integration of the Classical and the Popular creates a new but authoritative cultural and religious pattern that is viable within a greatly changed context.

In the context of my study, the Classical is represented in the widest sense by the Vedic (vaidika) tradition that has its source in and is based upon the Sanskrit sacred scriptures, the Vedas, which are traditionally divided into two sections, the earlier (pūrva) being called the karma-kāṇḍa, "the division concerning karma or ritual action," and the latter (uttara) being termed the jñāna-kāṇḍa, "the division concerning knowledge," of which the Upaniṣads are the "end" or culmination, the Veda-anta. More narrowly, my central concern will be with the orthodox Brāhmanic darśanas or traditions of systematic and critical religious thought, especially with the Vedānta or Uttara Mīmāṃsā darśana, the systematic interpretation of the latter part of the Vedas, the Upaniṣads.

The Popular, on the other hand, is represented most generally by the more emotionally and esthetically oriented Bhakti movements that provided an alternate path (mārga) or discipline (yoga) of salvation in addition to the Vedic Karma-mārga and Jñāna-mārga, a path that was open to the common person who was not qualified or eligible for the Vedic paths. More specifically and precisely, the Popular in my study is represented by the Tāntric (tāntrika[9]) traditions, which are based upon Sanskrit ritual texts called Tantras, Āgamas or Saṃhitās, scriptures which govern the theistic devotional and ritual practice in the temples that are dedicated to the deities Viṣṇu, Śiva or the Goddess (Devī, Śakti) and that from the middle of the first millenium C.E. have been the central loci for the development of Bhakti religion. These Vaiṣṇava, Śaiva and Śākta Tāntric traditions are defined in the most general and basic sense by their opposition to the Smārta traditions, Smārtas being those strict Vedic traditionalists who accept only smṛti or post-Vedic texts (e.g., such Dharma-śāstras as Manu, the Epics, the Bhagavad Gītā, and certain Purāṇas such as the Viṣṇu Purāṇa) which supposedly derive their authority directly from śruti or the "heard" or traditionally received Vedic revelation itself.[10] The Tantras or Āgamas, on the other hand, are considered to be new and independent post-Vedic (if not non- or anti-Vedic) revelations that provide alternate means of salvation or release (mokṣa) for a new age (the degenerate Kali Yuga) in which the Vedic revelation is more difficult to apply and for those who are not qualified or able to follow the Vedas.[11] The Vaiṣṇava Pañcarātra Tantras or Āgamas, the earliest of which date from the fifth century C.E.,[12] are the scriptural basis for Pāñcarātra as a Tāntric tradition and our first extant example of a fully developed Tāntric tradition, one which, while maintaining its opposition to certain aspects of the Vedic tradition (especially the Karma-mārga), gradually worked out an accomodation with other aspects, especially Vedānta and the Jñāna-mārga.

The Pañcarātra Āgama or revelation is often termed a "great ocean" containing many individual Āgamas or scriptures, traditionally reckoned at the sacred number of "108" but actually having included over 200 texts.[13] Traditionally, these Āgamas are also considered to have had four categories of major concerns and accordingly to have been divided into four sections or pādas:[14]

1) the jñāna-pāda, the section concerning "knowledge," the theological, cosmogonic and cosmological portion which deals with the nature of the Highest Godhead Viṣṇu, Vāsudeva or Nārāyaṇa and of the manifestation (sṛṣṭi) of the universe from Him. In this section, the peculiarly Pāñcarātrika vyūha-vāda or theory of "extension" (vyūha) or manifestation looms large. From the perspective of Vedānta, this vyūha theory is the distinguishing and most problematic aspect of Pāñcarātra; and we will recur to it at a number of points throughout this work.[15]

2) the yoga-pāda, the section dealing with meditation (upāsanā) or concentration, especially by means of sacred formulae or mantras.

3) the kriyā-pāda, concerning the "action" necessary for maintaining the temple as a place of worship, e.g., building and consecrating temples, making and installing icons, etc.

4) the caryā-pāda, detailing the codes of "conduct" for initiation (dikṣā), for the performance of daily ritual worship (pūjā) and festivals (utsavas), for social duty or dharma, etc. As has often been noted,[16] these Āgamas are primarily concerned with the more practical and ritual aspects such as "Action" (kriyā) and "Conduct" (caryā), while the pādas on jñāna and

yoga, especially the former, are often very brief and fragmentarily preserved, if they have not been lost altogether. Mitsunori Matsubara, who has made a thorough study of the *jñānapādas* of many of the extant Āgamas, has suggested the plausible hypothesis that the major reason for the loss or fragmentation of the theological sections was that this aspect was taken over by the Śrī Vaiṣṇava school of Viśiṣṭādvaita Vedānta while the Āgamas remained the dominating authorities for the temple ritual.[17] In this present work, we will examine this same process of merger or integration from the perspective of Vedānta and Yāmuna's sophisticated theological and philosophical works.

There has been a long but inconclusive debate about the meaning of the name "Pañca-rātra" (derived from the words *pañca*, "five," and *rātri*, "night").[18] Matsubara[19] and van Buitenen[20] have shown conclusively that the name is an ancient and sacred one whose meaning became obscure at a very early time. Matsubara rightly concludes that all that can be shown definitively is that from the earliest times the word Pañcarātra "is the name of a sacred text, called *upaniṣad*, *tantra*, *saṃhitā*, *āgama* or *śāstra*. . .. The word then naturally comes to mean the system or doctrine revealed in the sacred scripture."[21] Throughout this work I will use the word "Pañcarātra" to refer to the sacred revelation or the scripture or scriptures (Āgama[s], Tantra[s], etc.) in which the revelation is contained and the derivative "Pāñcarātra" to refer to the system or tradition based upon this revelation.[22]

To enter briefly into the more speculative realm of the "original" meaning of the term, most modern interpretations attempt to translate the word as "five nights," being influenced by the earliest known use of the term in the Śatapatha Brāhmaṇa XIII.6.1 for the Pañcarātra *sattram* or sacrifice or by later fanciful "folk" etymologies in the extant Āgamas.[23] My own interpretation, drawn from the *earliest* specifically *Pāñcarātrika* use of the term (in the Nārāyaṇīya section of the Mahābhārata),[24] takes the word as meaning "the night of the five."

In my view, the *locus classicus* of the Pāñcarātrika use of "Pañcarātra" as the name for a sacred revelation is the following passage from the Nārāyaṇīya:

idaṃ mahopaniṣadaṃ caturvedasamanvitam/
sāṃkhyayogakṛtaṃ tena _pañcarātrānuśabditam_//
nārāyaṇamukhodgītaṃ nārado srāvayat punaḥ/
brahmaṇaḥ sadane tāta yathā dṛṣṭam yathā śrutam//
[Mahābhārata (critical edition) 12.326.100-101][25]

Nārada, O sire, recounted again in the dwelling of Brahmā, exactly as he had seen and heard it, this great Upaniṣad, which is consistent with the four Vedas and established by Sāṃkhya and Yoga, which was entitled "Pañcarātra" by that (Nārada) and which had been recited from the very mouth of Nārāyaṇa.

The great Upaniṣad mentioned here obviously refers to the sacred revelation or secret instruction given by Nārāyaṇa to Nārada that had just been presented in the immediately preceeding portion of the Nārāyaṇīya [MBh(CE) 12.321.27-326.97].[26] Moreover, the term "Pañcarātra" is clearly indicated to be a _descriptive_ title for this Upaniṣad or secret dialogue between Nārāyaṇa and Nārada.

Thus, unless the text is hopelessly corrupt, the meaning of the name "Pañcarātra" should be indicated by the content of MBh(CE) 12.321.27-326.97; and I believe that, if we listen carefully to the text with regard to the most likely meanings of _pañca_ ("five") and _rātra_ ("night"), a clear, plausible and significant explanation emerges. For in this text only one set of "five" receives special emphasis and detailed analysis: the five material elements (_bhūtas_), "earth" (_pṛthivī_), "air" (_vāyu_), "ether" (_ākāśa_), "water" (_ap_) and the "fifth" (_pañcama_) "light" or "fire" (_jyotis_), which in the manifestation (_sṛṣṭi_) of the universe combine to form what is termed the physical "body" (_śarīra_) (_pṛthivī vāyur ākāśam āpo jyotiś ca pañcamam/ te sametā mahātmānaḥ śarīram iti saṃjñitam_// MBh(CE) 12.326.32).[27] Moreover, there is only one use of an image of "night," a somewhat indirect one but one that is again central to the content of the dialoque or Upaniṣad: Nārāyaṇa twice likens himself to the Sun in the sky and likens the dissolution (_pralaya_) or withdrawal of the physical universe into himself to the setting of the Sun at night.[28] This image of the setting Sun comes just after Nārāyaṇa discusses the supreme path of "cessation" (_nivṛttiḥ paramā_), the _nirvāṇa_ of all _dharmas_ (_nirvāṇam sarva-dharmāṇām_).[29] Significantly, Nārāyaṇa in this same passage reveals himself to be the same as the one called Kapila (the founder of Sāṃkhya-Yoga) and the Hiraṇyagarbha praised in the Vedas (cf. "idaṃ mahopaniṣadaṃ caturveda-samanvitam/ sāṃkhya-yoga-kṛtaṃ").[30]

Thus, it seems clear that in the Nārāyaṇīya, our earliest specifically Pāñcarātrika source, "Pañca-rātra" means "the Night (i.e., the dissolution) of the Five [Physical Elements]" and is a symbolic image for Nirvāṇa or Mokṣa, release from bondage to the physical body (śarīra) and the attainment of union with the Godhead Nārāyaṇa by means of the Knowledge (vidyā)[31] revealed in this great Upaniṣad entitled "Pañcarātra." Not only is this interpretation etymologically straight-forward and derived from an early and important Pāñcarātrika source, but it is also centrally significant for an understanding of the Pāñcarātra tradition[32] and especially of its relation to Vedānta. For, as we will see, an essential element in Yāmuna's integration of Vedānta and Pañcarātra is that they are both Mokṣa-śāstras and thus have precisely the same goal, the attainment of the Highest Human Good of "Release" and the attainment of Brahman, the Blessed Lord (Bhagavān) called Viṣṇu, Nārāyaṇa or Vāsudeva.[33]

Yāmuna's Role

This study then will explore the role of Yāmuna as a representative of the early Śrī Vaiṣṇava Brāhmans and Teachers and as an integrator of the Classical (vaidika) and the Popular (tāntrika), of the Vedānta darśana and the Pāñcarātra tradition of temple ritual and theistic devotion. Essentially, I will consider Yāmuna as a Vedāntin or Uttara Mīmāṃsaka on the basis of his Āgama-prāmāṇya ("The Authoritativeness of the [Pañcarātra] Revelation")[34] and his Ātma-siddhi ("The Determination and Manifestation of the 'Self'"),[35] his two most substantial, and substantially preserved, works that represent his major contribution to the development of Indian systematic and critical religious thought (darśana).[36] As will be argued throughout this work, but especially in Chapters IV and V, Yāmuna was the self-conscious representative of a tradition of Pāñcarātrika Vedānta, what will be called the "Miśra" tradition, into which he was initiated by his immediate Teacher and guru Rāma Miśra and which was based upon the Vedānta Sūtra commentary of a revered but obscure teacher named Śrīvatsāṅka Miśra, about whom nothing is known save what little can be gleaned from Yāmuna's extant works.

Yāmuna will also be considered as a representative of a logical and epistemological system (nyāya-śāstra) based upon the no longer extant Nyāya-tattva, a work by Nāthamuni (tenth century C.E.), Yāmuna's grandfather who has come to be recognized by Śrī Vaiṣṇavas as their first Teacher and the initiator of their distinctive intellectual tradition or darśana. I will argue (see Chapter V) that Yāmuna's most distinctive personal contribution to the development of the Śrī Vaiṣṇava darśana was the integration of Nāthamuni's sophisticated nyāya system into the "Misra" tradition of Pāñcarātrika Vedānta. The evidence is persuasive that Nāthamuni's and Yāmuna's family represented an extremely learned, cultured and prestigious class of Brāhmans whose Brāhmanic status could not in practice be called into question. As trained logicians and epistemologists or naiyāyikas, they had the dialectical skill and, as learned scriptural exegetes or mīmāṃsakas, the command of the Vedas to be able to defend effectively others whose Vedic and Brāhmanic status was not as secure as their own. In addition to being śiṣṭās (i.e., Brāhmans who are highly learned in the Veda and its auxilliary disciplines and who are therefore the exemplars of the Vedic tradition, the ones whose practice [śiṣṭācāra] is in effect the major determinant of what is and what is not "Vedic" at any given time[37]), Nāthamuni's family (the coṭṭai kulam[38]) were Vaiṣṇava Bhāgavatas who had as their family deity the Bhagavān Vāsudeva-Kṛṣṇa, after whom Yāmuna ("he who resides on the bank of the river Yamunā") was named. They were therefore open and sympathetic to the popular Vaiṣṇava Bhakti movements and important agents in the "classicization" or "Sanskritization" of them.

An interesting sociological side-light of my study is my exploration in Chapters III and V of the different classes or communities of Brāhmans involved in the integration of the Classical and the Popular within the Śrī Vaiṣṇava tradition. I will examine especially the relationship of Nāthamuni's and Yāmuna's family of śiṣṭa Bhāgavatas to certain other Brāhmanic classes whose status was more questionable because of their long-term involvement with non-Vedic popular movements, not only the "Miśras" who were related to Pāñcarātra but also certain Coḷiya or Pūrva-śikhī ("fore-lock") Brāhmans who were intimately involved with and, indeed, heavily represented among the Tamil Āḻvārs (see Chapter V). A distinctive aspect of my approach in this area is my correlation of the evidence from Yāmuna's extant works with that from a variety of other sources, especially Vedānta Deśika's voluminous works[39] and the earliest traditional biographical or hagiographical accounts dealing with the Guru-paramparā ("Succession of Spiritual Masters") written in Maṇi-pravāḷam (Sanskritized Tamil).[40] While these accounts are often exaggerated and must be used with critical caution, they are an essential aid for understanding the cultural and social context of the early Śrī Vaiṣṇava Teachers and often have the ring of authenticity about them.[41] Their vivid and not always complimentary portrayal of these figures indicates that, at least in part, they are preserving the characters of genuine individuals and not simply ideal types;[42] their presentation of Yāmuna as precocious, quick-witted, pugnacious, irascible and occasionally even harsh conforms well with the scrappy debater who loves to argue whom we will see emerging from his systematic and polemical works.

My central focus throughout this study, however, will be upon this latter category of Yāmuna's extant works and upon the issue of how he attempts to maintain the full harmony and compatibility between Vedānta and Pāñcarātra, a Tāntric tradition that was almost certainly rejected by Bādarāyaṇa, the Sūtrakāra who composed or compiled the Vedānta Sūtras, the very foundation stone of Vedānta as a darśana. Classical Vedānta recognized only a limited number of scriptures beyond the Vedas or śruti itself as authoritative. Yāmuna's successor Rāmānuja carefully restricted himself to the universally accepted sources. Yāmuna, too, when writing as a Vedāntin in a disciplined sense, limited himself in what he cited as authorities; but he insisted on arguing openly and vehemently that the Pañcarātra Āgamas, texts of dubious antiquity and clearly of non-Vedic origin, were equally as valid as the Veda, since they both were in accord with or based upon the omniscience (sārvajñya) of the Supreme Person, Viṣṇu. Yāmuna's attitude may also reflect his openness to the Āḻvārs' Tamil hymns, and is in some respects similar to the cosmopolitan approach of such Nyāya thinkers as Jayanta Bhaṭṭa and Bhāsarvajña in North India, who helped to enrich the classical Vedic traditions through the appropriation of popular devotional scriptures and movements.

Van Buitenen comments on the significance of Yāmuna's Āgama-prāmāṇya (AP) as follows:

> The revolution which he effected was in Vedānta tradition, and it has proved to be a crucial one. After Śankara who continued an orthodox tradition of monism, and Bhāskara who continued a not less orthodox tradition of dualism-monism, traditions both which based themselves principally on the Upaniṣads, Yāmuna gave Vedānta a completely new scope. Not only did he argue a theistic Vedānta--as others had done before--, he argued it with texts that so far had had no place in the tradition of uttaramīmāṃsā. The significance does not lie principally in the fact that he accepted as canonical a certain class of sectarian Vaiṣṇava texts, but that he argued it within the aupaniṣada tradition. Several schools had arisen which, while paying lip service to the Vedic scriptures, in practice ignored them in favour of more accessible and more popular texts. The interest and the importance of the Āgama-prāmāṇya lie in the author's intention of bringing within the Vedānta tradition, and thus in a way subjecting to this tradition, a body of religious literature that often had been denied to be a part of it.
>
> The motivation of this attempt was in part surely to restore to Vedānta thought the religious inspiration that, one cannot help but feel, was threatenend by the philosophical acrobatics of the monistic schools. This religious inspiration was for Yāmuna that of the religion of worship and devotion that had swept Southern India.[43]

One of the reasons, then, that Yāmuna is such a fascinating figure to study is that he represents a "revolutionary" integration of a number of developments that were taking place within Indian religion during the second half of the first millenium C.E. It was during this period that popular Bhakti movements using such vernaculars as Tamil and such Tāntric traditions as Pāñcarātra first rose to prominence. It was also during this period that Vedānta or Uttara Mīmāṃsā first asasumed a place of major importance as a distinct school of thought or darśana.[44] Moreover, this era, which we have called the end of the Classical (i.e., Vedic-Buddhist) period, was characterized by heavy but declining Buddhist influence. Such

Buddhist logicians and epistemologists as Dignāga (fourth or fifth century) and Dharmakīrti (seventh century) had established nyāya as the dominant mode of systematic thought; and Nāthamuni's nyāya-śāstra in the tenth century can be viewed as a fruit of this period.

By heritage, training and temperament, Nāthamuni's grandson Yāmuna was a dialectician, a naiyāyika. But by his time the greatest naiyāyikas and heterodox opponents, the Buddhists, had waned in influence, so Yāmuna turned his main polemic within the Vedic tradition and towards those mīmāṃsakas or interpreters of the Vedas whom he felt had reacted to the Buddhist challenge either by covertly accepting their position (Śaṅkara's followers whom Yāmuna calls Pracchanna Bauddhās or "Covert Buddhists") or by retreating into a defensive position so restricted in scope and significance as to be no longer worth defending (certain Pūrva Mīmāṃsakas or interpreters of the earlier portion of the Vedas, the karma-kāṇḍa). Yāmuna represents those within the Vedic tradition who were in search of a new, independent self-understanding that would be both faithful to their ancient heritage and responsive to the religious life of the day, particularly to the popular Bhakti and Tāntric movements that were acquiring large followings, building huge temples, producing voluminous bodies of scripture and becoming one of the most dominating and vital forces within Indian life.

Dates of the Early Śrī Vaiṣṇava Teachers

For the purposes of this study it is unnecessary to enter into a full discussion of the precise dates of the early Śrī Vaiṣṇava Teachers. I know of no reason to challenge the traditional view that Yāmuna died ca. 1036 or 1038 C.E.[45] There are, however, serious reasons for doubting the tradition that he lived a long life of 120 years (i.e., twice the normal span), having been born in 916 C.E.[46] In my opinion, he was probably given such a long lifetime and his birth date pushed back in order to relate him more closely to his grandfather Nāthamuni, after the latter's lifetime in turn had been moved back and made extraordinarily long (330 to 340 years, i.e., between 583 and 913 or 923 C.E.) in order to associate him with the Āḻvārs who traditionally lived many centuries before.[47] In turn, there is reason to believe that Rāmānuja's (probably genuinely) long life was moved back several decades to the traditional dates of 1017-1137 in order to enable him to receive the Ācārya's blessing or glance from Yāmuna.[48]

My own approach to the dating of these figures--which I plan to discuss more fully in a future publication--has been to attempt to correlate the traditional accounts of their lives with the plentiful epigraphical evidence that exists for South India from the beginning of the Coḷa period in the tenth century C.E. For example, the unanimous tradition is that both Nāthamuni and Yāmuna were born at Vīranārāyaṇa Puram (also called in Tamil Kāṭṭu-Mannār-gudi, "the settlement of Mannanār [Kṛṣṇa] in the wilderness") in the South Arcot District just north of the Coleroon branch of the Kāveri River. There is strong epigraphical evidence that this area was developed and settled by Parāntaka I (907-955 C.E.), also called Vīranārāyaṇa Coḷa, who built a huge irrigation tank and established a Vīranārāyaṇa Agrahāra (Brāhmaṇa village), both named after himself.[49] This act of colonizing this frontier region apparently had a fantastic effect upon the religious life of South India since, according to Vaiṣṇava and Śaiva traditions, not only did the collection and canonization of the Āḻvārs' hymns in the Divya-prabandha result through the efforts of Nāthamuni, but the hymns of the Śaiva poet-saints called the Nāyaṉārs were also canonized in the Tirumuṛai by Nambi Āṇḍār Nambi, who reputedly was a contemporary of Nāthamuni and who lived at Tirunarayur, only six miles from Vīranārāyaṇa Puram.[50] Therefore, a reasonable hypothesis would be that Nāthamuni was born at Vīranārāyaṇa Puram sometime shortly after 907 C.E. and flourished during the tenth century.

Both Nāthamuni and Yāmuna are closely associated in the traditional accounts with the Coḷa capital, Gaṅgai-koṇḍa-coḷa-puram, which was also located north of the Coleroon and only thirteen miles from Vīranārāyaṇa Puram. In the case of Nāthamuni this association is clearly impossible since Gaṅgai-koṇḍa-coḷa-puram was not founded by Rājendra I (1012-1044 C.E.) until sometime shortly after 1022 C.E.[51] However, the probability of Yāmuna's actually being associated with the Coḷa capital is strengthened by the existence of a locality in the immediate vicinity that goes by the name Āḷavandār-mēḍu and is remembered as the place which the Coḷa king gave to Yāmuna (Tamil, Āḷavandār) as a prize for winning a court debate and at which Yāmuna dwelt in honor for some time before being converted from his life of leisure by his Ācārya Rāma Miśra and being brought to the Śrî Rangam temple as the intellectual leader (darśana-pravartaka) of the Śrî Vaiṣṇavas.[52] Thus a reasonable hypothesis would be that Yāmuna flourished as a major figure for a relatively brief period sometime between 1022 and 1038. The probability that he was short-lived is strengthened by the traditional accounts of his poor health, perhaps by the fragmentary nature of his preserved works, and by the unanimous tradition that he died in disappointment at his failure to fulfill certain goals which were left as "three wishes" which had to be carried out by his great successor Rāmānuja.[53]

While the precise content of Yāmuna's three unfulfilled wishes varies in the different accounts, they always include his desire for an adequate commentary on the Vedānta Sūtras of Bādarāyaṇa (who is identified with Vyāsa, the author of the Mahābhārata) and his concern for honoring and fostering the popular Vaiṣṇava devotional movement, generally citing Nammāḻvār, the greatest of the Āḻvārs who sang the praises of Viṣṇu in Tamil.[54] Rāmānuja is honored as the one who fulfilled the goals of Yāmuna, establishing the Śrî Vaiṣṇava tradition as a viable synthesis of classical and popular religious ways, based upon the timeless wisdom of the Upaniṣads or Vedānta but open to the vital movements and practical needs of its day.

Hence we find in Yāmuna a seminal figure whose contribution, as a Vedāntin at least, lay not so much in what he actually accomplished as in what he boldly attempted to do and in what he inspired others to do on the basis of his insight and vision. In this study, I will attempt to recover some aspects of what Yāmuna attempted to do through an analysis of his two major extant works, the Āgama-prāmāṇya (AP), in which he defends the Pāñcarātra Tāntric tradition and attempts to integrate it fully into the Vedic and Vedāntic traditions, and the Ātma-siddhi (AtS), in which he proposes an interpretation of Vedānta that is in harmony and compatible with Pāñcarātra.

CHAPTER II

THE RELATION OF THE CLASSICAL VEDĀNTA TO THE POPULAR PĀÑCARĀTRA

In Yāmuna's case, the most fruitful way of exploring the integration of the Classical and the Popular is through a consideration of the manner in which he relates the Vedānta tradition to Pāñcarātra. In the Ātma-siddhi (AtS), his major Vedāntic work, Yāmuna self-consciously and explicitly places himself within the classical Vedānta or Uttara Mīmāṃsā darśana based upon Bādarāyaṇa's Vedānta Sūtras (VS), refers by name to many of the most prestigious among the preceding orthodox Vedāntins, and conducts himself throughout as one fully and securely at home within a classical and orthodox intellectual milieu.[1] In the Āgama-prāmāṇya (AP), on the other hand, Yāmuna argues for the authority of the Pañcarātra Āgama or Tantra, assuming a basically defensive--although also belligerent and self-assertive--posture against some prestigious orthodox opponents who present a strong case that this popular post-Vedic Tāntric tradition is unorthodox, heretical and to be excluded from the Vedic tradition (veda-bāhya).[2] This contrast between his two major extant works raises the question of how he reconciles his commitment to the orthodox Vedic and Vedāntic tradition with his commitment to the seemingly unorthodox or non-Vedic Pāñcarātra.

The success of Yāmuna and the Śrī Vaiṣṇava tradition in general at making such a reconciliation has been perhaps their greatest contribution to the ongoing evolution or development of Hindu religion, providing a model for the reinvigoration of the ancient classical traditions through the integration of vibrant contemporary movements.[3] The difficulty of their task was great, especially within the context of Mīmāṃsā, a tradition based upon a rational and systematic interpretation of the Vedas. As is clear from the AP, the greatest opposition to

Pāñcarātra came from within the ranks of Pūrva Mīmāṃsā, which has Vedic ritual action or karma as its major concern; the significance of this point will be pursued below.

However, even within Uttara Mīmāṃsā or Vedānta there was a strong traditional bias against Pāñcarātra. The seemingly dominant Vedāntic tradition maintains that Bādarāyaṇa at VS II.ii.42-45, the Utpatty-asaṃbhava-adhikaraṇa ("the Section on the Impossibility of Origination," hereafter UA Adhik.) refutes Pāñcarātrika doctrine as being incompatible with Vedānta on at least several essential points, especially in teaching that the individual self (ātmā or jīva) has an origin (utpatti) as a vyūha or "extension" of the Godhead or the Highest Self (paramātmā).[4] Van Buitenen has argued persuasively that there is a strong prima facie case for these four sūtras being a refutation of some system, although we have only commentatorial tradition for that system's being Pāñcarātra.[5] These sūtras come at the conclusion of a division of the VS called the Tarka-pāda, which is devoted to the refutation of opposing non-Vedāntic viewpoints by means of logical argumentation (tarka); and there is no persuasive, independent way of interpreting the bare words of the sūtras so as to reverse the presumption that they are also a refutation and to assert--as do Yāmuna and the later Śrī Vaiṣṇava tradition--that they represent Bādarāyaṇa's own final position or Siddhānta.

Moreover, the testimony of Śaṅkara (ca. eighth century) and Bhāskara (ca. early ninth century), the authors of the two earliest extant commentaries on the VS, strongly suggests that the dominant early Vedāntic tradition viewed the UA Adhik. as a refutation of Pāñcarātra.[6] Since Bhāskara is not known for his willing agreement with Śaṅkara on controversial points but in general follows him on the interpretation of the UA Adhik., their shared opinion is certain to have been a widely accepted one within Vedāntic circles for at least several centuries before the time of Yāmuna.[7]

This dominant orthodox opinion was challenged by Yāmuna, explicitly in the AP and--as I shall argue--implicitly in the AtS. Gerhard Oberhammer has provided a ground-breaking analysis of the section of the AP that contains Yāmuna's response to this interpretation of VS II.ii.42-45.[8] Oberhammer establishes that Yāmuna was not the first to challenge the orthodox interpretation of the UA Adhik. and that he was able to draw upon a number of earlier sources that had maintained that Bādarāyaṇa in these sūtras accepts the authoritativeness (prāmāṇya) of the Pañcarātra revelation or scriptures (āgama).[9] Oberhammer argues that Yāmuna in the composition of his exposition utilized in a positive manner four distinct sources: one being a refutation of a preliminary counter-position or pūrvapakṣa constructed primarily from Śaṅkara's commentary and secondarily from Bhaskara's; the other three being alternate interpretations of the UA Adhik. as favorable to the Pāñcarātra.[10] While the distinction between and interrelations among these sources and Yāmuna's own position are not as clear in Oberhammer's analysis as one would wish, he does demonstrate that there were, among the various traditions of commentary upon the VS, other voices that challenged the view that Bādarāyaṇa rejected the validity of Pāñcarātra.

In this connection it is necessary to note that even the dominant orthodox interpretation of such Vedāntins as Śaṅkara and Bhāskara did not constitute as thorough-going and unconditional a condemnation of Pāñcarātra as Oberhammer tends to assume.[11] Paul Hacker, in developing Śaṅkara's generally close and positive relation to Vaiṣṇava traditions and elements, remarks of Śaṅkara's commentary on the UA Adhik.,

> It is true that Śaṅkara rejects the theology of the Vaiṣṇava system of Pāñcarātra, but it is worthy of note that his criticism is not so unqualified here as in the case of Śaiva theology. He controverts only the vyūha theory of the Pāñcarātrins but expressly approves of a considerable part of their system. He admits that in some respects, e.g., in the doctrine of God being the material as well as the efficient cause of the world, this system agrees with his Vedānta . . .. I think it cannot be overlooked that a marked sympathy for the Vaiṣṇava religion speaks from these words. . . . he even identifies the Highest Self as taught by the Advaita system with . . . Nārāyaṇa, the Bhagavān, who is the highest deity of Vaiṣṇavism, and he expressly approves of Vaiṣṇava practices and devotion.[12]

As Hacker notes, Śaṅkara's main criticism of Pāñcarātra was directed against the vyūha theory, the most peculiar aspect of this tradition according to which the manifestation of the universe is explained in terms of "extensions" (vyūhas) of the

Highest Self (paramātmā).[13] However, it is significant that even here Śaṅkara's refutation is not a complete one. In indicating those aspects of the system which he does not reject, he admits that in a general sense the concept of the Paramātmā existing in a manifold way as vyūhas or "extensions" of Himself (ātmanā--ātmānam vyūha-avasthita) has a Vedic basis, quoting Chāndogya Upaniṣad 7.26.2.[14] At another point, he is willing to say that the entire universe has the character of a vyūha of the Lord (jagato bhagavad-vyūhatva).[15] Śaṅkara's objection is thus not to a general use of the concept vyūha but rather to certain faults which result from the specific manner in which the vyūha theory is developed within Pāñcarātra.[16]

Twice Śaṅkara refers to one specific aspect of the Pāñcarātrika vyūha theory, i.e., the ṣaḍ-guṇas or "Six Qualities" [1. jñāna ("knowledge"), 2. aiśvarya ("lordliness"), 3. śakti ("power"), 4. bala ("strength"), 5. vīrya ("immutability"), 6. tejas ("splendor")], which exist in co-equal fullness in Vāsudeva or Nārāyaṇa, the highest Godhead and vyūha (para-vyūha), with three other vyūhas becoming manifest through the dominance of successive pairs of these qualities.[17] Once again, while he criticized the manner in which these six guṇas are applied within the Pāñcarātrika vyūha theory, it is clear that he did not completely reject the basic position since in another place he himself ascribes these six to the Lord in their characteristically Pāñcarātrika enumeration. In his introduction to his commentary on the Bhāgavad Gītā, and in the course of presenting his own understanding of how and why Viṣṇu, called Nārāyaṇa, becomes the avatāra Kṛṣṇa, Śaṅkara uses the phrase sa ca bhagavān jñāna-aiśvarya-śakti-bala-vīrya-tejobhiḥ sadā sampannaḥ . . . ("And that Bhagavān who is always endowed with [the Six Qualities] jñāna, aiśvarya, śakti, bala, vīrya and tejas . . .").[18] Since Śaṅkara twice uses these Six Qualities in this particular sequence as a distinctive aspect of Pāñcarātrika doctrine, it does not seem hazardous to assert that his independent use of them in his Gītā commentary indicates his self-conscious willingness to identify himself with at least certain aspects of Pāñcarātra.[19]

Thus it would seem to be impossible to maintain Oberhammer's contention that Śaṅkara intends finally to reject the entire system of Pāñcarātra. As van Buitenen, widening the scope of the investigation to include Bhāskara as well, says,

> As both philosophers point out, it is not the general orthodoxy of Pāñcarātra as a system of religious practice which is at issue, but the orthodoxy, or conformity, of specific points of theological doctrine. Somewhat in contradiction with this view of the matter is the interpretation by both commentators of the last sūtras [sic] which clearly implies that Pāñcarātra is non-Vedic; but neither thinker gives much weight to this point, though it must be noted that for Yāmuna this was the fundamental objection raised against Pāñcarātra.[20]

Van Buitenen's first sentence supports the basic position I am outlining here; however, his second sentence indicates the major basis for Oberhammer's interpretation and raises an interesting question about who the real opponents of Pāñcarātra were, at least in Yāmuna's eyes. My basic argument will be, first, that there is no known specifically Vedāntic commentatorial source that attempts to maintain with any consistency or force the view that Pāñcarātra is completely heretical and excluded from the Vedic way (veda-bāhya) and, second, that this hostile assertion derives primarily from Pūrva Mīmāṃsā, not from Uttara Mīmāṃsā or Vedānta.

The first three sūtras of the UA Adhik. all deal with specific objections to different aspects or varieties of the vyūha theory (see Chapter VIII for a discussion of these sūtras). The last sūtra, II.ii.45, "vipratiṣedhāc ca," "and because of the conflict or contradiction," is more general and open-ended; and, as van Buitenen stated above, it is only in the interpretation of this sūtra that we appear to find a clear rejection of Pāñcarātra as a whole as non-Vedic. Both Śaṅkara and Bhāskara take this sūtra to mean "because of conflict" both internally between different aspects of Pāñcarātra and between Pāñcarātra and the Vedas (veda-vipratiṣedhaś ca).[21] By putting undue emphasis on the latter point, Oberhammer has Śaṅkara finally coming down on the side of rejecting the entire system of Pāñcarātra.[22]

However, as van Buitenen also points out above, the treatment of this sūtra by Śaṅkara, and even more so by Bhāskara, is exceedingly cursory and is so at a point where they were free to lodge against Pāñcarātra any and all charges they wished to muster. As S. K. Belvalkar notes with regard to Śaṅkara's commentary on this sūtra,

> One expects that Śaṅkarāchārya would pick many more holes into the system under cover of this last sūtra than what he has actually done. His "Veda-vipratishedha" is absolutely untenable. Rāmānuja has correctly pointed to the analogous passage in the Chhāndogya, VII.i.2-3, where the "Veda-nindā" ["scorn for the Vedas"] by Nārada is not really intended, and says that the words of dissatisfaction put in Śāṇḍilya's mouth are merely intended as "vakshyamāṇa-vidyā-praśaṃṣārtham." [i.e., "for the praise of the 'knowledge' being discussed (and not for the rejection of that which is scorned)."][23]

If veda-vipratiṣedha, i.e., "[Pāñcarātra as a whole is in] conflict with the Vedas," were Śaṅkara's final position, it would have been quite amazing for a scholar of his ability to allow it to rest upon what Belvalkar terms an "absolutely untenable" argument.

In both Śaṅkara's and Bhāskara's commentary, the "untenable" argument supporting the charge of veda-vipratiṣedha is based upon the variously quoted stock phrase concerning the sage Śāṇḍilya: "Not having been able to find the Highest Good in the four Vedas, Śaṇḍilya became learned in this [Pāñcarātra] system."[24] On the basis of such "scorn for the Vedas" (veda-nindā) found in Pāñcarātra, it is considered to be opposed to the Vedas. Rāmānuja's refutation of this argument, which Belvalkar affirms in the above quotation, is derived from Yāmuna's AP, as will be seen in Chapter IV. Here what it is essential to note are the contexts in which Yāmuna considers and refutes this charge in the AP. Yāmuna does not give the full statement and refutation of this charge within the context of his discussion of VS II.ii.42-45. Rather at that point, he gives only the most cursory restatement of the charge and a reference to his earlier refutation of it.[25] The full statement of the charge veda-vipratiṣedha in conjunction with the statement about Śāṇḍilya (in nearly the precise words that Śaṅkara uses) comes at the conclusion of the Pūrva Mīmāṃsā refutation of the Pañcarātra Tantra as totally outside the Vedic pale (veda-bāhya);[26] and Yāmuna's full refutation of the charge comes in the course of his reply to this Smārta opponent.[27]

Thus, the evidence of the AP suggests that the charge that Pāñcarātra as a whole is in conflict with the Vedas derives primarily from Pūrva Mīmāṃsā--not from Uttara Mīmāṃsā or Vedānta. Such "scorn for the Vedas" as found in the statement about Śāṇḍilya has force only within the context of the full Pūrva Mīmāṃsā argument, as one piece of evidence among many tending to indicate the non-Vedic character of Pāñcarātra. When Śaṅkara and Bhāskara abstract this more catchy than substantial objection from its Pūrva Mīmāṃsā context and use it as the sole basis for the charge of veda-vipratiṣedha, the charge becomes "absolutely untenable," little more than a pro forma vestigial traditional objection.

My contention is, therefore, that all known Vedāntic commentatorial sources reveal a more or less positive attitude toward Pāñcarātra, relative at least to the more hostile attitude that was dominant within Pūrva Mīmāṃsā. While the dominant tradition typified by Śaṅkara and Bhāskara recognized that there were objectionable aspects to Pāñcarātra, their criticism of this Tantra is quite muted, much less severe than their criticism of the Śaiva Māheśvaras or Pāśupatas (as noted by Hacker above) and even of such prestigious and orthodox systems as Sāṅkhya-Yoga and Vaiśeṣika, all of which Śaṅkara explicitly terms heretical (veda-bāhya) because they all commit the cardinal Vedāntic sin of denying that Brahman is not only the efficient (nimitta) but also the material (upādāna) cause of the universe.[28] Both Śaṅkara and Bhāskara begin the UA Adhik. by acknowledging that this cardinal fault cannot be lodged against Pāñcarātra, thereby placing it on a quite different level from the previous opponents.[29] It seems clear that they both felt that, by placing the refutation of Pāñcarātra last, Bādarāyaṇa was indicating that, of all the opponents cited, it was the one closest to Vedānta. As V. S. Ghate comments,

> The fact that this particular doctrine is refuted last of all, can be explained by the circumstance that it is the most allied to the Vedānta doctrine, and Saṁkara has admitted this at the beginning of the adhikaraṇa, as we have remarked above.[30]

Yāmuna and his sources in the AP, then, refuting the specific criticisms of Śaṅkara and Bhāskara and building upon the relatively favored status accorded to Pāñcarātra, take the further step of asserting that Bādarāyaṇa, in response to a

Pūrvapakṣa rejecting Pāñcarātra (II.ii.42-43), concludes the Tarka-pāda with his own Siddhānta, an affirmation of the authoritativeness of this Tantra (II.ii.44-45).[31] According to Oberhammer's analysis, Yāmuna's major source accepted the fact that there were conflicts between the Vedas or śruti and Pāñcarātra but asserted that Bādarāyaṇa affirmed both as equally authoritative alternatives (vikalpas).[32] Yāmuna's distinctive contribution was to take this general trend to its extreme by denying completely that there were any genuine conflicts between the two ways and asserting their total harmony and compatibility.[33]

It would be profitable at this point to consider the question of why Vedānta or Uttara Mīmāṃsā was relatively positive toward Pāñcarātra in striking contrast to the hostility of Pūrva Mīmāṃsā. This contrast becomes somewhat less surprising if viewed in the light of several general historical factors which I shall simply enumerate here:

1) Vedānta or Uttara Mīmāṃsā as a distinct darśana rose to prominence only in about the fifth century C.E.,[34] i.e., at the same time that such Tāntric traditions as Pāñcarātra became major factors in the religious life of India.[35] Before this time it would appear that Pūrva and Uttara Mīmāṃsā were simply the "earlier" and the "later" sub-divisions within one darśana (eka-śāstra), both being designated by the term Mīmāṃsā.[36]

2) Both Vedānta and such Tāntric traditions as Pāñcarātra arose at least partly in opposition to Pūrva Mīmāṃṣā and its path (mārga) or discipline (yoga) of Vedic karma or ritual action, criticizing the inadequacies of this path and arguing for the necessity of alternate or supplementary ways of salvation, the path of knowledge (jñāna) in the case of the former and alternate paths of ritual action in the latter.[37] Śaṅkara, the one figure most responsible for the establishment of Vedānta as a major distinct darśana, is, if anything, more critical of the Vedic karma than are the Tāntric traditions, in that he rejects the very rationale underlying the path of karma and argues for the complete discontinuity between it and the path of jñāna,[38] while the Tāntric traditions accept in general the

theoretical basis for and need of ritual action, simply asserting that the Vedic karma is inadequate for the present degenerate age, the Kali-yuga.[39]

3) As to the question of why Vedānta should be particularly favorable toward Pāñcarātra among the various Tāntric traditions, a relatively obvious answer is because Pāñcarātra was particularly favorably disposed towards Vedānta. While all the Bhakti and Tāntric traditions claimed to be "orthodox," the Vaiṣṇava popular movements in general were milder and less extreme in their variation from Vedic norms than were their Śaiva and Śākta counterparts and were more anxious and better able to demonstrate their continuity with the Vedas.[40] Pāñcarātra, a Vaiṣṇava Tāntric tradition that proposed an alternate ritual tradition, was obviously in conflict with the Vedic karma-kāṇḍa and Pūrva Mīmāṃsā, but compensated by laying great stress on its continuity with the Upaniṣads or Vedānta, the jñāna-kāṇḍa that gives true knowledge about the nature of Ultimate Reality (tattva-jñāna) or Brahman and of the Highest Human Goal of "Release" (mokṣa).[41]

My general hypothesis then, supported by the clear evidence of Yāmuna's AP, is that the primary source of opposition to Pāñcarātra came from Pūrva Mīmāṃsaka Brāhmans who had a vested interest in maintaining the Vedic karma or ritual tradition. The rise of alternate Tāntric ritual traditions was a great threat to such Smārta Brāhmans whose very livelihood depended upon the performance of Vedic ritual. On the other hand, Brāhmans who were not so committed to and dependent upon maintaining the Vedic karma were able to be somewhat more open-minded towards these new ritual traditions.[42] All Brāhmans who were committed to Vedānta as a distinct darśana would tend to fall into the latter, more open-minded category since the very "desire to know Brahman" (brahma-jijñāsā), with which the study of Vedānta begins, is based upon a realization of the limitations inherent in the performance of Vedic karma.[43]

However, since Vedānta or Uttara Mīmāṃsā only gradually grew out of a single Mīmāṃsā darśana in which obviously great emphasis would have been placed upon the necessity of Vedic karma as an essential prerequisite to the attainment of the Upaniṣadic jñāna, the traditional Mīmāṃsā prejudice against alternate ritual traditions could be expected to persist to some degree within the different traditions of Vedānta. Thus, it can be explained why such Vedāntins as Śaṅkara and Bhāskara, who were ambiguous but not wholly condemnatory toward Pāñcarātra, would be willing to repeat in passing the traditional stock Pūrva Mīmāṃsā objection of veda-vipratiṣedha, but without feeling it necessary to press the point or to support it adequately.

Implicit in this hypothesis is the assumption that Bādarāyaṇa himself (as opposed to all existing later Vedāntic commentaries) would have intended a much more thorough-going rejection of Pāñcarātra, since the VS would have been composed or compiled at a time when Vedānta was simply the latter (uttara) portion of the one Mīmāṃsā darśana. As Belvalkar notes, the tone of the last sūtra (vipratiṣedhāc ca) of VS II.ii.42-45 is "decidedly combative," echoing the last sūtras of several of the preceding sections in which the refutation preserved by the commentatorial tradition is more severe.[44] Thus it would seem very likely that Śaṅkara and Bhāskara preserve the charge veda-vipratiṣedha, even though it contradicts their general interpretation, because it has the weight of ancient tradition behind it, probably representing the viewpoint of the composer or redactor of the VS, Bādarāyaṇa himself.

As Vedānta diverged from Pūrva Mīmāṃsā and as the Tāntric traditions became increasingly influential and acceptable, the original harsh refutation would presumably have been toned down as much as possible within reasonable limits. And then, when there arose Vedāntins such as Yāmuna who were also committed to the Pāñcarātrika ritual tradition, no effort would have been spared to reverse the original rejection contained in the VS and to "classicize" or "Sanskritize" Pāñcarātra in such a way as to remove any obstacles to its full integration into the Vedic tradition.

To summarize in a preliminary manner, the most general and basic pattern which Yāmuna and his Vedāntic sources employed for the integration of Pāñcarātra was

1) to argue for its complete continuity and harmony with the Vedic jñāna or knowledge about the nature of Ultimate Reality as it was quintessentially revealed in the Upaniṣads or Vedānta and

2) to account for any actual or seeming conflicts or differences by means of the theory that Pāñcarātra provides an alternate (vikalpa), but equally valid, ritual path or discipline to the Vedic karma, a theory that was powerful and effective because it was derived from an established Vedic Mīmāṃsā principle of vikalpa or "Option" that had been developed to account for conflicts and differences among the different ritual branches (śakhās) within the Vedic tradition.[45]

It is clear that to Yāmuna the essential link between Pāñcarātra and the Vedic tradition was the knowledge (jñāna) revealed by the Upaniṣads, whereas the Vedic karma, while being useful for the attainment and enjoyment of certain lower "worldly" goals,[46] was non-essential and could be replaced by the Pāñcarātrika ritual discipline, which has as its goal the same Highest Human Good (paraṃ śreyas) as is revealed in the Veda (pañcarātra-śrutyor aikārthyam eva),[47] i.e., final "Release" (mokṣa),[48] which is defined in Vedānta and in the AtS as the attainment of Brahman (brahma-prāpti)[49] and in the Pañcarātra Āgama and the AP as the attainment of the Bhagavān (bhagavat-prāpti).[50]

Thus, in the integration of the Classical and the Popular in the case of Vedānta and Pāñcarātra, the revealed knowledge of the Upaniṣads, together with the Vedānta darśana based upon that knowledge, provides the essential classical norms to which Pāñcarātra must conform if it is to be accepted as Vedic. We may say that the Vedānta in general forms the central integrating core and is the primary "classicizing" or "Sanskritizing" agent that preserves the continuity of Vedic culture and religion throughout this process of change. On the other hand, the temple ritual and devotional practice of Pāñcarātra are the "popularizing" agents, the instrumental actions or means whereby the central insights, values and goals of the Vedānta are made vivid, vital and relevant to a wider audience in a new context.

This basic pattern or model for the integration of the classical Vedānta and the popular Pāñcarātra invites some general comments upon the respective roles of orthodoxy ("correct doctrines or belief") and orthopraxis ("correct practice or action") in maintaining the continuity, integrity and vitality of Vedic or Hindu culture and religion. After an earlier over-emphasis on highly abstract intellectual or mystical aspects, there has been a generally salutary swing to the other extreme with a stress upon concrete and immediate aspects of Hindu religious practice since, as van Buitenen asserts, "the norm for Hinduism generally is better described by orthopraxis than by orthodoxy."[51] In the present instance, however, we see that orthodox norms can also play a central role since for Yāmuna the crucial test was the conformity of Pāñcarātra with the Vedāntic "knowledge." As is always the case, it is best not to dichotomize and thereby "cut the nerve" of the living human reality in which both thought and practice, jñāna and karma, are essential complementary aspects. Indeed, Yāmuna, while being primarily concerned with the theoretical philosophical and theological side, takes as his task in the AP the demonstration that neither in doctrine nor in practice does the Pañcarātra revelation conflict with what is acceptable within the Vedic and Vedāntic traditions.

CHAPTER III

THE ĀGAMA-PRĀMĀṆYA: YĀMUNA'S DEFENSE OF THE PAÑCARĀTRA REVELATION

The Āgama-prāmāṇya, in which Yāmuna defends the authoritativeness (prāmāṇya) of the Pañcarātra revelation or scripture (āgama, tantra, śāstra), is an exceedingly significant text in Hindu religious and intellectual history. It was written by a learned and cultured (śiṣṭa) Brāhman whose Vedic credentials could not be effectively denied, but who was also open to the Pāñcarātra Tāntric tradition and was ready, willing and able to do vociferous battle on its behalf against some prestigious Smārta Brāhman opponents who detail at length its non-Vedic origins and associations. For Yāmuna's status as a śiṣṭa Brāhman, an exemplar of the Vedic tradition, we need not depend solely upon the perhaps exaggerated traditional Śrī Vaiṣṇava accounts: the fact shines through on every page that he has composed. Yāmuna writes with a sense of self-assurance and confidence, with a sophisticated philosophical skill and with a command of the Vedic sources that simply could not have been faked nor acquired easily or quickly--they must represent the fruits of generations of cultivation and training. Yāmuna himself attests to this fact when, in his concluding verses to the AP, he traces both the task and the dialectical style of the work back to the inspiration of his prestigious naiyāyika grandfather Nāthamuni.[1] As Nāthamuni's intellectual heir, Yāmuna conducts himself as a well-trained naiyāyika mīmāṃsaka who can meet his Brāhman opponents on their own ground and, as did the disciples of Nāthamuni, "crush the arrogance of those who scorn the Sātvata (i.e., Bhāgavata or Pañcarātra) teaching, having slashed their position to pieces by turning their own dialectial arguments (yuktis) against them."[2]

J. A. B. van Buitenen has presented in some detail certain of the more sociological aspects of Yāmuna's polemics with his Smarta opponents over the orthodoxy or orthopraxis of the supposedly disreputable Sātvatas, Bhāgavatas or Pāñcarātrins.[3] Van Buitenen's interesting account, however, is somewhat misleading because he tends to accept the Smārta viewpoint according to which all Bhāgavatas are to be lumped together and tarred with the same brush as could be applied to those most at variance with traditional Vedic and Brāhmanic norms. Essential to understanding Yāmuna's defense of Pāñcarātra and, even more so, to understanding why his defense was effective is the perception that there were significant differences or distinctions among those groups called "Bhāgavatas" and associated with the Pañcarātra Āgamas or the temples governed by these ritual texts. While, as Yāmuna is forced to admit, there were "Bhāgavatas" associated with Pāñcarātrika temples whose Vedic and/or Brāhmanic status was hard to maintain, Yāmuna also asserted--and the eventual success of his argument strongly suggests that he was telling the truth--that there were other classes of Bhāgavatas and Pāñcaratrins whose Brāhmanic status was nearly as secure and defensible as that of the Smārtas themselves.

An analysis of the AP reveals that Yāmuna, at least for the sake of argument, recognized four distinct categories or classes of Bhāgavatas or Sātvatas associated with Pāñcarātrika temples, the first two of which had low or questionable status while the last two had Brāhmanic standing that was defensible on Vedic and Mīmāṃsaka principles:

Bhāgavata Class I

There are some who are called Bhāgavatas or Sātvatas who are traditionally classed as *Vaiśya-vrātyas*, i.e., members of a community who were originally derived from the Vaiśya *varṇa*, the lowest of the three "twice-born" (*dvi-ja*) Vedic classes, but who lost their Vedic status altogether by forsaking the required Vedic *karma* or rites (especially the sacrament or *saṃskāra* of *upanayana* or initiation) and by devoting themselves instead to worship and service at temples of Viṣṇu (*viṣṇor āyatanāni*).[4] Yāmuna admits that there are such low or fallen outcastes associated with temples of Vāsudeva as servants and temple-guards (*prāsāda-pālakas*) who clean the temples (*āyatana-śodhana*), clear away and eat leftover food offering (*bali-*

nirharaṇa, naivedya-bhojana), and protect the sacred images (pratimā-saṃrakṣaṇa) and who are called "Bhāgavatas" because of this loose relation to the worship of the Bhagavān Vāsudeva-Kṛṣṇa.[5]

However, he claims that they are not Bhāgavatas or Pāñcarātrins in any strict formal sectarian sense because they cannot worship the Bhagavān directly (sākṣād-bhagavad-ārādhana-abhāva)[6] and because they do not, as do genuine Bhāgavatas or Pāñcarātrins, perform the temple and devotional ritual discipline that is established by the Pañcarātra scriptures and that is called "Pāñcakālikā" (bhagavac-chāstra-siddha-pāñcakālikā), a name derived from its being divided into five (pañca) parts each to be done during a certain portion or time (kāla) of the day:

1) Abhigamana, early morning ablutions and devotions;
2) Upādāna, preparation for worship and gathering of the materials to be offered, during the morning;
3) Ijyā, worship of the Lord (bhagavad-ārādhana, deva-pūjā) in the form of an icon (arcā) before the mid-day meal;
4) Svādhyāya, recitation and study of sacred scriptures, mantras and other religious books during the afternoon;
5) Yoga, meditation on the Bhagavān before sleep.[7]

Yāmuna's Smārta opponents attempt to include the genuine practicing Pāñcarātrins among the former class of outcaste (veda-bāhya) Vaiśya-vrātya "Bhāgavatas" and thus to discredit the Pañcarātra Āgama and all its adherents as non-Vedic--a procedure which Yāmuna regards as a blatant smear tactic.

Bhāgavata Class II

This category is composed of genuine Bhāgavatas or Pāñcarātrins who are professional temple priests or arcakas who perform the ritual worship (pūjā) before the sacred image or icon (arcā).[8] While Yāmuna argues that these arcakas are also genuine Brāhmans, he has difficulty doing so because there is a strong traditional prejudice against those who perform sacrifice or worship for others (para-artham) professionally or for their livelihood (vṛtty-artham). Those who perform temple worship (deva-pūjā) for their livelihood, who require an additional non-Vedic Tāntric initiation (dīkṣā) to do so, and who live off the temple treasury (deva-kośa-upajīvin) are called Devalakās by the Smārtas and are at best considered corrupt Brāhmans (upa-brāhmaṇās) who have lost their qualification (adhikāra) for performing the Vedic rituals (śrauta-kriyā) and are polluting to true Brāhmans.[9]

Yāmuna is hard pressed to defend these professional Pāñcarātrin temple priests against the charge of their being bad Brāhmans (daurbrāhmaṇya) because his opponents can cite the disapprobriation not only of orthodox smṛti literature such as Manu's Dharma-śāstra but even of a Pañcarātra Āgama, the Parama-saṃhitā, which says that not even in times of distress should one worship the God of gods for the sake of one's livelihood or any other gain.[10] Yāmuna, as a good Brāhman himself, is obviously bothered by the charges against this class of Bhāgavatas and can only put up a series of rather lame arguments in their behalf:

1) Not all Bhāgavatas worship Viṣṇu (Hari) for their livelihood (vṛtti) for many Sātvatas are seen to perform worship simply for themselves (sva-arthaṃ) and not for others for the sake of gain.[11]

2) Even if some good Sātvatas in hard straits (vṛtti-karśitāḥ) do so, they do not necessarily lose their Brāhmanic status thereby any more than do the Brāhman priests who perform such Vedic rituals as the Jyotiṣṭoma and receive a "gift" (dakṣinā) for their services; in both cases, they become bad Brāhmans only if they perform the ritual out of greed (dravya-lubdhena) and not as purified by faith (śraddhā-pūta).[12]

3) The smṛti statements about Brāhmans becoming corrupt Devalakās through becoming professional temple priests refer only to Brāhmans who worship gods other than Viṣṇu such as Rudra-Śiva and whose activities are not ordained and purified by the Pañcarātra Āgama and the proper initiatory rite (dīkṣā).[13]

While Yāmuna, as a devout Vaiṣṇava, may have considered argument 3) to be the strongest one, in terms of the effectiveness of his case among non-Vaiṣṇavas and non-Pāñcarātrins the first two were clearly the more decisive, i.e., that there were other Bhāgavata Brāhmans who were not tainted by being "professionally" involved with the performance of Pāñcarātrika temple ritual and could defend their less chaste fellows on the basis of principles and practices that were current and accepted within the Vedic tradition.

Bhāgavata Class III

This class consists of Bhāgavata Brāhmans who perform worship only for themselves (svārtham) in accordance with the Pāñcakālikā ritual ordained by the Pañcarātra Āgama but who also perform a distinctive series of forty sacraments (saṃskārās) or "rites of passage," a series that Yāmuna claims is a valid alternative or option (vikalpa) to the traditional Vedic one because it is based upon the now lost but inferable Ekāyana Śākhā or Branch of the Vājasaneya or Śukla Yajur Veda.[14] His Smārta opponents have grouped this class along with Classes I and II, claiming that their peculiar alternate series of saṃskārās stamps them as non-Vedic[15] and that the resort to a lost but inferable Vedic basis or śākhā was simply a deceitful trick to disguise their heretical character.[16]

However, Yāmuna has his opponents in a weak position because both the stratagems or principles involved (i.e., that of vikalpa or equally valid ritual options[17] and that of lost but inferable Vedic scriptures [pralīna-nitya-anumeya-śākhā-mūlatā][18]) have been devised by the Smārta Pūrva Mīmāṃsakas themselves in order to account for conflict between Vedic ritual injunctions and to provide a Vedic basis (veda-mūlatva) for Smārta practices that lack an extant "visible" Vedic injunction or text (pratyakṣa-śruti).[19] For even the most orthodox Smārta Brāhman must recognize that there are rites in accepted smṛti texts, such as the aṣṭakā in Manu's Dharma-śāstra,[20] for which there is no known extant Vedic injunction but for which an original but now lost Vedic basis must be presumed or inferred to have existed on the basis of the pramāṇa arthāpatti, "Presumption" or "Circumstantial-Implication," i.e., because without presuming such a Vedic basis there is no way of accounting for why such a revered and wise sage as Manu would have enjoined the aṣṭakā rite.[21]

While the Smārtas of course deny that this argument can be applied to establish a Vedic basis for the Pañcarātra Tantra, Yāmuna shows that every argument they use against the

Pañcarātra scriptures can be used with equal force against Manu's smṛti and demands that they justify their willingness to apply their argument from "Circumstantial-Implication" to establish the veda-mūlatva of Manu's composition while denying it in the case of Pañcarātra, which is accepted as Vedic by such great ancient sages as Nārada and Śāṇḍilya.[22]

Yāmuna is therefore able to dismiss the objection to accepting the lost but inferable Ekāyana Śākhā as the Vedic basis for these Bhāgavata Brāhmans' peculiar saṃskārās and to insist that their rituals are a valid option (vikalpa) to the usual Brāhmanic ones. Yāmuna states his case in a passage that merits a full translation:

> With regard to the objection made [by you, my worthy opponents,] according to which these Bhāgavatas are non-Brāhmanic (a-brāhmaṇyam) because they observe another series of sacraments (saṃskārās) beginning with the garbhādhāna ("the implanting of the seed in the womb") and ending with the dāha (cremation), here the fault is not with you, revered sirs, but with your ignorance! For these [Bhāgavata Brāhmans], who have been studying the Vājasaneya-śākhā in an [ancient and unbroken] family tradition (vaṃśa-paramparayā), perform the sacraments, garbhādhāna, etc., in accordance with the path (mārga) laid down by such Gṛhya or household sūtras as that by Kātyāyana. Indeed, those who perform the forty sacraments ordained by the Ekāyana-śrūti itself, while abandoning the duties established by the three Vedas (trayī-dharma-tyāgena) beginning with the recitation of the Sāvitrī [or Gāyatrī mantra at the rite of initiation], do not fall from their Brāhmanic status because of not following the rituals (karma) ordained by another śākhā, since they quite properly adhere to what is set forth by the Gṛhya-sūtras of their own śākhā. Otherwise, indeed, it would follow that all other Brāhmans would lose their Brāhmanic status because they do not perform the rituals enjoined by the śākhās of others. For everywhere customary activities (samācārās) are found to be regulated (vyavasthitās) according to differences of birth (jāti), Vedic branch (caraṇa), Vedic lineage (gotra) and personal qualification (adhikāra). Even if there is the rule that "one karma is meant for all śākhās," nevertheless nowhere do all duties (dharmās) come together as encumbent upon all the mutually distinct qualified performers (paraspara-vilakṣaṇa-adhikari-).
>
> And these [Bhāgavata] Brāhmans are distinct (vilakṣaṇās) from those "twice-born" (dvi-ja) who are qualified for the karma ordained by the Three Vedas (trayī-vihita), such as those sacrifices to Indra (aindra), Agni (āgneya), etc., that are means for the enjoyment of such [lower "worldly" or sensuous] goals

> as Heaven (svarga), sons (putra), etc., respectively.[23] [By contrast, these Bhāgavata] Brāhmans are mumukṣus or aspirants for [the Highest Human Goal of] "Release" (mokṣa), who are qualified for the karma that is the sole means (eka-upāya) for the attainment of the Bhagavān (bhagavat-prāpti), i.e., [the Pāñcakālikā ritual] abhigamana, upādāna, ijyā, etc., ordained by the Ekāyana-śruti and the vijñāna or meditative knowledge ordained by the Upaniṣads (trayy-anta). Therefore, it follows that neither of these two groups [i.e., the "worldly" twice-born Brāhmans who follow the Trayî-dharma nor the Bhāgavata mumukṣu Brāhmans] are non-Brāhmanic because they do not practice the karma ordained by the śākhā of the others. And since the eternal and faultless character (a-pauruṣeyatva) of the Ekāyana-śākhā has been established elaborately in Kāśmīra-āgama-prāmāṇya, it is not necessary to discuss the issue further here.[24]

Thus does Yāmuna give a not-so-subtle snub to his "wordly" Vedic opponents and give his clearest statement of the basic pattern for the integration of Pāñcarātra into the Vedic tradition, i.e., as an equally valid, and indeed superior, alternate ritual tradition that has the same goal as the Upaniṣads or Vedānta, "Release" (mokṣa) and the attainment of the Bhagavān or Brahman.[25] However, even in the case of this third class of Bhāgavatas, Yāmuna's argument is somewhat strained and would probably not have been effective if there were not a fourth class whose Brāhmanic status was much more secure.

Bhāgavata Class IV

This is a class of indisputably śiṣṭa Bhāgavata Brāhmans who perform faithfully both the path ordained by the Pañcarātra Tantra (pañcarātra-tantra-vihita-mārga) and the Vedic karma in accord with the strict Trayî-dharma.[26] Immediately following the long passage quoted above describing the Bhāgavata Brāhmans who have abandoned the Trayî-dharma for those rites ordained by the Ekāyana-śruti, Yāmuna qualifies his argument by asserting that "since genuine (prakṛtānāṃ) Bhāgavatas are clearly observed to be also associated with the rites of the Trayî-dharma such as the recitation of the Sāvitrî mantra, etc., it is therefore impossible to cast such aspersions upon them as the charge that they are vrātyas on the basis of the false assumptions that they have abandoned these Vedic rites."[27] Since this statement also comes immediately before the concluding verses dedicated to his learned and devout grandfather

Nāthamuni,[28] there can be no doubt that Yāmuna intended to place his own family (the coṭṭai kulam) among these śiṣṭa Bhāgavatas who observed both of these ritual paths, and little doubt that the effectiveness of his polemic in defense of the Pañcaratra Āgama derived largely from the fact that he was telling the truth.

Yāmuna's Smārta Pūrva Mīmāṃsaka opponents, citing Jaimini's Pūrva Mīmāṃsā Sūtra I.iii.2 (kartṛ-sāmānyāt pramāṇam), make clear that the real reason for inferring a Vedic basis for a rite enjoined only in a smṛti text such as Manu's Dharmaśāstra is that they are performed by the same agents (kartṛ-sāmānyāt) who perform the rites enjoined by śruti, i.e., by exemplary members of the three twice-born classes or varṇas (traivarṇikāḥ śiṣṭās) who have been educated in all aspects of the Vedic tradition by their fathers and teachers in unbroken succession.[29] In an immediate sense, it is only the practice of such learned and cultured exemplars (śiṣṭa-ācāra) that provides an adequate basis for the presumption that a text or practice with no known Vedic basis must originally have had one.[30]

Yāmuna again accepts the Smārtas' basic theory and turns it against them and in favor of the Pañcarātra revelation:

> And I have declared that [Pañcarātra] is accepted by Vedic people and by such great sages as Bhṛgu, Bharadvāja and Dvaipāyana who are the foremost among all orthodox people. Indeed, even now at the present time we see śiṣṭās who, with their minds set upon the Highest Good, perform such rites as temple-construction (prāsāda-karaṇa), the installation of images (pratimā-pratiṣṭhāpana), prostration (praṇāma), circumambulation (pradakṣiṇā) and festivals (utsava) according to the path ordained by the Pañcarātra Tantra, just as they perform such rites as the agnihotra, etc., that are ordained by "visible" extant Vedic texts (pratyakṣa-śruti-vihita). And it is not proper to claim that their [Tāntric] ritual acts are without a [Vedic] basis (nir-mūlam) because that would entail accepting that such similar [Smārta] rites as the sandhyāvandana and the aṣṭakā are also non-Vedic. Moreover, as has been said [by the Bhagavān Jaimini in Pūrva Mīmāṃsā Sūtra I.iii.7] "Or even when the source is not known, the necessary practices [of śiṣṭās] should be understood [as authoritative]," the conduct of śiṣṭās is authoritative (śiṣṭācārasya prāmāṇyam).[31]

Because he himself was one of these *śiṣṭās* and a learned *mīmāṃsaka*, Yāmuna was thus able to appeal persuasively and effectively to the very corner-stone of the Smārta Pūrva Mīmāmsā *darśana* in order to establish the *prāmāṇya* or authoritativeness of the Pañcarātra Āgama and the Tāntric ritual practices of its Bhāgavata adherents. In general, it may be stated that, once such *śiṣṭa* Brāhmans as Nāthamuni, Yāmuna and Rāmānuja in the case of the Vaiṣṇava Pañcarātra Tantra and Bhāsarvajña in the case of the Śaiva Pāśupata[32] became committed to these popular, originally non-Vedic traditions, it became impossible--on the basis of their orthodox Smārta opponents' own principles--for them to be excluded from the classical Vedic tradition. Thus such relatively open and cosmopolitan *śiṣṭa* Brāhmans are one of the most powerful and effective "classicizing" or "Sanskritizing" agents in the integration of the popular Bhakti and Tāntric traditions.

In Chapter V, I will further explore the integrative role of the early Śrī Vaiṣṇava Brāhman Teachers and especially the role of Nāthamuni's and Yāmuna's family (the *coṭṭai kulam*) of *śiṣṭa* Bhāgavatas or Kṛṣṇa devotees in defending, and continuing the efforts of, other classes of Brāhmans (the "Miśras" and the Coḷiyas) whose Vedic and Brāhmanic status had become questionable because of their involvement with the popular movements of Pāñcarātra and the Āḻvārs.

Yāmuna's Argument and Siddhānta

Yāmuna in the AP makes clear that there are essentially two categories of objections or issues raised against the validity of the Pañcarātra Āgama, one being largely sociological or practical in nature and the other primarily theological and theoretical. The former, with which we have just dealt, has to do with objections against the people who follow the injunctions of this Tantra.[33] While Yāmuna takes this sort of objection seriously and responds at length,[34] the AP is essentially a theoretical work of epistemology (*nyāya*) and scriptural theology (*mīmāṃsā*) and is thus structured in terms of Yāmuna's response to the latter type of objection, i.e., to the Pañcarātra revelation or scripture itself and to its source, the

Supreme Person (parama-puruṣa) or Bhagavān named Viṣṇu, Nārāyaṇa, Vāsudeva, etc.[35]

The Pūrvapakṣa section[36] is devoted to a presentation of all the criticisms lodged against the Pañcarātra Tantra by both the major schools of Pūrva Mīmāṃsā, the Bhāṭṭa and the Prābhākara, and to preliminary responses to these criticisms, primarily by a defender of Pañcarātra who argues from a Nyāya position (and with whom Yāmuna is closely allied) and secondarily by Yāmuna himself. The Bhāṭṭas begin the argumentation by driving a wedge between the words of the Vedas and all other words--the former being independently or innately authoritative (svataḥ prāmāṇya) because they are eternal, without any person (puruṣa) as an author and therefore devoid of all faults associated with persons (a-pauruṣeya), while all other words, being dependent upon fallible persons, can at the most have only a dependent authority that must be established by some other means of valid knowledge (pramāṇa).[37] The remainder of this first Bhāṭṭa Pūrvapakṣa is then devoted to maintaining that there is no pramāṇa that can conclusively establish the authoritativeness of the words of the Pañcarātra Tantra.[38]

While all of the major pramāṇas are considered and rejected, the option most relevant here is the one put forward by the Pāñcarātrika Naiyāyika, i.e., the perfect omniscient supersensual perception (pratyakṣa) of the Supreme Person. Against the Pūrva Mīmāṃsakas' objections that neither such perception nor such a Supreme Person exists,[39] this Pāñcarātrika Naiyāyika persists in arguing that they do and that the Pañcarātra scriptures based upon that Supreme Person's omniscient and flawless perception are equally and independently as authoritative as are the Vedas themselves.[40] The remainder of the Pūrvapakṣa and Yāmuna's theoretical Siddhānta are then devoted primarily to a debate, between the Pāñcarātrika Naiyāyika and Yāmuna on one hand and their Bhāṭṭa and Prābhākara opponents on the other, on whether and how the existence of such a perfect and omniscient Person can be established.[41]

In accord with the standard orthodox Nyāya procedure, the Pāñcarātrika Naiyāyika maintains that the existence of such a Supreme Person is established by means of the pramāṇa anumāṇa or Inference, the testimony of which is then confirmed by authoritative scriptural statements.[42] The Bhāṭṭas then respond at length showing that Inference is incompetent to establish such a Supreme Person, arguing, on the one hand, that Inference, being based upon sense perception, cannot establish super-sensual realities and, on the other hand, that Inference with regard to such a Supreme Person, being based upon analogies with human persons, necessarily ascribe to the former all the limitations and imperfections universally associated with the latter.[43] Thus, the Naiyāyika's inference that the Universe, the Vedas and the Pañcarātra Āgamas must have an intelligent creator because they are effects can at the most establish some person who has as his inherent attributes (svabhāvas) "properties like being in possession of a body, having something left to desire, being deprived of omnipotence and omniscience, etc."[44]--not a Supreme Person with the opposite necessary particulars (viśeṣās) such as being without a body, having his desires eternally satisfied and being omniscient.

The Bhāṭṭas go so far as to admit that the Naiyāyika Inference might actually be successful in establishing the desired Supreme Person if there were some other pramāṇa that could be applied to rule out the undesired particular properties; however, since the Bhagavān whose existence is to be established falls completely outside the scope of all other pramāṇas, the Naiyāyika Inference simply establishes the existence of some imperfect person of limited knowledge.[45] The Bhāṭṭas then conclude by reaffirming the unique status of the a-pauruṣeya Vedas and asserting that the Pañcarātra Tantra was composed simply by some human person in order to deceive the world.[46]

At this point Yāmuna himself enters the discussion for the first time with an objection against the Bhāṭṭas.[47] Van Buitenen's translation reads:

> Objection. This [the Bhātta's criticism of the Naiyāyika] would be true if proof of the existence of the Lord could only be sought on the strength of logical argumentation. As it is, this is a fallacy, for the great Lord is known on the authority of the upaniṣads. When we hear the multitudinous statements of the eternal Scriptures which set forth the existence of an omniscient and omnipotent supreme Personality who is capable of creating the entire universe, how then can we refuse to accept the

> authority of a tradition which derives from His immediate cognition?[48]

Yāmuna's statement here is somewhat ambiguous, apparently lending itself to opposed interpretations. Van Buitenen at first maintains that Yāmuna is concurring with the Bhāṭṭas' rejection of Inference as a means of proving the existence of the Supreme Person but asserting that His existence can be known _only_ from Scripture.[49]

My interpretation of the course of Yāmuna's argument at this point is quite different:

1) Yāmuna has the Pāñcarātrika Naiyāyika assert that Inference is a _pramāṇa_, noting in passing that the results of Inference are supported or strengthened by Scripture.

2) He then has the Bhāṭṭa Mīmāṃsakas argue that Inference by itself is not capable of establishing all that the Naiyāyika claims that it does.

3) Yāmuna next has the Mīmāṃsakas make the crucial admission that the Naiyāyika's use of Inference would be valid _if there were another pramāṇa that would be capable of ruling out certain undesired properties_. The Mīmāṃsakas, however, deny the existence of such an additional _pramāṇa_.

4) Yāmuna himself then grants that, _if_ there were no _pramāṇa_ other than Inference, the Mīmāṃsakas would be correct; _however, since there is another applicable pramāṇa_, i.e., Scripture, the Mīmāṃsakas' criticism of the Naiyāyikas is invalid.

If my understanding of the course of the argument is correct, Yāmuna, far from concurring with the Mīmāṃsakas here, intends to reject their criticism and to affirm or at least build upon the position of the Pāñcarātrika Naiyāyika.

My understanding would seem to be confirmed by Yāmuna's deceptively brief but explicit rejection of the Bhāṭṭas' major criticism of the Naiyāyika's Inference:

> And thus the faults of being non-omniscient, possessing a physical form, etc., that are implied by what is observed to be the general nature [of all perceptible creators and that would, if allowed to stand, negate the Inferences with regard to the Supreme Person] are excluded from the Lord whose various glorious qualities such as Knowledge, Lordliness, etc., are known from hundreds of Scriptural passages.[50]

And thus, since the faults cited by the Bhāṭṭas can be warded off by means of another pramāṇa, the Pāñcarātrika Naiyāyika's Inferences can be allowed to stand as valid, although not sufficient in and of themselves since they require the assistance of Scripture to establish fully the particularities of the Divine nature.[51]

In his defense of the Pāñcarātrika Naiyāyika against the Bhāṭṭas' criticism, Yāmuna has challenged the most basic Pūrva Mīmāṃsā assumptions about Scripture as a pramāṇa, especially the dictum that Scripture is a means of valid knowledge only as an injunction (vidhi) with reference to some kārya, a ritual action "yet to be established, a task yet to be undertaken, an act yet to be performed,"[52] but not as an indicative statement about the nature of some already established fact or entity (pariniṣṭhita-vastu, siddha-vastu) such as Brahman. Yāmuna, along with all Vedāntins, must deny this Pūrva Mīmāṃsā assumption and affirm that the primary purpose of the Upaniṣads is to give valid knowledge about the nature of Brahman or the Supreme Person.[53] Yāmuna's denial is answered quite sharply by the Prābhākaras, the other major school of Pūrva Mīmāṃsā who advocate most strongly and consistently the view that Scripture and indeed all language is meaningful and authoritative only when construed in an injunctive mode in relation to some kārya.[54] Thus the Prābhākaras deny once again that Scripture can be used as a pramāṇa with regard to an established entity like a Supreme Person and, therefore, reassert that no such person can be proven to exist. In the establishment of his Siddhānta, Yāmuna takes this Prābhākara position seriously as the major one that must be conclusively refuted before the Upaniṣads can be employed to establish the existence and nature of the Supreme Person.

Yāmuna's Siddhānta

Yāmuna first states his Siddhānta as a formal Inference expressed in verse or kārikā form and containing several points of ambiguity:

> vivādādhyasitaṃ tantraṃ pramāṇam iti gṛhyatām/
> nirdoṣajñānajanmatvāj jyotiṣṭomādivākyavat//[55]

Let it be accepted that this disputed [Pañcarātra] Tantra is pramāṇa

Because it has faultless knowledge (nirdoṣa-jñāna) as its source [or "because it is the source of faultless knowledge"], like the [Vedic] statements on such rites as the Jyotiṣṭoma.

The major source of ambiguity in this Inference lies in the issue of how to interpret its Reason (hetu), nirdoṣa-jñāna-janma-tvāt.[56] In my translation above I have given first my understanding, which agrees with that of Narasimhachary,[57] followed in brackets by a translation corresponding to those of van Buitenen and Oberhammer.[58] While this latter meaning could not have been Yāmuna's primary intention, I will argue that, as a poet-philosopher, he did intend for his ambiguous verse to evoke it as a secondary overtone.

Yāmuna begins his explication of his Siddhānta by a detailed and technical demonstration of the absence of all possible faults (doṣās) or logical fallacies (ābhāsās) from his Inference,[59] an exercise that contributes little to our positive understanding of his intended meaning. Yāmuna concludes this exercise by asserting that the Reason nirdoṣa-jñāna-janma-tvāt does not suffer from the fallacy of svarūpa-asiddhi, i.e., of being by its very nature not established as existing in the Subject (pakṣa) of the Inference, here Pañcarātra Tantra, because "the negation of hetu, and not the hetu, resides in the pakṣa."[60] At this point, Yāmuna's Pūrva Mīmāṃsā opponents, who hold that the negation of this hetu (i.e., "having faulty knowledge as its source") does indeed reside in this Tantra, challenge his assertion; and Yāmuna proceeds to develop his position through a debate with these opponents, especially the Prābhākaras.[61] I will first present my best understanding of the major points Yāmuna is making through this debate and then return to the issue of how to interpret Yāmuna's ambiguous Inference.

The text of the beginning of this debate reads:

Pūrva Mīmāṃsaka: Indeed how, in the case of these Pañcarātra Tantras [which you admit to be the statements of a person], can the assumption of faults (doṣas) be avoided, arising as it does from the [immediate observation of the] general nature of statements originating from [observable] persons [who are universally found to be fallible] (pauruṣeyatva-sāmānyād)?

Yāmuna: How, in the case of the Vedas [which you admit to be language-statements,] can this same assumption be excluded when it arises from the [immediate observation of the] general nature of language-statements (vākyatva-sāmānyād)?

If you reply "[Vedic language-statements can be distinguished from all other language-statements and can be shown to be free from the possibility of fault] because they are non-personal in origin (a-pauruṣeya-tva) [and therefore cannot possess the faults that arise only from fallible persons],"

then here also [these pauruṣeya Tantras can be distinguished from all other pauruṣeya statements and can be shown to be free from the possibility of fault] because they have been composed by the omniscient Supreme Person who is without any motive to deceive us (sarvajña-avāptakāma-parama-puruṣa-praṇītatayā) [and therefore cannot possess the faults that arise only from fallible persons].[62]

Thus, having understood [that the argument is just as strong in the case of the Pañcarātra Tantras as it is in the case of the Vedas], sir, keep quiet [about any charge that my Inference suffers from the fallacy of svarūpa-asiddhi because the Reason nirdoṣa-jñāna-janmatvāt is excluded from these Tantras]!

What I have been saying amounts to the following:

[First of all, the following statement is accepted as an] established axiom [by all the Mīmāṃsakas who are parties to this debate]: "Faults (doṣās) that destroy the authoritativeness (prāmāṇya) [of language-statements] never exist in language (śabda) because of the inherent nature of language itself (svato); rather, language as such is intrinsically authoritative (sva-tas . . . pramāṇatvam)."[63]

However, with regard to certain [language-statements] this [intrinsic authoritativeness] is destroyed because of a fault in the mind or intention of the speaker (vaktur āśaya-doṣeṇa); such is the case with such statements as "a herd of elephants is on my finger-tip."[64]

With regard to the collection of compositions here under discussion, i.e., the Pañcarātra Tantras , the very language of the Upaniṣads (trayī-mūrddha-dhvanir eva) excludes any doubt we may have as to the possibility of faults (doṣa) being associated with the mind of their composer.

Indeed, the Vedāntas speak of an omniscient Lord of the Universe who is supremely compassionate--how then could such [faults] as deceitfulness, etc., reside in Him?[65]

This section of text presents Yāmuna's direct statement of his intention in his initial versified Inference and is sufficient in and of itself to establish that his primary concern in proving his Thesis tantram pramāṇam is with showing that the sources (-janma-) of these compositions, i.e., the "mind," "intention," or consciousness of their author (vaktur āśaya-), is faultless (nirdoṣa-)--not with the text themselves being sources of faultless knowledge.

To maintain his Siddhānta, Yāmuna must refute the crucial objection posed by the Prābhākaras in the Pūrvapakṣa, since his entire argument stands or falls on the question of the validity of his using Scripture, especially the Upaniṣads or Vedāntas, as a pramāṇa that excludes all faults from the "mind" or consciousness of the Author of the Pañcarātra Āgamas. At this point, a Prābhākara objector reminds him of their still unrefuted objection that Vedic language-statements (śabdas) have no authoritativeness with regard to an established entity (siddhe vastuni) such as the postulated Supreme Author, since language is meaningfully denotative only when construed in an injunctive mode in relation to some kārya.[66]

Yāmuna begins to attack this Prābhākara position by arguing that worldly language-statements (laukikās) are regularly seen to be concerned with established objects (siddham apy artham) and meaningfully convey their denotative capacity (śaktim) simply through their normal modes of application (prayogataḥ) with regard to these objects just as they do when applied in an injunctive mode to a kārya.[67] Thus, on the basis of normal usage (vyavahāra-upapatteḥ),[68] it must be denied that language-statements are denotative only when construed in relation to a kārya (kārya-anvita-abhidhānam) and affirmed that they are denotative of their own objects in whatever mode they are construed (sarvatra-anvita-abhidhānam).[69]

The Prābhākaras, however, make a hard and fast distinction between normal worldly language-statements, which to them are not pramāṇas at all,[70] and Vedic scriptural ones, which are the only type of śabda that is pramāṇa since it alone gives valid knowledge about kāryas that are not previously known by means of any other pramāṇa (māna-antara-apūrve kārye). While Yāmuna goes into considerable detail in refuting this exceedingly complex (gaurava) theory, his main concern is to maintain that, even if Vedic śabda were to have such an object and

and function, that would be no reason 1) to assume that such an object and function are the only or even the primary ones that valid śabda can have, 2) to deny the capacity of śabda to denotate its own object no matter what the nature of that object is and 3) to deny the validity of worldly śabda with regard to the objects that legitimately come within its scope.[71] Thus Yāmuna denies the absolute distinction that the Prābhākaras attempt to make between worldly (laukika) śabda and Vedic (vaidika) and reaffirms that valid knowledge or cognition with regard to established objects is given by worldly śabda and, by implication, by all śabda, including the Upaniṣads.[72]

The Prābhākaras then maintain that it is not valid to generalize about the nature of śabda as a pramāṇa on the basis of the kind of knowledge or cognition given by laukika-śabda since the validity of such cognitions depends not on the pramāṇa śabda but rather on anumāna or Inference.[73] Their argument is based upon the commonly accepted proposition that valid knowledge or cognition (pramā or pramiti) must be definite (niścaya), free from any doubt whatsoever. Since worldly śabda is so often found to be in error, doubt is associated with the knowledge that results from it and such śabda cannot be deemed an independent pramāṇa or means of valid knowledge. Whatever degree of definite validity such knowledge attains results secondarily from an Inference that the speakers of these statements are āptās, qualified and knowledgeable persons. Thus, the types of objects (i.e., established entities) presented by worldly śabda cannot be said to be established by the pramāṇa śabda, since such worldly statements are not independently and inherently valid but rather are dependent upon the cognition of the speaker (vaktr-anubhava-paratantratayā).

While this argument of the Prābhākaras would be a strong one from the perspectives of the Naiyāyikas and the Buddhists, who assume that the validity or authoritativeness of knowledge is extrinsic (parataḥ prāmāṇyam),[74] within the Mīmāṃsā context it is a weak and inconsistent one, since the Prābhākaras, along with all other Mīmāṃsakas, begin with the assumption of the intrinsic authoritativeness (svataḥ prāmāṇyam) of all knowledge.[75] Thus, to deny Yāmuna's arguments based upon the nature of laukika-śabda, the Prābhākaras have been forced to contravene their own first principles.

Having maneuvered his opponents into such a weak position, Yāmuna returns to restate and develop certain crucial aspects of his Siddhānta as briefly stated in the section quoted in full above. He restates the basic Mīmāṃsaka position that the fact that certain śabda is secondarily (guṇataḥ) or extrinsically (parataḥ) shown to be false (vitatha) or non-authoritative (a-prāmāṇyam) because of faults in the "mind" or "intention" of the speaker (vaktṛ-āśaya-doṣa-vaśīkārād) does not mean that śabda abandons its axiomatic essential nature of being intrinsically authoritative (svataḥ prāmāṇyam), i.e., of independently and immediately communicating or revealing valid knowledge or cognition of its object (svabhāvato 'rtham avagamayan śabdaḥ).[76] Thus, to a hearer, who has been taught the particular language, śabda immediately (sahasā--eva) reveals its object; it does not wait until the hearer acquires knowledge of the source (mūla-jñānam) of the śabda.[77] In accord with the principle of the extrinsic invalidity (parataḥ aprāmāṇyam) of knowledge, later and secondarily knowledge of the source might arise that would reveal faults in the speaker that would invalidate the particular śabda as pramāṇa, without however affecting the basic nature of śabda itself.[78] If all śabda, including worldly, did not immediately communicate its object, then all worldly discourse and activity would be impossible, including the Prābhākara recourse to Inference.[79]

Therefore, Yāmuna asserts, a cognition that concerns an established object (siddha-viṣayā buddhiḥ) and that is produced by a worldly śabda is a valid cognition based upon the pramāṇa śabda, not upon anumāna.[80] Consequently, the pramāṇa is meaningfully denotative not only with regard to a kārya but also with regard to established entities. Thus, Yāmuna returns to the point at which he had originally been challenged by the Prābhākaras and says,

> And therefore, [because śabda can be denotative of an established entity,] those statements of the Vedāntas (vedānta-vacāṃsi) . . . that reveal a Person who is absolutely different (vilakṣaṇa-puruṣa-) [from all other persons in that he is without fault] are means of valid knowledge (pramāṇa) with regard to Him (tatra) because [as śabda] they have the

> nature of being the cause of definite uncontradicted knowledge about such an object as that [established entity which is the Supreme Person] (tad-visaya-asandigdha-aviparyaya-vijñāna-hetu-tvāt).[81]

Yāmuna then concludes his refutation of the Prābhākara objection by proposing his own general definition of pramāṇa, which he feels is simpler and more straightforward than the Prābhākara's complex and convoluted one:

> Therefore, indubitable and uncontradicted knowledge (asandigdha-aviparyasta-vijñānam) is pramāṇa, regardless of such distinctions as whether it refers to something already established, to something still to be done or whatever.[82]

Before concluding the statement of his Siddhānta, Yāmuna must refute an earlier objection of the Bhāṭṭas[83] that, even if Scriptural śabda is a means of valid knowledge with regard to an established entity like a person, it cannot establish omniscient perception (sārvajñya) as a quality of any person because other pramāṇas such as Perception and Inference definitely establish that perception, by its very nature being limited by its dependence upon particular sense organs, cannot possibly be omniscient or all-encompassing. While the pramāṇa śabda gives us knowledge about matters beyond the scope of other pramāṇas, the knowledge it gives about such super-sensible matters cannot be such as to conflict blatantly with the clear testimony of our normal experience.

Yāmuna replies to this argument by showing that the clear testimony of the Upaniṣads is that the Perception of the Supreme Person is absolutely unique and distinct from normal sense-perception and that therefore the nature of the former cannot be determined on the basis of analogy with the latter.[84] His main evidence is drawn from the Śvetāśvatara Upaniṣad in which it is said that the Supreme Person "sees without eyes and hears without ears" (SvetUp 3.19) and that His "activity of knowledge and power is inherent and natural" (svābhāvikī jñāna-bala-kriyā, SvetUp 6.8), i.e., not dependent upon or limited by anything (i.e., sense-organs) other than His own nature.[85] According to Yāmuna, these scriptural statements must be accepted in their primary denotative sense (mukhya-vṛtti) because there is no other pramāṇa that is competent to contradict their primary sense and thus necessitate a secondary metaphorical interpretation (guṇa-vāda).[86] Since the character of the Supreme Person is established by Scripture (śāstra) which is the most powerful of all pramāṇas (pramāṇa-goṣṭhī-jyeṣṭena śāstrenaiva) and the only one competent to give complete and valid knowledge of super-sensible matters, the scriptural testimony as to the inherent omniscient perception of the Supreme Person must be accepted.[87]

Thus, Yāmuna concludes that the primary purpose of the Upaniṣads, the jñāna-kāṇḍa of the Vedas, is not--as is the case with the karma-kāṇḍa--to give injunctions (vidhi) that serve man by telling him how to act in accord with Dharma, but rather to be of service to man (pum-artha-tā) by giving true knowledge of Brahman that has as its fruit the highest bliss (brahma-vijñānaṃ mahānanda-phalaṃ).[88]

Then Yāmuna sums up his Siddhānta in a prose sentence that is the equivalant of his initial verse Inference:

> To sum up, when the Bhagavān is thus established as one who is the sole depository of such auspicious qualities as unfalsifiable (avitatha), natural (sahaja) and all-encompassing direct cognition (sarva-sākṣātkāra); compassion; etc., as is understood from hundreds of quoted Scriptural statements, then the prāmāṇya of the [Pañcarātra] Tantra is conclusively established because it has as its source the [faultless] cognition of the [Bhagavān] (tad-anubhava-mūla-tayā tantra-prāmāṇyam).[89]

The Reason given in this statement, i.e., tad[bhagavad]-anubhava-mūla-tayā, once again establishes quite clearly that the Reason nirdoṣa-jñāna-janma-tvāt in Yāmuna's initial Inference has as its primary meaning "because it has the faultless knowledge (nirdoṣa-jñāna = tad-anubhava = avitatha-sahaja-sarva-sākṣātkāra) of the Bhagavān as its source."

Indeed, there is in the AP no usage of any similar phrasing in a contextually equivalent situation (i.e., where the issue is the Reason for the Thesis tantram pramāṇam) that supports the alternative interpretation employed by van Buitenen and Oberhammer.[90] While there is one construction that in isolation could be taken to support their translations, the context at that point concerns the pramāṇatva of the Upaniṣads (vedānta-vacāṃsi), not the Pañcarātra Tantra, and the issue is not the establishment of the Upaniṣads' pramāṇatva in general (which is presupposed), but rather their being pramāṇa with regard to a particular kind of object, i.e., an established entity.[91]

Having thus resolved the issue of the primary meaning of Yāmuna's Siddhānta, it remains to consider the ambiguity in the statement of his initial Inference that provided a basis for van Buitenen's and Oberhammer's interpretation. This ambiguity is partially based upon an ambiguity within Indian epistemological discussion with regard to the word pramāṇa in Yāmuna's Thesis tantraṃ pramāṇam. Pramāṇa can be used 1) for a "means of valid knowledge or cognition" or 2) for the result or fruit of such a means, i.e., "valid knowledge or cognition" itself, which is more accurately designated by pramā or pramiti.[92] Pramāṇa can also be used in the more general sense of an "authority," "something that is true, valid or authoritative;" and van Buitenen and Oberhammer are doubtless correct in choosing such a general, vague and ambiguous phrasing for their translations of Yāmuna's tantraṃ pramāṇam.[93]

However, they should not have let the matter rest with this vague rendering since Yāmuna himself goes on to give, at several points, clear indication of the ways he employs the term pramāṇa in its technical usage. He also gives a strong indication of the primary sense that should be given to it in the context of his Siddhānta.

First of all it is clear that Yāmuna does follow the general practice of using pramāṇa in two senses, sometimes for the "means of valid knowledge or cognition"[94] and sometimes for the "valid knowledge or cognition itself."[95] However, while Yāmuna uses pramāṇa in both senses, in the course of presenting his Siddhānta he explicitly defines it only in the latter sense, a fact that should be given great weight in determining the primary sense of Yāmuna's initial Inference. As presented above, Yāmuna defines pramāṇa as "indubitable and uncontradicted knowledge" (asandigdha-aviparyasta-vijñānaṃ pramāṇam).[96]

Combining this definition of pramāṇa with the results of our previous discussion, we arrive at the conclusion that Yāmuna's primary intention in his initial Inference was to assert that:

> this disputed Pañcarātra Tantra is indubitable and uncontradicted knowledge because it has the faultless knowledge of the Bhagavān as its source, just as the Vedic statements . . . are such valid knowledge because they are non-personal in origin (apauruṣeyatvāt) and therefore also free from fault with regard to their source.

Presumably, van Buitenen and Oberhammer have been led astray in their interpretation of nirdoṣa-jñāna-janmatvāt because Yāmuna's definition of the term pramāṇa and primary concern with the pramāṇa-vāda in general are not the same as those often encountered in Indian epistemological discussion. In addition to one's normal expectation that pramāṇa refers to the means of valid knowledge, the pramāṇa-vāda is often primarily concerned with producing, and guaranteeing the validity of, valid knowledge in the sense of accurate cognition (pramā) within the consciousness of a cognizer (pramātṛ).[97] In line with such a concern, the interpretation that this Tantra is pramāṇa "because it produces faultless knowledge" would seem to make sense. However, this concern, while present in the AP, is not Yāmuna's major focus. Rather, his prior and primary concern is to establish that the language-statements contained within the Pañcarātra Āgamas are valid and without error. And within Yāmuna's Mīmāṃsā context it is clear that the crucial step in establishing this point conclusively is the excluding of the very possibility of what Yamuna terms a kāraṇa-doṣa, a fault in the cause or source of the language-statements.[98]

While Yāmuna's primary intention is thus to exclude any kāraṇa-doṣa, he does recognize another kind of fault that can invalidate knowledge; and he may well have constructed his Reason nirdoṣa-jñāna-janmatvāt in a deliberately ambiguous manner so as to exclude secondarily this second type of fault. In the course of denying that his argument can be applied to establish the authoritativeness of other Tantras such as those of the Kāpālikās, the Kālāmukhās, the Pāśupatās and the Śaivās, Yāmuna is challenged by an objector who asserts that, since in Yāmuna's darśana it is an axiom that knowledge is intrinsically valid (svataḥ pramāṇam vijñānaṃ), all Tantras should be accepted as valid. Yāmuna agrees that all knowledge is intrinsically valid but counters the objection by observing that the presumed validity of knowledge is vitiated either 1) by bādha, i.e., by being contradicted by another, more powerful pramāṇa, or 2) by kāraṇa-doṣa.[99] Yāmuna asserts that both these faults are clearly present in the cases of the other Tantras, implying the absence of both in the case of Pañcarātra.

Yāmuna does explicitly exclude the possibility of bādha or contradiction with regard to Pañcarātra;[100] and in this connection, he does occasionally quote an example of knowledge or cognition that has arisen from the Pañcarātra Āgamas and shows that it also is not vitiated by a fault of bādha.[101] In such a context there would seem to be justification for interpreting nirdoṣa-jñāna-janmatvāt as meaning "because it is the source of faultless knowledge," i.e., cognition whose validity is not destroyed by bādha. Since such an interpretation is grammatically possible, since Yāmuna would certainly have agreed with its intention and since he was a skillful poet as well as dialectician, it seems quite likely to me that he self-consciously composed his versified Inference so as to allow for this secondary interpretation on the basis of the double sense of the term pramāṇa and the ambiguity inherent in the compound nirdoṣa-jñāna-janmatvāt. If such were the case, then in addition to his primary meaning given above, Yāmuna would also have meant to assert that

> this disputed Pañcarātra Tantra is a means of indubitable and uncontradicted knowledge or cognition because it is a source of knowledge or cognition that is free from the fault of being contradicted by any other pramāṇa, just as is the case with the Vedic statements. . .

It still remains to ask the question as to whether or not the ambiguities contained within Yāmuna's statement of his Siddhānta can be understood and expressed in a unified systematic manner. According to Yāmuna, all existing knowledge or cognition (vijñāna) is to be presumed to be intrinsically true or valid (svataḥ pramāṇam vijñānaṃ). However, if a particular vijñāna is secondarily (guṇataḥ) or extrinsically (parataḥ), i.e., upon later examination, found either to be uncertain or doubtful (sandigdha) or to be false or contradicted (viparyasta), then it is a-pramāṇa or invalid.[102] Therefore, pramāṇa is defined (i.e., distinguished from all cognition that is a-pramāṇa) as knowledge or cognition that is 1) indubitable (a-sandigdha) and 2) uncontradicted (a-viparyasta). Thus, in the definition asandigdha-aviparyasta-vijñānam, the first defining characteristic corresponds to and excludes the vitiating factor of kāraṇa-doṣa (faults in the cause of the knowledge that make us doubtful as to its validity), while the second defining characteristic corresponds to and excludes the vitiating factor of bādha (definite contradiction or falsification by another, more powerful knowledge or cognition whose validity is assured). Any knowledge or cognition that is free from these two classes of vitiating faults (nirdoṣa-jñāna-) must be accepted as being inherently or intrinsically pramāṇa, taken first in the sense of pramā but also in the sense of the cause of other valid knowledge or cognition (-asandigdha-aviparyaya-vijñāna-hetu-tva.)[103]

Expressing Yāmuna's initial Inference in terms of this systematic analysis yields:

> this disputed Pañcarātra Tantra is indubitable and unfalsifiable knowledge as well as the means of such knowledge among men. It is the former because it has as its source the Bhagavān's knowledge that is free from all faults, both faults inhering in itself or the Bhagavān that would produce doubts about the validity of this Tantra and faults arising from contradiction by another more powerful valid knowledge that would show the Bhagavān's knowledge and its results to be false. It is the latter because it in turn is the source of knowledge that is also free from both these types of faults.

Having thus completed his general theoretical argument for the prāmāṇya of the Pañcarātra Tantra by establishing that the Upaniṣads reveal the existence of a perfect, compassionate and omniscient Supreme Person who is competent to produce such a revelation, Yāmuna then takes two further steps necessary to buttress his Siddhānta. The first is to establish, on the basis of extensive quotation from śruti and smṛti, that the innately omniscient one (sahaja-sarvajñāna-vān) revealed by the Upaniṣads is no other than the one named Viṣṇu, Hari, Vāsudeva or Nārāyaṇa who composed the Pañcarātra Āgamas.[104] This discussion is of significance primarily because, as Yāmuna explicitly states, it summarizes at least a portion of his no longer extant composition, the Puruṣa-nirṇaya.[105]

This first additional step concludes Yāmuna's positive statement of his Siddhānta; however, he must take one further negative step, i.e., he must deny that his own argument (nyāya) in defense of the Pañcarātra Tantra can be extended to the other Tantras adhered to by such worshippers of Rudra-Śiva as the Kāpālikas, the Kālāmukhas, the Pāśupatas and the Śaivas.[106] The most remarkable aspect of this section is the degree to which Yāmuna sides with the orthodox Smārta Pūrva Mīmāṃsaka opponents of Pāñcarātra against these Śaiva Tantras. He applies, and with equal vehemence, all of his own critics' arguments against these other Tantras, e.g., they teach doctrines and practices in contradiction of the Vedas and Vedānta, they were composed by fallible persons with the intention of deceiving the world, they are adhered to by those outside the varṇa-āśrama system, etc. Yāmuna thus makes every effort to distinguish Pāñcarātra from these other non-Vedic Tāntric traditions which he views as heretical deviations and to align it with the Vedic tradition and the beliefs and practices of the most learned śiṣṭa Brāhmans.

The remainder of the AP is devoted to the refutation of the various criticisms still remaining unanswered from among those presented in the Pūrvapakṣa. It is in this section of the text that Yāmuna responds at great length to the charge, made by the Bhāṭṭas near the end of the Pūrvapakṣa,[107] that Bādarāyaṇa rejects Pāñcarātra in the Vedānta Sūtras.[108] In Chapter IV, we will analyze this section in which Yāmuna attempts to overcome this major obstacle to the harmonization of Vedānta and Pāñcarātra.

CHAPTER IV

YĀMUNA AND HIS VEDĀNTIC SOURCES IN THE ĀGAMA-PRĀMĀṆYA AND THE ĀTMA-SIDDHI

The major statement of Yāmuna's self-conscious position on the relation between Vedānta and Pāñcarātra, and a major source for our knowledge of the general character and sources of his Vedāntic tradition, is the section of the Āgama-prāmāṇya in which he refutes the charge that Bādarāyaṇa rejected Pāñcarātra in the Vedānta Sūtras. In the first part of this chapter, this section of the AP will be analyzed in order to isolate and characterize the sources of Yāmuna's tradition of Pāñcarātrika Vedānta. In the second part, an attempt will be made to relate these sources to the ones that Yāmuna explicitly cites in his major Vedāntic work, the Ātma-siddhi.

In the Pūrvapakṣa section of the AP, the criticisms related to VS II.ii.42-45 or the Utpatty-asambhava-adhikaraṇa (UA Adhik.) were brought in piecemeal and generally dealt with briefly as relatively minor aspects of the larger Pūrva Mīmāṃsaka argument against Pāñcarātra.[1] On the other hand, Yāmuna's refutation of the charge that Bādarāyaṇa rejected Pāñcarātra is long and elaborate[2]--a contrast indicative of Yāmuna's great personal concern to be able to claim the support of the VS for Pāñcarātra and to assert the complete harmony and compatibility of this Tantra with Vedānta.

As emphasized previously, Yāmuna deals with the charge that Pāñcarātra as a whole is in conflict with the Vedas (veda-vipratiṣedha) as deriving from his Pūrva Mīmāṃsaka opponents and effectively eliminates this extreme position before beginning to consider Bādarāyaṇa's viewpoint directly. Thus, Yāmuna points out to the Pūrva Mīmāṃṣaka critics that such statements as Śāṇḍilya's "scorn of the Vedas" (veda-nindā) cannot be employed to deny the Vedic character or basis (veda-mūlatva) of Pāñcarātra because such "scorn" is not actually meant to criticize or reject that which is scorned but rather to praise that which is compared with the scorned object.[3] And Yāmuna is able to cite sufficient instances of similar veda-nindā within the Vedas themselves and within such accepted smṛti literature as the Mahābhārata to make his argument quite a strong one, as has been attested by Belvalkar (see Chapter II) with regard to Rāmānuja's restatement of Yāmuna's argument.[4] Yāmuna also cites instances of "praise of the Vedas" (veda-praśaṃśā) found within the Pañcarātra Āgamas.[5]

Finally, Yāmuna says that the statement that Śāṇḍilya was not able to find the Highest Good or Goal of man (paraṃ śreyas, puruṣārtham) in the four Vedas is not intended to mean that this Highest Good is not in the Vedas but only that Śāṇḍilya was not able to find it in and through them. Thus, when the statement is correctly interpreted as meaning "not finding that Goal of man which is in the Vedas and desiring it, he became learned in the Pañcarātra scripture [in order to attain that same Goal]," we see that it actually declares that Pañcarātra and the Veda have precisely the same goal or meaning (pañcarātra-śrutyor aikārthyam eva).[6]

Having thus forestalled the charge that Pañcarātra as a whole is in conflict with the Vedas, Yāmuna moves quickly to deny that Bādarāyaṇa rejected Pāñcarātra in any sense whatsoever. The beginning point and cornerstone of Yāmuna's argument is the identification of Bādarāyaṇa, the author of the VS, with Dvaipāyana (Vyāsa or Veda-Vyāsa), the author of the Mahābhārata.[7] Since Dvaipāyana in the Mahābhārata shows himself to be an exemplary Bhāgavata and praises Pañcarātra as a great Upaniṣad that is consistent with the four Vedas (mahopaniṣadaṃ caturveda-samanvitam),[8] how then could he reverse himself in the VS and reject Pañcarātra which is "his own supreme teaching, the very essence of the meaning of the Vedānta" (vedānta-sāra-sarvasvam ātmīyaṃ paramaṃ matam)?[9] Thus we are brought to the issue of how, according to Yāmuna and his Vedāntic sources, Bādarāyaṇa's sūtras dealing with Pañcarātra are to be understood.

A. Yāmuna's Vedāntic Sources in the Āgama-prāmāṇya

Gerhard Oberhammer's previously mentioned analysis[10] provides the most fruitful starting point for a discussion of the section of the AP dealing with the UA Adhik. In the terms of his primary focus, i.e., on isolating and distinguishing the sources upon which Yāmuna drew in composing or compiling this section, his study is painstaking and generally accurate and helpful; with some objections and modifications, his hypotheses as to Yāmuna's major Vedāntic sources will be accepted and built upon in this study.

However, Oberhammer's general approach has severe limitations and requires balancing by a different, although complementary, perspective. His preoccupation with Yāmuna's sources leads him to devote little effort to understanding Yāmuna himself, whose own position is in effect reduced to what is left over after the ideas of his sources are subtracted.[11] Oberhammer's analysis leaves the impression that Yāmuna quite mechanically compiled a collection of mutually inconsistent sources and then tacked on at the end his own peculiar, and also inconsistent, contribution.[12] Even if Yāmuna's individual contribution was as meager as Oberhammer maintains, Yāmuna's integration of his sources into his presentation was not as mechanical, riddled with logical inconsistencies and lacking in creativity as Oberhammer suggests.

Within Biblical studies in recent years there has been an increasing recognition of the limitations and dangers inherent in such a preoccupation with reducing literary documents to their sources to the exclusion of an adequate appreciation for the significance and creativity of the integrative role of the redactor.[13] It is, after all, through the efforts of the redactor that his sources continue to live, to exert influence upon succeeding generations, and eventually to be available for and worthy of critical analysis. The literary document that the redactor creates is as it were the living body or whole of which the sources are the vital organs or parts. Exploratory surgery is often helpful and necessary but is to be performed only for the benefit of the living whole, not simply for the sake of appreciating the structure and function of the heart, the lungs, etc. A complete dissection is justified only if the body is dead or we consider the living organism to be of insignificant value compared with the knowledge to be gained from the dissection.

The latter is apparently Oberhammer's attitude. He considers Yāmuna's integration to be a secondary scholastic effort flawed with internal contradictions[14] and feels that more can be gained by a dissection that reveals the nature of Yāmuna's primary sources that were more internally consistent and viable options.[15]

Yāmuna is a much more significant figure than Oberhammer's emphasis suggests. Oberhammer's reduction of Yāmuna's position to only that which is uniquely his own individual contribution, while serving a useful purpose in terms of a study of historical development, is based upon certain modern preconceptions about the role and importance of individual originality, preconceptions that can have seriously distorting effects upon a study of traditional developments. From a traditional perspective, which would have included Yāmuna's own self-consciousness about his role, Yāmuna's unique personal or individual contribution, over and above what is handed down by his sources, should have been <u>zero</u>--his intention was simply to recover and restate clearly the meaning of his sources so as to make it available to his contemporaries.[16] From such a perspective, originality is simply irrelevant to an assessment of the significance and creativity of Yāmuna's integration of his sources.

Moreover, from an historical perspective that is sensitive to this traditional viewpoint but also recognizes the significance of individuals and of originality in the historical process, Yāmuna's own position should be viewed not simply as what is left over after the ideas of his sources have been subtracted, but rather as <u>both</u> the ideas from his sources that he accepts <u>and</u> his own original ideas or, better, as the <u>pattern</u> that integrates into a coherent whole both his sources' ideas and his own. It is the integrative power of such a pattern that is the source of the impact and creativity of a seminal thinker like Yāmuna, enabling him, from a traditional perspective, to recover a threatened or lost wholeness or, from an historical perspective, to create a new wholeness or coherence through a synthesis of old and new ideas.

Thus, while I will build upon Oberhammer's analysis of Yāmuna's sources, my primary concern will be with Yāmuna himself, his relationship to the various sources that Oberhammer distills, and his attempt to integrate these sources into a coherent whole. According to Oberhammer, Yāmuna's section on VS II.ii.42-45 presupposes six distinct and independent earlier discussions of these sūtras.[17] Yāmuna's position is unambiguously negative with regard to only one of these, i.e., the dominant orthodox Vedāntic opposition presented as a Pūrvapakṣa drawn primarily from Śaṅkara but at points from Bhāskara.[18] With regard to the other five, his attitude and relationship is positive; but he draws substantially upon only four of these and with varying degrees of dependence. The discussion can proceed more effectively if these five sources are first sketched as they have been isolated and characterized by Oberhammer.

Source I[19]

According to Oberhammer, Yāmuna first drew upon a work by some earlier Pāñcarātrin for a sūtra by sūtra refutation of the dominant orthodox Vedāntic interpretation. Apparently this source, at least as represented in the AP, did not provide its own positive interpretation of these sūtras but simply established the untenability of the opposition's position. Oberhammer distinguishes this source primarily by the distinctive vyūha theory that it employs to refute such specific charges as that Pāñcarātra teaches that the individual self (jīva) has an origin (utpatti) or is produced.[20]

Source II[21]

Oberhammer derives this source from the first of the three alternative positive interpretations of VS II.ii.42-45 that Yāmuna gives. All three of these positive interpretations reveal the same basic structural characteristic in distinction from the dominant Vedāntic position, i.e., sūtras 42-43 are taken as representing an orthodox Pūrvapakṣa in opposition to Pāñcarātra, while sūtras 44-45 are seen as Bādarāyaṇa's response and Siddhānta in defense of the prāmāṇya of this Tantra. Once again, Oberhammer sees the distinguishing characteristic of this source to be its vyūha theory which, in comparison with that of Source I, is more fully developed in a śākta direction, i.e., employing a bipolar view of the Godhead and the concept of Vāsudeva's *śakti* to account for the cause and effect relationship (*kārya-kāraṇa-bhāva*) between the various *vyūhas*.[22]

Source III[23]

This source is represented by the second, briefly stated positive alternative that Yāmuna proposes. As Oberhammer notes, this new interpretation represents a basic shift in perspective. Previously the discussion had proceeded on the basis of the assumption that the *prāmāṇya* of Pañcarātra stands or falls on the question of the conformity of specific doctrines with, and their derivation from, the Vedas (*veda-mūlatva*).[24] Now the debate begins to center directly on the more general and basic issue of the primary or ultimate basis for the *prāmāṇya* of this Tantra, a shift that brings the discussion back to the central concern of the AP.[25]

The major clear point made by this source is that there is no possibility of Pañcarātra being false or invalid because Brahman, who is without any fault, is the cause of its validity, i.e., this Tantra has *āpta-ukta-tva*, the character of having been spoken by an *āpta*, a reliable speaker. Since the procedure of basing the *prāmāṇya* of Scripture upon the criterion of *āptoktatva* is characteristic of the orthodox Nyāya *darśana*, Oberhammer sees in this source influence from the side of Nyāya and complete opposition to the Mīmāṃsā theory in which the *prāmāṇya* of Scripture is based upon either *apauruṣeyatva* or *veda-mūlatva*.

Oberhammer also argues in favor of the possibility, which he admits cannot be established with any certainty, that this source is to be identified with the anonymous Pāñcarātrika Naiyāyika who appears in the Pūrvapakṣa section of the AP. While Oberhammer admits 1) that there is a way of interpreting the position of this source in a manner that would be consistent with Mīmāṃsā presuppositions and 2) that the concluding phrase of this section provides a basis for doing so, he views the concluding phrase as a later addition from another source and stresses the opposition and conflict between the Nyāya and the Mīmāṃsā perspectives.

While Oberhammer is quite correct in noting the Nyāya influence in this source, I feel he is misleading in stressing the opposition between Nyāya and Mīmāṃsā. It is quite clear to me that this source, as utilized and understood by Yāmuna in the context of the AP, was intended to represent a harmonious blending of Nyāya and Mīmāṃsā principles.[26] While it is of course possible that this harmonization was a foreign imposition by Yāmuna upon his source, it is also possible that Yāmuna himself was simply continuing a tradition of such harmonization and that it was original to this source.[27]

Source IV[28]

Yāmuna's third and final positive interpretation of VS II.ii.42-45 provides the primary basis for this source. This final location, together with the fact that it is the only alternative that is developed at great length, indicates that this interpretation, if not Yāmuna's own creation, stems from a source with which he identified himself sufficiently to enable him to allow its position to stand substantially as his own Siddhānta on Bādarāyaṇa's position with regard to Pañcarātra. While Oberhammer, with his concern for distinguishing this source from Yāmuna, stresses their differences, it is clear that in Yāmuna's own mind there were no contradictions between his own position and that of this his major source.[29]

The major distinctive tenet of this source is that the Pañcarātra Tantra, even when in conflict with the Veda, is independently authoritative as an alternative (vikalpa) to it.[30] According to Oberhammer, this position presupposes the existence of genuine contradictions between the Veda and Pañcarātra, contradictions that are never denied by this source.[31] In his opinion it is only Yāmuna who imports, in a secondary scholastic manner and in conflict with the original intention of this source, the viewpoint that these contradictions are only apparent or seeming ones and that actually or ultimately there are no genuine contradictions between the two revelations.[32]

While there is evidence to support Oberhammer's general hypothesis that this position comes from some source other than Yāmuna himself, in my opinion he does not correctly assess the influence of contextual considerations in determining to some degree the difference between Source IV's and Yāmuna's positions vis-à-vis the conflicts between Pañcarātra and the Veda.[33] Thus, the context of VS II.ii, the Tarka-pāda that is devoted to a rational analysis and rejection of systems that are in conflict with Vedānta, requires, if Pañcarātra is to come under discussion at all, the intial assumption of points of difference which at least some Vedāntins would have interpreted as contradictions. Within such a context the well-established Mīmāṃsā principle of vikalpa[34] provides a powerful and generally accepted device or model for accounting for such differences. However, Yāmuna in the independent context of the AP, while accepting the principle of vikalpa as one way of relating the two, is free to move beyond the stated position of Source IV and make explicit certain aspects of his source's ultimate theological position that were only implicit in the section included at this point in the AP.

Moreover, a strong case can be made that Yāmuna's extension of Source IV was a legitimate and consistent one. Indeed, when Source IV acknowledges that both the Pañcarātra Tantra and the Veda are intrinsically authoritative (svataḥ prāmāṇya),[35] it obviously cannot assume any final contradiction between them on ultimate matters. Further, the principle of vikalpa can be applied only where the two options serve the same purpose[36] and is thus not in conflict with Yāmuna's position that "Pañcarātra and śruti have precisely the same goal or meaning" (pañcarātra-śrutyor aikārthyam eva).[37] Moreover, when Source IV at one point bases the pramāṇatva of both Pañcarātra and the Veda upon the logical Reason nirdoṣa-vijñāna-kāraṇatvād[38] and at another asserts that Pañcarātra is pramāṇa because it has as its basis (mūlatva) "the jñāna of the Bhagavān whose unfalsifiable and innate immediate perception of all dharma, adharma, etc., is understood from hundreds of śrutis" (śruti-śata-samadhigata-),[39] we see that there is in fact very little theoretical difference between Source IV and Yāmuna's Siddhānta in the AP as presented in Chapter III.

However, in my judgment Oberhammer's analysis does reveal some genuine differences of emphasis and attitude between Yāmuna and his major source--differences probably of a more practical than theoretical nature. Not only is Source IV more willing than Yāmuna to acknowledge and deal with serious--if not ultimate--conflicts, it is also willing to be at least tentatively and argumentatively critical of the Veda itself,[40] in striking contrast to Yāmuna who to my knowledge is never even hypothetically critical of the Veda. It is possible that the author of Source IV, living some time before Yāmuna,[41] wrote in a context in which the conflicts between the Vedic tradition and the Tāntric tradition Pāñcarātra were more bitter and unavoidable than at Yāmuna's time when such Tāntric traditions, althought not without orthodox critics, were more generally acceptable and ready for a fuller integration and harmonization with the Vedic tradition.[42]

It should also be noted that, as with Source III, Source IV is heavily influenced by the Nyāya theory of āptoktatvam although here indisputably being developed within a Mīmāṃsa context and in accord with Mīmāṃsā presuppositions. Also characteristic of this source is a heavy emphasis upon nyāya in the broad sense of rational rules or principles of scriptural exegesis and hermeneutics--its sytle is that of a naiyāyika of the Mīmāṃsā tradition, similar to that of Kumārila Bhaṭṭa with whom, as Oberhammer substantiates, this source is in constant debate.

Source V: The Bhāṣyakāra[43]

After Yāmuna completes his interpretation of the UA Adhik. as based upon Source IV, an opponent raises a final objection based upon the position of an anonymous Bhāṣyakāra or "Commentator," a personage who is a prestigious authority to Yāmuna but whose position, at least on the surface, conflicts with Yāmuna's own. In contrast to the positions of both Yāmuna and Source IV, this Bhāṣyakāra has made "the declaration that those aspects [of Pañcarātra] that are contradicted [by the Vedas] are non-authoritative" (viruddha-aṃśa-aprāmāṇya-abhidhānaṃ). Yāmuna's reply to this objection acknowledges the fact that the Bhāṣyakāra has made such a statement but attempts to explain its purpose or intention in such a way that finally there is no conflict between their positions:

> Although [any apparent] contradition [between the Vedas and Pañcarātra] had been removed through being subjected to a dialectial rational analysis, indeed that [statement, i.e., viruddha-aṃśa-aprāmāṇya-abhidhānaṃ,] was meant to convey "Let there not be disrespect or rejection of the Veda by those of weak minds who are not strong enough to fathom the deep ocean of rational analysis (gambhīra-nyāya-sāgaram) [that must be comprehended before the seeming contradictions can be resolved]." Indeed, the situation is precisely

> the same as with the declaration of Bhagavān Jaimini[44] that fruits come from karma [alone and not from a divine being] which is meant to strengthen the faith [of the weak minded] in karma, [not to deny that in actuality fruits come ultimately from Brahman].[45]

One of the major contributions of Oberhammer's study is what he has been able to recover about the position of this briefly cited anonymous Bhāṣyakāra or at least about his position as traditionally represented. Oberhammer argues persuasively that this position, referred to even more anonymously as that of "others" or "some," figures prominently in the Śrī Bhāṣya (ŚBh) of Rāmānuja and even more so in the supercommentary (Śruta-Prakāśikā) of Sudarśanasūri. Significantly, the position has shifted from that of a prestigious if problematic authority to one that is viewed simply as an opponent.

As in the AP, Rāmānuja and Sudarśanasūri deal with this position at the conclusion of their commentaries on the UA Adhik. (VS II.ii.39-42 according to Rāmānuja's enumeration). Rāmānuja concludes his discussion of the last sūtra (vipratiṣedhāc ca) by refuting at some length the position put forth "by others" (paraiḥ) that Bādarāyaṇa intended to deny the prāmāṇya of only those parts of Pañcarātra that are contradicted by the Vedas. Apparently according to this position also, Bādarāyaṇa is to be identified with the author of the Mahābhārata (MBh); but it is held that Bādarāyaṇa did not place Pañcarātra on a different level from that of those other orthodoxly acceptable Āgamas that he praised in the MBh alongside Pañcarātra and the Vedas, i.e., Sāṃkhya, Yoga and Pāśupata. Since all agree that in the VS Bādarāyaṇa rejected aspects of these latter three, it follows that he also rejected certain contradicted aspects of Pañcarātra even though he lauds it in the MBh.[46]

The above is all we can learn about this source from Rāmānuja, but Sudarśanasūri, in his long concluding excursus, presents a number of quotations or close paraphrases that he clearly intends to represent the position of Rāmānuja's "others." While Oberhammer argues that these quotations are taken from Yāmuna's Bhāṣyakāra's commentary on the VS,[47] I doubt that his hypothesis can be maintained in all its particulars. While I agree that Yāmuna, Rāmānuja and Sudarśanasūri were all reacting to what they would have considered to be the same position--and one based upon the Bhāṣyakāra's commentary, the evidence strongly suggests that they were actually responding to a tradition that maintained this interpretation rather than to precisely the same written source.[48]

According to Sudarśanasūri's account of this tradition's viewpoint, Yāmuna's Bhāṣyakāra would have operated upon the basic Mīmāṃsaka principles of the intrinsic validity (svataḥ prāmāṇya) and the extrinsic invalidity (parataḥ aprāmāṇya) of all knowledge. Therefore all four of the Āgamas praised by Bādarāyaṇa in the MBh were originally wholly authoritative and totally without conflict with the Vedas, since their original propounders (ādi-vaktṛ-)[49] are omniscient lords (īśvarās) who are completely without any of the faults (doṣāḥ) that would vitiate their intrinsic validity. However, in the case of each of these four Āgamas, non-authoritative aspects in conflict with the Vedas crept in because of faults in the intellects of the composers of later books (grantha) that were based upon and attempted to interpret the original Āgama (avāntara-grantha-kartṛ-buddhi-doṣād). Therefore, Bādarāyaṇa in the Tarka-pāda of the VS intended to refute those secondary, non-Vedic aspects that were imposed upon the original Āgamas by later fallible human authors who did not correctly grasp the intention of the original infallible composers.

From the manner in which the Bhāṣyakāra's traditional position is presented by Yāmuna, Rāmānuja and Sudarśanasūri, it is clear that all three of these Śrī Vaiṣṇava authors viewed it as being somewhat less hostile and more open toward Pañcarātra than was the dominant Vedāntic position of Śaṅkara and Bhāskara. Indeed, as Oberhammer maintains, essentially the same modified vyūha theory that Śaṅkara rejects ad VS.II.ii.44, is accepted by this tradition according to one fragment given by Sudarśanasūri.[50] Thus, the position of this prestigious and relatively catholic or cosmopolitan Vedāntin must have been of great historical significance in the effort to open Vedānta to such new Tāntric movements as Pāñcarātra and to provide a theoretical or theological basis for the integration of aspects of these movements. However, from Yāmuna's perspective the Bhāṣyakāra's position was problematic, and from the later Śrī Vaiṣṇava viewpoint wholly unacceptable, because it was not willing to accord a special supreme status to Pāñcarātra among the new movements.

B. Yāmuna's Vedāntic Sources in the Ātma-siddhi: the "Commentator" and the Bhagavān Śrīvatsāṅka Miśra

I wish now to enter into the area of my major concern, i.e., Yāmuna's own self-conscious attitude toward and relationship with his Vedāntic sources as revealed through a correlation of the above sources derived from the AP (especially Source IV and the Bhāṣyakāra) with those explicitly referred to in the AtS. To deal with the prestigious anonymous "Commentator" first, Oberhammer has pointed out the possible identity of the Bhāṣyakāra of the AP with a Bhāṣyakṛt mentioned by Yāmuna in the introduction to the AtS.[51] Indeed, the case for the identification of these two "Commentators" is much stronger than indicated by Oberhammer who does not marshall the evidence as effectively as possible.

In his introduction to the AtS, Yāmuna claims an identity of purpose or intention between his composition and the works of a particular line of Vedāntins who are contrasted with a host of other Vedāntins or Mīmāṃsakas whose works are flawed with error and therefore confusing and untrustworthy. The tradition of Vedānta with which Yāmuna thus self-consciously aligns himself is described by the following words:

> . . .the Bhagavān Bādarāyaṇa has composed sūtras that have precisely the same purpose [as my present work] and these sūtras were explained by the Bhāṣyakṛt, whose language is both concise and profound, and then they were expounded in great detail by the Bhagavān Śrīvatsāṅka Miśra himself, whose language is a deep ocean of nyāya (gambhīra-nyāya-sāgara-). . .[52]

Oberhammer's argument for the identity of the AP's Bhāṣyakāra and the AtS's Bhāṣyakṛt is based largely upon the synonymity of the two terms and upon the fact that Yāmuna presents each as a praiseworthy or venerable authority.[53] However, in both contexts there is a certain ambiguity and moderation in the praise given that, if properly understood, strengthens the presumption of the identity of these two Commentators.

It is quite striking that in the AtS the Bhāṣyakṛt is not accorded the epithet Bhagavān while both Bādarāyaṇa and Śrīvatsāṅka Miśra are. In like manner, in the AP where the statement of Yāmuna's Bhāṣyakāra (bhavatāṃ bhāṣyakārāṇāṃ) is likened to that of Bhagavān Jaimini (bhagavato jaimineḥ), the term of veneration Bhagavān ("the Blessed Lord") is once again not employed in the case of this figure.[54] While both Oberhammer and van Buitenen take the work bhavatāṃ as an adjective agreeing with bhāṣyakārāṇāṃ and as being the equivalent of the word bhagavato modifying jaimineḥ,[55] Yāmuna's characteristic usage of the term bhavant suggests that they are not correct in doing so. Yāmuna, in accord with general śāstric usage, usually employs bhavant as a mocking term of insincere respect to be used in addressing one's opponents.[56]

Now, the phrase bhavatāṃ bhāṣyakārāṇaṃ appears in an objection that is addressed to Yāmuna himself. At another point in the AP in another objection directed against Yāmuna, the same word bhavatām occurs in an unambiguous sense that is suggestive both as to how to interpret the present phrase and as to Yāmuna's relation to the Bhāṣyakāra. At that point, the objector says with regard to Yāmuna,

> Indeed, according to the darśana of your lordship, knowledge is intrinsically valid (svataḥ pramāṇaṃ vijñānaṃ bhavatāṃ nanu darśane).[57]

Here the phrase bhavatāṃ. . .darśane clearly means "in your [i.e., Yāmuna's] darśana." Thus, the phrase bhavatāṃ bhāṣyakārāṇāṃ should be taken to mean "of the Commentator of your lordship," i.e., of Yāmuna himself.[58]

If this interpretation of the phrase bhavatāṃ bhāṣyakārāṇāṃ is correct, i.e., if Yāmuna himself has his opponent in effect identify this authority as "Yāmuna's Commentator," then he obviously would have had a high degree of self-conscious committment to this interpretor of the VS and the identification with the Bhāṣyakṛt of the AtS would be rendered highly probably. When shortly the relationship of Source IV to Yāmuna and to the "Commentator" is considered, it will be seen that there is further corroborating evidence in support of this identification.

However, before turning to Source IV, the issue of the identity of Yāmuna's anonymous "Commentator" should be considered. Oberhammer tentatively assumes him to be Dramiḍācārya on the basis that several of the printed texts of the AtS have the reading dramiḍa-bhāṣyakṛtā.[59] While Oberhammer is aware that the Chowkhamba Sanskrit Series edition reads only bhāṣyakṛtā, he apparently has not utilized the Annamalai University edition that is the closest we have to a critical edition[60] and that also has the anonymous reading. Van Buitenen, who utilized this latter edition, has sharply rejected the tendency to identify Yāmuna's Bhāṣyakṛt with the Dramiḍa-bhāṣyakāra and has countered by identifying him with Bodhāyana, the Vṛtti-kāra whom Rāmānuja, at the beginning of his ŚBh, claims to follow in his interpretation of the VS.[61] However, van Buitenen's argument is not convincing;[62] and, while certainty is impossible, what evidence there is weighs more heavily in favor of the traditional identification with the Dramiḍa-bhāṣyakāra.[63]

There are some suggestive parallels between Yāmuna's Bhāṣyakāra and the Dramiḍa-bhāṣyakāra as known from other sources. In the AP, the Bhāṣyakāra is cited in a way that suggests that he is a prestigious authority for both Yāmuna and his opponents. Such a widely inclusive authoritativeness is a prime characteristic of Dramiḍācārya, whose support is claimed by Vedāntins of several different schools and whose words are subjected to widely divergent interpretations.[64] Moreover, Yāmuna's Bhāṣyakāra is open to the authority of smṛti texts, and such would also appear to be the case with Dramiḍācārya.[65]

Most suggestive of all is a parallel that involves directly some central characteristics of Yāmuna's Bhāṣyakāra's position as presented in the AP, i.e., 1) the determination of the invalidity of other texts in terms of conflict with the Vedas (viruddha-aṁśa-aprāmāṇya-abhidhānam) and 2) the resolution of seeming or apparent contradictions between the Vedas and other texts (yadi api virodhaḥ kṛtvā cintayā parihṛtas). Kuppuswami Sastri expounds one reference to Dramiḍācārya as follows:

> Again in the Śaṁkara-Bhāṣya on III.8 to 10 of the Chāndogyopaniṣad, Śaṁkara is found relying upon Dramiḍācārya's explanation to meet a difficulty arising from an inconsistency between the Chāndogyopaniṣad and the Paurāṇika account of the time of sunrise and sunset in the different parts of the world of the Gods: "atroktaḥ parihāra ācāryaiḥ" (Śaṁkara-Bhāṣya on the Chāndogya--Anandāśrama edition, page 145). In this connection Ānandagiri says--"yady api śrutivirodhe smṛtir apramāṇam, tathāpi yathā-kathaṁcid-virodha-parihāraṃ dravidācārya-uktam upapādayati" 66

Here in another independent tradition of Vedānta we find Dramiḍācārya[67] invoked as an authority for the resolution of a seeming contradiction (-virodha-parihāram) between śruti and smṛti. Thus, I feel that the evidence weighs in favor of the hypothesis that Yāmuna's "Commentator" was the ancient, widely accepted authority, Dramiḍācārya. However, the evidence is far from conclusive; and this working hypothesis must be utilized in only the most tentative manner.

Yāmuna's Source IV: Śrīvatsāṅka Miśra

Turning now to Source IV, Oberhammer has also suggested a relationship between Yāmuna's major Vedāntic source in the AP and the Bhagavān Śrīvatsāṅka Miśra who figures so prominently in Yamuna's Vedānta tradition as given in the introduction to the AtS.[68] The most obvious link between this Śrīvatsāṅka Miśra and Yāmuna's discussion of VS II.ii.42-45 is the key phrase gambhīra-nyāya-sāgara-. In the AtS Yāmuna typifies his venerable predecessor as "one whose language is a deep ocean of nyāya" (gambhira-nyāya-sāgara-bhāṣiṇā).[69] In the AP Yāmuna uses the same phrase while explaining the true intention of his Bhāṣyakāra's statement, i.e., that it was intended to prevent "disrespect of the Veda among those of weak minds who are not strong enough to fathom the deep ocean of nyāya" (gambhīra-nyāya-sāgaram avagāṭhum aparibṛḍhānāṃ komala-manasāṃ vedānādaro).[70]

Now in its context in the AP, this phrase obviously refers to the extensive logical argumentation that Yāmuna has just presented in order to resolve any seeming contradictions and that, according to Oberhammer's analysis, is based almost in its entirety upon Source IV. That such is the case, i.e., that the gambhīra-nyāya-sāgaram referred to is the logical argumentation of Source IV, is shown quite clearly by the words used by Yāmuna to introduce his final interpretation of VS II. ii.42-45:

> yad vā sūtrāṇāṃ nyāya-pradarśana-paratvāt
> pañcarātra-śrutayor asantam api virodhaṃ kṛtvā
> 'tra cintyate tathā hi/[71]
>
> Or [finally there is another interpretation:] Because the concern of [this portion of the Vedānta] Sūtras is with instruction by means of nyāya or logical argumentation [alone without the aid of Scriptural authority, Bādarāyaṇa], although in fact there is no contradiction between Pañcarātra

> and the Veda, first posits one [in order to be able to submit Pañcarātra to a dialectical rational analysis in accord with the concern of this portion of the Vedānta Sūtras] and then here [i.e., at VS II.ii.42-45] conducts this analysis as follows: . . .

Here we see that, in distinguishing it from the preceding alternatives, Yāmuna particularly characterizes his final interpretation by its emphasis upon nyāya.

Thus his later use of the phrase gambhīra-nyāya-sāgaram in association with his Bhāṣyakāra as well as the similarity of the words used in both cases to describe their dialectical procedures (cf. virodhaṃ kṛtvā--atra cintyate with virodhah kṛtvā cintayā parihṛtas) conclusively establish that Yāmuna was stating that his Bhāṣyakāra's interpretation of Bādarāyaṇa's sūtras could be properly understood only in the light of his own final interpretation as based upon Source IV. If Source IV and the Bhagavān Śrīvatsāṅka Miśra are identified on the basis of the key phrase gambhīra-nyāya-sāgara, then this line of Vedāntic interpretation derived from the AP corresponds completely with Yāmuna's own explicit statement of his Vedānta tradition in the AtS:

AP		AtS
Bhagavān Bādarāyaṇa	- - - - - - -	Bhagavān Bādarāyaṇa
Bhāṣyakāra	- - - - - - - - - - - -	(?dramiḍa-?) Bhāṣyakṛt
Source IV	- - - - - gambhīra-nyāya-sāgaram - -	Bhagavān Śrīvatsāṅka Miśra
Yāmuna	- - - - - - - - - - - - - - -	Yāmuna

This correlation makes abundantly clear the significance of the little known figure Śrīvatsāṅka Miśra for Yāmuna and his tradition of Vedānta. That he was Yāmuna's most prestigious and most direct Vedāntic authority is clear simply from the manner in which he is referred to in the AtS.[72] Not only is this Bhagavān referred to more reverently than is the Bhāṣyakṛt, but he even receives more emphasis (śrīvatsāṅka-miśreṇa--api) than does the Bhagavān Bādarāyaṇa himself. Yāmuna would seem to be indicating that in the AtS he is depending upon Śrīvatsāṅka Miśra's commentary for his fullest understanding of Bādarāyaṇa's sūtras (vistṛtāni. . .tāni)--in a manner similar to that in which Rāmānuja at the beginning of the ŚBh states his dependence upon the extensive commentary (vistīrṇām brahma-sūtra-vṛttim) by the Bhagavān Bodhāyana.[73] The image of "an ocean" is a common one for an extensive and somewhat archaic text that can no longer be "navigated" or comprehended easily and whose message must therefore be restated more briefly and in a more contemporary idiom.[74] The AtS can thus be taken as Yāmuna's self-conscious attempt to restate clearly, concisely and persuasively Śrīvatsāṅka Miśra's interpretation of the Vedānta Sūtras.

When Śrīvatsāṅka Miśra is identified with Source IV in the AP, Yāmuna's dependence upon this Vedāntic authority is strikingly confirmed since, according to Oberhammer's analysis, he in effect allowed Source IV's interpretation to stand as his own Siddhānta on Bādarāyaṇa's position regarding Pañcarātra.

This Śrīvatsāṅka Miśra presents a mystery. Why, if he was of such great signficance for Yāmuna, has this figure and his work seemingly disappeared without leaving a trace within the later Śrī Vaiṣṇava tradition? Vedānta Deśika in his voluminous works has preserved references to and fragments from the works of many, often less significant authors; but none of his references or fragments have yet been related to this figure. Is it possible to recover anything about this mysterious figure and the impact of his tradition of Vedānta upon the development of the Śrī Vaiṣṇava tradition?

While we are once again entering the realm of speculation, it seems to me that there are some hypothetical suggestions that deserve to be put forward. At the beginning of the ŚBh, Rāmānuja twice refers to pūrvācāryās or "previous teachers"; and, according to Vedānta Deśika's commentary in the Tattva-ṭīkā, he had two distinct groups of previous teachers in mind.[75] The first reference occurs in Rāmānuja's second dedicatory verse where he says that the teaching he is putting forth had been "well protected by the pūrvācāryās" (pūrvācārya-surakṣitām). The second occurs in the immediately following introductory prose sentence in which Rāmānuja states that "the pūrvācāryās have summarized the extensive Brahmasūtra-vṛtti composed by the Bhagavān Bodhāyana" (bhagavad-bodhāyana-kṛtām vistīrṇām brahmasūtra-vṛttim pūrvācāryāḥ saṃcikṣipuḥ) and indicates that he will explain the words of the sūtras in accord with the teachings of that vṛtti.

Vedānta Deśika says that in the latter case the pūrvācāryās meant are "Brahmanandin (Ṭaṅka), etc." (atra pūrvācāryā brahmanandyādayaḥ).[76] Vedānta Deśika's testimony is corroborated by, or perhaps based upon, a passage in the Vedārthasaṁgraha where Rāmānuja lists a series of famous śiṣṭās who have accepted the path he prescribes, beginning with Bhagavān Bodhāyana and followed immediately by Ṭaṅka, Dramiḍa and others.[77] It is interesting to note that Ācārya-Ṭaṅka begins Yāmuna's list of relatively untrustworthy and misleading authors whom he contrasts with the authorities upon whom he depends in the AtS.[78] According to Vedānta Deśika, Rāmānuja also considered this class of pūrvācāryās not to be fully representative of the genuine orthodox tradition as indicated by the fact that he follows the teachings of Bodhāyana's Vṛtti and not the summaries of these pūrvācāryās (parokter anāpta-sampradāyatvaṃ vyañjayitum āha--tanmatānusāreṇa iti).[79]

On the other hand, according to Vedānta Deśika the pūrvācāryās referred to in Rāmānuja's second dedicatory stanza are those who are fully orthodox and are represented preeminently by Yāmuna and the Vedāntic tradition presented in his AtS.[80] Vedānta Deśika's interpretation here would seem to be confirmed by the facts:

1) that Rāmānuja's first dedicatory stanza to the ŚBh is clearly patterned after that of the AtS[81] and

2) that, in the second dedicatory verse to Rāmānuja's more independent and more sectarian work, the Vedārthasaṁgraha (VAS), Yāmuna is referred to by name and in precisely the same connection, i.e., as a protector of the true teaching against erroneous viewpoints.[82]

Rāmānuja says that the correct teaching has been "well protected" (-su-rakṣitām) by these pūrvācāryās. Vedānta Deśika makes a distinction, however, between simple protection (rakṣā) and su-rakṣā.[83] The former refers to oral instruction (aupadeśikī rakṣā) by an ācārya that prevents one from being led astray by heretical or erroneous teachings. Su-rakṣā, on the other hand, refers to such instruction contained within a book and is superior because it is not lost with the passage of time, etc. (grānthikī tu kālāntarādy-anucchedāt surakṣā uktā).

Vedānta Deśika then states his interpretation of Rāmānuja's pūrvācārya-surakṣitām in the form of a verse:

rakṣitatvaṃ tu rāmāryais
trayyantārthe hi sūcitam/
ātmasiddhyādibhiḥ proktaṃ
yāmunāryanibandhanaiḥ// [84]

But the protection [of which Rāmānuja speaks] is that taught (sūcitam) with regard to the meaning of the Vedānta (trayy-anta-) by the noble Rāma and that expounded by such compositions of the noble Yāmuna as the Ātmasiddhi, etc.

Vedānta Deśika here clearly indicates that this Rāma provided the purely oral "protection" or Vedāntic instruction (aupadeśikī rakṣā) on the basis of which Yāmuna in his books, especially the AtS, provided the surakṣā referred to by Rāmānuja. This "noble Rāma" (Rāma-ārya) thus must refer to Yāmuna's immediate guru, the third ācārya or Teacher in the Śrī Vaiṣṇava "Succession of Spritual Masters" (Guru-paramparā), who, according to the traditional biographers, converted Yāmuna by means of daily oral instruction on the Bhagavad Gītā,[85] brought Yāmuna to the Śrī Rangam temple to hold the "Chair of the Teacher" (ācārya-pīṭham) and commissioned Yāmuna to search for a darśana-pravartaka ("Propagator of the darśana") the equal of himself, a search that culminated in the eventual bringing of Rāmānuja to Śrī Rangam.[86]

Now Vedānta Deśika in the above verse would seem to place Yāmuna's book, the Ātma-siddhi, in precisely the same relationship of dependence upon this Rāma's oral instruction on Vedānta as that which Yāmuna in the AtS itself indicates with regard to the extensive written commentary on the Vedānta Sūtras by the Bhagavān Śrīvatsāṅka Miśra. Indeed, the word sūcitam used for Rāma's teaching may indicate oral instruction on the Vedānta Sūtras since Vedānta Deśika later uses the related work sūcaka for the way in which sūtras use a few syllables to "string together" or teach many meanings.[87] Moreover, this Rāma, Yāmuna's Teacher, is usually known as Rāma Miśra.[88]

On the basis of this correlation of the evidence from Vedānta Deśika's Tattva-ṭīkā with that from the AtS, a highly probable hypothesis would be that at Yāmuna's time (i.e., early in the eleventh century) Rāma Miśra was the contemporary exponent of a tradition of Vedānta based upon the extensive Vedānta Sūtra commentary by the Bhagavān Śrīvatsāṅka Miśra--what I will henceforth identify as the "Miśra"[89] tradition of Vedānta, a tradition that Yāmuna apparently both continued and eclipsed before being partially eclipsed himself by Rāmānuja's tradition based upon Bodhāyana's Vṛtti.

To summarize the results of my investagations in this chapter, we have seen that Yāmuna in the first half of the eleventh century was building upon a long and substantial tradition that was attempting to work out a harmonization between Pāñcarātra and Vedānta.[90] Of major importance among these predecessors was "Yāmuna's Commentator," a prestigious and relatively ancient anonymous commentator upon Bādarāyaṇa's VS, who, in a cosmopolitan but critical manner, attempted to moderate Bādarāyaṇa's original rejection of Pāñcarātra and to open the Vedāntic tradition to such new Tāntric movements as Pāñcarātra (but only as one among others) by accepting such aspects of these movements as were not in conflict with the Vedas. If, as I tentatively suggest, this "Commentator" is identified with the ancient Vedāntic authority Dramiḍācārya, then we would see this process of accomodation and integration extending right back to the period of our earliest extant Pañcarātra Āgamas and our earliest view of Tāntic religion in general. Van Buitenen, who does not accept this identification, places Dramiḍācārya at least three centuries before Śaṅkara, i.e., in the fifth century A.D.[91]

Even more central and determinative for Yāmuna's tradition of Pāñcarātrika Vedānta was the Bhagavān Śrīvatsāṅka Miśra (Source IV), whom Oberhammer places in the early ninth century.[92] Yāmuna depends upon this authority not only for his fullest understanding of Bādarāyaṇa's sūtras but also for the interpretation of his "Commentator's" language which was "concise and profound" and therefore ambiguous and subject to various interpretations. This Miśra tradition moved beyond the position of "Yāmuna's Commentator" by granting Pāñcarātra a supreme place among the Tāntric movements and by denying that Bādārayaṇa rejected Pāñcaratra even in part. No longer is conformity to the Veda the sole basis of this Tantra's authority, but even in the cases where there is a (seeming) contradiction or conflict, the injunctions of the Pañcarātra Āgamas are independently authoritative as equally valid alternatives (vi-kalpas) leading to the same end.

It was this Miśra tradition of Pāñcarātrika Vedānta into which Yāmuna was initiated by his Teacher, Rāma Miśra. In the following chapters, we will inquire more directly into Yāmuna's own distinctive place in and contribution to the development of this tradition of Vedānta.

CHAPTER V

NĀTHAMUNI AND YĀMUNA: THE EARLY ŚRĪ VAIṢṆAVA TEACHERS AS INTEGRATORS OF THE CLASSICAL AND THE POPULAR

Building upon the preceding analysis of Yāmuna's sources, we may now begin to discuss his own place and role in the development of the Śrī Vaiṣṇava tradition and school of Vedānta. By virtue of what did Yāmuna come to be the preeminent Protector (su-rakṣitṛ) of the true teaching and the transitional figure between the Miśra tradition of Pāñcarātrika Vedānta and Rāmānuja's Bodhāyana tradition? On this question the testimony both of Yāmuna himself and of the later Śrī Vaiṣṇava tradition is quite clear: he derived his position through the virtue of his grandfather, Nāthamuni, who has become enshrined as the first Ācārya or Teacher in the Śrī Vaiṣṇava Guru-paramparā ("Succession of Spiritual Masters") and has come to be considered the initiator of the distinctively Śrī Vaiṣṇava intellectual tradition.[1]

In the devotional and poetic context of his hymn, the Stotra-ratna (SR), Yāmuna reveals an extraordinary degree of attachment to and dependence upon his grandfather, dedicating four verses (the first three and the final one) to him and another verse to the great family or lineage (vaṃśe mahati) of which Nāthamuni is the exemplar,[2] a family traditionally known in Tamil as the coṭṭai kulam and in Sanskrit as the Kṛṣṇa-vaṃśa because it was especially blessed by the Bhagavān Kṛṣṇa, after whom Yāmuna was named.[3] Moreover, the Āgama-prāmāṇya, as already emphasized in Chapter III, is concluded by two verses, both of which explicitly refer to Nāthamuni, the first being dedicated directly to his praise as a great bhakta and yogī and as the source of a line of disciples who have defended the Pañcarātra teaching by means of dialectical argumentation (yuktis).[4] From this verse, it is clear that Yāmuna self-consciously identified both the task and the style of argumentation of the AP with those of Nāthamuni--or at least of his disciples.

This observation raises the question of the degree to which the content of the AP is dependent upon Nāthamuni's logical and epistemological treatise (nyāya-śāstra), the Nyāya-Tattva (NyT).[5] While Gerhard Oberhammer has not pursued this question, in a note he observes that, while there is no indication that Nāthamuni commented upon the Vedānta Sūtras, it is not unlikely that a section of the NyT might have been devoted to VS II.ii.42-45 or the Utpatty-asambhava-adhikaraṇa and thus have provided the basis for one of the sources outlined in Chapter IV.[6] Once Yāmuna's major Source IV is ruled out by its identification with the Vedāntin Śrīvatsāṅka Miśra, it is clear that Source III is the most likely possibility. Oberhammer shows that the interpretation of Source III involves a basic shift in perspective and concern from those of Source I and II,[7] without, however, stressing sufficiently the implications of the fact that this shift brings Source III's discussion of VS II.ii.42-45 back into line with the general concern and position of the AP itself.[8] Since Yāmuna explicitly aligns the AP with Nāthamuni, once we grant the assumptions 1) that one of his sources was the NyT and 2) that it is not Source IV, then there would seem to be a strong prima facie case in support of the hypothesis that Source III was the NyT.

There are some other considerations that lend support to this hypothesis. Oberhammer stresses the heavy influence from the side of Nyāya that is evident in Source III. According to Vedānta Deśika, the NyT was a nyāya-śāstra, an alternate logical and epistemological system to the mainline Nyāya-Vaiśeṣika tradition.[9] According to Oberhammer, Source III is concerned not with the meaning and validity of specific doctrines or statements but rather with the general issue of the basis of authoritativeness (prāmāṇya) itself--a concern that accords well with the nature of the NyT as a nyāya-śāstra since, according to Jayanta Bhaṭṭa, the prime characteristic of Nyāya as a distinct darśana is precisely its being a prāmāṇa-vidyā, a discipline dealing with the bases of valid knowledge (pramā), in distinction from Mīmāṃsā that is a vākya-artha-vidyā, a discipline concerned primarily with the meaning of specific scriptural statements (vākyas).[10] Moreover, Narasimhachary notes that the verse used to summarize the position of Source III is evocative of the verse which, according to tradition, Nāthamuni began the NyT.[11]

While such evidence is too weak and general to establish a positive identification of Source III with the NyT, the similarities between the two suggest some interesting possibilities that deserve to be mentioned, especially in connection with the Ātma-siddhi where Yāmuna's material dependence upon the NyT is somewhat more clearly defined.[12] As presented in Chapter IV above, Oberhammer stresses the Nyāya, as opposed to Mīmāṃsā, character of Source III. However, he also indicates that it is possible to interpret the position of Source III in a manner that is harmonious with Mīmāṃsā presuppositions. Vedānta Deśika stresses that the NyT, in contrast to the orthodox Nyāya darśana, presents a system of nyāya that is harmonious or compatible with Uttara Mīmāṃsā or Vedānta (vedānta-anukūlam nyāya-śāstram) and that was accepted and followed by Yāmuna.[13] Vedānta Deśika's statement is supported by the evidence of the AtS in which Yamuna explicitly integrates the insights of the NyT into his system of Vedānta.

In the AtS, Yāmuna draws upon the NyT most heavily while debating with the Prābhākaras and in a manner that clearly suggests that in his own mind he is continuing a debate in which Nāthamuni himself had participated in the NyT.[14] In both the AtS and the AP, the Prābhākaras present the most fundamental objections to the integrity of Vedānta as a distinct darśana. Thus, Nāthamuni's position in the AtS as an opponent of the Prābhākaras would support the contentions that his nyāya-śāstra was developed in a Mīmāṃsā context and that it tended to lend support to a Vedāntic position.

Now, whether or not Source III was the NyT, there can be no doubt that Yāmuna intended the position of Source III to be interpreted as an harmonious blending of nyāya and mīmāṃsā principles. Oberhammer's concern to determine the differences between Yāmuna and his sources is misleading at this point in that is obscures the fact that the central point emphasized by Source III is precisely the same as the one emphasized in

Yāmuna's own Siddhānta, i.e., the undeniability of the validity of the Pañcarātra Tantras because of the impossibility of any faults residing in the Supreme Person who is their cause or source.[15] Since in the case of Source III Yāmuna states this primary point very briefly, it is obvious that Yāmuna intended to have this summarily stated position interpreted in accord with his earlier and fuller statement of his own Siddhānta and in accord with the basic Mīmāṃsā principle of svataḥ-prāmāṇya.[16]

While it cannot be proven conclusively that Source III and Nāthamuni's NyT were one and the same, it would appear that Source III holds a position relative to Yāmuna that is at several points analogous to that of the NyT as revealed by the AtS and by Vedānta Deśika, i.e., it appears to be a nyāya source that, at least in Yāmuna's own eyes, is compatible with Mīmāṃsā and Vedānta and that Yāmuna accepts, builds upon and integrates into his own Vedāntic position.

In pursuing this line of investigation, we should note Oberhammer's tentative suggestion that Source III may be identical with the anonymous Pāñcarātrika Naiyāyika who appears in the Pūrvapakṣa of the AP and upon whose position Yāmuna also builds.[17] Oberhammer argues that nothing prohibits this identification and that, unless we wish to multiply without reason Yāmuna's sources, we should seriously consider the possibility of their being the same. On the basis of such an argument, one could also argue for the identification of 1) the Pāñcarātrika Naiyāyika of the Pūrvapakṣa, 2) Source III and 3) the NyT of Nāthamuni who is named in the concluding verses of the AP.

However, the precise wording of Yāmuna's concluding reference to his grandfather suggests another possibility. Yāmuna says,

> Let triumph Nāthamuni . . . whose disciples (-śiṣyair) have crushed the arrogance of those who scorn the Pañcarātra teaching, having slashed their teaching to pieces by turning their own dialectical arguments (yuktis) against them.[18]

Thus Yāmuna does not say that Nāthamuni himself defended Pañcarātra against the attacks of its opponents, but rather that his disciples or students (śiṣyās) did so. Thus, strictly speaking, the anonymous Pāñcarātrika Naiyāyika, who in the AP attacks the critics of Pāñcarātra and whose position Yamuna himself defends and builds upon, would seem to fit more closely the position of one of Nāthamuni's disciples than that of Nāthamuni himself.

According to the traditional Śrī Vaiṣṇava biographical accounts, the disciple who preserved and handed on Nathamuni's śāstra was Puṇḍarīkākṣa (Tamil, Uyyakkoṇḍār), the second Teacher in the Guru-paramparā.[19] Thus this figure would be a likely candidate for the Pāñcarātrika Naiyāyika of the AP. This possibility receives support from the Śata-dūṣaṇī of Vedānta Deśika which preserves two stanzas from an anonymous work of Puṇḍarīkākṣa that "convincingly prove the logical and dialectical character of the work."[20] Vedānta Deśika quotes Śrī Puṇḍarīkākṣācārya as the authoritative interpreter of a dialectical polemical principle or procedure that had been established by the Tarka-tattva (presumably another name for the Nyāya-tattva) and that accords very well with the negative dialectical method of attacking the enemies of Pāñcarātra that Yāmuna ascribes to the disciples of Nāthamuni.[21] Thus it would appear quite possible that the Pāñcarātrika Naiyāyika, and perhaps Source III also, represents not the NyT itself but rather Puṇḍarīkākṣa's now lost work, which would have been based upon Nāthamuni's nyāya-śāstra.

The fact that Yāmuna ascribes the defense of Pāñcarātra to Nāthamuni's disciples, not to Nāthamuni himself, and the possibility that Puṇḍarīkākṣa was one of these disciples are suggestive of many intriguing possibilities to which we will want to return later in this chapter. For the present it is sufficient to stress Yāmuna's distinctive and self-conscious position as the heir of a nyāya tradition that included--in some indeterminate relationship--Nāthamuni and his NyT, Source III and the Pāñcarātrika Naiyāyika (Puṇḍarīkākṣa?) and that--at least in Yāmuna's own eyes--was positively related to and compatible with both Mīmāṃsā and Vedānta on the one hand and the Pañcarātra Tantra on the other. It would appear that Yāmuna's preeminence among the early Śrī Vaiṣṇava Teachers was derived from his merging and integrating this prestigious nyāya tradition with the Miśra tradition of Vedānta, a tradition that itself placed a heavy emphasis on nyāya or rational argumentation (gambhīra-nyāya-sāgaram) and that--on the basis of

Śrīvatsaṅka Miśra's identification with Source IV--was also positively related to Pāñcarātra.[22]

The Early Śrī Vaiṣṇava Teachers

It would seem possible that the traditional structuring of the relations between the first four Teachers or Ācāryas--Nāthamuni, Puṇḍarīkākṣa, Rāma Miśra and Yāmuna--reflects and dramatizes Yāmuna's central role as the integrator of these two intellectual traditions. In the various accounts, the relationships among these early figures are confused and fluid.[23] According to one version, all four were alive at the same time, with Nāthamuni dying when Yāmuna was seven years of age.[24] According to another, seemingly more reasonable account, Nāthamuni died quite some time before Yāmuna's birth, with Puṇḍarīkākṣa's and Rāma Miśra's periods as Teacher filling in the intervening time.[25]

Puṇḍarīkākṣa and Rāma Miśra are a closely linked pair in the biographies. They are both reputed to have been direct disciples of Nāthamuni, although Rāma Miśra, the younger of the two, is subsequently portrayed as Puṇḍarīkākṣa's disciple and successor. They both came from villages very close to the Śrī Rangam temple, perhaps the most important center for the development of the Pāñcarātrika Śrī Vaiṣṇava tradition, and went to live as disciples with Nāthamuni at his home, Vīra-nārāyaṇa Puram (Tamil, Kāṭṭu-mannār-gudi).[26] Although Puṇḍa-rīkākṣa was a Brāhmaṇa of relatively low status, he became, through his very humbleness, one of Nāthamuni's favored disciples[27] and was commanded by his Ācārya to hand on his *śāstra* to his grandson Yāmuna.[28] However, Puṇḍarīkākṣa, to his great disappointment, failed to accomplish this task; and at the end of his life he passed on this sacred Teacher's command to Rāma Miśra, who since Nāthamuni's death had been Puṇḍarīkākṣa's disciple.[29] As I have already indicated, it was Rāma Miśra who succeeded in fulfilling Nāthamuni's command and who brought Yāmuna to Śrī Rangam as the leading Teacher and *darśana-pravartaka* ("Propagator of the Darśana") of the movement.[30]

Yāmuna, a precocious and pugnacious young man, had already won fame and fortune as a debater and dialectician, having outwitted the chief minister (*purohita*) of the Coḷa king in a debate.[31] Because of this conquest, the Coḷa queen dubbed him Āḷavandār (Tamil, "one who came to rule")[32] and the Coḷa king (Rājendra I or Gaṅgai-koṇḍa-coḷa?, 1012-1044 C. E.) granted him a substantial prize,[33] literally "half his kingdom" (ardha-rājyam) but probably the more modest prize of a place to live within or near the royal capital of Gaṅgai-koṇḍa-coḷa-puram, a site which is still identified as Āḷavandār-mēḍu, "the mound or ruin of Yāmuna."[34] Yāmuna called his wife to live with him and, enjoying royal pleasures (rāja-bhoga), supposedly became forgetful of the spiritual and intellectual heritage of his grandfather.

Rāma Miśra, unable to gain an audience with the now famous Yāmuna, devised a clever ploy to gain his attention by appealing to his hedonistic life-style.[35] He went into Yāmuna's kitchen and inquired of the cook what his master's favorite vegetable was. Then for six months he brought it daily to the cook. He then stopped supplying it; and, after four days when Yāmuna asked about it, he finally got Yāmuna's attention. When Rāma Miśra was ushered into his presence, Yāmuna showed him great honor and offered to reward him for his kind service; Rāma Miśra, however, replied that he did not want to receive anything but rather to give Yāmuna the "eternal treasure" that his grandfather had left for him.[36] Yāmuna then allowed Rāma Miśra to see him daily and for the next eighteen days received instructions on the eighteen chapters of the Bhagavad Gītā which contains the essence of Vedānta.[37] Rāma Miśra then gave him instruction in the great mantra, the Carama Śloka or "final word" of the Gītā (XVIII.66) that teaches taking refuge in or absolute surrender (śaraṇāgati, prapatti) to Kṛṣṇa, after which Yāmuna is ready to receive Nāthamuni's "treasure." He is therefore taken to the Śrī Rangam temple and shown this "eternal treasure," the sacred image of the Lord Ranga-nātha (Tamil, Perīya Perumāḷ). Yāmuna is overcome with devotion; and, reciting hymns of the Āḻvārs, he surrenders to the Lord and renounces his former wayward life, becoming a Renouncer (sannyāsin) and the leading Ācarya of the Śrī Vaiṣṇavas centered at Śrī Rangam.[38]

A number of points in this traditional account should be noted:

1) Yāmuna is established as the leading Śrī Vaiṣṇava Ācārya through the sustained and combined efforts of Puṇḍarīkākṣa, who was the teacher of a <u>śāstra</u> or system based upon Nāthamuni's NyT, and Rāma Miśra, who--as I have argued--was the teacher of a Vedānta system based upon the commentary of Śrīvatsāṅka Miśra.

2) It is the Uttara Mīmāṃsaka or Vedāntin Rāma Miśra, not the Naiyāyika Pundarīkākṣa, who was successful in bringing Yāmuna to the Śrī Rangam themple.

3) In one version quite a point is made of the contrast between Nāthamuni's extremely high status as a learned and cultured <u>śiṣṭa</u> Brāhman and the relatively lower status of Puṇḍarīkākṣa who is said to be a <u>Pūrva-śikhī</u> (one who wears his hair tuft on the fore-part of the head),[39] i.e., a representative of the Coḷiya Brāhmans, a relatively ancient class in South India (associated in some way with the Coḷa kings or region) whose status was low among the orthdox because of its close associations with such popular Non-Vedic movements as Tāntric temple worship and the largely non-Brāhmanic Tamil hymnic Bhakti movement (as we shall see, all of the Brāhman Āḻvārs were Coḷiyas).[40] Puṇḍarīkākṣa's Tamil name Uyyakkoṇḍār as well as his favored status as one of Nāthamuni's major disciples were derived from the gracious and humble manner in which he bore an insult from some of Nāthamuni's snobbish high class in-laws who refused to allow him to eat within their house and fed him cold left-over rice in the servants' area.[41]

4) While Rāma Miśra's Brāhmanic caste status is not specified, he is treated as one of quite high status as can be inferred from the use of the honorific Miśra and, even more so, from the fact that he is able to gain access to Yāmuna's well-guarded kitchen and is allowed to provide Yāmuna with his favorite vegetable.[42] When this prestigious Vedāntin Miśra is related to the Bhagavān Śrīvatsāṅka Miśra whom Yāmuna honors in the AtS and when we note the presence of several other prestigious and scholarly Miśras in the early Śrī Vaiṣṇava development,[43] we have a basis for speculating that these Miśras were representative of some sort of class, community or element among the Śrī Vaiṣṇava Brāhmans who enjoyed a relatively high status and maintained a tradition of Vedic and Vedāntic learning.

The title "Miśra" has become one of the most common "surnames" among all divisions of Northern Brāhmans[44] and has on occasion been used as a clue indicating the Northern provenance of obscure authors.[45] While the presence of a number of Miśras in South India among the early Śrī Vaiṣṇava community reveals this latter procedure to be a dubious one, the strong Northern associations of the title do lead one to wonder if its use in the South might be indicative of relatively recent immigration by scholarly Brāhmans brought down from the North to "raise," i.e., "Brāhmanize" or "Sanskritize," the cultural and educational level of the South.[46]

If so, such Miśras would derive their relatively high status from their Vedic learning and from their close association with the North; and they would not have had this status diminished through a close and long-term association with the non-Brāhmanic Tamil movements--at least not to the same degree as occurred in the case of the Pūrva-śikhī or Coḷiya Brāhmans. The hypothesis would be that these learned, relatively high status Miśras would be closely associated with the popular but Sanskritic Pāñcarātra Tāntric temple tradition, which in its earlier phases also had strong Northern associations,[47] but relatively loosely linked with the non-Sanskritic Tamil elements that went into the formation of the Śrī Vaiṣṇava tradition.

At least the first part of this hypothesis is supported by the identification of the AP's Source IV, a profound and learned Vedic scholar or Mīmāṃsaka who defends the Pañcarātra Tantra as an equally valid alternative (vikalpa) to the Vedas, with the revered Śrīvatsāṅka Miśra of the AtS. It is then the "noble Rāma" (rāma-ārya), the contemporary leader of these Miśras who adhere to both Vedānta and the Pañcarātra Tantra, who becomes Yāmuna's Teacher and establishes him at that major center of Śrī Vaiṣṇava Pāñcarātrika Tāntric developments, the temple at Śrī Rangam.

In light of the important role of these Miśras in the integration of Vedānta and Pāñcarātra, it is interesting to speculate upon the somewhat obscure meaning and etymology of the honorific miśra. From at least the late seventh to early eighth centuries C.E. (i.e., the period of Prabhākara Miśra and Maṇḍana Miśra[48]), it has been used simply as a vague honorific with little regard for its literal meaning of "mixed, blended, combined, manifold."[49] That such is also the way in which the word has been used among Śrī Vaiṣṇavas is shown by Vedānta Deśika's use of Rāma-ārya for Rāma-miśra in the verse quoted in Chapter IV.[50] However, there have been some efforts to relate it to its original meaning, e.g., a Miśra is one who "mixes" or "combines" the two Mīmāṃsās, Pūrva and Uttara,[51] or one who "mixes" the duties of the two stages of life (āśramas) of Householder and Renouncer.[52] In terms of this sense of a "Miśra" as a "mixer," "combiner" or, as I will prefer, "integrator," it is interesting to note that perhaps the most famous Miśra of all, Vācaspati Miśra, is best known by the title Sarva-tantra-svatantra, "one who was an independent master of all systems."[53] In like manner, the most famous Miśra among the Śrī Vaiṣṇavas, Kureśa or the second Śrīvatsāṅka Miśra, Rāmānuja's brilliant and learned chief disciple and scribe, is also distinctively characterized as sarva-śāstra-artha-kovidaḥ or sarva-śāstra-viśāradaḥ.[54] Thus a plausible and direct connotation of the honorific miśra would be of a scholar with a "manifold" or "many-sided" ability to combine or integrate diverse systems and ideas, in the present case to integrate Vedic and Tāntric systems, Vedānta and Pāñcarātra.

It is further interesting to note that the word miśra is occasionally used with specific reference to the mixing or combining of Vedic and Tāntric rites, as for example Bhāgavata Purāna XI.27.7, where Kṛṣṇa speaks of a threefold sacrifice or rite as "Vedic, Tāntric or a mixture [of the two]" (vaidikas tāntriko miśra).[55] Thus it would seem quite possible that some of the prestigious and learned Miśra Brāhmans who became influential during the latter half of the first millenium C.E. (the period of the rise both of Vedānta as a distinct darśana and of the Tāntric traditions) were so designated because they were "Integrators" of Vedānta and Pāñcarātra. Whether or not this is the correct interpretation of the honorific miśra, it is nevertheless the case that the Miśra Brāhmans among the Śrī Vaiṣṇavas were in fact performing such an integrative function.

5) Yāmuna is the first member of Nāthamuni's great family of śiṣṭa Brāhman Bhāgavatas to reside as Teacher at the Śrī Rangam temple. While in some late accounts Nāthamuni is made to reside there,[56] in the earlier accounts it is quite clear that Nāthamuni was born, lived and died at Vīranārāyaṇa Puram or Kāṭṭu-mannār-gudi, having only a few brief associations with Śrī Rangam.[57] Puṇḍarīkākṣa and Rāma Miśra came from Śrī Rangam to Nāthamuni's home to study with him; he did not go to Śrī Rangam to teach.[58] His intellectual and hereditary line becomes fully a part of the tradition developing around Śrī Rangam only when Rāma Miśra brings Yāmuna there, commanding him, "Do not leave Śrī Rangam but find another darśana-pravartaka like yourself,"[59] a command that eventuated in the bringing of Rāmānuja to Śrī Rangam.

The five points above, when taken together with the fact that Yāmuna ascribes the defense of Pāñcarātra to Nāthamuni's disciples and not to Nāthamuni himself, suggest an interesting hypothesis, one that gains in plausibility the more it is pursued. This hypothesis is that Nāthamuni himself was less closely associated with the popular non-Vedic and non-Brāhmanic elements--not only Pāñcarātra but also the Tamil hymns of the Āḻvārs--that went into the formulation of the Śrī Vaiṣṇava tradition than were his disciples Puṇḍarīkākṣa and Rāma Miśra and his grandson Yāmuna. Rather he may have been the exemplar of a family of śiṣṭa Vaidika Brāhmans who, while certainly being Vaiṣṇava Bhāgavatas or devotees of Kṛṣṇa, had not yet fully embraced the temple-oriented Pāñcarātra Tāntric tradition.

Now what are the factors, in addition to those already cited, that tend to increase the plausibility of this hypothesis? One major factor is the self-consciousness, on the part of both Yāmuna himself and the later Śrī Vaiṣṇava tradition, of a radical change in type of religiosity between that represented by Nāthamuni on the one hand and by Yāmuna on the other. While Nāthamuni is praised as a passionate and unrestrained bhakta or devotee who has taken refuge at the feet of the Lord, he is most distinctively characterized as a self-possessed and self-disciplined yogī who has attained complete knowledge through the prowess of his own yoga, as indicated by the phrase sva-yoga-mahima-pratyakṣa-tattva-trayaḥ that Yāmuna uses to describe Nāthamuni at the end of the AP and that has become the single most well-known testimony to Nāthamuni's greatness among Śrī Vaiṣṇavas.[60]

In addition to his NyT, Nāthamuni is reputed to have composed the Yoga-rahasya ("The Secret of Yoga"), a treatise on Pātañjalian aṣṭānga-yoga.[61] According to Śrī Vaiṣṇava tradition, Nāthamuni's tradition of classical yoga with its emphasis on individual effort and achievement and self-control has been completely lost; and it was lost by his grandson Yāmuna precisely because he became so attracted to and preoccupied with a popular temple-oriented Tāntric style of religion, combined with the highly emotional and poetic style of devotion and self-surrender typified by the Tamil hymns of the Āḻvārs.[62] As I have developed elsewhere, Yāmuna's references to Nāthamuni and his great family in his devotional hymn, the Stotra-ratna, also reflect just such a change.[63]

Another major factor, one that is perhaps even more intriguing and suggestive, concerns Nāthamuni's relation to the hymns of the Āḻvārs. As indicated above, Yāmuna is reputed to have lost Nāthamuni's "secret of yoga" (yoga-rahasya) because he became entranced by a particularly moving rendition of one of these Tamil hymns that led him to go on a pilgrimage to worship at a temple, thus forgetting to keep the appointment at which he was to have been initiated into this "secret" by another of Nāthamuni's disciples.[64] There would seem to be substantial evidence in support of Yāmuna's association with and attraction to the Āḻvārs' hymns in that Nammāḻvar is apparently praised in verse 5 of the SR, a hymn that at a number of other points reflects the Āḻvārs' influence.[65] On the other hand, the evidence for Nāthamuni's association with the Āḻvārs' hymns is suprisingly inconclusive.

Traditionally, Nāthamuni's single most important contribution to the development of the Śrī Vaiṣṇava movement is reputed to have been the miraculous recovery of the almost completely lost hymns of the Āḻvārs through his own yogic powers (sva-yoga-mahima-), the collection of them into the Divya-prabandham ("Divine Collect"), and the arranging to have them set to music and institutionalized as part of the temple ritual at Śrī Rangam.[66] In light of the great emphasis that the later tradition places upon this aspect of Nāthamuni's contribution, it is indeed striking that Yāmuna, who is unusually profuse in his praise of his grandfather, makes no clear, explicit reference to Nāthamuni's association with the Āḻvārs' hymns.

While there are two references that directly or indirectly associate Nāthamuni with "faultless and pleasing words" or utterances and that could in a vague general manner be taken to include the Āḻvārs' hymns of praise, among other literary compositions, there are strong arguments against restricting these general references so as to take them as specific references to Nāthamuni's recovery of these hymns.[67] Indeed, it would seem possible that these two general references by Yāmuna together with his testimony to Nāthamuni's yogic powers, instead of reflecting Nāthamuni's activities as traditionally recounted, could have been the source for the traditional miraculous account. At any rate, simply on the basis of Yāmuna's silence, it would appear probable that the traditional reconstruction has exaggerated the extent of Nāthamuni's personal involvement in the integration into the Śrī Vaiṣṇava tradition of the popular, non-Brāhmanic temple-oriented Vaiṣṇava Bhakti movement of the Āḻvārs.[68]

As in the question of Nāthamuni's relation to Pāñcarātra, so also in the question of his relation to the Āḻvārs, the role of his śiṣya Puṇḍarīkākṣa may well have been of crucial importance. In addition to being remembered as the perpetuator of Nāthamuni's śāstra that was employed in defence of Pāñcarātra, Puṇḍarīkākṣa, as previously noted, is also reputed to have been a representative of a class of Brāhmans known as Coḷiya or Pūrva-śikhī. Among the twelve Āḻvārs, all of those explicitly identified as Brāhmans--Madhura Kavi, Toṇḍaraḍipoḍi and Periyāḻvār--supposedly came from this same class.[69] Although a relatively ancient class, these Coḷiyas also had relatively low status among Brāhmans, probably to a large degree precisely because of their involvement with the largely non-Brāhmanic Tamil hymnic movement, just like the village of Brāhmans, mentioned in the Shilappadikaram, who became "addicted" to the non-Vedic practices of music and dancing and "for this sin . . . lost their rank."[70]

In general, these Coḷiya Brāhmans are typified as humble and simple devotees and servants of the Lord; they are also depicted as unlearned in the Vedic lore. Perhaps most typical of them was Periyāḻvār (Sanskrit, Viṣṇu-citta), the humble flower gardener and maker of garlands who while he "was a very good man and ordinarily read he hardly had done his Veda and was not a scholar."[71] According to the traditional biographical account, the Pāṇḍya king in Madurai commanded all the Vedic scholars in his kingdom to hold a court debate in order to "hear from them the purport of the Vedānta."[72] The Lord then appeared to Periyāḻvār in a dream and ordered him to attend the debate and win the prize offered:

> "What" exclaimed Periy-āzhvār, "boor and illiterate that I am, I am to be deputed to an intellectual tournament! Lord, look at my hands cicatriced by constant plying with the garden implements. To me it seems the height of folly that a poor gardener fit only for humble service to Thee, should dare to appear in the midst of wisemen and throw down the gauntlet! I am unlearned in the Vaidika Lore, and yet Thou desirest me to cut a figure amongst the rare literati that will assemble! How canst Thou have thought of such an impossible thing?"[73]

Nevertheless, through the grace of the Lord and his own simple but profound insight, this "dullard who knows not a letter of Vedānta" revealed the essence of the Vedānta according to Pāñcarātra and won the debate, humbling all the proud and learned Brāhmans.[74]

While such simple devotion and devotees remained at the heart of the inspiration of the Śrī Vaiṣṇava tradition, the traditional Guru-paramparās are essentially accounts of a long-term search by such pious but unlearned Brāhmans as these Coḷiyas for Vedicly trained scholars and śiṣṭās who could meet their orthodox critics on their own ground.

While these Coḷiya or Pūrva-śikhī Brāhmans are not traditionally reputed to have been arcakas or professional temple priests and thus do not fully correspond to the low status Brāhmans of Bhāgavata Class II derived from the AP (see Chapter III), they clearly represent Bhāgavatas who would be hard pressed to maintain their Vedic orthodoxy against strict Smārta opponents because of their intimate involvement with popular Bhakti and Tāntric religious practices.[75] They represent, however, an essential link between the Vedic tradition and the burgeoning popular movements and active agents in the integration of the latter.

In the preserved biographical accounts, the search by these lower status Brāhmans for a śiṣṭa darśana-pravartaka revolves primarily around Nāthamuni, Yāmuna and Rāmānuja. However, my reconstruction would assume that this search also would have involved the Bhagavān Śrīvatsāṅka Miśra, an earlier darśana-pravartaka whose efforts at defending the validity of the Pañcarātra Tantra and at integrating it into the Vedic and Vedāntic tradition were relatively unsuccessful, probably because of his relative openness to the recognition of conflict between the two ways and of the necessity at the practical level of making a choice between the two options (vikalpas). The class of Miśra Brāhmans that this major figure represents clearly corresponds to the Bhāgavata Class III of the AP, those who had abandoned the duties or rites established by the Three Vedas (trayī-dharma-tyāga) and who performed an alternate series of sacraments based upon the Ekāyana Śākhā as well as the Pāñcakālikā rites established by the Pañcarātra Tantra.[76]

The Guru-paramparā accounts then pick up the search for a darśana-pravartaka at the point which to the later Śrī Vaiṣṇava tradition signified the beginning of its successful culmination: the integration of Nāthamuni's and Yāmuna's great śiṣṭa family or lineage, the foremost represetatives of the Bhāgavata Class IV that is also the essential basis for the success of the argument of the AP (see Chapter III). In the Guru-paramparās, the great prestige of this family, while stemming partly from its high degree of Vedic learning and culture, derives even more from its being especially beloved of Kṛṣṇa; the family is known as the coṭṭai kulam with Kṛṣṇa being called the God of the coṭṭai kulam.[77]

Over the centuries the etymological meaning of the name coṭṭai kulam has been lost; but in my opinion the word coṭṭai (Tamil, "crookedness," "a crooked sword or club") must refer to the crooked shepherd's staff (Sanskrit, yaṣṭi) that is a distinguishing iconographical characteristic of Mannanār, the form of Kṛṣṇa enshrined at Nāthamuni's and Yāmuna's home temple at Vīranārāyaṇa Puram or Kāṭṭu-mannār-gudi ("the settlement of

Kṛṣṇa in the wilderness"), at least as I have seen and photographed Mannanār/Kṛṣṇa as depicted between Nāthamuni and Yāmuna on a Gopuram tower at the Śrī Rangam temple.[78]

Of course, Yāmuna's very name is a sign of this special relationship to Kṛṣṇa, being a name of this avatāra of Viṣṇu and, as the traditional accounts imply, being chosen by Nāthamuni himself because of his special attachment to the sacred places on the banks of the river Yamunā at which Kṛṣṇa sported and at which Nāthamuni and his family almost settled permanently while on a pilgrimage to the places sacred to Kṛṣṇa in North India.[79] Thus, Nāthamuni and his family were Vaiṣṇava Bhāgavatas or devotees of Kṛṣṇa, in accord certainly with the Bhagavad Gītā and such acceptably orthodox Purāṇas as the Viṣṇu Purāṇa, but not necessarily with the Pañcarātra Tantras or the ecstatic hymns of the Āḻvārs.

Thus, according to my hypothesis, the traditional Guruparamparās record the turning of the Pāñcarātrika Coḷiya and Miśra Brāhmans, in the persons of their leading representatives, Puṇḍarīkākṣa and Rāma Miśra respectively, to Nāthamuni and his śiṣṭa Vaidika Bhāgavata lineage, the coṭṭai kulam, in their search for an adequate darśana-pravartaka. Nāthamuni would have been the promulgator of a nyāya-śastra, a system of polemics, logic and epistemology, developed in accord with Mīmāṃsā and Vedānta on the one hand and Purāṇic Bhāgavata theistic Bhakti on the other. If not himself a Pāñcarātrin, as I am suggesting, Nāthamuni must have been willing to give instruction in his śāstra to other Bhāgavatas who were committed to that Tāntric tradition. Such Pāñcarātrins as Puṇḍarīkākṣa and Rāma Miśra would then have been able to apply the principles learned from Nāthamuni and his NyT in order to defend Pāñcarātra against its opponents and provide a more adequate and sophisticated epistemological basis for their darśana.

Obviously, such Pāñcarātrins would greatly prize the intellectual leadership of one who possessed not only the dialectical skill and epistemological sophistication that derived from Nāthamuni's śāstra, but also the great status of actually being a member of the coṭṭai kulam. Puṇḍarīkākṣa, the intellectual leader of the relatively low-status Pūrva-śikhī or Coḷiya Brāhmans, was unable to win such a prize. However, the "noble Rāma," a Miśra Brāhman of higher status who taught a system of Vedānta based upon commentary of the Bhagavān Śrīvatsāṅka Miśra, was able to win Yāmuna--a Poet-Philosopher who became "addicted" to the popular Tamil devotional and poetic type of religion without losing his grandfather's dialectical skill--as a defender of the Pañcarātra Tantra and as the *darśana-pravartaka* for the Miśra tradition of Pāñcarātrika Vedānta.

The impact of Nāthamuni's physical and intellectual heir upon this Vedānta tradition was so great as to constitute in effect a *new beginning*; and the Śrī Vaiṣṇava tradition, in tribute to the source of Yāmuna's greatness, came to recognize as their first Ācārya, and as the initiator of their distinctive Vedānta *darśana*, Nāthamuni, who was himself not a Vedāntin and who was probably not as personally involved with or committed to the popular elements that went into the composition of the Śrī Vaiṣṇava movement as the traditional accounts suggest.

Thus Yāmuna's distinctive role in the intellectual development of the Śrī Vaiṣṇava tradition was the integration of a classically oriented *nyāya* tradition based upon Nāthamuni's NyT with a Vedānta tradition that was closely allied with the popular Pāñcarātra Tāntric tradition and based upon the Vedānta Sūtra commentary of the Bhagavān Śrīvatsāṅka Miśra. That this commentary, which should be viewed as the true beginning point of the distinctively Śrī Vaiṣṇava Vedānta *darśana*, should have been eclipsed by Yāmuna's AtS and is now lost should not surprise us overly much, since this latter work was itself partially eclipsed by Rāmānuja's *Śrī Bhāṣya* and has been only fragmentarily preserved. We may perhaps assume that, in addition to losing Nathamuni's "secret of yoga," Yāmuna also lost some of his grandfather's family's great *śiṣṭa* status by his whole-hearted championing of originally non-Brāhmanic modes of religion. Thus, it was necessary for the more cautious and prosaic, but impeccably Vedic, Rāmānuja to complete the process of "classicization," "Brāhmanization" or "Sanskritization" through which the popular movements were fully integrated into the classical Vedic tradition.[80]

While Rāmānuja partially eclipsed Yāmuna and the AtS is only partially preserved, the extant fragment of the AtS, Yāmuna's major systematic Vedāntic work, is a substantial and exceedingly significant one and provides our only basis for a comprehensive understanding of Yāmuna's interpretation of the Miśra tradition of Pāñcarātrika Vedānta. Hence we must now turn to an analysis of the AtS in an attempt to recover Yāmuna's Vedāntic system, the pattern into which he integrated his intellectual and religious sources and through which he revitalized them, providing the impetus and inspiration for the later culmination in Rāmānuja's magisterial systematization.

PART TWO:

YĀMUNA'S VEDĀNTA

CHAPTER VI

THE ĀTMA-SIDDHI: BREAKING THE CODE

A. Introduction: Critical Problems in the Analysis of the Extant Text

The *Ātma-siddhi* is without doubt Yāmuna's most significant extant contribution to the development of classical Indian systematic religious thought (*darśana*); but its significance has thus far been understood only incompletely or "fragmentarily"--largely, of course, because the text itself has been preserved only "fragmentarily." However, a rather large "fragment" of the AtS has been preserved, including an introductory section that is clearly intended to be a preliminary survey or outline of all the topics to be covered in the work. As we shall see, this section also contains, stated in a preliminary summary manner, Yāmuna's own final positions or Siddhāntas on all of these topics. Thus, if we were able to understand thoroughly this introductory section and Yāmuna's summary Siddhāntas, we would be able to recover his Vedāntic system in its entirety.

However, since most of the extended discussion or argumentation that was to follow this summary plan or outline is no longer extant, this introduction appears--as indeed Yāmuna intended it to appear--as a confusing welter of conflicting opinions; and thus Yāmuna's Vedāntic Siddhāntas and system are presented to us in the form of a puzzle, as it were in a coded message for which we do not possess the full code. Nevertheless, we do possess a portion of the code since a major block of Yāmuna's extended discussion is extant and provides the basis for the full understanding of two of the major topics outlined in the introductory section. Thus, I feel that it is possible to "break the code" partially and to recover, if not Yāmuna's entire system in its fullness, at least a fuller understanding of some of his Vedāntic Siddhāntas and of certain aspects of the basic pattern of his thought.

Beyond the difficulties inherent in the text itself, another reason that the AtS has not been adequately understood is that those who have devoted the most serious study to this work are themselves Śrī Vaiṣṇavas whose main, and quite legitimate, interest has been to understand the text in terms of the developments and categories of the later Śrī Vaiṣṇava thought--particularly that of Rāmānuja, who drew much of his inspiration from the compositions of Yāmuna. While I too am interested in Yāmuna's relationship to Rāmānuja and could not personally have made any headway in this study without the dedicated effort and kind personal assistance of many present-day Śrī Vaiṣṇava scholars, to say nothing of the centuries upon centuries of traditional scholars who have preserved the materials that make my study possible, I believe that as an outsider I can best complement--and, in certain important aspects, supplement and correct--these previous traditionally oriented studies by attempting to achieve a more independent perspective upon the AtS and upon Yāmuna's contribution in its own right.

While it will never be possible to recover Yāmuna's own system completely, much more than has been done can be done through a coordinated analysis of the different sections of the AtS that have been preserved. I will first present a general survey of the basic structure of the extant portion of the text and then indicate how my detailed and coordinated analysis will proceed in this attempt to break the AtS's code.

The Structure of the Extant Portion

Yamuna begins the AtS with two verses: the first a dedicatory verse asking for the blessing of the Highest Person accompanied by Śrī, i.e., Viṣṇu; and the second giving the name of the work, its justification (the many contradictory conceptions of the individual self [ātmā] and the Highest Self [paramātmā]), and its purpose (the elucidation and resolution of the conflicting viewpoints).[1]

He then presents an introductory section that is extremely important as it presents a large number of opinions--including his own--on the various topics to be considered and, as has been indicated, provides the only basis for recovering

Yāmuna's Vedāntic system in any degree of wholeness.[2] The central purpose of this introduction is to restate in prose and substantiate in some detail the justification of and purpose for his writing the AtS. Yāmuna first establishes the importance of his topic by noting that all schools agree that "Knowledge of the ātmā is the cause of the Highest Good" (ātma-jñānaṃ niḥśreyasa-hetur) and that many Vedāntic passages declare that knowledge of the essential nature of the higher and the lower ātmā is the means to release (para-avara-ātma-tattva-jñānasya--apavarga-sādhanatvaṃ).[3]

However, this seemingly universal agreement on the importance of this matter does not render further discussion of it superfluous because various religious leaders teach such a confusing welter of conflicting opinions (vipratipattis) with regard to the individual ātmā and the Highest ātmā.[4] Yāmuna then proceeds to demonstrate this welter of opinions, giving series (to be referred to in the following as "Pratijñā Series") of summarily stated theses or "propositions" (pratijñās) on all the major points of dispute. These Pratijñā Series outline the following disputed topics:

I. the ātmā (ātma-viṣaye),[5]

II. the paramātmā (paramātma-viṣaye),[6]

III. the relationship between them (ātma-paramātmanoḥ sambandhe);[7]

IV. the nature of the Highest Human Goal of "Release" (mokṣa), i.e., the attainment of Brahman (parama-puruṣārtha-bhūte brahma-prāpti-lakṣaṇa-mokṣe),[8]

V. means for attaining that Goal (tat-sādhanato).[9]

Faced with all these ambiguous and conflicting opinions and not able to discern the relative strengths and weaknesses of the arguments put forth in support of them, even sincere and intelligent seekers, bewilderedly expending their energies on the doubts arising from first one viewpoint and then another, would not be able to exert themselves single-mindedly toward the attainment of the Highest Human Goal as long as this ātmā and paramātmā are not authoritatively and definitively established in terms of

(i) their essential natures (svarūpataḥ),

(ii) the means of attaining valid knowledge of them (pramāṇataḥ),

(iii) the relationship between them (saṃbandhataḥ),

(iv) the nature of the state of attainment of the Highest Good (prāptitaḥ), and

(v) the means whereby that Highest Good is attained (tat-sādhanataś ca).[10]

Therefore, Yāmuna has undertaken this work in order to illuminate clearly all these points and to remove thereby the obstacles which the present confusion poses to sincere seekers for the Highest Good.

In conclusion of this introductory section and in anticipation of the objection that Bādarāyaṇa's Vedānta Sūtras, by the very definition of a sūtra,[11] were written with precisely the same intention of making these matters unambiguously clear (asaṃdigdhaṃ), and that therefore the present work is superfluous, Yāmuna states,

> Even though the Bhagavān Bādarāyaṇa has composed sūtras having precisely this same purpose and these sūtras were explained by the Bhāṣyakṛt, whose language is both concise and profound, and expounded in great detail by even [such a teacher as] the Bhagavān Śrīvatsāṅka Miśra, whose language is a deep ocean of nyāya (gambhīra-nyāya-sāgara), nevertheless, many persons have had their judgment corrupted by their giving credence to various writings of uneven quality that have correct and incorrect ideas interwoven through them like warp and woof (sita-asita-vividha-nibandhana),[12] books such as those composed by Acārya-ṭaṅka, Bhartṛprapañca, Bhartṛmitra, Bhartṛhari, Brahmadatta, Śaṅkara, Śrīvatsāṅka, Bhāskara, etc.[13] Since persons who have been confused in this way do not understand things as they really are and have many erroneous conceptions, the undertaking of this work or discussion (prakaraṇa) with the aim of establishing a [clear, comprehensive and definitive] understanding (pratipatti) of the [ātmā and the paramātmā] is proper.[14]

The significance of the first part of this statement and the Vedāntic authorities cited therein has been developed at length in Chaper IV. However, two points should be reemphasized:

1) By this testimony Yāmuna self-consciously places himself within a well-established tradition of Vedānta, identifying completely the intention of Bādarāyaṇa's sūtras with that of the AtS, acknowledging two other revered teachers in his line of interpretation, and recognizing--and challenging--many of the most prestigious of his Vedāntic predecessors. Thus, while on the basis of his AP Yāmuna's credentials as a Vedāntin

might be doubted,[15] in the AtS he carefully and self-consciously placed himself within, and throughout operates as a member of, the tradition and universe of discourse of the Vedānta or Uttara Mīmāṃsā darśana.[16]

2) Although, as previously noted,[17] Yāmuna in the AtS explicitly quotes Nāthamuni's Nyāya-tattva as an authority and although the AtS, on the basis of a statement by Vedānta Deśika, has been considered a work or discussion (prakaraṇa) based upon the Nyāya-tattva (nyāya-tattva-śāstra-prakaraṇam hi ātma-siddhi),[18] Nāthamuni is not mentioned in this introductory statement as one of the authorities upon whom this Vedāntic work (prakaraṇa) is based. This fact illustrates quite dramatically that Nāthamuni was not a Vedāntin and that Yāmuna was integrating his grandfather's nyāya-śāstra into a new context, the Vedāntic tradition based upon the VS commentary of Śrīvatsāṅka Miśra.[19]

Having justified his undertaking and given a brief outline of all the views to be refuted and topics to be elucidated, Yāmuna then begins the extended discussion of the topics. As in the introduction, he proposes to deal first with all the major disputes concerning the individual ātmā and states in a Summary Śloka or verse all of his own final positions or Siddhāntas that he will establish:

> dehendriyamanaḥprāṇadhībhyo 'nyo 'nanyasādhanaḥ/
> nityo vyāpī pratikṣetram ātmā bhinnaḥ svataḥ sukhī//[20]

The ātmā is that which is

(1) other than the body (deha),
the external sense-organs (indriya),
the internal sense-organ or mind (manas),
the breath or vital force (prāṇa),
and consciousness (dhī);

(2) not dependent on any other means for its revelation or manifestation (an-anya-sādhanaḥ);

(3) eternal (nityo);

(4) pervasive (vyāpī);

(5) different in each body (pratikṣetram. . . bhinnaḥ);

(6) innately blessed with "happiness" (svataḥ suhkī).

Yāmuna then begins to argue for these Siddhāntas in detail, proposing and refuting the various Pūrvapakṣas or preliminary opposed viewpoints in the process of gradually building toward his own conclusion. While Yāmuna's complete argumentation is available for only topics (1) and (2) of this Summary Śloka--with the extant text of the AtS ending after only a few lines devoted to topic (3)--the order within these two complete discussions reveals a high degree of correlation with the structure and order of both the Summary Śloka and the summary propositions or Pratijñās. It is only by discovering the precise nature of this mutual correlation of order, structure and content among these two types of summary statements (to be hereafter designated by "Summary Śloka Śiddhāntas or Topics" and "Pratijñās" or "Pratijñā Series") on the one hand and the "Extended Discussion" (as the extant portion of the full argumentation shall henceforth be termed) on the other that it is possible to recover the structure and argument of the extant "fragment" of the AtS and to attempt to "break the code" in which Yāmuna's Vedāntic Siddhāntas are presented in the introductory section.

Critical Problems in the Interpretation of the Pratijñā Series

J. A. B. van Buitenen, in his attempt to unravel and interpret Yāmuna's major Siddhāntas from the Pratijñā Series, maintains that

> His principal tenets can best be described in his own words, taken from the beginning of the Ātmasiddhi, where he enumerates a great many different views that were held by Indian schools of thought before him on the cardinal truths. Generally his own opinion concludes the series of theories as a preliminary thesis to be demonstrated later on.[21]

Pandit U. T. Vīrarāghavācārya, the leading contemporary Śrī Vaiṣṇava interpreter of Yāmuna's thought, in his Sanskrit commentary on the AtS, the Gūḍha-prakāśa, confirms van Buitenen's assertion that the final member of each Pratijñā Series is a preliminary statement of Yāmuna's own Siddhānta.[22] However, van Buitenen's analysis underestimates the difficulties involved; and, according to my own analysis, his attempt to isolate and interpret Yāmuna's main tenets goes astray at several crucial points, as do the attempts of all other previous interpreters of these Pratijñās.

I would first like to outline some of the major complexities and problems involved in analyzing these Pratijñā Series:

1) First of all there is the problem of determining the general structure of this section, i.e., how many and what topics are being considered and where does the Pratijñā Series on a particular topic begin and end? In general these questions can be answered clearly, but in several important instances my analysis indicates that all previous interpreters have been misled.

2) A more major difficulty is that of determinining where, within each Pratijñā Series, Yāmuna's Siddhānta begins and ends. Van Buitenen has exemplified this issue in criticizing R. Ramanujachari's translation of the Siddhānta on the relationship (saṃbandha) between the ātmā and paramātmā.[23] However, the complexity of the problem is indicated by the fact that I, while acknowledging van Buitenen's interpretation as superior to Ramanujachari's, must recommend even further modification.[24] Moreover, on occasion, it seems necessary to accept as part of the Siddhānta some point that is explicitly stated only in a preceeding opposition Pratijñā but which is not rejected and is explicitly or implicitly accepted by the succeeding Pratijñās.

3) Once each Siddhānta is isolated there remains the problem of interpreting the very concise technical language in which they are given. Only in the case of the first two Summary Śloka Topics for which the Siddhānta is developed at length in the Extended Discussion is it possible to overcome this problem completely.

Previous Efforts

All previous attempts to analyze Yāmuna's Pratijñā Series have been dependent, directly or indirectly, upon the interpretations of one or both of the traditional Śrī Vaiṣṇava scholars who have written modern Sanskrit commentaries on the Siddhi-traya. Abhinavadeśika Śrī Uttamūr T. Vīrarāghavācārya, referred to above and reputed to be the most learned Vaḍagalai Śrī Vaiṣṇava Pandit in Madras City, is the first and probably most significant source. Professor R. Ramanujachari has told me that, when he was in the process of translating the Siddhi-traya in collaboration with Pandit K. Srinivasacharya, who had primary responsibility for editing the text, they would regularly consult Pandit Vīrarāghavācārya for the elucidation of obscure passages.[25] This edited text and translation appeared serially between 1935 and 1943.[26] It is certainly no coincidence that Śrī Vīrarāghavācārya's brief commentary, or rather gloss and notes (ṭippaṇādi), called Gūḍha-prakāśa (hereafter GPrak), was published in 1942.[27] While van Buitenen was not to my knowledge aware of this gloss, he was, as indicated above, aware of Ramanujachari's translation. While he exercised some criticism over this translation, he basically followed the structure given by it and was therefore indirectly, but substantially, influenced by Pandit Vīrarāghavācārya's interpretation.[28]

In 1954, a Teṅgalai Śrī Vaiṣṇava scholar, P. B. Aṇṇaṅgarācārya, the Head Pandit of the Svāminārāyaṇa Saṃskṛta Pāṭhaśālā at Vaḍṭal in Gujarat, published a fuller commentary on the Siddhi-traya, entitled the Siddhāñjana-vyākhyā (hereafter SVy).[29] While the scholarship of this work is not as critical or insightful as that of the GPrak, this fuller commentary, if used critically, is another major source for the interpretation of the AtS. Dr. M. Narasimhachary, whose study, written in 1966, is the fullest secondary work on Yāmuna in English, was largely dependent upon these two Śrī Vaiṣṇava commentaries for his interpretation of the AtS.[30] He read Yāmuna's philosophical texts with U. T. Vīrarāghavācārya[31] and used P. B. Aṇṇaṅgarācārya's edition as the text of reference in his thesis.[32] When I read the AtS with Dr. Narasimhachary, he repeatedly referred to one or the other of these Pandits as his authorities.[33]

Thus, all previous efforts to interpret Yāmuna's Pratijñās depend primarily upon the analysis of Pandit Vīrarāghavācārya and secondarily upon that of Pandit Aṇṇaṅgarācārya, with the partial exception of J. A. B. van Buitenen's brief treatment. Therefore, in my analysis I will be responding primarily to these modern Sanskrit commentaries and van Buitenen's analysis and only secondarily and occasionally to the other presentations.

B. The Recovery of the Structure and Argument of the Extant Text

As has been stated, the basis for and first step in this attempt to recover and understand Yāmuna's Vedāntic Siddhāntas is the correlation of the Extended Discussion of the first two topics set out in the Summary Śloka with the corresponding Pratijñā Series. These Summary Śloka Topics again are:

(1) the demonstration that "the ātmā is that which is other than the body, the external sense-organs, the internal sense-organ or mind, the breath or vital force, and consciousness" (deha-indriya-manaḥ-prāṇa-dhībhyo 'nyo);

(2) the establishment that the individual ātmā "does not depend on any other means for its revelation or manifestation" (an-anya-sādhanaḥ).

I will now attempt to isolate the Pratijñā Series that correspond to and summarize the argumentation on these two topics, to demonstrate their correlation with the extended discussion, and thus to establish fully and precisely their meaning. In the following chapters, I will then attempt, on the basis of the present analysis, to translate and interpret the significance of the remaining Pratijñā Series and Siddhāntas for which the full discussion is no longer extant.

Pratijñā Series I.A and I.B

The following gives my translation of the Pratijñā Series which must be correlated with the Extended Discussion of Summary Śloka Topics (1) and (2), i.e., Series I.A on the svarūpa ("own-form" or essential nature) of the invidividual ātmā and Series I.B on the question of pramāṇa or means of valid knowledge with regard to the same. (See Chapter VII for the Sanskrit text and an annotated version of this translation.) The Pratijñās that my analysis reveals to be Yāmuna's Siddhāntas will be indicated by capital letters:

I. With regard to the individual ātmā, [many opposing theses have been propounded on the following topics]:

   A. Thus [concerning the dispute as to what is the essential nature or "unique form" (svarūpa) of the entity that is designated by the term "ātmā"],

I. A. 1. certain persons call the physical body (deham) itself the ātmā;

2. others, the external sense-organs (indriyāṇi);

3. others [say] "the internal sense-organ or mind" (manas);

4. still others, the breath or vital force (prāṇam);

5. others [declare that what is called the ātmā is] nothing but cognition or consciousness (bodha-mātram) that in and of itself is devoid of any individual self-consciousness (an-ahaṅkāram) but which has superimposed (adhyasta) upon it the character of being an individualized active knower (jñātṛ);

6. others [call ātmā] that [entity] that is distinct from the body, the external sense-organs, the internal sense-organ, the vital force and cognition (bodha); [that is formless, all-pervasive and of infinite dimension] like ether, etc; that does not have consciousness associated with its essential nature (a-cit-svabhāvam); that is the substratum in which inhere such adventitious (āgantuka) special qualities as cognition (bodha), pleasure (sukha) and pain (duḥkha), etc.; and that is the object of the cognition "I" (ahaṃkāra-gocaram);

7. BUT OTHERS [YĀMUNA HIMSELF] DECLARE [THE ātmā TO BE] THIS SELF-LUMINOUS ONE (svayam-jyotiṣam imam) THAT MANIFESTS ITS OWN ESSENTIAL FORM (svarūpa) WITHOUT BEGINNING AND WITHOUT END; THIS ONE THAT IS NONE OTHER THAN THAT WHICH HAS CONSCIOUSNESS AS ITS SOLE ESSENTIAL ATTRIBUTE (bodha-eka-svabhāvam eva), BUT THAT APPEARS TO POSSESS SUCH INAUSPICIOUS ATTRIBUTES (a-śiva-guṇas) AS THE PAIRS OF DESIRE AND AVERSION, PLEASURE (sukha) AND PAIN, ETC., WHICH ARE IMPUTED TO IT BECAUSE OF PARTICULAR RESTRICTING CONDITIONS (upadhāna) OF THE INTERNAL SENSE-ORGAN (antaḥkaraṇa)--AS IS THE CASE WITH A CRYSTAL THAT HAS ONLY WHITENESS THROUGH ITS OWN ESSENTIAL ATTRIBUTE (svabhāva) [OF LUMINOSITY] BUT SEEMS TO HAVE SUCH ATTRIBUTES AS REDNESS IMPUTED TO IT BECAUSE OF PARTICULAR RESTRICTING CONDITIONS (upadhāna) [SUCH AS THE REDNESS OF A NEARBY ROSE].

a. However, others [while basically agreeing with the position of Pratijñā I.A.7, hold it to be incomplete because they believe that the ātmā] has both consciousness (jñāna) and bliss (ānanda) as its essential attributes (svabhāva), [not consciousness alone].

b. OTHERS [YĀMUNA HIMSELF], [IN RESPONSE TO THIS OBJECTION AND IN DEFENSE OF THE ADEQUACY OF PRATIJÑĀ I.A.7, SAY] "THAT WHICH IS INNATELY ESSENTIAL TO THIS [ātmā] IS NEVER ANYTHING OTHER THAN A PARTICULAR STATE OF CONSCIOUSNESS (bodha) [ALTHOUGH IT IS TRUE THAT THIS CONSCIOUSNESS] ACQUIRES SUCH DESIGNATIONS AS

I. A. 7. b.(cont.)

BLISS (ānanda), HAPPINESS (sukha), ETC., WHEN IT CONFORMS TO ITS [BLESSED] SUBSTRATUM (āśraya).

B. In the same manner, they teach [the following conflicting theories on the question of the means (pramāṇa) whereby the ātmā is known or cognized]:

1. [the ātmā is] to be comprehended through inference (anumāna);
2. to be known only through scriptural revelation (āgama);
3. to be known [as the object] of a special immediate cognition by the internal sense-organ (mānasa-pratyakṣa);
4. to be immediately apprehended (pratyakṣo) as the subject and only as the subject (grāhakatayā--eva) [and only] during [and by means of] each cognition of an object (sakala-viṣaya-vittiṣu);
5. [BUT ACCORDING TO MY (YĀMUNA'S) VIEW, THE ātmā IS]

   a. SELF-LUMINOUS (svayaṃjyotiḥ), POSSESSING BEGINNINGLESS AND ENDLESS MANIFESTATION (prakāśa) OF ITS OWN ESSENTIAL FORM (svarūpa) IN AS MUCH AS IT POSSESSES COGNITION OR CONSCIOUSNESS (jñāna) AS ITS ESSENTIAL ATTRIBUTE (svabhāva);

   b. [HOWEVER,] EVEN THOUGH BEING OF SUCH [AN ESSENTIAL NATURE AND THEREFORE BEING KNOWN INDEPENDENTLY OF ANY OTHER MEANS, STILL THE OTHER MEANS OF KNOWLEDGE ARE NOT TO BE DISCARDED AS USELESS AND FUTILE BECAUSE THE ātmā IN THE EMBODIED STATE DOES NOT MANIFEST ITSELF CLEARLY AND DISTINCTLY AND] APPEARS IMMEDIATELY, EXACTLY AS IT IS, [ONLY] AT THE END [OF A LONG COURSE OF DISCIPLINE--AFTER HAVING GRADUALLY BEEN PERCEIVED] CLEARLY, MORE CLEARLY AND FINALLY WITH PERFECT CLARITY, AS ESSENTIALLY DIFFERENT FROM ALL OTHER THAN ITSELF, [AT FIRST] BY MEANS OF SCRIPTURAL REVELATION (āgama) AND INFERENCE (anumāna) AND [FINALLY THROUGH THE IMMEDIATE SUPERSENSUOUS] PERCEPTION BORN FROM yoga.

With regard to both the overall structure of these Pratijñā Series and the location of Yāmuna's Siddhāntas within them, my interpretation differs from all previous ones. It will thus be necessary to establish the validity of my understanding by a systematic analysis of the correlation between these Series as presented in my translation and Yāmuna's Extended Discussion on the same topics.

The Correlation of Pratijñā Series I.A and I.B

Dealing first with Pratijñā Series I.A, my analysis reveals Pratijñā I.A.7 to be Yāmuna's Siddhānta. In contrast, Vīrarāghavācārya and Aṇṇaṅgarācārya take this Pratijñā to be a Sāṅkhya position[34] while van Buitenen apparently interprets it as being Bhāskara's aupādhika-vāda.[35] Moreover, all three of these scholars agree that this Series consists of nine distinct Pratijñās, with the last one (my I.A.7.b) representing Yāmuna's Siddhānta. While there is no doubt a connection between the two additional Pratijñās (that I designate as I.A.7.a and I.A. 7.b) and the immediately preceeding Series, and I also accept the latter one as a Siddhānta of Yāmuna, these additional Pratijñās are not simply a continuation of the same series but rather represent a new Series or sub-series on a closely related topic or point of dispute that was brought up by Yāmuna's Siddhānta in I.A.7--the issue of whether or not ānanda or "bliss" is essentially and eternally associated with the ātmā. When Yāmuna states that the ātmā has "consciousness alone as its essential attribute" (bodha-eka-svabhāva), the question "What of ānanda?" is implicitly raised and then answered with this brief Series.

While my major argument for taking Pratijñā I.A.7 as Yāmuna's Siddhānta must await the demonstration that it does correspond to his detailed conclusion in the Extended Discussion, there is one preliminary consideration that presents a strong prima facie case in favor of my position. According to all previous interpretations, there are only five Pratijñā Series concerning the individual ātmā, covering only five out of the six topics proposed for discussion in the Summary Śloka. The basic structure of the remainder of that portion of the introduction concerned with the individual ātmā is as follows:

tathā . . . iti/[36]
tathā . . . iti/[37]
tathā . . . iti/[38]
. . . iti ca tathātathā pratipadyante/[39]

> With regard to the various other points of dispute (tathātathā), they also put forth many conflicting understandings:
>
> Thus (tathā) [with regard to the pramāṇa or means of valid knowledge of the ātmā, they teach] ". . ." (Pratijñā Series I.B);
>
> In the same manner (tathā) [with regard to the parimāṇa or dimension of the ātmā, they teach] ". . ." (Series I.C);
>
> Again (tathā) [on the duration of the ātmā, they say] ". . ." (Series I.D);
>
> and [on the number of ātmās, they declare] ". . ." (Series I.E).

These four points correspond respectively to Summary Śloka Topics (2), (4), (3), and (5) (see above). If the usual interpretation of the first nine Pratijñās as one Series is accepted, then it must also be accepted that Yāmuna has not explicitly outlined the proposed discussion on Summary Śloka Topic (6), "The ātmā is that which is. . .innately blessed with happiness (svataḥ sukhī)." Both Vīrarāghavācārya and Aṇṇaṅgarācārya recognize this lack of symmetry and attempt to account for it. As Vīrarāghavācārya says, "By means of the word 'tathātathā' [that indicates additional points of dispute not explicitly mentioned], the absence of a statement of the ātmā's innate happiness can be understood."[40] While this explanation is conceivable, Yāmuna's introduction is unusually extensive,[41] giving the impression that it was meant to include all of the major topics. Moreover, it is undeniable that the two Pratijñās that come immediately after I.A.7 in the first series are concerned precisely with the issue raised by Summary Śloka Topic (6), i.e., the relation between ānanda or sukha and the ātmā.

Therefore, I feel that the prima facie evidence supports my contention that the eighth and ninth Pratijñās given by Yāmuna are a new Series or sub-series outlining the positions to be discussed in the svataḥ sukhī section of the AtS--a section that unfortunately is no longer extant but that is alluded to in anticipation twice in the extant Extended Discussion.[42]

A legitimate question at this point would be why Yāmuna did not give the Pratijñās on this topic in the same order as followed in the Summary Śloka and the Extended Discussion.

First of all it should be noted that while Yāmuna's general pattern is to adhere closely to a predetermined sequence, he does not do so rigidly or invariably. For example, in the Pratijñā Series he presents first the topic of the dimension of the ātmā (Series I.C) and then that of its duration (Series I.D), while this sequence is reversed in the Summary Śloka [Topics (4) and (3)] and the Extended Discussion.[43] Moreover, I believe it is possible to present a plausible, if not demonstrable, rationale for the shift in the order of the discussion of svataḥ sukhī. As I have already indicated, the issue of the relation between ānanda and the ātmā is raised quite naturally by the way in which Yāmuna phrases his immediately preceeding Siddhānta, i.e., bodha-eka-svabhāvam, the ātmā has bodha or consciousness as its sole svabhāva. To "some" debaters, ānanda should be included as a svabhāva of the ātmā and they so state in I.A.7.a. Yāmuna then responds with his second Siddhānta that in effect says "no, ānanda does not deserve to be included as an essential attribute of the ātmā! The only attribute that is essentially related to the ātmā is bodha. Ānanda and sukha are simply names applied to a particular state of bodha when it has achieved compatibility with its substratum or support (āśraya), i.e., in the first instance the individual ātmā to which it is related and ultimately the Paramātmā, knowledge of whom produces supreme happiness (niratiśaya-sukha[44])."

In the Summary Śloka and the Extended Discussion, Yāmuna may have moved the discussion of svataḥ sukhī to the final position because this "innate happiness" of the ātmā is characteristic of it only in the highest ideal state of mokṣa or final release from suffering. Yāmuna does deal with the topic of mokṣa near the end in the Pratijñā Series (Series IV) and in his Siddhānta uses the phrase niratiśaya-sukha.[45] It is generally true that the discussion of ānanda occurs in the context of the ānanda-mokṣa-vāda, the dispute as to whether the ātmā in release is characterized by bliss.[46]

Thus, in Pratijñā Series I.A only the first seven Pratijñās are related directly to the extant Extended Discussion on Summary Śloka Topics (1) and (2). I will now explicate the the structure and meaning of Pratijñās I.A.1-7 as revealed by their correlation to the Extended Discussion. As indicated before, the purpose of the proposed discussion is the determination of the essential nature or "unique form" (svarūpa) of that entity that is called "ātmā" and that is the underlying basis or principle of consciousness which appears as the knower (jñātṛ), the subject of the cognition "I" (aham iti, ahaṅ-kāra, ahaṃ-pratyaya) in such cognitions as "I know."[47] The course of the argument proceeds "inward" or "backward" within the human person from grosser entities to more subtle ones. He first presents four views that are probably stereotypes representing different gradations of a Cārvāka or "materialist" position[48]--moving from the visible gross body (Pratijñā I.A.1);[49] to the invisible but elemental external sense organs (I.A.2);[50] to the internal, and to some non-elemental, sense-organ or mind (I.A. 3);[51] and finally to the subtle breath or life-force (I.A.4),[52] which deserves a certain pride of place among the materialist options because even certain Upaniṣadic references can be cited in favor of prāṇa as the ultimate principle.[53] These four are to be rejected because they are all insentient and thus unable to provide a basis for the existence of the ātmā who appears as a sentient being (cetana).[54]

Thus the argument leads to a fifth option (Pratijñā I. A.5), namely that it is merely consciousness itself (bodha-mātram) that is the ātmā and that only appears to be a distinct knower or subject of consciousness.[55] As the detailed discussion clearly shows, this Pratijñā is deliberately stated ambiguously so as to lump together and "tar with the same brush" both "the professed or honest Buddhists and the covert or deceitful ones" (saugatāḥ prakaṭāḥ pracchannāś ca),[56] the former being represented by such Vijñāna-vādins as Dharmakīrti who see consciousness as momentary[57] and the Pracchannas by such followers of Śaṅkara as Sureśvara and Vimuktātman who see it as eternal.[58] While these two schools differ radically on this point, Yāmuna sees them as at one in maintaining that the ultimate principle or "ātmā" 1) is absolutely pure, undivided simple consciousness that is devoid of any attribute (dharma or guṇa) whatsoever (bodha-mātram); 2) therefore, whether momentary or eternal, is ultimately devoid of any individual self-consciousness or cognition of "I" (an-ahaṅ-kāram), and 3) is regarded to be a distinct, active knower or agent in the act of cognition only because of ignorance (avidyā) (adhyasta-jñātṛ-bhāvam).

In the Extended Discussion, Yāmuna, in a preliminary and largely negative manner, defines most of his own Siddhānta on the ātmā's svarūpa through his absolute opposition to all of the above "Buddhistic" points--i.e., the ātmā in its irreducible essence or "unique form" is not merely consciousness itself but is rather the possessor of consciousness (jñāna-vān), the knower (jñātṛ), the independent and eternal entity that appears directly as the self-luminous "I" in all acts of cognition and that has consciousness as its attribute (dharma, guṇa).[59] Thus, he concludes his discussion of what is not the ātmā, i.e., of Summary Śloka Topic (1), to which Pratijñās I.A.1-5 correspond.

One of the major puzzles that needs to be solved in a systematic analysis of the extant text of the AtS is posed by the fact that, through the establishment of Yāmuna's Siddhānta on Summary Śloka Topic (1), there is a complete and clear-cut correlation between 1) Pratijñā Series I.A, 2) the Summary Śloka, and 3) the Extended Discussion, but that immediately thereafter the correlation between the first of these and the latter two seemingly breaks down. Thus, before we can meaningfully proceed with the explication of Pratijna Series I.A, it is necessary to deal with this puzzle at some length and attempt to "decode" or recover the correlation which Yāmuna intended.

In the Extended Discussion, after his refutation of the Pratijñā I.A.5 (the Buddhists and the Pracchanna Kevaladvaitins) and his response, Yāmuna, instead of proceeding to present the position of Pratijñā I.A.6, seemingly abandons the order of Pratijñā Series I.A and introduces the topic proposed by Pratijñā Series I.B with the words:

> kiṃ punar asmin dehādi-vyatirekiṇi cetane pratyag-ātmani pramāṇam/[60]
>
> What then is pramāṇa or means of valid knowledge or cognition with regard to this sentient individual ātmā [who has thus been shown to be] entirely different from the physical body, etc.?

This progression is quite in accord with the order of Yāmuna's Summary Śloka which proposes as Topic (2) the demonstration that the ātmā is an-anya-sādhanaḥ, "not dependent upon any other means (sādhana) for its manifestation." This fact, together with the previously noted fact of the order in which the topics of duration and dimension are considered,[61] reveals that the over-all structure of the Extended Discussion is determined primarily by the Summary Śloka rather than by the Pratijñā Series.

However, as we have seen, there is certainly also some degree of correlation between the Extended Discussion and the Pratijñā Series. Indeed, the Extended Discussion meant to deal with Summary Śloka Topic (2) on pramāṇa once again begins by showing a complete and clear-cut correlation with Pratijñā Series I.B throughout the first four Pratijñās and then ends with a paragraph clearly patterned after I.B.5.b. But once again, somewhere in between the correlation seems to be lost or obscured.

Despite this confusion, I believe that it is possible to rediscover the sense in which Yāmuna understood the correlation between Pratijñā Series I.A and I.B on the one hand and the Summary Śloka and the Extended Discussion on the other. Solving the puzzle requires first of all the recognition of the following two points:

1) that, as in the case of Pratijñā I.A.5, Pratijñā I.A.6 does not represent simply one opponent but rather is a cleverly worded synthesis of the teachings of a closely related group of schools of thought, i.e., the Nyāya-Vaiśeṣikas and certain Neo-Mīmāṃsakas (later representatives of both the Bhāṭṭa and the Prābhākara schools of Pūrva Mīmāṃsā) whom Yāmuna considers to be dependent upon the Nyāya-Vaiśeṣika teachings (nyāya-vaiśeṣikās tan-mata-upajīvinaś ca--abhinava-mīmāṃsakāḥ);[62]

2) that, with certain parenthetical or transitional exceptions, the group of debators represented by the Pūrvapakṣas in Pratijñā Series I.B (i.e., Pratijñās I.B.1-4) is identical with the group represented by Pratijñā I.A.6.

This group represented by Pratijñā I.A.6 and by Pratijñās I.B.1-4 is comprised of debators who are in essential agreement with Yāmuna's Siddhānta on Summary Śloka Topic (1), i.e., deha-indriya-manaḥ-prāṇa-dhībhyo 'nyo. That such is the case is indicated quite strikingly by the fact that Yāmuna begins Pratijñā I.A.6 with the equivalent phrase deha-indriya-manaḥ-prāṇa-bodha-vilakṣaṇam.[63] Thus, once Yāmuna completes the essentially negative task of showing what entities are not the ātmā, the discussion shifts to one carried on essentially between disputants who are agreed on this negative conclusion. However, before the discussion can proceed with the positive task of determining the precise character of the entity that is the ātmā, it is necessary first to establish what is the basis or means (pramāṇa) of positive valid knowledge about this uniquely distinctive ātmā.

Therefore, when the Extended Discussion begins to consider Pratijñā Series I.B after the refutation of Pratijñā I.A.5, it is not actually abandoning the order of Series I.A. Rather, Yāmuna is inserting into Series I.A at this point another issue that must be settled before the discussion as to the svarūpa of the ātmā can proceed.[64] Accordingly, Yāmuna presents and refutes the various viewpoints on the topic of pramāṇa held by the various opponents represented by Pratijñā I.A.6:

> Pratijñā I.B.1 (anumāna-samadhigamyaḥ): the position of the Nyāya-Vaiśeṣikas, with the Sāṅkhyas considered parenthetically, ostensibly because they also employ anumāna as a pramāṇa for the ātmā but actually in order to take another swipe at the Pracchanna Buddhists or Kevalādvaitins whom Yāmuna feels are also dependent upon the Sāṅkhya view of the ātmā.[65]
>
> Pratijñā I.B.2 (āgama-eka-vedyaḥ): the view of certain Śrotriyās, i.e., unthinking and uncritical Mīmāṃsakas or Scripturalists who are presented as a transition between the Nyāya-Vaiśeṣikas and Yāmuna's major Neo-Mīmāṃsaka opponents.[66]
>
> Pratijñā I.B.3 (mānasa-pratyakṣa-vedyaḥ): that of Neo-Mīmāṃsakas of the Bhāṭṭa school of Pūrva Mīmāṃsā.[67]
>
> Pratijñā I.B.4 (grāhakatayā--eva sakala-viṣaya-vittiṣu pratyakṣo): that of Neo-Mīmāṃsakas of the Prābhākara School of Pūrva Mīmāṃsā.[68]

After rejecting these four Pūrvapakṣas, Yāmuna begins to present directly his Summary Śloka Siddhānta (2), an-anya-sādhanaḥ, with almost all of the remaining extant text being devoted to this task.[69] The key to understanding the correlation of this section of the Extended Discussion with the Pratijñā Series is the realization that Yāmuna's phrasing an-anya-sādhanaḥ, while being most ostensibly a summary of his Siddhānta on the topic of pramāṇa, also represents and corresponds to his Siddhānta on the svarūpa of the ātmā, because according to Yāmuna the way in which the ātmā is known is integrally related to, and in fact dependent upon, its svarūpa or essential nature. Thus, Yāmuna begins his presentation of his Siddhānta ananyasādhanaḥ with a brief statement[70] of his position that serves two purposes:

1) it corresponds to Pratijñā I.B.5.a (Yamuna's major theoretical portion of his Siddhānta on the topic of pramāṇa) and thus "rounds off" or temporarily concludes the parenthetical discussion of Pratijñā Series I.B;[71] and

2) it also serves as a preliminary statement of Pratijñā I.A.7, (his direct positive Siddhānta on the topic of svarūpa) and as a bridge or transition back to the discussion of Pratijñā Series I.A.[72]

Thus, the Extended Discussion finally returns to Pratijñā I.A.6, which is at this point explicitly designated as the position of the Nyāya-Vaiśeṣikas and certain Neo-Mīmāṃsakas who are aligned with them and presented as an objection to Yāmuna's preliminary statement of his Siddhānta.[73] Before returning to the explication of Pratijñā Series I.A and the significance and meaning of this position therein, however, let us complete this outline of the correlation between the Pratijñā Series and the Extended Discussion.

After allowing the exponent of Pratijñā I.A.6 to criticize his own position thoroughly and to state their own viewpoint, Yāmuna begins his elaborate and systematic argument in support of his Siddhānta on the true nature of the individual ātmā.[74] This argumentation serves to establish his Siddhānta an-anya-sādhana as being based upon and in accord with the svarūpa or essential nature of the ātmā. As will be established in detail below, this section of the Extended Discussion is fully in accord with the position of Pratijñā I.A.7, which is thus conclusively established as Yāmuna's Siddhānta on the svarūpa of the individual ātmā. Since the content and terminology of Pratijñā I.B.5.a are essentially identical with those of I.A.7,[75] my argument will also establish that the former represents the major theoretical aspect of Yāmuna's Siddhānta on the issue of pramāṇa.

After completing his full systematic theoretical statement on the svarūpa of and pramāṇa for the ātmā, Yāmuna then concludes his Extended Discussion of Summary Śloka Topic (2) with a brief paragraph that relates this theoretical discussion to his practical religious concern, i.e., how ignorant persons can actually come to a true immediate knowledge or apprehension of their ātmās.[76] This concluding paragraph corresponds quite clearly with Pratijñā I.B.5.b, the last member of Pratijñā Series I.A and I.B remaining to be accounted for.

Thus is concluded my solution of the puzzle of the correlation between Pratijñā Series I.A and I.B on the one hand and the Extended Discussion of Summary Śloka Topics (1) and (2) on the other. For ready reference, this correlation is restated in chart form in Appendix II which is given at the back of this work. If my analysis is correct, then the long lost "code" of at least the first portion of the Pratijñā Series has been recovered--revealing that Pratijñās I.A.7, I.A.7.b, I.B.5.a, and I.B.5.b represent Yāmuna's own Siddhāntas. The final guarantee of the validity of this analysis will come from the detailed demonstration in the remainder of this chapter that the contents of Pratijñās I.A.7, I.B.5.a, and I.B.5.b do in fact correspond to Yāmuna's views as presented in the extant Extended Discussion.

Since in the Extended Discussion most of Pratijñā Series I.B is dealt with before proceeding with the discussion of Pratijñā I.A.6 and Yāmuna's Siddhāntas, and since the group of debators represented by Pratijñā I.A.6 is identical with the major Pūrvapakṣas of Series I.B, certain key aspects of the discussion of that Series must be stressed here for a full understanding of Pratijñā I.A.6 and its relationship to Yāmuna's Siddhāntas.

As has been seen, the Nyāya-Vaiśeṣikas and Neo-Mīmāṃsakas represented by Pratijñā I.A.6 are in agreement with Yāmuna's negative Siddhānta that the ātmā is different from the body, the external sense-organs, the internal sense-organ, the vital force, and cognition or consciousness (bodha). Moreover, there are other substantial areas of more positive agreement.

They also concur with Yāmuna's conclusion, in opposition to the Buddhists and Pracchannas of Pratijñā I.A.5, that the ātmā is not mere consciousness itself but is the possessor of consciousness, the entity that appears in the cognition "I" (ahaṃkāra-gocaram)[77] and that is the support (ādhāra) or substance in which such internal special qualities (asādhāraṇa-guṇas) as consciousness inhere.[78] However, there are also major areas of disagreement, especially with regard to 1) the manner in which the ātmā appears or is manifested in cognition as the "I," the subject, and 2) the nature of the relationship between the ātmā and its quality or attribute, consciousness or cognition.

With regard to the first of these two points of disagreement, Yāmuna's Nyāya-Vaiśeṣika and Neo-Mīmāṃsaka opponents do not believe that the ātmā appears or is manifested in cognition immediately and/or independently. This point is the major one at issue in Pratijñā Series I.B, and it is with reference to this issue that Yāmuna formulated his summary of his Siddhānta as an-anya-sādhana, "not established, manifested or known by means of anything other [than itself]." According to Yāmuna, the ātmā must be and is the only independent (svatantra, svayaṃjyotis, svataḥsiddha) element associated with consciousness or cognition.[79] On the other hand, his opponents all make the ātmā dependent (paratantra) on something else for its manifestation as the "I," the subject, the knower, the possessor of knowledge or cognition.

According to the Nyāya-Vaiśeṣikas (Pratijñā I.B.1), knowledge of the ātmā arises only indirectly in dependence upon the pramāṇa anumāna, i.e., an inferential process based upon the assumption that such internal special qualities (viśeṣa-guṇas) as consciousness (jñāna, bodha), happiness (sukha), etc., must inhere in some substance (dravya) or substrate (āśraya), which substance, by the elimination of all other possibilities, is shown to be the ātmā.[80] In the case of the Neo-Mīmāṃsakas of the Bhāṭṭa school (Pratijñā I.B.3), it is admitted that there is an immediate cognition of the ātmā as "I" (ahamity aparokṣāvabhāsaḥ pratyayaḥ), but this cognition is held to be dependent upon a variety of the pramāṇa pratyakṣa (perception) known as mānasa-pratyakṣa or perception by means of the internal sense-organ (manas, antaḥkaraṇa, svānta).[81]

The Prābhākara Neo-Mīmāṃsakas (Pratijñā I.B.4) also agree that the ātmā is immediately perceived (pratyakṣo) but deny that it ever appears as the object of a cognition arising from any pramāṇa. Rather, the ātmā is directly manifested as the subject and the subject alone (grāhaktayā--eva) in every cognition of an object.[82] However, according to the Prābhākaras, this manifestation of the ātmā (ātma-siddhi) does not occur independently but is dependent upon cognition (saṃvit) itself, which alone is independently self-manifest (svataḥ siddhi) and which has as its nature the ability to manifest other things: its objects to the ātmā as objects and the ātmā as the subject, the "I," that possesses the particular cognition.[83] Thus, as with the Buddhists by whom it is generally recognized the Prābhākaras were greatly influenced,[84] momentary, fleeting cognition is itself the only active independent element or principle in consciousness; and the ātmā, while acknowledged as an eternal immutable substance, plays an essentially passive and dependent role.

Thus, Yāmuna feels that all of his Nyāya-Vaiśeṣika and Neo-Mīmāṃsaka opponents tend to reduce the ātmā to a dependent, passive and finally non-essential element in consciousness. This tendency is indicated in Pratijñā I.A.6 by the somewhat difficult to interpret phrase, ākāśādivad, "like ether, etc."[85] While in certain contexts ākāśa-ādi could be taken to represent the five insentient mahābhūtas or material elements as Ramanujachari has done,[86] in terms of the usage most characteristic of Nyāya-Vaiśeṣika[87] and of the AtS,[88] ākāśa is clearly meant to represent entities that are all-pervasive (vibhu) or omnipresent (sarva-gata), of infinite or unlimited dimension (parama-mahat), and formless (a-mūrta).

This view of the ātmā as all-pervasive functions primarily to preserve its eternality (nityatva) precisely by removing the necessity of its participating in the activity, change and impermanence of normal phenomenal consciousness or cognitive experience--since the ātmā is omnipresent, it does not have to move from place to place in order to experience or cognize different objects. However, in Yāmuna's opinion, those who adopt this view go too far and pay far too great a price in their attempt to safeguard the eternality and immutability of the ātmā against the Buddhist critique of everything as momentary, for in the end they make it impossible for the ātmā to be essentially related to consciousness or cognition at all.

This point, then, brings us to the second major area of disagreement between Yāmuna and his Nyāya-Vaiśeṣika and Neo-Mīmāṃsaka opponents, i.e., the nature of the relationship between the ātmā, the subject or possessor of consciousness, and consciousness or cognition itself, the property, quality or attribute or the ātmā. This disagreement is indicated most starkly and dramatically by the phrase in Pratijñā I.A.6, a-cit-svabhāvam "[the ātmā] does not have consciousness (cit) associated with its essential nature or as an essential attribute (svabhāva)." Thus, as is also indicated by the following phrase, āgantuka-bodha-sukha-duḥkhādy-asādhāraṇa-guṇa-ādhāram, consciousness or cognition (bodha) is regarded as no different from other internal special qualities (asādhāraṇa-guṇas) such as pleasure (sukha) and pain (duḥkha) that are simply adventitious (āgantuka), only accidentally, occasionally, non-essentially and non-eternally related to the ātmā. In the Extended Discussion, these opponents at several points[89] argue at length for the adventitious and non-eternal character of consciousness and for the view that it is related to the ātmā only in the bound embodied state and cannot in the very nature of things exist in the state of release (mokṣa, apavarga),[90] which is defined as the absolute cessation of all special qualities of the ātmā--such as cognition, pleasure, pain, etc.[91]

Thus, when Pratijñā I.A.6 states in response to I.A.5 that the ātmā is "other than. . .consciousness," it is actually proposing that this "other" is an entity that is essentially insentient (a-cit-svabhāvam). However, the ātmā is apparently different from the first four insentient entities in being non-material (a-bhautika) and possessing the potential (citi-śakti)[92] of becoming, in the embodied state, the entity referred to by the cognition "I" (ahaṃkāra-gocaram) and thus the subject who possesses consciousness or cognition as an adventitious quality (āgantuka-guṇa).

Before proceeding to the consideration of Yāmuna's Siddhānta, it will be useful to restate briefly and in slightly different terms the course of the argument leading up to

Pratijñā I.A.7. The first five Pratijñās represent positions that in Yāmuna's opinion are clearly heretical or outside the Vedic pale (veda-bāhya) and that must be excluded before proceeding with the positive determination of the manner in which the ātmā is known or manifested (ātma-siddhi) and of its essential nature (svarūpa) when truly known as revealed. Pratijñās I.A.1-4 are all excluded as variations of the Cārvāka or Materialistic position in which the sentient ātmā is derived from some insentient entity or entities. Pratijñā I.A.5 is explicitly labeled the position of Buddhists, the greatest heretics and rejectors of the eternality (nityatva) of the ātmā and of Brahman that are essential presuppositions of the Vedic way.

While it is clear that practially all of the problems and issues dealt with in the AtS stemmed ultimately from the Buddhist critique of eternality, Yāmuna in the eleventh century came at a date when the Buddhists themselves were no longer a major factor. The living problems and issues which Yāmuna himself had to face were ones arising from the overreaction of various Vedic thinkers to the Buddhist challenge. Thus, most of the Extended Discussion on Pratijñā I.A.5 is actually devoted to a rejection of the Pracchanna or covert Buddhists, the Kevalādvaitins who follow Śaṅkara's interpretation of Vedānta and who in Yāmuna's opinion deceitfully claim to be Vedic while actually adhering to a variety of Vijñāna-vāda Buddhism that is heretical and destructive of the Vedic way.[93] In order to preserve the eternality of Brahman or the Paramātmā these Pracchannas teach that it is absolutely immutable (kūṭastha) consciousness utterly devoid of such distinctions as knower and known, subject and object.[94] Thus they deny the ultimate validity of the individual ātmā, the "I," the subject, knower or agent in the act of cognition; teach its final destruction or annihilation in the state of release just as do the Buddhists;[95] and thus destroy the very basis of the Vedic way which in Yāmuna's view presupposes for its validity the existence of an eternal individual knower or agent who will desire the fruits or goals described in the Vedas and follow the injunctions prescribed therein for the attainment of these goals.

To Yāmuna's practical and realistic mind, no sane person would desire mokṣa if it involved the destruction of himself; and thus the Vedantic injunctions would fall into desuetude because no one would desire to follow them:

> Moreover, he who considers himself to be afflicted by the miseries of worldly existence, whether in truth or in error, and thinks 'I am suffering pain,' and in whom the desire for release has arisen, making him reflect: 'How may I become tranquil and blissful, setting aside this entire collection of miseries?', he alone enters upon the means for realisation. If (on the other hand) he were to realise 'I should be no more if I practised the means (for the attainment of release),' he would run away at the very mention of the topic of release. As a consequence of this, since there can be none possessing the requisite qualifications (to enter upon the study of the scripture), the entire upaniṣadic texts and all the śāstras relating to liberation would lose their validity.[96]

In Pratijñā I.A.6 then, Yāmuna turns to those defenders of the Vedic way who agree with him on the necessity of an ultimately real and eternal individual ātmā. However, as we have seen, these Vedic thinkers go to another extreme that is in certain aspects more disastrous and destructive than the Pracchannas' position, for not only is individual self-consciousness destroyed in mokṣa but all consciousness whatsoever disappears in that state, making it an even less attractive goal. This dilemma, in which mokṣa comes to be conceived of as the totally negative goal of the end or cessation of human misery (duḥkha-anta), is also forced upon the Nyāya-Vaiśeṣikas and Neo-Mīmāṃsakas by their response--albeit a totally negative and hostile one--to the Buddhist analysis of the momentariness and non-eternality of normal human cognitive activity. That such is the case is clearly indicated in the case of the Prābhākaras whose view of momentary cognition as the sole independent self-luminous element in consciousness reveals unmistakable Buddhist influence. These Vedic thinkers believed that the only way to preserve the eternality of the individual ātmā was to exclude it from any essential involvement in normal cognitive activity. Yāmuna, on the other hand, in his Siddhānta will attempt to establish the manner in which an eternally self-conscious ātmā can be related to normal human cognition and experience.

Before turning directly to Pratijñā I.A.7, there is a methodological point that should be stressed. As has been noted, there are substantial areas of agreement between the position of Pratijñā I.A.6 and that of Yāmuna. Obviously, as is often the case in Indian dialectics, the argument of the series has been proceeding from the more opposed viewpoints to those more in agreement with the Siddhānta. Even more significantly, certain points with which Yāmuna is in total or substantial agreement find their explicit statement only in Pratijñā I.A.6 (i.e., deha-. . .bodha-vilakṣaṇam and ahaṃkāra-gocaram) but are implicitly presupposed by I.A.7. Thus, as indicated in the discussion of critical problems, in interpreting the Siddhāntas of a series it is sometimes necessary to accept--either as they stand or modified to conform to the Siddhānta--certain aspects that are stated explicitly only in previous Pratijñās.[97]

Yāmuna's Siddhānta on the Svarūpa of the Individual Ātmā (Pratijñā I.A.7)

I now turn to my interpretation of Pratijna I.A.7 and my demonstration that it represents Yāmuna's Siddhānta on the svarūpa of the individual ātmā. As has been pointed out, the contemporary Śrī Vaiṣṇava opinion is that this is a Sāṅkhya Pūrvapakṣa[98] while van Buitenen ascribes it to Bhāskara's interpretation of Vedānta.[99] While I disagree with these interpretations, it will become clear that Yāmuna's position is closely related to the Yoga school of Sāṅkhya and is in certain respects a mode of Vedānta similar to Bhāskara's Bhedābheda-vāda and Aupādhika-vāda.

In terms of its place within the sequence of Pratijñā Series I.A, this Pratijñā is intended to establish that the asserion that the ātmā is "distinct from or other than consciousness" (bodha-vilakṣaṇam), which was made in opposition to the Buddhists and Pracchannas, need not necessarily imply that it is essentially insentient (a-cit-svabhāvam). Thus, I.A.7 must indicate what is the correct relationship between the ātmā and consciousness on the one hand and on the other must distinguish consciousness from the other non-essential adventitious internal special qualities with which consciousness is classified by Pratijñā I.A.6 (āgantuka-bodha-sukha-duḥkhādy-asādhāraṇa-guṇas).

The three basic points made by Pratijñā I.A.7 can be summarized in a preliminary manner as follows:

1) The ātmā within each person is that being that is called "self-luminous" in the Upaniṣads and that eternally and independently manifests its svarūpa (ātma-svarūpa-siddhi[100]) as the "I" (aham ity eva hi tasya svarūpam[101]), the knower (jñātṛ) or subject in all consciousness and acts of cognition; i.e., the ātmā in and of itself manifests itself as eternal "self-consciousness" (anudita-anastamita-svarūpa-prakāśam svayaṃjyotiṣam).[102]

2) The relationship between each ātmā and its consciousness is that the latter is the former's sole svabhāva, i.e., the only special property or quality (a-sādhāraṇa-dharma, viśeṣa-guṇa) that is essentially and inseparably related to its possessor (dharmin, guṇin), that is the "Distinguishing Class Property" that resides in or within its possessor's svarūpa (svarūpa-upādhi-dharma-tva[103]), and that thus exists as long as, and is invariably manifest along with, the individual in which it resides (yāvad-āśraya-bhāvin[104]), i.e., eternally in the case of consciousness which has the svarūpa of the eternal ātmā as its substratum (āśraya) (bodha-eka-svabhāvam eva).[105]

3) All other internal special qualities, such as happiness (sukha) and pain (duḥkha), etc., that the ātmā appears to possess are not essential to it but are imputed to or imposed upon (aupādhika) the ātmā and its consciousness by such conditioning factors (upadhānas) as the sense-organs, especially the internal one (antaḥ-karaṇa), in contact with the objects being cognized (antaḥ-karaṇa-upadhāna-āpādita-rāga-dveṣa-sukha-duḥkha-ādy-aśiva-guṇa-nirbhāsam).[106]

I will now proceed to substantiate these summary interpretations by reference to the Extended Discussion. For the sake of methodological clarity and to make my argument as conclusive as possible, I will wherever possible restrict my evidence to those sections of the Extended Discussion about which there is no dispute between myself and the various Śrī Vaiṣṇava interpreters as to the fact that they definitely represent Yāmuna's own views.

Essential to the understanding of Pratijñā I.A.7 and its relation to the course of Yāmuna's argument is the perception that the phrase bodha-eka-svabhāvam eva [see point 2) above] does not--as the modern Śrī Vaiṣṇava interpretation of this as the position of the Sāṅkhya dṛśi-mātra-ātma-vādins assumes it does[107]--mean the same thing as the phrase bodha-mātram in Pratijñā I.A.5, but, rather, is meant to contrast sharply with it. Prerequisite to this perception is the insight that Yāmuna makes a rather unusual distinction between the terms svabhāva and svarūpa--a distinction that was also maintained and developed by Rāmānuja[108] and that is a peculiar and essential basis for the Śrī Vaiṣṇava Viśiṣṭādvaita Vedānta darśana.

Since the key to understanding Pratijñā I.A.7 as Yāmuna's Siddhānta on the svarūpa lies in the proper understanding of the term svabhāva, it is best to present his technical usage of this latter term before considering the other aspects of his position. Yāmuna wishes to maintain on the one hand that consciousness is an innate property or quality related eternally to tha ātmā and on the other that this same consciousness participates in the ever-changing cognition of objects and is thus in some sense or manner also occasional (āgantuka, kādācitka). Shortly after the major statement of his Siddhānta, one of his Neo-Mīmāṃsaka opponents, probably a Bhāṭṭa who holds cognition to be an impermanent action (kriyā),[109] takes Yāmuna to task, asking him in effect how consciousness can be at one and the same time both an eternal property of the ātmā and an occasional activity like the cognition of objects:

> Indeed cognition (jñāna), which has been accepted [by you] as that which effects the manifestation of objects, is occasional (āgantuka) and has the form of an activity (kriyā-rūpa); therefore how can that be a svabhāva of the ātmā?[110]

In response to this question Yāmuna proceeds to establish the sense in which jñāna is an ātma-svabhāva. Since all agree that motion or action (kriyā, karma) is impermanent and non-eternal, Yāmuna first denies that jñāna must itself be an activity in order to be the cause (nimitta) that produces as an effect (kārya) the manifestation of objects (artha-siddhi, -prakāśa), citing as proof other instances in which an effect is produced without any activity on the part of its cause.[111] Essential to Yāmuna's position is the distinction that both consciousness and the ātmā itself have the capacity of participating in or possessing activity (kriyā-vat-tva) without themselves being activity or being non-eternal because of their association with it.[112] Thus, Yāmuna concludes his first step in showing the manner in which jñāna is an ātma-svabhāva by saying,

> Hence, [it is not necessary to maintain that the manifestation of objects which is peculiar (praty-asādhāraṇa) to a particular person is produced by an adventitious special action which inheres in that person (tat-samaveta-āgantuka-asādhāraṇa. . . -kriyā-janya);[113] rather] all that needs to be said is that the aforesaid peculiar property (dharma) [i.e., "manifestation of objects" (artha-siddhi, artha-prakāśa)] has as its cause another special property (asādhāraṇa-dharma) inhering in the person. And that latter special property is indeed accepted to be the consciousness (caitanya) of the ātmā in the same way as luminosity (tejasvitva) [or light is the special property] of the sun.[114]

Thus, one aspect of consciousness's being a svabhāva is its being a special property (asādhāraṇa-dharma) of the ātmā, i.e., something that distinguishes an ātmā alone and no other category of reality.[115] However, the term dharma is a very ambiguous one as is indicated by Yāmuna's use of it in the above quotation with regard to two distinct types of categories, "manifestation of objects" and consciousness. Being one of the most widely and variously used terms in Indian religious thought, even in Yāmuna's immediate technical intellectual context dharma has a wide range of usages. In its widest sense, it can indicate any property that is characteristic of an entity or category (padārtha) which is thus called the dharmin, "the possessor of that property."[116] In a somewhat narrower, technical Nyāya-Vaiśeṣika usage, a dharma refers to a property that is related to its possessor (dharmin) or substratum (āśraya, ādhāra) by a special relation called samavāya or "Inherence" in which the dharma is dependent upon (paratantra) and unable to exist separately from (a-yuta-siddha) its dharmin.[117] Even in this technical definition, dharma can still refer to any one of five different categories (padārthas) that can be a property inhering in a substratum: substance (dravya), quality (guṇa), motion (karma, kriyā), universal (sāmānya) or particular (viśeṣa).[118]

However, in a further, very common specialization of meaning, dharma is often used interchangeably and synonymously with one of the more important of these five categories of properties, i.e., guṇa, quality or attribute, but with the often confusing complication that the usage of dharma can very easily slip over into its more general senses.[119] A further complication is posed by the fact that, while the thinkers in Yāmuna's milieu in a very general way accept and operate according to Nyāya-Vaiśeṣika categories and principles, many among them--including Yāmuna and his grandfather Nāthamuni--do not feel bound by these technical definitions and modify them as they find necessary.[120] Thus, Yāmuna often seems to use dharma synonymously with guṇa but with the effect of broadening the meaning of the latter category beyond its strict Nyāya-Vaiśeṣika definition.[121]

Thus far in his attempt to define consciousness as an ātma-svabhāva, all Yāmuna has done is to establish that it is not a dharma or property having the form of an activity (kriyā-rūpam) and therefore is not necessarily impermanent and occasional. Now he must proceed to prove that it is a dharma that is innately and eternally related to the ātmā. To do so, Yāmuna employs what is his favorite example (dṛṣṭānta) or analogy for the relationship between the ātmā and consciousness, i.e., that between the sun and its luminosity (tejasvitva, prakāśa) or light (āloka). Yāmuna's Nyāya-Vaiśeṣika and Neo-Mīmāṃsaka opponents had inferred the occasional and non-eternal nature of jñāna as a property of the ātmā on the basis of such cognitions as "I know" and "I knew" that they claim show the ātmā (the "I") to be related to discrete acts of cognition which exist for only a limited time (kāla-avaccheda-pratīter), in the same way as the cognitions "I go" and "I went" show the ātmā to be only occasionally or adventitiously associated with actions which exist only for limited times.[122]

Yāmuna shows that their reasoning is inconclusive because we experience similar cognitions ("The sun illuminates this place." "It illuminated it." "It will illuminate it.") with regard to the sun and its luminosity which both Yāmuna and his opponents accept as an essential property of the sun.[123] Just as Yāmuna's opponents would explain that, although luminosity is an essential property of the sun, it appears to be temporally limited because it is only occasionally related to or in contact with any particular place, so Yāmuna may say,

> Here also then [in the case of the manifestation of objects by the ātmā's consciousness], the particular object to be manifested or cognized, i.e., the one that at the moment exists in such a state as to be compatible with being brought into close contact (pratyāsatti) with the sense-organs, etc., delimits the essential quality of the ātmā, consciousness (svābhāvikam ātmanaś caitanya-guṇam avacchinatti).[124]

Thus, in both cases, the temporally limited (kāla-avaccheda) or occasional (āgantuka) character of the illumination or cognition is caused by the temporary occasional nature of the relationship (sambandha) or contact (pratyāsatti) of luminosity or consciousness with the particular place or object--not by the nature of luminosity or consciousness or by the nature of their relationship with the sun or the ātmā. According to Yāmuna, it is in such a way that we can understand the occasional nature of cognition while still accepting consciousness as an essential quality of the ātmā (svābhāvikam ātmanaś caitanya-guṇam).

Yāmuna's opponents then ask him how in the case of the consciousness of the ātmā it can be definitely established that the temporal distinction (bheda) between cognitions is aupādhika, i.e., caused by its relationship to other conditioning factors (upādhis), as is the case with the luminosity (prakāśa) of the sun (dyumaṇi) or of a jewel (maṇi), and not svābhāvika, i.e., a bheda caused by the occasional non-eternal nature of consciousness itself, as is the case with such actions (kriyās) as "going," "cooking," etc.[125]

In response to this question, Yāmuna gives his definitive statement of the sense in which consciousness is the svabhāva of the ātmā:

> tādrūpyeṇa--eva pratyakṣatvāt/ na hi jātu cid a-cid-rūpo 'yam ātmā loṣṭādivad dṛṣṭacaraḥ/
>
> yaś ca yadguṇatayā--eva sākṣād-bhavati, sa tat-svabhāvaḥ, marud iva sparśa-guṇatayā--eva--adhyakṣyamāṇaḥ/
>
> yo yat-svabhāvo na bhavati, sa tad-virahenāpi svarūpata upalabhyate, gamanādi-rahitatayā--iva devadattādiḥ/[126]

> [The difference (bheda) between past, present and future cognitions is aupādhika and not svābhāvika] because [the ātmā] is perceived, directly experienced or cognized, only as having such a form [i.e., as possessing consciousness as a property or quality], for at no time has the ātmā been seen to exist in an insentient form [a form without consciousness] as if it were a clod of earth, etc.
>
> And that which is perceived or directly cognized only as possessing a certain thing as a quality (guṇa) possesses that thing as its svabhāva, as for example air, being perceived (i.e., "felt") only as possessing the quality, touch (sparśa), [posseses that quality as its svabhāva].
>
> That which does not possess a certain thing as a svabhāva is experienced in its own unique form (svarūpatas) even without that thing, as for example [the individual] Devadatta, [being found to exist at times] as devoid of such [actions] as going, [does not possess such an action as a svabhāva]. [Therefore, consciousness is a svabhāva of the ātmā since the latter is perceived only as possessing the former as its quality.]

Thus, a svabhāva is a special property (asādhāraṇa-dharma) or quality (viśeṣa-guṇa) that is essentially related to, and necessarily and invariablly accompanies and appears with, its possessor (dharmin, guṇin), which in its turn never exists, and is never perceived in and of itself (svarūpatas), without this essential attribute.

While there are further subtleties and complications to be considered, it is clear that the above is the sense in which the term svabhāva is used in the phrase bodha-eka-svabhāvam eva in Pratijñā I.A.7. Sprinkled throughout passages that indisputably represent Yāmuna's own positions are found similar phrases such as:

(1) jña-svabhāvasya aham-arthasya,

(2) caitanya-svabhāvatayā svayaṃjyotiṣṭvāt,

(3) ātmā tu prakāśa-svabhāva eva,

(4) cit-svabhāvasya puṃsaḥ svābhāvikī citiḥ,

(5) bodha-svābhāvye hi puruṣasya,

(6) bodha-svabhāvatvād eva--asya,

(7) puṃso bodha-svabhāvatvam,

(8) ātma-svabhāva-bhūtāyāś citer,

(9) bodha-svabhāvatām asya,

(10) ātma-svabhāva-bhūtasya caitanyasya,

(11) caitanya-svabhāva eva--ayam ātmā,

(12) caitanya-svabhāvaḥ parisphurann apy ayam ātmā.[127]

And when Yāmuna at one point explicitly excludes all the other generally accepted special qualities (viśeṣa-guṇas) of the ātmā, such as suhka and duḥkha, etc., from the special status accorded to bodha,[128] we see that the phrase bodha-eka-svabhāvam eva in Pratijna I.A.7 conforms fully to Yāmuna's position as stated in the Extended Discussion.

In Pratijñā I.A.7, the status of such inauspicious qualities (a-śiva-guṇas) as suhka and duḥkha was explained through the use of the example (dṛṣṭānta) of a sphaṭika-maṇi or crystal jewel that has only the color white through its essential quality (svabhāva-dhavalam) of luminosity (prakāśa) but that appears to have other different qualities such as redness that are imputed to it because of the close presence of particular conditioning factors (upadhānas) such as a red rose. As we have seen, in the Extended Discussion Yāmuna's favorite example for dealing with such aupādhika bhedas or non-essential differences or distinctions caused by the presence or close association of conditioning factors (upādhis) is the Sun and its luminosity. However, at one point the example of a maṇi or jewel and its luminosity is cited in a manner that clearly suggests that it could be used interchangeably with that of the Sun and its light (dyumaṇi-maṇi-prakāśāder iva--aupādhiko 'yaṃ bhedaḥ).[129]

At the points in the Extended Discussion at which Yāmuna explicitly deals with the status of such qualities as sukha and duḥkha, he does not employ the sphaṭika-maṇi analogy, but the content of what he says agrees with what is stated in Pratijñā I.A.7, i.e., that such qualities are not essentially related to the ātmā or consciousness but are caused by the conditioning factors (upadhānas) of the states of the sense-organs, especially the internal sense-organ (antaḥ-karaṇa) or mind (manas).[130] However, his treatment of this question receives little emphasis in the extant portion of the Extended Discussion, being dealt with briefly and somewhat inconclusively with reference to either the sukha-duḥkha-adhikaraṇa of Nāthamuni's NyT or the no longer extant portion of the AtS dealing with svataḥ sukhī for a fuller discussion.[131] The sphaṭika-maṇi analogy may have been developed systematically in the course of this no longer extant portion of the Extended Discussion.

It is now time to turn to a more systematic discussion of Yāmuna's Siddhānta on the svarūpa of the ātmā as it is presented in the Extended Discussion itself. As in the AP, Yāmuna begins and summarizes the major statement of his Siddhānta with an inference expressed in verse or kārikā form:

> atrāhur ātmatattvajñāḥ svataś caitanyam ātmanaḥ/
> svarūpopādhidharmatvāt prakāśa iva tejasaḥ//[132]
>
> Here, the knowers of the reality of the ātmā say that the consciousness of the ātmā is innate or essential (svataś) to it,
>
> Because consciousness has the character of a property (dharma) that is the svarūpa-upādhi, [of the class or category ātmā, the common qualifier that resides in and distinguishes an ātmā from everything else and that is dependent upon and inseparably and invariably existing with the ātmā in which it resides]; like the luminosity (prakāśa) of fire.

As was also the case in the AP, the major problem in understanding this inference and Yāmuna's Siddhānta lies in the fact that the Reason (hetu) svarūpa-upādhi-dharma-tvāt, like the one nirdoṣa-jñāna-janma-tvāt, is ambiguous and susceptible of varied interpretations. Once again, it seems likely that the ambiguity was deliberate and self-conscious on the part of the poet-philosopher Yāmuna.

As Vīrarāghavācārya notes, this Reason can be construed either as "because it has the character of a property (dharma) that possesses the svarūpa as its upādhi" or as "because it has the character of a property that is the or an upādhi of [in] the svarūpa."[133] Ramanujachari chooses the first of these options, according to which upādhi must be taken to mean "cause" (nimitta) or "causal or determining factor" (prayojaka), and translates the Reason as "for, it is a quality dependent on the soul itself."[134] There is no doubt that an essential step in Yāmuna's argument is the assertion that consciousness is "dependent on, produced by, essentially connected with and consequent on the svarūpa" (svarūpa-prayukta) and therefore exists as long as the ātmā exists (yāvad-āśraya-bhāvin), i.e., eternally.[135] Therefore, it seems likely to me that Yāmuna deliberately constructed his Reason so that it could be taken in such a sense, only, however, as a secondary overtone following upon its primary meaning for which it must be construed as in the second option. It is necessary at this point to establish this fact and to determine as precisely as possible what Yāmuna means by the terms upādhi and svarūpa-upādhi.

Immediately following the above verse, Yāmuna continues his statement of his Siddhānta as follows:

> Except for its being the substratum of consciousness (caitanya-āśraya-tām), there is no other svarūpa of the ātmā;
>
> For that which is devoid of consciousness, like a pot, etc., is not an ātmā.
>
> And Self-hood (ātma-tva) cannot be distinguished simply on the basis of the capacity or potency to produce consciousness (citi-śakti), because, in such a view, the result would be destruction (nāśa) of the ātmā in release (mukti).
>
> Indeed, according to the doctrine of Nyāya-Vaiśeṣika, release (mokṣa) is defined as the absolute cessation (ātyantika-uparama) of all special qualities of the ātmā (vaiśeṣika-ātma-guṇas) such as cognition (buddhi), pleasure (sukha) and pain (duḥkha), etc., and there is simply no means (pramāṇa) that is competent to establish that an entity which is absolutely devoid of an effect (atyanta-lupta-kāryam) has the potency or capacity of producing that effect; [therefore an ātmā distinguished only by the potency of producing consciousness (citi-śakti) cannot be proven to continue to exist in release].
>
> An effect (kārya) such as pleasure and pain, cognition (jñāna), etc., being observed as being related to a qualified entity such as the body, etc. (dehādi-viśiṣṭa-sambandhitayā), establishes that the capacity or potency of producing the effect itself (ātma-utpāda-śaktim) exists only in a qualified entity (viśiṣṭa-vartinīm eva), just as smoke [being observed only in relation to a fire qualified by wet fuel] establishes that the capacity of producing smoke exists only in a fire that is associated with or qualified by wet fuel (ardrendhana-sambandhini dhūma-dhvaje), and as a rice sprout establishes such a capacity only with regard to a rice seed that is still associated with or qualified by its husk (sa-tuṣa-taṇḍule).
>
> Moreover, when the distinguishing or delimitation of ātmā from all that is not ātmā is possible simply when consciousness exists (bodhe saty eva--ātmano 'nātma-vyavacchede sambhavati), be done with this unnecessary resort to the potency (śakti) to produce consciousness [as the distinguishing characteristic of ātmā].136

If my understanding of this statement--Yāmuna's first extended comment upon his versified inference--is correct, then Yāmuna's primary concern with consciousness is as a qualifier (viśeṣaṇa), distinguisher or "delimiter" (vyavacchedaka, avacchedaka) that is a common property (sāmānya, sāmānya-dharma) of all ātmās and distinguishes them as a class from all other classes.[137]

Now, there is a technical usage of the term upādhi in such a sense within Nyāya-Vaiśeṣika, one that became increasingly important within the Navya-Nyāya or New Logic that was beginning to develop around Yāmuna's time. Sāmānya or "Generality," one of the basic Vaiśeṣika Categories (padārthas), was apparently originally a somewhat fluid concept, denoting primarily a common property of a class of entities but one that is also capable of being termed secondarily a viśeṣa or specific property when viewed as that by which the class is distinguished (vyavacchidyate) from all else.[138] Within this category it became necessary to distinguish between, on the one hand, those Generalities that are strictly Generic Properties or Characters, termed jātis and conceived of as eternal and unitary properties or "universals" residing in individuals (vyaktis) through a special relation of samavāya (Inherence), and, on the other, those which are merely common to some class of individuals but are not distinct eternal properties that meet the technical definition of a Generic Property (jāti).[139] This latter type of Sāmānya came to be termed upādhi.[140]

Originally the primary concern was with jāti, with which the Category Sāmānya proper is often identified, while an upādhi was viewed as a non-essential adventitious Class Property that is only indirectly connected with or "imposed" upon a class of objects through our cognition of them.[141] Hence upādhi is standardly translated as "imposed property"[142] as opposed to the Generic Property jāti which provides the essential basis for the existence of its class or genus and which is immediately given when an individual of the genus is cognized.[143]

However, in Navya-Nyāya the concept upādhi in the above and other closely related senses assumed a much more important place as the concept of jāti became increasingly problematic and hard to defend and was accordingly relegated to a more restricted role.[144] This process of revaluation was part of a general reaction against the traditional Vaiśeṣika Categories and the problems and absurdities which their rigid divisions involved. Specifically at issue here was the relationship between the Categories jāti and samavāya (Inherence). According to Nyāya-Vaiśeṣiká, a jāti is related to its individual manifestations (vyaktis) by the relation samavāya. However, both jāti and samavāya are distinct Categories so one must ask what relation relates samavāya to jāti and so on in an infinite regress.[145]

Commenting upon this regressus ad infinitum, Bimal Krishna Matilal, upon whose outstanding analysis of Navya-Nyāya I am primarily depending, says,

> The Naiyāyika averts the difficulty by pointing out that it arises because of the tacit assumption that all relations are essentially different from the relata and hence should be tied by a second relation. There is, however, no a priori necessity, so claims Nyāya, for the relation to be taken as numerically different in all cases from its relata. Nyāya thus postulated a "peculiar" kind of relation, a svarūpa relation, which is not to be taken as different from its relata. . . . Besides avoiding the paradox, there is another advantage of this expedient of the svarūpa relation. Nyāya thus avoided the danger of the multiplication of entities or categories through what we have called "hypostatic abstraction" of any futher relation.
>
> . . .The Nyāya doctrine of the svarūpa or self-linking relation to solve the above paradox may seem to be alarmingly simple. . . . On the whole we can regard the Nyāya doctrine of the svarūpa relation as a heuristic device to explain certain epistemological facts. It also provided Nyāya with a way out of a maze of unnecessary abstract entities.[146]

Matilal, in continuing the above discussion, reveals how this svarūpa relation and the concern for a way out of the traditional Nyāya-Vaiśeṣika "maze" of abstract entities and properties are related to the development of the concept upādhi:

> . . .Let us call a property "intrinsic" if it is denoted by a term abstracted from what we have called an "adjective" term. . .by adding suffixes of the type '-tva' or '-tā.' The general tendency of the Naiyāyikas was to construe any such simple property denoted by such a substantivized term as a separate entity. This tendency was also aided by the easy grammatical device of the Sanskrit language by which abstract terms can be formed even out of already abstract expressions. But the Naiyāyikas also saw the danger of unnecessarily multiplying such abstract properties. Thus to avoid this obvious charge,

> they had to stipulate that each such intrinsic property, unless it is construed as a jāti or generic property (which implies that it is a separate real), is related to its locus through a relation of selfsameness, i.e., a svarūpa relation. This stipulation implies, from the Nyāya point of view, that we can, for the sake of convenience and simplicity, use these expressions without committing ourselves to the existence of such abstract entities.
>
> To push the point a little further: the class of the so-called intrinsic properties (as I am using the term here) can be divided into two groups, one being the class of what Nyāya calls jāti 'generic properties,' and the other class of what it calls upādhi 'imposed properties'. . . . In the traditional Nyāya-Vaiśeṣika system a jāti was accepted as a separate category, and hence it should be ontologically different from its locus or its manifestations (vyakti). But apart from these, all other intrinsic properties are earmarked as 'imposed' (aupādhika), and ontologically each of them is to be identified with its locus or subjunct. It may incidentally be noted that the old doctrine of jāti was seriously criticized by the Buddhists and that as a result while the later orthodox school built up a strong defense against the criticism of the Buddhists, they also tended gradually to narrow down the scope of jāti in such a way that finally only a small subclass of our intrinsic properties could be regarded as jāti.[147]

Thus we see how the concept of upādhi, as an "intrinsic" but "imposed" property that is distinguishable from, but not ultimately different than, its locus or possessor, increased in significance as the scope of jāti became reduced. Moreover, as Matilal says of the related svarūpa relation, "with the advent of the svarūpa relation in this way, the position of samavāya itself in the Nyāya system was left dwindling."[148] Both Matilal and Ingalls, upon whose work Matilal's is based, note that the svarūpa relation can also be called a viśeṣaṇatā-viśeṣa-sambandha (Ingalls: "Particular Qualification Relation"; Matilal: "qualifier-ness relation"), i.e., a relation having the nature of that between a qualifier and the thing qualified (viśeṣaṇa-viśeṣya-bhāva) in a determinate (savikalpaka) or qualificative cognition (viśiṣṭa-jñāna).[149] As Ingalls says, the viśeṣaṇas ("qualifiers," "distinguishers," "limitors," "conditioners") in these viśiṣṭa-jñānas "are always either generic characters (jāti) or imposed properties (upādhi)."[150]

The most important type of such an upādhi was called a-khaṇḍa-upādhi, "an indivisible and unanalyzable imposed property," i.e., a viśeṣaṇa that is cognized as residing in, and being possessed by, a particular entity, but that cannot be analyzed as belonging to one of the traditional fundamental and separate Categories (padārthas) and thus must be classified as inseparable or indivisible (a-khaṇḍa) from, and related by a svarūpa relation to, the particular entity that it qualifies or distinguishes in cognition.[151]

Thus, the concepts a-khaṇḍa-upādhi and svarūpa relation came to be of increasing importance as the Navya-Naiyāyikas attempted to deal with cognitive experience and evidence that could not be made to conform to the rigidity of the traditional Viśeṣika Categories--especially that of samavāya as a separate eternal relation.[152] Indeed, in the case of the innovative Raghunātha Śiromani, they come close to routing the traditional categories from the field altogether.[153] As Matilal comments,

> It may sound paradoxical, but it seems to me that the introduction of svarūpa relation into the Nyāya-Vaiśesika system is a little like the proverbial camel's head under the tent (one might call it, facetiously, a Vedāntin's head): carried to its logical conclusion, the doctrine destroys the traditional system of categories.[154]

While a full consideration of the relation of Yāmuna's tradition of Nyāya to Navya-Nyāya lies beyond the scope of the present work, the Navya-Nyāya developments of a-khaṇḍa-upādhi and svarūpa relation would seem to provide the best general context for the understanding of Yāmuna's svarūpa-upādhi. To pursue Matilal's "facetious" analogy, we might say that in Yāmuna's case the Vedāntin camel has moved into the tent and made it his own, for here we see the integration of these Nyāya developments into an explicitly Vedāntic system.

As was developed in Chapter V, Yāmuna's distinctive contribution was the integration of Nāthamuni's Vedāntically compatible Nyāya system (vedāntānukūlam nyāyaśāstram) into the Miśra tradition of Vedānta. According to Vedānta Deśika, Nāthamuni "scorned Akṣapāda, etc., and composed another way of Nyāya called the Nyāya-Tattva";[155] and Vedānta Deśika makes it quite clear that the major objection to the orthodox Nyāya founded on Akṣapāda's Nyāya-Sūtras was the intrusion of the

Vaiśeṣika Categories that occurred with the development of the syncretistic Nyāya-Vaiśeṣika school.[156]

Thus the Śrī Vaiṣṇava tradition of Nyāya based upon Nāthamuni's NyT was also a "New Logic" developed in reaction to the problems caused by the Vaiśeṣika Categories--although in the Śrī Vaiṣṇava case the departure from the "Old Logic" was more extreme because it became integrated into Vedānta while Navya-Nyāya remained formally within the Nyāya-Vaiśeṣika darśana and could not dismiss outmoded Categories as completely as the Śrī Vaiṣṇavas did.[157] For example, the Category of samavāya as a separate eternal relation caused many problems for the Navya-Naiyāyikas but generally they felt compelled to accept it,[158] while Yāmuna, following Nāthamuni, explicitly rejects it as a distinct Vaiśeṣika Category and defines it as simply a particular type of the more basic and general class saṃyoga or simple relation or close association.[159]

As has been noted before, Yāmuna's dependence upon Nāthamuni's NyT in the AtS is quite clearly established by one explicit reference to this work and by the large number of points at which the form of reference or the peculiar terminology make it probable that he is following or interpreting his grandfather.[160] However, the form of Yāmuna's explicit reference to the NyT, when taken together with the fact that Nāthamuni is not mentioned among the Vedāntic authorities cited in in the introduction of the AtS, is very suggestive. While developing his definition of prakāśa (manifestation in consciousness or cognition), Yāmuna for the one and only time quotes the precise words of the NyT. However, the words which Yāmuna quotes are not Nāthamuni's definition of prakāśa but rather form a short phrase dealing with a related topic from which Yāmuna then derives his own definition.[161] What this fact suggests is that, while Yāmuna was dependent on Nāthamuni for much of his inspiration and many of his ideas, his dependence was not mechanical or imitative; rather, as stated before, Yāmuna was actively developing Nāthamuni's nyāya-śāstra within a new and different context, i.e., Vedānta.

This view of the relationship between Yāmuna and Nāthamuni is in turn suggestive vis-à-vis Yāmuna's use of the terms upādhi and svarūpa-upādhi. While Yāmuna employs this terminology in his kārikā or verse summary of his Siddhānta, the term upādhi is rarely resorted to in the following Extended Discussion; and Yāmuna, as we have seen, deliberately develops the alternative terminology of svabhāva which, if my understanding is correct, corresponds to svarūpa-upādhi. Thus, a plausible hypothesis would be that Yāmuna employed the terminology svarūpa-upādhi in his kārikā because of the status it enjoyed as stemming from Nāthamuni's "new" nyāya-śāstra, but felt compelled to redefine this terminology and to develop more adequate alternatives because of certain limitations inherent in the term upādhi as utilized within Navya-Nyāya and within other darśanas and schools of Vedānta.

If my understanding is correct, Yāmuna's distinction between svabhāva and svarūpa roughly corresponds to that between an a-khaṇḍa-upādhi and its āśraya, i.e., an intrinsic inseparable property (dharma) or qualifier (viśeṣaṇa) and the entity in which it resides and which is qualified (viśeṣya, viśiṣṭa) by it. As we have seen, Yāmuna clearly states that the irreducible essence or core of the ātmā's svarūpa is its being the āśraya of consciousness (caitanya-āśrayatāṃ muktvā svarūpaṃ na--anyad ātmanaḥ).[162] At another place, Yāmuna emphatically makes the same point:

> 'aham' ity eva hi tasya svarūpam/ jñānam api hi tad-dharmatvena tasya--eva prakāśate, jñānaṃ me jātam iti/[163]
>
> For that alone (eva) which appears in the cognition "I" is the svarūpa of that [ātmā], for knowledge (jñāna) appears to that one alone (eva) as its property (dharma), as in "knowledge is born in me."

Thus, the svarūpa of the ātmā is most strictly defined in terms of its being the possessor (dharmin, jñāna-vān) or substratum (āśraya) of the property (dharma) of consciousness, its svabhāva or svarūpa-upādhi.

However, as we have seen, an entity cannot appear or be cognized svarūpa-tas, as it is in and of itself, without its svabhāva; and thus it is possible for the term or category svarūpa to be used in such a way as to include within itself the svabhāva, i.e., a svabhāva cannot finally be categorized as something different from its svarūpa; it is an upādhi in or "within" the svarūpa. It is at this point that the Navya-Nyāya overtones of the term svarūpa-upādhi as presented by Matilal above are most relevant, in a positive sense, to Yāmuna's usage of svarūpa and svabhāva. As we have seen, an a-khaṇḍa-upādhi, being related to its āśraya by a svarūpa relation, is distinguishable from, but not finally different than, its possessor. Again, Matilal is worth quoting on this "relation of selfsameness":

> An imposed property (upādhi). . ., although it is said to be related to its locus by a svarūpa relation, is not held to be different from its locus. It may be asked, how does it differ from the identity relation? We may now try to distinguish them by appealing to the notion of occurrence-exacting and non-occurrence-exacting relations. Identity is a non-occurrence-exacting relation such that, given a = b, we cannot use the expression "a occurs in b" or "a is a locus of b." But a svarūpa relation, holding between an imposed property and its possessor, is said to be occurrence-exacting in the sense that, given such a relation relating a and b, we can use the expression "a occurs in b" or "b is a locus of a," although in the final analysis, i.e., when we talk in terms of categorical predicates to be attached to a or b, a can be identified with b.[164]

Thus it would seem that the related concepts of a-khaṇḍa-upādhi and svarūpa relation provide a model for the relation between the ātmā and its property consciousness that avoids both the extremes of absolute difference (atyanta-bheda), as advocated by Yāmuna's Nyāya-Vaiśeṣika and Neo-Mīmāṃsā opponents, and of absolute non-difference (atyanta-abheda) or identity (tādātmya), as advocated by the Buddhists and the Pracchanna Kevalādvaitins.

Yāmuna must be invoking some such model by his use of the term svarūpa-upādhi and in his development of the svarūpa/svabhāva distinction and relation. In the latter development, by using two terms that are usually taken synonymously as signifying the "essential nature" of an entity and by sometimes treating the svabhāva as included within the svarūpa, he is asserting that, while consciousness is distinct and distinguishable from the ātmā, it is ultimately and eternally inseparably related to it.

It would also seem possible that the very term viśiṣṭa-advaita ["the non-duality of that which is qualified or distinguished (viśiṣṭa)"],[165] which in later centuries came to be the designation of the Śrī Vaiṣṇava Vedānta darśana, also reflects the influence of some such model as the Navya-Nyāya svarūpa relation, which, as we have noticed, is also called a "qualifier-ness (viśeṣaṇa-tā) relation," having the nature of the relationship between a qualificand (viśeṣya), [i.e., an object cognized as qualified (viśiṣṭa)], and the qualifier (viśeṣaṇa) which distinguishes the object in the cognition (viśeṣaṇa-viśeṣya-bhāva).[166]

Unfortunately, in the extant Extended Discussion, Yāmuna's views on the svarūpa/svabhāva relation between the ātmā and consciousness (dharma-dharmi-saṃbandha) are presented only briefly and somewhat obliquely, with his full discussion being postponed until the no longer extant section dealing directly with the question of relation (saṃbandha-vimarśe);[167] therefore, it is not possible to determine his position with any fullness or precision.[168]

However, in a passage quoted above, Yāmuna places great emphasis upon the point that the svarūpa of the ātmā must be viśiṣṭa, "qualified or distinguished" by consciousness (caitanya, bodha), if it is to have the potency (śakti) of producing as an effect (kārya) the cognition (jñāna) or manifestation (prakāśa) of objects.[169] While Yāmuna does not to my knowledge explicitly employ the pair viśeṣaṇa-viśeṣya (preferring the pairs dharma-dharmin and guṇa-guṇin),[170] he does on occasion use the term viśeṣaṇa or its equivalent prakāra for the svabhāva consciousness.[171] Moreover, in the Śrī Bhāṣya, Rāmānuja explicitly develops the svarūpa/svabhāva distinction in terms of the viśeṣaṇa-viśeṣya relation.[172] Thus, it does not seem overly speculative to assert that Yāmuna's Vedānta and the Viśiṣṭā-advaita school that evolved from it were influenced at least indirectly by such Navya-Nyāya developments as the a-khaṇḍa-upādhi and the svarūpa sambandha, probably through the agency of Nāthamuni's "New" Nyāya.

However, the positive parallels between Navya-Nyāya's a-khaṇḍa-upādhi and svarūpa relation and Yāmuna's svarūpa-upādhi or svarūpa/svabhāva distinction must not be pushed too far as there are some very large differences. Matilal maintains that these Navya-Nyāya concepts were developed largely as a pragmatic heuristic device that permitted the use of such "intrinsic imposed properties" without impinging upon the traditional fundamental categories:

> Whenever they were faced with some unanalyzable and apparently irreducible predicate-concept, they sought to parse it away as an akhaṇḍa-upādhi (unanalyzable imposed property) which is predicable of some individual but does not itself constitute a separate fundamental category. In other words, such an imposed property can very well be said to characterize some individual or other but does not become a separate entity by hypostatic abstraction over and beyond the individual itself. They also parsed the tie connecting that property to the individual as a kind of svarūpa or self-linking relation. . . .and they asserted that a svarūpa relation by definition does not involve any ontological commitment. . .[173]

By contrast Yāmuna's svarūpa/svabhāva distinction does involve a very definite ontological commitment in that for him the distinction or difference between the ātmā and its consciousness is as crucial and necessary as is their inseparability or non-difference. It is more than probable that this committment was the major factor in Yāmuna's development of the term svabhāva[174] in preference to svarūpa-upādhi. For the term upādhi has very definite connotations of something that either is itself an adventitious "conditioning factor" or is caused or "imposed" by such an adventitious or accidental factor. Yāmuna himself uses the bare term upādhi in such a sense when, as we have seen above, he refers to the occasional temporally limited (kāla-avaccheda) distinctions within consciousness as aupādhika bhedas[175] and when, in the context of discussions with the Pracchana Kevalādvaitins, he uses such phrases as ajñāna-upadhi, avidyā-upādhike jīve, māyā-avidyādy-upādhayaḥ.[176] Apparently the phrase svarūpa-upādhi was intended to overcome the overtones which the term upādhi by itself carried with it.

While, as I have noted, Yāmuna rarely recurs to the terminology svarūpa-upādhi, he does do so in a section that comes near the end of the extant Extended Discussion and just after the conclusion of the systematic argumentation of his Siddhānta. This is the section, to which reference has already been made, in which Yāmuna distinguishes consciousness from all of the other so-called special qualities of the ātmā (ātma-viśeṣa-guṇa) which are adventitious (āgantuka) and with which consciousness is compared and classified by Yāmuna's Nyāya-Vaiśeṣika and Neo-Mīmāṃsaka opponents. Once again svarūpa-upādhi appears in a verse although in this case the terminology is also employed in the following prose:

> svarūpopādhayo dharmā yāvadāśrayabhāvinaḥ/
>
> naivaṃ sukhādi bodhas tu svarūpopādhir ātmanaḥ//[177]
>
> Properties that are svarūpa-upādhis exist as long as their substratum (āśraya) exists;
>
> Pleasure (sukha), etc., are not so; but consciousness (bodha) is a svarūpa-upādhi of the ātmā.

Immediately following this verse and obviously referring to all the argumentation following his first use of the term svarūpa-upādhi, Yāmuna states

> yathā ca bodha-upādhir ātma-bhāvas, tathā--upapāditam/[178]
>
> And the way in which Self-hood (ātma-bhāva) possesses consciousness as its upādhi or "Distinguishing Class Property" has been established.

If my understanding of these statements is correct, they confirm that Yāmuna in this context employs upādhi as a type of Sāmānya or "Distinguishing Class Property or Qualifier" and that a svarūpa-upādhi at least, far from being accidental, is essentially related to and co-existent with the individual class-member whose svarūpa is its āśraya (yāvad-āśraya-bhāvin).

Later in this same prose section, we find Yāmuna's final extant usage of the terminology svarūpa-upādhi. After showing that the Upaniṣads establish that consciousness is svābhāvika and eternal because it is dependent upon the svarūpa (svarūpa-prayuktaṃ) of the indestructible eternal ātmā,[179] Yāmuna reiterates his argument for the eternality of consciousness as follows:

> na hi sati padārthe tat-svarūpa-upādhayo na bhavitum arhanti, sati kanaka iva paiṅgaḷyaṃ, prabhā--iva ca pradīpe/ [180]
>
> For when an object (padārtha) exists, svarūpa-upādhis of that object cannot not exist, as for example when gold exists so must its distinguishing yellow color and when flame exists so must its radiance (prabhā).

This instance would appear to confirm my understanding that svarūpa-upādhi is the equivalent of svabhāva, a property which must always be perceived when the object itself is and without which the object in and of itself (svarūpatas) cannot appear. That is, such a svarūpa-upādhi or svabhāva is svarūpa-prayukta, "connected with, consequent upon, based on and dependent upon the svarūpa," which, as I have argued, was probably a secondary meaning intended by Yāmuna in his Reason svarūpa-upādhi-dharma-tvāt.[181]

It is now necessary to consider briefly the remaining portion of Pratijñā I.A.7, anudita-anastamita-svarūpa-prakāśaṃ svayaṃjyotiṣam, which phrase also forms the major portion of Pratijñā I.B.5.a, a fact the significance of which has been noted several times previously.[182] It is this phrase that corresponds most directly to Summary Śloka Siddhānta (2), an-anya-sādhanaḥ. That this phrase corresponds with and faithfully represents Yāmuna's own position as expressed in the Extended Discussion can be established quite easily by the following examples:

(1) caitanya-svabhāvatayā svayaṃjyotiṣṭvāt;

(2) samasta-vṛtti-prayastamaye 'pi svayaṃjyotir ayam ātmā--avatiṣṭhata iti ca vakṣyāmaḥ;

(3) an-anyāpekṣā hy ātma-svarūpa-siddhiḥ;

(4) na ceha--ātma-svarūpa-bodhasya jātu cin nirodho janma vā, nitya-ātma-sattā-prayuktatvāt;

(5) anavarata-anuvṛtta-bodhatayā sthitam eva puṃso bodha-svabhāvatām;

(6) nitya-prakāśaś ca ātmā;

(7) svatas-siddha-prakāśa-tvam apy asya;

(8) ātma-svabhāva-bhūtāyās. . .sva-ātma-avabhāsinyāḥ saṃsāra-apavarga-avasthayoḥ na jātu cid viparilopo vidyate;

(9) tathā 'svena bhāsā svena jyotiṣā' [Bṛhadāraṇyaka Up. IV.iii.9]. . .iti/ tathā apavarga-daśāyām eva chandogāḥ 'na paśyo mṛtyuṃ paśyati na rogaṃ nota duḥkhatām/ sarvaṃ ha paśyaḥ paśyati' [Chāndogya Up. VII.26.2]. . . iti/ . . .iti-ādyāḥ sakala-karaṇa-uparama-daśāyām apy ātmanaḥ prabodham abhidadhānāḥ śrutayo bodha-svabhāvatām asya dṛḍhayanti/[183]

The passage from the Bṛhadāraṇyaka Upaniṣad cited in passage (9) above concludes with the words atra--ayaṃ puruṣaḥ svayaṃjyotir bhavati[184] and is obviously the Upaniṣadic authority which Yāmuna meant to evoke when he concluded Pratijñā I.A.7, his Siddhānta on the svarūpa of the individual ātmā, with the words svayaṃjyotiṣam imam.[185]

Yāmuna's Siddhānta on the Means of Knowing the Individual Ātmā (Pratijñās I.B.5.a-b)

The basic structure of Pratijñā Series I.B., its correlation with the Extended Discussion and the basic points which Yāmuna is making through it have already been developed at some length above. My basic contribution over previous interpretations is the determination that, in addition to Pratijñā I.B. 5.b, Pratijñā I.B.5.a (jñāna-svabhāvatayā--anudita-anastamita-svarūpa-prakāšaḥ svayamjyotiḥ) also forms part of Yāmuna's Siddhānta and indeed represents his major theoretical statement on the issue of the pramāṇa or means of valid knowledge of the individual ātmā, with I.B.5.b dealing with certain practical concerns and problems raised by his theoretical position.

Thus we see that both Pratijñā Series I.A and I.B conclude not with the major statement of Yāmuna's Siddhānta but with some form of addendum or sub-series (Pratijñās I.A.7.a-b and I.B.5.b) which deals with issues or problems raised by his Siddhānta but which are in a sense incidental to the primary topic at hand. The failure to understand this tendency of Yāmuna's has hampered the efforts of all previous interpreters of these Pratijñā Series. As we shall see in the next chapter, a correct understanding of this structural trait may provide one of the essential keys for decoding Yāmuna's Siddhāntas from several other crucial but problematic Pratijñā Series.[186]

Since the similarity, or even identity, of expression and terminology between Pratijñās I.A.7 and I.B.5.a makes it obvious that the two must represent the same position,[187] it is unnecessary here to argue further the fact that I.B.5.a represents Yāmuna's Siddhānta or to expand upon his basic theoretical perspective. However, the manner in which Pratijñā I.B.5.a is phrased highlights an aspect of Yāmuna's position that has not yet been adequately stressed.

As has been indicated, Yāmuna's basic emphasis is upon the dependence (paratantra-tva) of the svabhāva consciousness upon the svarūpa of the ātmā (svarūpa-prayukta) which is itself independent or self-manifest (svatantra, svatassiddha, svayaṃjyotis). However, in Pratijñā I.B.5.a Yāmuna says that the ātmā is "self-luminous, possessed of eternal illumination of its svarūpa or eternal self-consciousness, in as much as, insofar as, or because it possesses consciousness as its svabhāva (jñāna-svabhāvatayā)." Thus, while consciousness is essentially dependent upon the ātmā, there is also a sense in which knowledge of the ātmā, its manifestation to itself in consciousness, is dependent upon its possessing consciousness as its svabhāva.

In this light, it is interesting to look again at Yāmuna's most definitive statement of what a svabhāva is:

> And that which is perceived or directly cognized (sākṣād-bhavati) only as possessing (i.e., "in as much as or because it possesses") a certain thing as its quality (yad-guṇa-tayā--eva) possesses that thing as its svabhāva. . .[188]

The example which Yāmuna gives at this point, i.e., air or wind (marut) which possesses the quality touch (sparśa) as its svabhāva, is of special significance, because the substance air is directly "perceived"--insofar as it is perceived at all and not simply inferred[189]--not simply "only as possessing the quality touch" but "only by means of or because of it," i.e., the invisible air or wind is immediately tactually perceived ("felt") and cognized or known only through its svabhāva touch. In the same way then, the ātmā is directly perceived and cognized as it is in its "own-form" (svarūpatas) only as possessing its svabhāva consciousness and only because it has consciousness as its svabhāva.

Yāmuna would also seem to be indicating this aspect of the relationship between the svarūpa of the ātmā and its svabhāva or svarūpa-upādhi consciousness in the important passage quoted above[190] in which it is maintained that unless the svarūpa of the ātmā is essentially and eternally qualified (viśiṣṭa) by consciousness, its attainment of release would be the equivalent of attaining a state of destruction (nāsa) or non-existence since there would be no means (pramāṇa) of gaining knowledge of, and proving the existence of, an ātmā absolutely devoid of consciousness. In that passage, he also makes the point that the potency or power (śakti) to produce an effect (kārya) such as jñāna, i.e., the cognition or manifestation of an object (artha-siddhi, artha-prakāśa), exists only in a qualified entity (viśiṣṭa-vartinīm eva), just as the capacity to produce the effect smoke exists only in a fire related to wet fuel and the capacity to produce a rice sprout exists only in a rice seed still associated with its husk.[191]

Thus, the śakti[192] to produce the manifestation of the svarūpa of the ātmā (svarūpa-prakāśa, ātma-svarūpa-siddhi) as the entity cognized as "I" (ahaṃkāra-gocaram) can exist only in an ātmā whose svarūpa is qualified (viśiṣṭa) by the svarūpa-upādhi or svabhāva consciousness. While consciousness is dependent upon and cannot exist apart from the svarūpa of the ātmā (svarūpa-prayukta), it is also true that "there is no other svarūpa for the ātmā except for its being the abode of consciousness" (caitanya-āśraya-tāṃ muktvā svarūpaṃ nānyad ātmanaḥ).[193] Thus for Yāmuna neither can the ātmā exist apart from, nor can it be known other than through or by means of, its svabhāva consciousness, its svarūpa-upādhi, the property that resides in or "within" its svarūpa, distinguishing and making manifest what it is in its uniqueness.

In conclusion to deal briefly with Pratijñā I.B.5.b, Yāmuna has maintained that the ātmā knows or is conscious of itself independently of any other means (an-anya-sādhanaḥ). His position is based upon the essential nature of the ātmā in and of itself as distinct from everything else. However, a central concern of the present series is with how ignorant persons, bound in the embodied state (saṃsāra), can come to know this ātmā. From such a perspective, anyone who maintains that the ātmā is eternally and independently known opens himself to the charges of having destroyed the distinction between the embodied state of bondage (saṃsāra) and the desired goal of release (mokṣa) and of having destroyed the motivation for and necessity of employing the various means meant to release one from bondage, i.e., of having destroyed the basis of all religious life.[194]

Therefore, in Pratijñā I.B.5.b, Yāmuna wishes to ward off these charges and to indicate that some of the means, which he has rejected as independently adequate, do have a valid role to play in the attainment of a full immediate cognition or realization of the ātmā as it really is. As Yāmuna states, in an only slightly expanded version and in conclusion of the integral portion of the AtS that has been preserved,

> Even though this ātmā, having consciousness as its svabhāva (caitanya-svabhāvaḥ), manifests itself in such a way (i.e., independently), nevertheless, like a fish swimming in a deep lake and like milk mixed with water, it does not appear clearly, having distinguished [itself from all other than itself]. Therefore, [while the pramāṇas Inference and Scriptural Revelation do not themselves manifest the ātmā,] the various Inferences given above and the Scriptural statements, when accompanied by rigorous rational argumentation with the purpose of establishing an undestanding of the ātmā, are accepted [as pramāṇas or means of attaining an increasingly clear apprehension of it]. Those who are not satisfied even with [the knowledge of the ātmā gained from] these [Scripture and Inference], having first thrown off all obscuring impurities and stains through the practice of the preliminary stages of yoga such as yama, niyama, etc., exert themselves in order to attain immediate knowledge or perception (aparokṣa-jñāna) of the ātmā as distinct from all other objects, an immediate perception that arises from the predominance of [the purest guṇa] sattva and from having eliminated the impurities of [the guṇas] rajas and tamas by the purifying process of the practice of restricting [mental activity from other objects and concentrating upon the ātmā alone]. And that this immediate perception [of the ātmā] arises at the culmination of the highest stage of concentration (bhāvanā) is accepted by all parties without dispute; therefore, it is not necessary for me to exert myself here in order to prove this point.
>
> Thus the ātmā, although manifesting itself independently (svatassiddhyan) is illuminated clearly and distinctly by Scripture (āgamena), Inference (anumānataḥ) and Perception (pratyakṣeṇa) born from the practice of yoga.[195]

This concluding emphasis upon yogic perception as the preeminent means of attaining immediate knowledge of the individual ātmā is probably another indication of Yāmuna's debt to the spiritual and intellectual heritage of Nāthamuni, whom Yāmuna remembers as a great yogī and who is reputed to have written a work called the Yoga-rahasya.[196] At several points in the extant text of the AtS, Yāmuna also refers to Patañjali and his Yoga-sūtras in respectful terms and attempts to show that the position put forward in the AtS is not in conflict with the Yoga-sūtras.[197] While Yāmuna's respect for yogic insight might seem to conflict with the traditional account that he lost Nāthamuni's "secret of yoga" (yoga-rahasya) because of his preoccupation with the ecstatic hymns of the Āḻvārs, a story that

I have accepted as in accord with the evidence of the _Stotra-ratna_,[198] it need not necessarily do so. As Professor D. H. H. Ingalls has observed, it is quite common for Indian thinkers to maintain the prestige of yogic perception as a source of transcendental insight and revelation long after the actual practice of _yoga_ has ceased.[199] Thus, Yāmuna may be honoring yogic perception primarily as the _pramāṇa_ that gave authority to the teachings of the great sages of the past,[200] such as his grandfather Nāthamuni, upon whose _śāstra_ the AtS is in part based and who "possessed immediate perception of the three elements of ultimate reality through the power of his own _yoga_" (_sva-yoga-mahima-pratyakṣa-tattva-trayaḥ_).[201]

CHAPTER VII

THE SIDDHĀNTAS OR CONCLUSIONS OF YĀMUNA'S VEDĀNTA

In this chapter, I will present an annotated translation of the introductory section of the Ātma-siddhi along with a transliteration of the Sanskrit text. My goal will be to "decode" the Pratijñā Series not dealt with in Chapter VI and to isolate all of Yāmuna's Vedāntic Siddhāntas ("Established or Final Conclusions"). The Pratijñās or Theses that I consider to be Yāmuna's will be given in capital letters.

In addition to my recovery in Chapter VI of two of Yāmuna's major and previously unrecognized Siddhāntas on the individual ātmā (i.e., Pratijñā I.A.7 on its essential nature or svarūpa and Pratijñā I.B.5.a on the pramāṇa or means of knowing or cognizing it), I argue in this chapter for the recognition of two other major and until now "lost" Siddhāntas:

> Pratijñā II.A.3 on the svarūpa of the Paramātmā or Highest Self;
> Pratijñā III.C.1 on the relation (saṃbandha) between the individual ātmā and the Paramātmā.

If my analysis is correct, all of Yāmuna's major Siddhāntas will have been recovered; and it will now be possible to sketch at least the rough outlines of Yāmuna's system of Vedānta and to see more clearly his place in the development of the Śrī Vaiṣṇava Viśiṣṭādvaita school.

The notes to this chapter will dwell primarily upon the Siddhāntas not considered in Chapter VI, attempting to interpret them in the light of the extant corpus of his works. Appendix III at the conclusion of the book presents the skeletal outline structure of the Pratijñā Series and is a major interpretive key in my attempt to decode them and to recover the Siddhāntas of Yāmuna's Vedānta.

The Introduction to the Ātma-Siddhi

Let become mine an abundance of devotion
to the Highest Person,
To the blessed Lord with his consort Śrī,[1]
who is cared for lovingly
by hosts of eternally free beings
whose own delight consists
in rendering this service,
To Him whose desire Primordial Material Nature,
Sentient Beings, Time, the Manifest
Universe, and Released Beings
all follow eternally.[2]

Manifold are the contradictory teachings
about the ātmā and the Paramātmā;

Hence, for the sake of clearing up this
confusion, this Ātma-siddhi,
"The Determination and Revelation of
the True Nature of the Individual Self and
of the Highest Self,"[3] is proclaimed.[4]

---

prakṛti-puruṣa-kāla-vyakta-muktā yad-icchām
anuvidadhati nityam nitya-siddhair anekaiḥ/
sva-paricaraṇa-bhogaiḥ śrīmati prīyamāṇe
bhavatu mama parasmin pūruṣe bhakti-bhūmā//

viruddhamatayo 'nekās santy ātma-paramātmanoḥ/
atas tatpariśuddhyartham ātma-siddhir vidhīyate//

This text is based upon the Annamalai University edition (AtS, pp. 1-8) by R. Ramanujachari and K. Srinivasacharya, unless otherwise indicated (see Chapter I, n. 35).

Indeed, all schools of thought would agree with the statement "Knowledge of the ātmā is the cause of the attainment of the highest good;" moreover, many Upaniṣadic statements are heard to declare that knowledge of the essential nature of the Higher and the lower ātmā is the means of attaining release, as is seen in the following examples:

> Having known the ātmā and the Divine Controller to be different and being satisfied, then one thereby attains immortality;[5]
>
> If he should know the ātmā . . . ,[6] the knower of the ātmā crosses beyond grief;[7]
>
> One who knows Brahman attains the highest.[8]

However, it is also true that--even in the midst of this [universal and scripturally supported agreement that knowledge of both the individual and the Highest ātmā is the cause of the attainment of the Highest Good]--the various religious teachers teach a confusing welter of conflicting conceptions (vipratipattis) with regard to both this individual ātmā and the Other or Highest ātmā.

The extent of this confusing disagreement [is exemplified by the following series of mutually conflicting opinions on the various topics of dispute that will be considered and clarified in this work]:[9]

---

sammataṃ hi sarvasamayeṣu "ātmajñānaṃ niḥśreyasahetur" iti/ śrūyate ca "pṛthag ātmānaṃ preritārañ ca matvā juṣṭas tatas tena--amṛtatvam eti" "ātmānaṃ ced vijānīyat" "tarati śokam ātmavit" "brahmavid āpnoti param" ityādiḥ para-avara-ātma-tattva-jñānasya--apavarga-sādhanatvaṃ pratipādayan vedānta-vākyagaṇaḥ/

tatra--asminn ātmani parasmiṃś cānekavidhā vipratipattayas tīrthakarāṇām/

tadyathā

Pratijñā Series

I. With regard to the individual ātmā, [many opposing theses (pratijñās) have been propounded on the following topics:]

A. Thus [concerning the dispute as to what is the essential nature or "unique form" (svarūpa)[10] of the entity that is designated by the term "ātmā"],

1. certain persons call the physical body itself the ātmā;[11]
2. others, the external sense-organs;
3. others [say] "the internal sense-organ or mind;"
4. still others, the breath or vital force;
5. others[12] [declare that what is called the ātmā is] nothing but cognition or consciousness (bodha-mātram) that in and of itself is devoid of any individual self-consciousness (an-ahaṃkāraṃ) but which has superimposed (adhyasta) upon it the character of being an individualized active knower (jñātṛ);
6. others[13] [call ātmā] that [entity] that is distinct from the body, the external sense-organs, the internal sense-organ, the vital force and cognition (bodha);[14] [that is formless, all pervasive and of infinite dimension] like ether, etc. (ākāśādivad);[15] that does not have consciousness associated with

---

I. ātma-viṣaye

A. tāvat

1. deham eva ke cid ātmānam ācakṣate;
2. indriyāṇy anye;
3. mana ity anye;
4. prāṇam apare;
5. adhyasta-jñātṛ-bhāvam an-ahaṃkāraṃ bodha-mātram itare;
6. deha-indriya-manaḥ-prāṇa-bodha-vilakṣaṇam, ākāśādivad, a-cit-svabhāvam, āgantuka-bodha-sukha-duhkhādy-asādhāraṇa-guṇa-ādhāram, ahaṃkāra-gocaram apare;

I. A. 6. (cont.)

its essential nature (a-cit-svabhāvam); that is the substratum in which inhere such adventitious (āgantuka) special qualities as cognition (bodha), pleasure (sukha) and pain, etc.; and that is the object of the cognition "I" (ahaṃkāra-gocaram);[16]

Yāmuna's Siddhānta

7. BUT OTHERS [YĀMUNA HIMSELF][17] DECLARE [THE ātmā TO BE] THIS SELF-LUMINOUS ONE (svayaṃ-jyotiṣam imam)[18] THAT MANIFESTS ITS OWN ESSENTIAL FORM (svarūpa) WITHOUT BEGINNING AND WITHOUT END; THIS ONE THAT IS NONE OTHER THAN THAT WHICH HAS CONSCIOUSNESS AS ITS SOLE ESSENTIAL ATTRIBUTE (bodha-eka-svabhāvam eva), BUT THAT APPEARS TO POSSESS SUCH INAUSPICIOUS ATTRIBUTES (a-śiva-guṇas) AS THE PAIRS OF DESIRE AND AVERSION, PLEASURE (sukha) AND PAIN, ETC., WHICH ARE IMPUTED TO IT BECAUSE OF PARTICULAR RESTRICTING CONDITIONS (upadhāna) OF THE INTERNAL SENSE-ORGAN (antaḥ-karaṇa)--AS IS THE CASE WITH A CRYSTAL (sphaṭika-maṇi) THAT HAS ONLY WHITENESS THROUGH ITS OWN ESSENTIAL ATTRIBUTE (svabhāva) [OF LUMINOSITY] BUT SEEMS TO HAVE SUCH ATTRIBUTES AS REDNESS IMPUTED TO IT BECAUSE OF PARTICULAR RESTRICTING CONDITIONS (upadhāna) [SUCH AS THE REDNESS OF A NEARBY ROSE].

I. A. 7. apare tu bodha-eka-svabhāvam eva, svabhāva-dhavalam iva sphaṭika-maṇim upadhāna-viśeṣa-āpādita-aruṇima-guṇa-ādi-nirbhāsam, antaḥkarana-upadhāna-āpādita-rāga-dveṣa-sukha-duḥkhādy-aśiva-guṇa-nirbhāsam, anudita-anastamita-svarūpa-prakāśaṃ, svayaṃjyotiṣam imam abhidadhati/

Sub-series on the "Essential Happiness" of the ātmā[19]

I. A. 7. a. However, others [while basically agreeing with the position of Pratijñā I.A.7., hold it to be incomplete because they believe that the ātmā] has both consciousness (jñāna) and bliss (ānanda) as its essential attributes (svabhāva), [not consciousness alone].[20]

Yāmuna's Siddhānta

b. OTHERS [YĀMUNA HIMSELF],[21] [IN RESPONSE TO THIS OBJECTION AND IN DEFENSE OF THE ADEQUACY OF PRATIJÑĀ I.A.7., SAY] "THAT WHICH IS INNATELY ESSENTIAL TO THIS [ātmā] IS NEVER ANYTHING OTHER THAN A PARTICULAR STATE OF CONSCIOUSNESS (bodha) [ALTHOUGH IT IS TRUE THAT THIS CONSCIOUSNESS] ACQUIRES SUCH DESIGNATIONS AS BLISS (ānanda), HAPPINESS (sukha), ETC., WHEN IT CONFORMS TO ITS [BLESSED] SUBSTRATUM."

B. In the same manner, they teach[22] [the following conflicting theories on the question of the means (pramāṇa) whereby the ātmā is known or cognized:][23]

1. [the ātmā is] to be comprehended through Inference;[24]
2. to be known only through Scriptural Revelation;[25]
3. to be known [as the object] of a special immediate cognition by the internal sense-organ (mānasa-pratyakṣa);[26]
4. to be immediately apprehended as the subject and only as the subject (grāhakatayā--eva) [and only]

I. A. 7. a. anye tu jñāna-ānanda-svabhāvam;

b. āśrayānukūlya-pratilabdha-ānanda-sukhādi-vyapadeśa-bodha-viśeṣa evāsya svābhāvika ity anye/

B. tathā

"1. anumāna-samadhigamyaḥ;

"2. āgama-eka-vedyaḥ;

"3. mānasa-pratyakṣa-vedyah;

"4. grāhakatayā--eva sakala viṣaya-vittiṣu pratyakṣo;

I. B. 4. (cont.)

during [and by means of] each cognition of an object (sakala-viṣaya-vittiṣu pratyakṣo);[27]

Yāmuna's Siddhānta

5. [BUT ACCORDING TO MY (YĀMUNA'S)[28] VIEW, THE ātmā IS]

a. SELF-LUMINOUS (svayaṃjyotiḥ), POSSESSING BEGINNINGLESS AND ENDLESS MANIFESTATION (prakāśa) OF ITS OWN ESSENTIAL FORM (svarūpa) IN AS MUCH AS IT POSSESSES COGNITION OR CONSCIOUSNESS (jñāna) AS ITS ESSENTIAL ATTRIBUTE (svabhāva);[29]

b. [HOWEVER,] EVEN THOUGH BEING OF SUCH [AN ESSENTIAL NATURE AND THEREFORE BEING KNOWN INDEPENDENTLY OF ANY OTHER MEANS, STILL THE OTHER MEANS OF KNOWLEDGE ARE NOT TO BE DISCARDED AS USELESS AND FUTILE BECAUSE THE ātmā IN THE EMBODIED STATE DOES NOT MANIFEST ITSELF CLEARLY AND DISTINCTLY AND] APPEARS IMMEDIATELY, EXACTLY AS IT IS [ONLY] AT THE END [OF A LONG COURSE OF DISCIPLINE--AFTER HAVING GRADUALLY BEEN PERCEIVED] CLEARLY, MORE CLEARLY AND FINALLY WITH PERFECT CLARITY, AS ESSENTIALLY DIFFERENT FROM ALL OTHER THAN ITSELF, [AT FIRST] BY MEANS OF SCRIPTURAL REVELATION (āgama) AND INFERENCE (anumāna) AND [FINALLY THROUGH THE IMMEDIATE SUPERSENSUOUS] PERCEPTION BORN FROM YOGA.[30]

I. B. "5. a. jñāna-svabhāvatayā--anuditānastamita-svarūpa-prakāśaḥ svayaṃjyotiḥ,

b. īdṛśo 'py āgama-anumāna-yoga-ja-pratyakṣaiḥ svetara-sakala-vilakṣaṇa-svābhāvyena viśada-viśadatara-viśadatamatayā --antato yathāvad aparokṣyata"

iti/

I. C. Similarly, [with regard to the dimension, magnitude or spatiality (parimāṇa) of the ātmā, they teach that the ātmā][31]

1. is of unlimited dimension [and all-pervasive];[32]
2. has the dimension of an atom (aṇu);[33]
3. has the dimension of the body (śarīra) [in which it dwells;][34]

Yāmuna's Siddhānta

4. [WHILE I (YĀMUNA) MAINTAIN THAT THE ātmā,] BEING DEVOID IN ITS ESSENTIAL FORM (svataḥ) OF [ANYTHING CORRESPONDING TO THE TECHNICAL NYĀYA-VAIŚEṢIKA QUALITY] "parimāṇa," IS DELIMITED BY THE DIMENSION (parimiti) [OR CONFIGURATION] OF THE ENTITY PERVADED [BY IT] (vyāpya-vastu).[35]
   a. Also, [on the related sub-topic of the mode or manner in which the ātmā pervades an entity,[36] some teach that] the pervasion (vyāptir) is by means of consciousness alone (caitanya-mātreṇa);[37]

Yāmuna's Siddhānta (?)

   b. [OTHERS (YAMUNA?) SAY IT IS EFFECTED] THROUGH HIS ESSENTIAL FORM (svarūpeṇa).[38]

I. C. tathā

"1. parama-mahān;

"2. aṇu-parimāṇaḥ;

"3. śarīra-parimāṇaḥ;

"4. svataḥ parimāṇa-rahito 'pi vyāpya-vastu-parimiti-kṛta-pariccheda"

iti/

"a. vyāptir api caitanya-mātreṇa;

"b. svarūpena"

iti/

I. D. Likewise, they teach [the following opinions as to the duration of the ātmā:][39]

1. [the ātmā is] momentary;[40]
2. exists only as long as there is life in the body;
3. persists until the dissolution (praḷaya) of the manifested universe;
4. exists until release (mokṣa) is attained;[41]
5. absolutely immutable (kūṭa-stho);[42]

Yāmuna's Siddhānta

6. ETERNAL (nitya).[43]

E. And [finally, on the general topic of the individual ātmā,] they maintain [with regard to the issue of whether there is only one ātmā or many of them:][44]

1. [the ātmā] in all bodies is one and the same;[45]

Yāmuna's Siddhānta

2. IS MANIFOLD [AND DISTINCT] IN EACH BODY.[46]

I. D. tathā

"1. kṣaṇikaḥ;

"2. yāvac-charîra-uṣma-sthāyî;

"3. ā-prākṛta-praḷaya-avasthāyî'

"4. ā-mokṣa-sthāyî;

"5. kūṭastho;

"6. nitya"

iti/

E. "1. sarva-śarîreṣv ekaḥ;

"2. pratikṣetraṃ nānā-bhūta"

iti ca tathātathā pratipadyante/

Pratijñā Series on the Paramātmā

II. In the same manner, with regard to the Paramātmā also [the various teachers have proposed conflicting theses on the following topics:]

A. [On the dispute as to the existence and essential nature (svarūpa) of the Paramātmā as the Divine Lord (īśvara-vāda)]

1. Certain persons do not even accept the existence of such an omniscient and omnipotent Lord (samasta-vastu-sākṣātkāriṇaṃ sarva-śaktim īśvaram).[47]

2. Some[48] accept [the Paramātmā or Brahman] as having as his sole essence (eka-rasa) immutable consciousness (kūṭastha-vijñāna) devoid of such mental constructs (vikalpa) as the distinction (bheda) between knowledge (miti), means of knowledge (māna), knower (mātṛ) and object of knowledge (meya) and between a ruling Lord (īśvara) and those he rules;[49] but they claim that [when conceived of as a personal Lord or Īśvara] he is imaginary (kālpanikam) in as much as he is merely a mental construct (vikalpa) embodying the magnificence of [the "Six Qualities" (ṣaḍ-guṇas)] knowledge, lordliness, etc. (jñāna-aiśvarya-ādi-mahima),[50] which are delimited (avacchinna) by such distinctions (bheda) as [the material evolutes] ether, etc., which are projected (upadarśita) by beginningless ignorance (anādy-avidyā).

II. tathā paramātma-viṣaye 'pi

A.

1. ke cit samasta-vastu-sākṣātkāriṇaṃ sarva-śaktim īśvaram eva na--abhyupagacchanti/

2. abhyupagacchanto 'py eke pratyastamita-miti-māna-mātṛ-meya-īśvara-īśitavya-ādi-bheda-vikalpa-kūṭastha-vijñāna-eka-rasam anādy-avidyā-upadarśita-viyad-ādi-bheda-avacchinna-jñāna-aiśvarya-ādi-mahima-vikalpatayā kālpanikam ācakṣate/

II. A. (cont.)

Yāmuna's Siddhanta

3. BUT (tu) OTHERS [YĀMUNA][51] DECLARE THAT [THE PARAMA-ĀTMĀ] IS OF PRECISELY THE SAME "SOLE ESSENCE" OR svarūpa AS STATED [IN PRATIJÑĀ II.A.2] (yathokta-svarūpam eva)[52] [BUT THAT AS THE LORD (īśvara) OF THE MANIFEST UNIVERSE HE IS NOT IMAGINARY (kālpanikam) BUT IS RATHER] A "QUALIFIED" (upahitam) BEING OR REALITY: [ON THE ONE HAND] POSSESSING [OR BEING QUALIFIED BY] SUCH PERFECTIONS AS OMNISCIENCE, ETC., WHICH ARE ACQUIRED (samāsādita) BY HIM IN AS MUCH AS HE IS QUALIFIED BY MĀYĀ (māyā-upahitatayā), HIS WONDROUS POWER [THE ŚAKTI OR GODDESS ŚRĪ[53]], WHOSE OWN NATURE (svabhāva) IS TO EVOLVE (vivarta) THE MANIFOLD UNIVERSE IN DEPENDENCE UPON HIMSELF (svādhīna); [AND ON THE OTHER HAND BEING QUALIFIED (upahitam) IN THAT] HE POSSESSES ALL THE DIFFERENT CLASSES OF LIVING BEINGS (jīvas) WHICH ARE PRODUCED AND GOVERNED (prakalpita) BY HIM THROUGH THE APPLICATION OF THE RESTRICTING CONDITIONS OF avidyā [or karma] (avidyā-upadhānena) IN AS MUCH AS HE IS ESSENTIALLY POSSESSED OF THE PROPERTIES OF avidyā [or karma] (tad-guṇa-sāratayā).[54]

B. Likewise (tathā), [on the dispute as to in what manner the Paramātmā is the source or cause and controller of the manifestation of the physical universe (kāraṇa-vāda, pariṇāma-vāda)],[55]

II. A. 3. apare tu yathokta-svarūpam eva avidyā-upadhānena tad-guṇa-sāratayā prakalpita-brahma-ādi-sthāvara-paryanta-vividha-jīva-bhedaṃ svādhīna-vicitra-vivarta-svabhāva-māyā-upahitatayā samāsādita-sārvajñya-ādi-saṃpadam upahitam imam abhidadhati/

B. tathā

II. B. 1. Others [denying that the Paramātmā manifests the universe through being qualified by the power Māyā that is dependent upon Himself (svādhīna-. . .-māyā-upahitatayā)] maintain that He manifests the perfection of universal lordship [over the universe] in a strictly determined way (niyama) by means of a particular modification of independent material nature (svatantra-pradhāna-pariṇāma)--[a modification] rendered possible by the fact that the independent material nature is composed of the most excellent [type of physical "quality," the guṇa] sattva.[56]

2. Others, even though not accepting [that the Paramātmā as Īśvara is] a "qualified" being (an-upahitam api), believe that the Paramātmā is subject to modification (pariṇāminam) [i.e., in manifesting the universe He undergoes modification within Himself rather than in His qualities].[57]

3. Others, even though denying that the Paramātmā undergoes modification within Himself (a-pariṇāminam api), imagine that the one sentient being that is everywhere one and the same (ekam eva cetanam) passes into the various states of Viśva (consciousness in the waking state), Taijasa (consciousness in dream state) and Prājña (consciousness in deep sleep) in as much as it is reflected (pratibimbitatayā) in the "mirrors" or internal sense-organs (antaḥkaraṇa) of the various beings that have come into existence from a part of His own Māyā.[58]

II. B. 1. anye prakṛṣṭa-sattva-upādāna-nimitta-svatantra-pradhāna-pariṇāma-viśeṣa-mātra-niyama-nirvāhita-sarva-aiśvarya-maryādam ādriyante/

2. an-upahitam api pariṇāminam apare pratipedire/

3. a-pariṇāminam api sva-māyā-aṁśa-bhūta-vicitra-antaḥkaraṇa-darpaṇa-tala-pratibimbitatayā pratipanna-viśva-taijasa-prājña-bhāvaṃ tam ekam eva cetanam itare rocayante/

II. B.

Yāmuna's Siddhānta

4. BUT OTHERS [YĀMUNA,[59] REAFFIRMING IN ACCORD WITH HIS SIDDHĀNTA II.A.3. THAT THE PARAMĀTMĀ AS THE CAUSE AND THE LORD OF THE UNIVERSE MUST BE ACCEPTED AS A "QUALIFIED" (upahitam) BEING] MAINTAIN THAT THE LORD IS A PARTICULAR PERSON (puruṣa-viśeṣam īśvaram)[60] WHO IS A GREAT OCEAN OF ALL AUSPICIOUS QUALITIES (kalyāṇa-guṇas),[61] WHICH ARE ESSENTIAL (svābhāvika) TO HIM AND OF BOUNDLESS EXCELLENCE, FOREMOST AMONG WHICH ARE [THE "SIX QUALITIES" (ṣaḍ-guṇas)] JÑĀNA AND BALA ("KNOWLEDGE" AND "STRENGTH"), AIŚVARYA AND VĪRYA ("LORDLINESS" AND "IMMUTABILITY"), AND ŚAKTI AND TEJAS ("POWER AND "SPLENDOR") [WHICH IN THE MANIFESTATION OF THE UNIVERSE ARE MANIFEST AS THE VYŪHAS SAṂKARṢAṆA (jñāna and bala), PRADYUMNA (aiśvarya and vīrya) AND ANIRUDDHA (śakti and tejas)];[62] [A PERSON] WHO ALSO POSSESSES AND HAS DEPENDENT UPON HIMSELF (svādhīna) THE VARIOUS ESSENTIAL NATURES (svarūpa), EXISTENCES (sthiti) AND ACTIVITIES (pravṛtti) OF THE THREE-FOLD SENTIENT AND INSENTIENT BEINGS.[63]

C. Likewise, with regard also to the particular details (viśeṣas) concerning that [unique Person (puruṣa-viseṣa)],[64]

1. they debate as to whether he has four, three, two or ONE [YĀMUNA'S VIEW] forms (mūrtis) by rejecting those forms which they do not accept among the four,

---

II. B. 4. anye tu svādhīna-trividha-cetana-acetana-svarūpa-sthiti-pravṛtti-bhedaṃ svābhāvika-niravadhika-atiśaya-jñāna-bala-aiśvarya-vīrya-śakti-tejaḥ-prabhṛti-sakala-kalyāṇa-guṇa-mahārṇavaṃ puruṣa-viśeṣam īśvaram ātiṣṭhante/

C. tathā tad-viśeṣe 'pi

1. hari-hara-viriñci-bhāskara-ātmanā--anabhimata-tat-tan-mūrti-parityāgena ca catus-tri-dvy-eka-mūrtitayā vivadante/

II. C. 1. (cont.)

Bhāskara (Sūrya), Viriñci (Brahmā), Hara (Śiva) and HARI (VIṢṆU) [YĀMUNA'S CHOICE].

2. They put forth conflicting arguments on particular questions concerning His form (mūrti-viśeṣas), e.g.,
   a. Is it ETERNAL [YĀMUNA] or non-eternal?
   b. Is it elemental or NON-ELEMENTAL [YĀMUNA]?
   c. Is it for His own sake or for the sake of others?
3. [They also teach differently] concerning His attendants, His abode, etc.

D. In the same way, also with regard to the means of attaining valid knowledge or cognition [of the Paramātmā] (pramāṇato 'pi),
1. some [say, "Such knowledge comes] only from Scripture";[65]
2. others, "[from Scripture] and Inference";[66]

Yāmuna's Siddhānta

3. OTHERS [YĀMUNA], "[FROM SCRIPTURE, INFERENCE] AND FROM BEING COMPREHENDED BY EXTRAORDINARY PERCEPTION."[67]

II. C. 2. mūrti-veśeṣa-viṣayāś ca
   a. nityatva-anityatva-
   b. bhautikatva-abhautikatva-
   c. svārtha-parārthatvādi-
      vitarkāḥ prādurbhavati,
3. parijana-sthānādi-gocarāś ca/

D. tathā pramāṇato 'pi
1. "ānuśravika eva"--ity eke/
2. "ānumānikaś ca"--ity anye/
3. "viśiṣṭa-pratyakṣa-samadhigamyaś ca"--ity apare/

Pratijñā Series on the Relation between the ātmā and the Paramātmā

III. Thus, also with regard to the relation (saṃbandha) between the individual ātmā and the Paramātmā, there are numerous theories (nānāvidhā vādāḥ):[68]

A. Certain persons [say], "The relation, as it is based upon difference (bheda) caused by beginningless 'Ignorance' (anādy-avidyā), has the form of that between a ruling Lord (Īśvara) and those He rules, etc., but from the viewpoint of ultimate reality there is just one entity (paramārthatas tv ekaṃ tattvam)."[69]

B. Others [say], "Even though there is no difference [in nature] (vyatireka-abhāve), the embodied ātmā (jīva) is separate (atirikta) [from the Paramātmā]."[70]

Yāmuna's Siddhānta

C. BUT (tu)

1. OTHERS [YAMUNA] SAY, "[THE STATEMENTS IN UPANIṢADS THAT DECLARE THE ABSOLUTE] UNITY (aikyam) [OF THE PARAMĀTMĀ] ARISE FROM HIS ESSENTIAL NATURE (svatas) [AS DISTINCT FROM EVERYTHING ELSE, WHILE THOSE DECLARING] DIFFERENCE (bheda) ARISE FROM HIS RELATION TO ALL THOSE PROPERTIES OR ATTRIBUTES THAT 'QUALIFY' HIM (upādhi-to). THEREFORE (iti) [THE TRUE NATURE OF THE RELATION BETWEEN THE ātmā AND THE PARAMĀTMĀ] IS bhinna-abhinnatvam (ONE OF BOTH DIFFERENCE AND NON-DIFFERENCE) IN THAT [THE PARAMĀTMĀ'S] svarūpa IS QUALIFIED (viśiṣṭa-svarūpa-bhāvena) [BY THE ātmā, I.E., THE ātmā IS DISTINCT FROM THE

III. tathā ātma-paramātmanoḥ saṃbandhe 'pi

A. "anādy-avidyā-upādāna-bheda-āspado 'yam īśvara-īśitavyādi-rūpaḥ saṃbandhaḥ, paramārthas tv ekaṃ tattvam" iti ke cit/

B. "vyatireka-abhāve 'py atirikto jīva" ity anye/

C. 1. "svatas tv aikyam upādhito bheda iti
viśiṣṭa-svarūpa-bhāvena
bhinna-abhinnatvam itare/

III. C. 1. (cont.)

PARAMĀTMĀ'S svarūpa BUT IT IS NON-DIFFERENT IN THAT IT IS HIS QUALITY (svarūpa-upādhi, svabhāva)].[71]

C. 2. "WHILE DIVERSITY (nānātva) [OR DIFFERENCE] DEFINITELY EXISTS,[72] THERE IS ALSO A RELATION (anvayaḥ) [BETWEEN THE ātmā AND THE PARAMĀTMĀ] CALLED 'NON-DIFFERENCE' (abheda) THAT CAN BE DEFINED AS HAVING THE NATURE OF THE RELATION BETWEEN A WHOLE AND ITS PARTS (aṃśa-aṃśi-bhāva);[73] OR AS 'INHERENCE' (samavāya), [I.E., A FORM OF CONJUNCTION (saṃyoga)] DEFINED AS A DEPENDENCE RELATION (paratantratā) [IN WHICH THE PROPERTY (dharma) CAN NOT EXIST APART FROM ITS POSSESSOR (dharmin)];[74] OR AS [A RELATION] HAVING THE FORM OF THAT BETWEEN AN 'ACCESSORY' (śeṣa) AND ITS 'PRINCIPAL' (śeṣin) [IN WHICH THE śeṣa EXISTS FOR THE PURPOSE OF SERVING THE śeṣin[75] AS IN THE RELATIONS] HAVING THE NATURE OF THAT BETWEEN AN OWNER AND HIS OWN [RIGHTFUL POSSESSIONS] (sva-svāmi-bhāva) OR OF THAT BETWEEN A MASTER AND HIS SERVANT OR SLAVE."[76]

IV. In the same manner, they maintain various divergent viewpoints even with regard to the Highest Human Goal (parama-puruṣārtha) of Release (mokṣa) that is defined as the attainment of Brahman (brahma-prāpti):

A. [Release] is defined as the annihilation of one's essential nature (svarūpa);

B. as the cessation of "Ignorance" (avidyā);

III. C. 2. "nānātve saty eva abhedo nāma--anvayaḥ
aṃśa-aṃśi-bhāva-lakṣaṇaḥ samavāyaḥ
paratantratā-lakṣaṇaḥ śeṣa-śeṣitva-rūpaḥ
sva-svāmi-bhāvaḥ bhṛtya-svāmi-lakṣaṇa" iti ca
nānāvidhā vādāḥ/

IV. tathā parama-puruṣārtha-bhūte brahma-prāpti-lakṣaṇa-mokṣe 'pi

A. "svarūpa-ucchiti-lakṣaṇaḥ,

B. "avidyā-astamaya-lakṣaṇaḥ,

IV.

C. as the destruction of all special qualities of the ātmā without exception;[77]

D. it has the form of isolation (kaivalya);

E. it is defined as similarity to the nature of that [Brahman];

F. as the inflow of the qualities of that (Brahman];

G. as the attainment of the image of that [Brahman];

H. as the manifestation of the [ātmā's] essential form (svarūpa) as possessed of innate ānanda, etc.[78]

Yāmuna's Siddhānta

I. AS ABSOLUTE SERVITUDE (kiṅkaratva) TO THAT [BRAHMAN] BROUGHT ABOUT BY THE AWAKENING OF SUPREME HAPPINESS (sukha) BORN FROM THE EXPERIENCE OF [BRAHMAN'S] QUALITIES.[79]

V. Also, with regard to the means (sādhana) whereby that [Release] is attained [the various viewpoints are]

A. It is to be attained by the discipline of action (karma-yoga);

B. by the discipline of knowledge (jñāna-yoga);

C. by one [of the above two] assisted by the other;

IV. C. "niśśeṣa-vaiśeṣika-ātma-guṇa-uccheda-lakṣaṇaḥ,
D. "kaivalya-rūpaḥ,
E. "tad-bhāva-(sādharmya-)lakṣaṇaḥ,
F. "tad-guṇa-saṃkrānti-lakṣaṇaḥ,
G. "tac-chāyāpatti-lakṣaṇaḥ,
H. "sāṃsiddhika-ānanda-ādi-svarūpa-āvirbhāva-lakṣaṇaḥ,
I. "tad-guṇa-anubhava-janita-niratiśaya-sukha-samunmeṣa-upanīta-ātyantika-tat-kiṅkaratva-lakṣaṇa"
iti tathātathā vivadante/

V. tat-sādhanato 'pi
A. "karma-yoga-labhyaḥ,
B. "jñāna-yoga-labhyaḥ,
C. "anyatara-anugṛhīta-anyatara-labhyaḥ,

V.

D. by both [karma-yoga and jñāna-yoga];

Yāmuna's Siddhānta

E. IT IS TO BE ATTAINED BY MEANS OF THE DISCIPLINE OF UNDIVIDED AND ABSOLUTE LOVING DEVOTION (aikāntika-ātyantika-bhakti-yoga) ON THE PART OF ONE WHOSE MIND HAS BEEN PURIFIED BY BOTH [karma-yoga and jñāna-yoga].[80]

The above being the case, [even] the wise, seeing the ambiguous and conflicting opinions of these debaters and not being able to discern the relative strengths and weaknesses of the arguments put forth in support of the various positions, become confused regarding them and thus would not be able to attain the Highest Human Goal (parama-puruṣārtha) as long as the ātmā and the Paramātmā are not definitively and authoritatively established in terms of

(i) their essential natures or "own-forms" (svarūpataḥ),
(ii) the means of attaining valid knowledge of them (pramāṇataḥ),
(iii) the relationship between them (saṃbandhataḥ),
(iv) the state of the attainment of the Highest Good (prāptitaḥ), and
(v) the means whereby that state is attained (tat-sādhanataś ca).

V. D. "ubhaya-labhyaḥ,
E. "ubhaya-parikarmita-svāntasya--aikāntika-ātyantika-bhakti-yoga-labhya"

iti/

tadevam anavasita-viśeṣa-vimarśaka-jana-vimati-darśanāt tat-tat-pakṣa-sādhana-bala-abala-anavagamāc ca, tatas tataḥ sandihānāḥ prekṣāvanto na tāvat parama-puruṣārthāya ghaṭeran, yāvad ayam ātmā paramātmā ca

(i) svarūpataḥ
(ii) pramāṇataḥ
(iii) saṃbandhataḥ
(iv) prāptitaḥ
(v) tat-sādhanataś ca

na nirṇīyeta/

Therefore, this [work] is undertaken in order to reveal the truth on all these points.

Even though the Bhagavān Bādarāyaṇa has composed sūtras having precisely this same purpose and these sūtras were explained by the "Commentator" (bhāṣyakṛt),[81] whose language is both concise and profound, and expounded in great detail by even [such a teacher as] the Bhagavān Śrīvatsāṅka-miśra,[82] whose language is like a deep ocean of nyāya (gambhīra-nyāya-sāgara), nevertheless, many persons have had their judgment corrupted by their giving credence to various writings of uneven quality that have correct and incorrect ideas interwoven in them like warp and woof,[83] such books as those composed by such writers as Ācārya-ṭaṅka,[84] Bhartṛ-prapañca,[85] Bhartṛ-mitra, Bhartṛ-hari, Brahma-datta,[86] Śaṅkara, Śrīvatsāṅka,[87] Bhāskara,[88] etc.[89] Since persons who have been confused in this way do not understand things as they really are and have many erroneous conceptions, the undertaking of this discussion (prakaraṇa) with the aim of establishing a [clear, comprehensive and definitive] understanding (pratipatti) of the [ātmā and the Paramātmā] is proper.

With regard to this [discussion, I will begin by giving in a Summary Śloka all of the Siddhāntas which I will establish

---

iti tat-pratibodhāya idam ārabhayate/

yadi api bhagavatā bādarāyaṇena idamarthāny eva sūtrāṇi praṇītāni, vivṛtāni ca tāni parimita-gambhīra-bhāṣiṇā bhāṣyakṛtā,[81] vistṛtāni ca tāni gambhīra-nyāya-sāgara-bhāṣiṇā bhagavatā śrīvatsāṅkamiśreṇa--api, tathāpi ācāryaṭaṅka-bhartṛprapañca-bhartṛmitra-bhartṛhari-brahmadatta-śaṅkara-śrīvatsāṅka-bhāskara-ādi-viracita-sitāsita-vividha-nibandhana-śraddhā-vipralabdha-buddhayo na yathāvad anyathā ca pratipadyanta iti tat-pratipattaye ca yuktaḥ prakaraṇa-prakramaḥ/

tatra

for the topics outlined in Pratijñā Series I. A-E above concerning the individual ātmā]:

The ātmā is that which is

(1) other than the body, the external sense-organs, the internal sense-organ or mind, the breath or vital force, and consciousness;
(2) not dependent on any means other than itself for its revelation or manifestation;
(3) eternal;
(4) pervasive;
(5) different in each body, and
(6) innately blessed with "happiness."

---

dehendriyamanaḥprāṇadhībhyo 'nyo 'nanyasādhanaḥ/

nityo vyāpī pratikṣetram ātmā bhinnaḥ svataḥ sukhī//

CHAPTER VIII

YĀMUNA'S PĀÑCARĀTRIKA VEDĀNTA:
THE SVARŪPA/SVABHĀVA DISTINCTION AND RELATION AS AN INTEGRATING PRINCIPLE

In Part One of this book, we examined Yāmuna's defense of the popular Pāñcarātra tradition; and I argued that his distinctive contribution was the integration of Nāthamuni's classically oriented epistemological system (nyāya-śāstra) into the "Miśra" tradition of Pāñcarātrika Vedānta based upon the Vedānta Sūtra commentary of the Bhagavān Śrīvatsāṅka Miśra. In the development of the Śrī Vaiṣṇava school of Viśiṣṭādvaita Vedānta, Yāmuna thus stands as the transitional figure between this "Miśra" tradition and Rāmānuja's more Vedically conservative Vedānta based upon the commentary (Vṛtti) of Bodhāyana (see Chapter V). In Chapters VI and VII of Part Two, I have laid the analytical foundation for a recovery of Yāmuna's own interpretation of Vedānta by isolating four of his major but previously "lost" or unrecognized Vedāntic Siddhāntas (Pratijñās I.A.7, I.B.5.a, II.A.3 and III.C.1) and by analyzing fully his basic theoretical and epistemological position with regard to the nature of the individual ātmā.

In this concluding chapter, I would like to demonstrate the manner in which Yāmuna's basic theoretical principle, the svarūpa/svabhāva distinction and relation (see Chapter VI), is a response to, and an attempt to overcome, the fundamental theoretical problematic in the relation between Vedānta and Pāñcarātra, especially with regard to the central and in the end definitive Vedāntic issue of the relationship (saṃbandha) between the Godhead (Brahman or the Paramātmā) on the one hand and the individual ātmā and the manifest universe on the other. My discussion will proceed again in the terms of the Vedāntic commentatorial discussion of Pāñcarātra in the context of Vedānta Sūtras II.ii.42-45, the Utpatty-asaṃbhava-adhikaraṇa

(UA Adhik.) and especially in terms of Śaṅkara's discussion of the Pāñcarātrika Vyūha theory.[1] After discussing Śaṅkara's and Yāmuna's adversary, but in some respects surprisingly close and positive, relation in terms of the Vyūha theory and the Vedāntic kāraṇa-vāda or dispute about causality, we will want to conclude with a brief discussion of Yāmuna's relation to his intellectual heirs, Rāmānuja and the Viśiṣṭādvaita school of Vedānta.

Before proceeding, however, it is best to emphasize my justification for calling Yāmuna's a system of "Pāñcarātrika Vedānta," for there are some, like Gerhard Oberhammer, who, apparently reflecting a conservative Vedic or Brāhmanic bias, would maintain that either one is a Pāñcarātrin (i.e., a supporter of the Vyūha theory) or one is a Vedāntin, but not both.[2] As we have seen in Chapter II and will see again below, such a hard and fast distinction is difficult to maintain even for a Vedāntin like Śaṅkara who is willing to accept a form of vyūha theory and to use such characteristically Pāñcarātrika categories as the "Six Qualities" (ṣaḍ-guṇas).[3] In the case of a Vedāntin like Yāmuna, such an exclusive categorical division is absolutely inappropriate, for not only did he defend and advocate the Vyūha theory in the Āgama-prāmāṇya[4] but he also explicitly integrated this characteristically Pāñcarātrika doctrine into one of his Vedāntic Siddhāntas on the Paramātmā. In Pratijñā II.B.4, one that unquestionably represents Yāmuna's own position,[5] he concludes with the words

> svābhāvika-niravadhika-atiśaya-jñāna-bala-aiśvarya-vīrya-śakti-tejaḥ-prabhṛti-sakala-kalyāṇa-guṇa-mahārṇavaṃ puruṣa-viśeṣam īśvaram.
>
> The Lord is a particular Person who is a great ocean of all auspicious qualities (kalyāṇa-guṇas), ones that are essential (svābhāvika) to Him and of boundless excellence, foremost among which are [the "Six Qualities" (ṣaḍ-guṇas)] jñāna and bala, aiśvarya and vīrya, śakti and tejas.

The significance of Yāmuna's phrasing is not simply that he explicitly mentions the "Six Qualities" (ṣaḍ-guṇas) but that he presents them in an order or "arrangement" that unmistakably identifies them with their functions in the Vyūha theory of manifestation or "extension." According to this theory,[6] the ṣaḍ-guṇas exist in co-equal fullness in the Godhead or highest Vyūha (para-vyūha) named Nārāyaṇa or Vāsudeva. The other three Vyūhas, while still possessing all of the Six Qualities, become manifest through the "re-arrangement" of them so that particular pairs become predominant:

Saṃkarṣaṇa: 1) Jñāna ("Knowledge") and 4) Bala ("Strength")

Pradyumna: 2) Aiśvarya ("Lordliness") and 5) Vīrya ("Immutability")

Aniruddha: 3) Śakti ("Power") and 6) Tejas ("Splendor").

Since Yāmuna presents the Six Qualities in precisely this order, it is clear that he was openly and self-consciously integrating this Pāñcarātrika view of the Godhead with the Upaniṣadic view of the Paramātmā or Brahman as one major aspect of his attempt to demonstrate the complete compatibility of Pāñcarātra and Vedānta. It should also be emphasized that Yāmuna does not use these six auspicious qualities (kalyāṇa-guṇas) simply as an outpouring of praise and devotion, as is generally the case whenever Rāmānuja repeats this phrase,[7] but rather that, in the context of the argument of Pratijñā Series II.A-B, his use of the Vyūha theory performs a definite Vedāntic function, i.e., defining the manner in which the Paramātmā is the material cause (upādāna-kāraṇa) of the manifest universe.[8]

The Basic Issues in the Relation between Vedānta and Pāñcarātra

I will now proceed to delineate the specific issues with regard to this Pāñcarātrika Vyūha theory that were problematic from the perspective of Vedānta. As the very name Utpatty-asaṃbhava-adhikaraṇa ("The Section dealing with the Impossibility of Origination [utpatti]") indicates, most of the issues were concerned with the problem of causality (kāraṇa-vāda) and especially the relationship (sambandha) between cause (kāraṇa) and effect (kārya). In the first instance the UA Adhik. is concerned with an early, relatively primitive version of the Vyūha theory--one closely related to that found in the Nārāyaṇīya section of the Mahābhārata[9]--in which the Vyūhas are identified with elements of a variant Sāṅkhyan scheme of manifestation (pariṇāma), with Vāsudeva, the Paramātmā, being the Highest Cause (parā prakṛti) and his three "extensions" being successively manifested effects (kāryas): Saṃkarṣaṇa, the jīva (taken as the individual ātmā); Pradyumna, the manas ("mind");

and Aniruddha, the ahaṃkāra ("ego-factor").[10]

Traditionally, the major specific issue within the context of Vedānta was that raised by the first sūtra (II.ii.42), utpatty-asaṃbhavāt ("because of the impossibility of origination"), from which the entire adhikaraṇa derives its name. This issue was whether or not this Vyūha theory, by identifying the Vyūha Saṃkarṣaṇa with the jīva or ātmā, teaches that the latter is produced or had an origin (utpatti) since it is said that the former is produced from Vāsudeva, the Paramātmā (vāsudevāt saṃkarṣaṇa utpadyate).[11] According to Pāñcarātra's Vedāntic opponents, it does teach that the jīva has an utpatti and is therefore unacceptable because such an ātmā would be an effect (kārya) capable of change and modification (i.e., a vikāra) and therefore would suffer from the fault of non-eternality (a-nityatva) and other attendant faults, contradicting the Upaniṣadic teaching of the ātmā's eternality (nityatva) and destroying the very basis of and motivation for the Vedic religious way.[12]

The other major issues are all raised with regard to a somewhat different interpretation of the Vyūha theory, one that corresponds more closely to the later, more fully developed theories of the Pañcarātra Āgamas themselves. The charges against the previous more primitive interpretation derived from the close association of the Vyūhas with the process of manifestation of the "impure" universe (a-śuddha-sṛṣṭi) composed of non-eternal products or effects (kāryas). The more sophisticated and normative Vyūha theory attempts to avoid such problems by interposing a long series of steps between the manifestation of the Vyūhas and that of the impure and ephemeral physical universe.[13] The former is a "pure manifestation" (śuddha-sṛṣṭi) that takes place solely within the Godhead himself through a rearrangement of his Six Qualities, Jñāna, etc., and thus is not in any way implicated in the imperfections inherent to the "impure manifestation." Thus, criticisms based upon the nature of effects (kāryas) and their relationship to causes (kāraṇas) as observed in the mainfestation of the physical universe are deemed simply not to be applicable to the process of the appearance of the Vyūhas.

According to both Śaṅkara and Bhāskara, the third sūtra, II.ii.44, vijñānādibhāve vā tadapratiṣedhaḥ ("Or, if [the Vyūhas] are vijñāna, etc., there is non-rejection of that"), signals a shift to a discussion and rejection of this more sophisticated and normative Vyūha theory.[14] However, it may be instructive to note the striking difference between the treatment of this theory by Bhāskara and that by Śaṅkara. Bhāskara's treatment is quite cursory, formal and never completely distinguished or separated from his criticism of the earlier Vyūha theory upon which he places greater emphasis throughout all four sūtras.[15] On the other hand, Śaṅkara's criticism of this later theory, which is more characteristic of fully developed Pāñcarātrika doctrine, is more extensive than that of the earlier version.[16]

Moreover, Śaṅkara treats this later theory as quite distinct from the earlier and does not--as does Bhāskara--attempt to discredit it by "tarring it with the same brush" as was used against the earlier view. Rather, he feels it necessary to accord this Vyūha theory the dignity of an independent and rather exhaustive logical analysis. Indeed Śaṅkara concludes his criticism by acknowledging that the entire universe has the nature of a vyūha of the Lord (samastasya--eva jagato bhagavad-vyūhatva) so it is wrong for Pāñcarātrins to limit the number of vyūhas to only four.[17] This contrast between Bhāskara and Śaṅkara suggests that the former had little personal involvement with the more fully developed Pāñcarātra and was simply repeating traditional objections that were formulated in opposition to an early form, while Śaṅkara was responding to a living Pāñcarātra tradition with which--as was also argued in Chapter II--he had a close personal involvement that was critical but not wholly negative.[18]

Thus it would appear likely that it is in Śaṅkara's criticism of the more developed Pāñcarātrika Vyūha theory that we may find some of the living issues that were in dispute between Vedānta and Pāñcarātra in the centuries preceding Yāmuna during which a closer relationship between these two traditions was being worked out.

Śaṅkara begins his commentary on the third sūtra by distinguishing this discussion from that of the earlier Vyūha theory. He acknowledges that the Pāñcarātrins do not really mean to identify Saṃkarṣaṇa, Pradyumna and Aniruddha with the gross evolutes jīva, manas and ahaṃkāra as has been assumed by the previous discussion.[19] Rather, as Śaṅkara presents the normative Pāñcarātrika position,

> īśvarā eva--ete sarve jñāna-aiśvarya-śakti-bala-vīrya-tejobhir aiśvarair dharmair anvitā abhyupagamyante, vāsudevā eva--ete sarve nirdoṣā niradhiṣṭhānā niravadyās ceti/[20]

> All these [three Vyūhas] are to be accepted as nothing but Supreme Lords endowed with the lordly qualities of Jñāna, Aiśvarya, Śakti, Bala, Vīrya and Tejas; [as is said,] "All these are nothing but Vāsudevas, without fault, without cause and perfect."

According to Vācaspati Miśra, nir-adhiṣṭhānā means nir-upādāna, "without material cause"; and hence these Vyūhas are nir-avadya, "not to be spoken against" or criticized as subject to such faults as non-eternality (a-nityatva) which are found in effects produced from a material cause.[21] Thus the Pāñcarātrin Pūrvapakṣa to the third sūtra denies that the fault of utpatty-asaṃbhava as developed in the first two sūtras obtains with regard to the Vyūhas so conceived.[22]

Śaṅkara then interprets the third sūtra to mean "even if the Vyūhas are so understood, there is non-rejection of that [fault of utpatty-asaṃbhava]," but it obtains in a different manner or sense than that in which it was taken in the first two sūtras.[23] The manner in which Śaṅkara then proceeds to find fault with this theory is by showing it to be flawed with internal contradictions--no matter how the process of "origination" (utpatti), manifestation or appearance of the Vyūhas and their relationship to Vāsudeva are understood. He poses the alternatives that either 1) these four must be accepted as Supreme Lords who possess precisely the same qualities (tulya-dharmāṇas) but are absolutely distinct from one another[24] or 2) they must be understood as Vyūhas or modifications of one and the same Lord who all possess precisely the same qualities.[25] In the first case the issue of "origination" would not arise, but such a positing of many Supreme Lords is useless and absurd as well as contradicting the established position of the Pāñcarātrins themselves who hold that "the one Lord Vāsudeva alone is the supreme reality" (bhagavān eva--eko vāsudevaḥ paramārtha-tattvam).[26]

Thus the second alternative must be the one accepted by the Pāñcarātrins and in this case the fault of utpatty-asaṃbhava again obtains. As Śaṅkara says in the final portion of his comment on the third sūtra,

> For it is not possible [to say, as you Pāñcarātrins do,] that there is an origination (utpatti) [or production] of Saṃkarṣaṇa [as an effect] from Vāsudeva [as the cause], nor of Pradyumna from Saṃkarṣaṇa, nor of Aniruddha from Pradyumna, because of the lack of any distinction (atiśaya) [among them in that they all have precisely the same qualities (tulyadharmāṇas)]. For it is only by virtue of there being some distinction that it is possible to speak of one object as the cause (kāraṇa) and another as an effect (kārya), as in the case of clay and a pot; in the absence of some such distinction, it is simply not possible to say meaningfully or with any correspondence to actual reality, "[This is] effect; [this is] cause." [While it may be argued that the cause-effect relationship can be validly applied in the case of the Vyūhas because of the distinctions that the Six Qualities exist in their co-equal fullness only in Vāsudeva, the cause, while they exist with different pairs in dominance in the other Vyūhas, the effects, such an argument is contradicted by the fact that] those who follow the Pañcarātra-siddhānta do not grant that any difference (bheda) between the four whatsoever is created by the proportion (tāratamya) or relative dominance of Jñāna, Aiśvarya, etc. among them. For they maintain that all the Vyūhas are equally Vāsudevas without any distinctions (nir-viśeṣā). Moreover, [if the Pāñcarātrins insist on viewing these Vyūhas as having an origination one from another and as being related as cause and effect,] then the vyūhas of the Lord can not be fixed as only four in number, for it is understood that the universe in all its parts, from Brahmā down to a clump of grass, has the character of a vyūha of the Lord (bhagavadvyūhatva).[27]

Śaṅkara's criticism here of the fully developed Pāñcarātrika Vyūha theory is very suggestive, both of the real issues involved in the dispute between Vedānta and Pāñcarātra and of the close relationship of even a Vedāntin of Śaṅkara's position to this Tāntric tradition. For the remarkable thing is that, in criticizing or showing the internal contradictions in either of the alternative ways of understanding this theory, Śaṅkara in both cases is able to conclude his criticism by citing a Pāñcarātrika statement or position that not only reinforces his criticism but would also seem in large part to be acceptable to and in agreement with his own position, judging by his own introductory presentation of the system and its acceptable aspects.[28] Moreover, the statement with which he concludes his comment on the third sūtra reminds us that there is a way of formulating the concept of vyūhas so as to make it Vedāntically acceptable to Śaṅkara.[29] Perhaps the clearest way of formulating the issues involved is by comparing the vyūha theory that Śaṅkara accepts with the Pāñcarātrika one he has criticized.

In his introduction to the UA Adhik., while indicating those aspects of Pāñcarātrika doctrine which are not to be rejected as in conflict with the Vedas, Śaṅkara says,

> That part of this teaching which says "He who is the well-known Nārāyaṇa, higher than the unmanifest, the highest Self, the Self of all, having divided[30] himself by himself (ātmanā-ātmānam) exists manifoldly in vyūhas (anekadhā vyūha-avasthita)" is not rejected, because the manifold existence (anekadhā bhāvasya) of the Paramātmā is understood from such Scriptures as "He exists as one, becomes three-fold, . . ." (sa ekadhā bhavati tridhā bhavati, Chāndogya Upaniṣad 7.26.2).[31]

The passage which Śaṅkara quotes from the Chāndogya Upaniṣad (ChUp) obviously refers to the process of manifestation (sṛṣṭi) given in perhaps the most important of all Upaniṣadic or Vedāntic texts, the Sad-vidyā (ChUp 6).[32] In this process, Sat (Brahman or Absolute Being), which before the origination (utpatti) of the universe was one only (ekam eva) without a second (a-dvitīyam), decided to become many ("bahu syām") and emitted or manifested 1) tejas (heat, fire), which also decided to become many and produced 2) āpas (waters), which in like manner produced 3) anna (food, earth).[33]

When it is noted that Sat is termed the Parā Devatā (the Highest Deity) and the other three emanations are also called Devatās,[34] the formal parallelism with Vāsudeva as the Para Vyūha and his three Vyūhas becomes strikingly and surprisingly clear. As in the Pāñcarātrika theory, the manifestation of these Devatās represents a subtle stage preceeding the production of the gross phenomenal universe. Then the Devatā Sat decides to enter into these three Devatās by means of "this living self" (anena jīvena--ātmanā) and, by dividing and combining them in different proportions in a process of triplication,[35] to make manifest names-and-forms (nāma-rūpe vyākarot), to produce the manifold individual modifications (vikāras) or effects (kāryas) that make up the phenomenal universe.[36]

As we have seen from Śaṅkara's commentary on the UA Adhik., he is willing to admit that all of these modifications (vikāras) of Sat can be called vyūhas of the Lord (bhagavad-vyūhatva). However, as is clear from his commentary on the ChUp, what he is unwilling to admit is that any such modification can be eternally and ultimately real in the same sense as is Sat, the one and undivided ultimate cause and reality (paramārtha-tattva). Every effect in and of itself is ultimately false or "untrue" (an-ṛta)[37] and non-eternal, since as a modification distinct from its cause it is nothing but a "name," (nāma), merely (-mātram) something distinguished by "speech" or for the purposes of worldly verbal conventions (vācārambhaṇam vikāro nāmadheyam).[38] Only that which is not an effect, which is never subject to modification and change, to origination (utpatti) and destruction (vināśa) can be ultimately real and eternal.[39]

Thus, Sat alone, the final and independent uncaused Cause (kāraṇa), is ultimately real. And this Ultimate Cause must be defined so as to be absolutely and unalterably distinguished from and opposed to all that characterizes an effect, lest it also be found to be an ultimately unreal effect and the universe be without any final basis. Hence, Sat must be without birth (a-ja), without death (a-mṛta), without fear (a-bhaya), without stain (nir-añjana), without a second (a-dvitīya), without activity (niṣ-kriyam), without qualification or distinction (nir-viśeṣa), without parts (nir-avayava, niṣ-kala), etc.[40]

We are now in a position to perceive the basic underlying issues involved in Śaṅkara's criticism of the fully developed Vyūha theory, issues that are somewhat obscured in the context of the UA Adhik. in which the traditional emphasis was on the earlier, more primitive version. The related issues which form the fundamental problematic in the relationship between Vedānta and Pāñcarātra are

1) the status and relationship of distinctions (viśeṣas) within the Godhead itself[41] and

2) the relationship (sambandha) of the one, immutable eternal Godhead or Ultimate Cause to the

> manifold, mutable and non-eternal created Universe of sentient and insentient beings.

From Śaṅkara's perspective the basic flaw in Pāñcarātra is not the specific distinctions (i.e., the Six Qualities and the resulting Vyūhas) that it ascribes to Vāsudeva, the Highest Cause (parā prakṛti) and sole Ultimate Reality (paramārtha-tattva), but rather that it recognized any distinction whatsoever within Him.[42] Whatever has internal distinctions must necessarily have parts (avayavas) in a particular relationship. Whatever is a whole composed of parts (avayavin) must necessarily be an effect (kārya), i.e., its parts must have been brought together in their particular relationship by some external agency at some point of origination (utpatti). Moreover, it must necessarily be subject to destruction (vināśa), the separation of its parts, and therefore non-eternal (a-nitya). Thus, Vāsudeva so conceived cannot be the eternal Ultimate Cause and Reality. Either an Ultimate Cause who is totally without distinctions (nir-viśeṣa) and parts (nir-avayava) must be accepted or there will be an infinite regress (an-avasthā) in which the universe will be without any eternal basis.

Thus Śaṅkara feels that Pāñcarātra abridges the absolute distinction and opposition between the nature of the Ultimate Cause and that of all non-eternal effects that must be maintained to preserve the eternality of Brahman as the cause of the universe. Since the preservation of the eternality of Brahman as the Ultimate Cause has traditionally been a central concern of Vedānta, Śaṅkara's criticism poses a major challenge to such champions of Pāñcarātra as Yāmuna in their attempts to maintain its compatibility with Vedānta. However, it must always be remembered that Śaṅkara's interpretation of Vedānta is not the only one and that, while his tradition may have become the dominant orthodoxy in later centuries, Śaṅkara in his own day was one of the greatest mavericks and innovators Vedānta has ever known. Indeed, it is possible to argue very plausibly that, with regard to the fundamental problematic given above, the dominant Vedāntic orthodoxy of Śaṅkara's time and before would be more in accord with and sympathetic to the fully developed Pāñcarātrika Vyūha theory than to Śaṅkara's radical position.

There is a growing scholarly consensus[43] that Bādarāyaṇa in the Vedānta Sūtras taught a form of pariṇāma-vāda (Theory of Modification or Transformation) in which Brahman itself, as both the efficient (nimitta-kāraṇa) and the material cause (upādāna-kāraṇa) of the Universe, passes through a process of modification (pariṇāma) into the condition of effect.[44] Śaṅkara's criticism of this primitive Vedāntic Pariṇāma-vāda, is even more severe than that of the Pāñcarātrika Vyūha-vāda, since the former theory even more blatantly propounds a Brahman who is subject to modification (pariṇāma-vad brahma).[45]

However, Śaṅkara's position is not without major problems of its own within the context of Vedānta and its basic principles or axioms. Śaṅkara's interpretation of Vedānta is in large part an extreme reaction to the Buddhists' teaching of the momentariness of all that exists (yat sat tat kṣanikam) and their consequent denial of the eternality of the Vedic Brahman or ātmā. Śaṅkara's main concern and intention is to preserve Brahman/ātmā as an eternal basis by distinguishing it radically from all non-eternal "momentary" phenomena.

While the eternality and immutability of Brahman is certainly an essential Vedāntic tenet, an equally essential, and even more peculiarly Vedāntic (as opposed to generally Vedic) principle is that Brahman is related to the manifested phenomenal universe as its material cause (upādāna-kāraṇa).[46] Once one accepts this latter principle as an axiom--as every Vedāntin, including Śaṅkara, must, then there is simply no straightforward, consistent, non-paradoxical way to avoid the conclusion that Brahman must in some sense be capable of undergoing some form of modification. Once one denies this conclusion--as Śaṅkara does--one forecloses the logical possibility of relating Brahman to the universe. Just as the Buddhists, once having defined reality (sat) as momentary, cannot logically and non-paradoxically affirm any eternal reality, so Śaṅkara once having defined Brahman (Sat) as absolutely immutable (kūṭastha) and undivided (nir-avayava), cannot logically relate this Brahman to the mutable and manifold effected universe. While Śaṅkara struggles mightily to do so,[47] he is in the end forced to grant the impossibility when he claims that the status of phenomenal realities or "names-and-forms" (nāma-rūpa) is a-nirvacanîya, incapable of logical determination or definition.[48]

When the relationship between Śaṅkara's Vedānta and the orthodox Pariṇāma-vāda is compared with that between Śaṅkara's and the normative Pāñcarātrika Vyūha theory, it is clear that the basic issues and fundamental problematic are precisely the same in both cases: how both to maintain the integrity of the Godhead and to relate it to the phenomenal universe.[49] It would appear that by the time of Śaṅkara, if not before, the Vyūha theory had moved if not into Vedānta itself[50] then at least into the general universe of Vedāntic discourse.

As has been pointed out above, the intention behind the development of the later Vyūha theory is precisely the same as that of Śaṅkara: to preserve the purity of the Godhead by separating it from the impure manifest universe. If Śaṅkara could criticize it for not going far enough, the advocates of this Vyūha theory could with equal justice, and with the support of many orthodox Vedāntins, maintain that he had gone too far and had utterly destroyed the basis for any relationship (saṃbandha) between the Godhead and the world and for a unified, coherent world-view. Thus, one of Yāmuna's basic concerns in the integration of Vedānta and Pāñcarātra was to establish a more adequate basis both for maintaining the integrity and eternality of Brahman and for providing an authentic and meaningful relationship between Brahman and the world of sentient and insentient beings.[51] In Yāmuna's opinion, and in that of Rāmānuja and the later Viśiṣṭādvaita tradition, his svarūpa/svabhāva distinction and relationship could provide such an integrating principle, a point to which I will return below.

The UA Adhik. concludes with the sūtra (II.ii.45) vipratiṣedhāc ca, ("and because of conflict"), which is taken to mean both internal conflicts within Pāñcarātra and conflict of Pāñcarātra with the Vedas. Under the latter is given the charge based upon the scorn of the Vedas (veda-nindā) by Śāṇḍilya, which, as has been shown in Chapter II, is a formal traditional criticism derived from a Pūrva Mîmāṃsā context and of no relevance for our present concern with the specific points at issue between Uttara Mîmāṃsā and Pāñcarātra. However, the specific criticisms given under the former category of internal conflicts are of great significance in that the very general nature of this sūtra gives to the critic the opportunity to present whatever he personally feels to be especially damning for Pāñcarātra. Śaṅkara and Bhāskara differ on the criticism that they bring to bear at this point; and, as Ingalls claims is often the case where these two differ,[52] it appears quite likely that Bhāskara is simply repeating a traditional objection while Śaṅkara is giving his own distinctive criticism.

As has been indicated above, Bhāskara deals with the later Vyūha theory simply as a variation of the earlier version around which the UA Adhik. was originally structured. Thus, the internal conflict which Bhāskara points out is presented as one between the earlier and later forms of Vyūha theory.[53] On the other hand, Śaṅkara's specific criticism at this point is once again directed exclusively against the later Vyūha theory and even more directly against what we have already identified as his major concern vis à vis this theory: the problems occasioned by the recognition of distinctions (*viśeṣas*) within the Godhead. As he says

> vipratiṣedhaś cāsmiñ chāstre bahuvidha upalabhyate guṇa-guṇi-tva-kalpanā-ādi-lakṣaṇaḥ/ jñāna-aiśvarya-śakti-bala-vīrya-tejāṃsi guṇāḥ, ātmāna eva--ete bhagavanto vāsudevā ityādidarśanāt//[54]
>
> And self-contradiction is found in this system in many ways as in its conception of the nature of the relationship between a quality and the possessor of the quality (*guṇa-guṇi-tva-kalpanā*), etc.; for we see such self-contradictory statements as that "[the *ṣaḍ-guṇas*] Jñāna, Aiśvarya, Śakti, Bala, Vīrya and Tejas are qualities (*guṇas*) [of selves, i.e., of the Paramātmā and the Vyūhas; and] that they are also themselves selves, Lord Vāsudevas, [i.e., the possessors (*guṇins*) of themselves].

While some of the details of this criticism are unclear, its general thrust is quite clear; and the problem it raises is of great significance to our discussion for two reasons:

1) Again the criticism is concerned with an issue that is of major importance *within* Vedānta and especially within Śaṅkara's interpretation in which, in accord with his view of two levels of reality and truth, there must be a clearly defined distinction between the higher formless (*a-mūrta*)

Brahman who is absolutely without qualities (nir-guṇa, nir-viśeṣa) and the lower formed (mūrta) Brahman who possesses qualities (sa-guṇa, sa-viśeṣa) and to whom the myriad qualities mentioned in the Vedas and Upaniṣads must be ascribed. As before, it is clear that many orthodox Vedāntins would have sided with Pāñcarātra against Śaṅkara in the attempt to maintain a close and real, but ambiguous and hard to define, relationship between the Godhead and its qualities.

2) Yāmuna's most distinctive and crucial theoretical contribution can be viewed as a direct response to this criticism of Pāñcarātra's guṇa-guṇi-tva-kalpanā and as an attempt to resolve the underlying issue so as to remove what, in Śaṅkara's own independent judgment, was the major obstacle to the Vedāntic acceptability of the later Pāñcarātrika Vyūha theory.

Yāmuna's Response to Śaṅkara's Critique

As has been developed in Chapter VI, Yāmuna employs a rather unusual distinction that is clearly an essential basis for his entire Vedāntic system, the distinction between the often synonymously employed terms svarūpa ("own form") and svabhāva ("own nature"). Svarūpa corresponds here to the possessor of a quality (guṇin, dharmin), the thing modified or specified (viśeṣya), the substrate (āśraya) in which a quality inheres; while svabhāva indicates a quality (guṇa, dharma, viśeṣaṇa, upādhi) which is essentially and inseparably related to the svarūpa (svarūpa-prayukta) and which is always without exception experienced when its svarūpa is experienced. Thus, the svabhāva is a quality (guṇa) that is so inextricably associated and experienced with the svarūpa that it can in certain circumstances and for certain purposes be included within the svarūpa itself and thus appear to be taken to be identical with its own possessor (guṇin). As has been shown in Chapter VI, in the case of the individual ātmā, the svarūpa is the "I" (aham), the self-conscious knower (jñātṛ), while the svabhāva is knowledge or consciousness (jñāna, bodha, samvit, caitanya, etc.). In the present chapter, our primary concern is to investigate how Yāmuna applies this distinction in the case of the Paramātmā and His relationship (sambandha) to His own qualities, the individual ātmā and the manifest universe.

In order to understand the precise relevance of Yāmuna's svarūpa/svabhāva distinction to the present discussion, it is necessary to clarify exactly how Śaṅkara's criticism of Pāñcarātra's conception of the relationship (saṃbandha) between a quality and its possessor (guṇa-guṇi-tva-kalpanā) applies to the Vyūha theory. In all of Śaṅkara's previous criticisms, his points have been clear because they have been directly related to and based upon the statements of Pāñcarātrika doctrine given within the body of his own commentary. In the present case, however, Śaṅkara is apparently assuming on the part of the reader some independent knowledge of this Vyūha theory since he has not previously explained how the Six Qualities are assumed to be identical with "selves, Lord Vāsudevas." All that he has previously stated is that the three Vyūhas or Lords (īśvarāḥ), which are themselves possessors (guṇins) of the Six Qualities, are assumed to be Vāsudevas.

Vācaspati Miśra in his paraphrase of Śaṅkara's criticism simply indicates that Pāñcarātra's position is self-contradictory because "having said that the qualities, Jñāna, etc., are different (bheda) from the selves who possess them, then again it declares that they are non-different (abheda) in the statement 'they are themselves selves, Lord Vāsudevas.'"[55] Vācaspati Miśra's comment here is worthy of note because of its indication that he classifies this Vyūha theory as a variety of Bhedābheda-vāda (the teaching that the relationship between Brahman and other aspects of reality is one of both difference and non-difference), a position which--as was the case with Pariṇāma-vāda--may well have more in common with that of Bādarāyaṇa's Vedānta Sūtras than does Śaṅkara's innovative viewpoint.[56] This point is of special interest in light of the term bhinnābhinnatvam used to characterize the relationship (saṃbandha) between the Paramātmā and the ātmā in Pratijñā III.C.1, which according to my analysis is Yāmuna's Siddhānta (see Chapter VII). However, Vācaspati Miśra's restatement, while it makes the meaning of what Śaṅkara said somewhat clearer, is of no assistance in supplying that which has been left unsaid but which is necessary for a full understanding of how Śaṅkara's criticism is related to the Vyūha theory.

Hence, it is necessary at this point to turn to the Pañcarātra Āgamas themselves for assistance. In the Ahirbudhnya Saṃhitā (AhirS), a Pañcarātra Āgama probably composed a few centuries before Śaṅkara,[57] we find an account of the Six Qualities and their relations to the Godhead that will be helpful both in making Śaṅkara's criticism clearer and in understanding how Yāmuna's svarūpa/svabhāva distinction and relation are related to the thought of the jñāna-pādas of the Āgamas. In the second chapter of the AhirS it is stated that the Supreme Brahman, the Cause of all causes (sarva-kāraṇa-kāraṇam), is both devoid of all qualities (sarva-upādhi-vivarjitam) and of the nature of the Six Qualities (ṣāḍguṇyam).[58] Immediately the query is raised of how Brahman who is devoid of qualities (guṇa-hīnam) can be praised as ṣāḍguṇya.[59] In answer, it is first stated that when Brahman is said to be without qualities (nirguṇam) it means that it is not associated with qualities derived from material nature (a-prākṛta-guṇa-sparśam).[60] Thus we see that we are dealing here with an example of the later Vyūha theory to which Śaṅkara was responding and in which the Vyūhas and the ṣaḍ-guṇas are disassociated from the impure creation (a-śuddha-sṛṣṭi) and viewed as "pure manifestations" (śuddha-sṛṣṭi) within the Godhead.[61]

The text, AhirS II.55cd-62, then proceeds to explain in what sense Brahman is ṣāḍguṇya, and it is here that we find a specific example of the way in which, as Śaṅkara charged, Pāñcarātra obscures the distinction between guṇa and guṇin:

> Hear, O Nārada, faultless one, the One of the "Six Qualities" (ṣāḍguṇyam) being recounted by me//55cd//
>
> The analysts of qualities declare that the foremost Quality (guṇam prathamam) is named Jñāna and that it is the opposite of insentient matter (a-jaḍam), self-aware (svātma-saṃbodhi), eternal (nityam) and all penetrating and comprehending (sarva-avagāhanam)//56//
>
> That (Jñāna) is praised as both the svarūpa of Brahman and its Quality (svarūpaṃ brahmaṇas tac ca guṇaś ca)// 57ab//
>
> She who has the nature of being Prakṛti, the Primordial Material Nature from which the physical universe springs (jagat-prakṛti-bhāvo), is praised as [the Quality] Śakti//57cd//
>
> The analysts of the true nature of these Qualities have declared that the one named Aiśvarya applies to him

> whose agency is supremely independent (kartṛtvam. . . svātantrya-paribṛṃhitam)//58//
>
> The Quality named Bala is declared to apply to the one who is constantly active in the universe but without the slightest effort (śrama-hānis)//59//
>
> The Quality Vīrya is another name for Acyuta, the "unfallen" or immutable one, and applies to the one who, even though being the material cause (upādāna) of the universe, is devoid of modification (vikāra-viraho)//60//
>
> The Quality Tejas is declared to apply to the one who is not dependent on any assistants or accessories (sahakāry-anapekṣā)//61ab//
>
> These Five, Śakti, etc., have been praised as the Qualities of Jñāna (ete śaktyādayaḥ pañca guṇā jñānasya kīrtitāḥ)//61cd//
>
> Jñāna alone is the Highest Form of Brahman, the Paramātmā. (jñānaṃ eva paraṃ rūpam brahmaṇaḥ paramātmanaḥ)//62ab//
>
> That Highest Brahman, the One of the Six Qualities (ṣāḍguṇyam), magnified by its union with its own Śakti (sva-śakti-paribṛṃhitam), made the auspicious resolution, "May I become manifold" (bahu syām, Chāndogya Upaniṣad 6.2.3)//62cf//62

This passage is of special interest in several regards. First of all, it illustrates clearly Śaṅkara's charge of guṇa-guṇi-tva-kalpanā in that Jñāna is called first a guṇa (II.56) and then a guṇin, the possessor of the other five guṇas (II.61cd). More to the point, the guṇa Jñāna itself is expressly called both the svarūpa of Brahman and its guṇa (II.57ab). It is clear then that Śaṅkara's critique is not without basis and that Pāñcarātra does in one and the same statement call Jñāna both a guṇa and identical with Brahman, its own possessor or guṇin.[63]

Of even greater interest is the clear parallel between this passage from the AhirS and Yāmuna's theory of the relation between consciousness (bodha=jñāna) and the svarūpa of the individual ātmā. As we have seen, consciousness is the sole essential quality or svabhāva (bodha-eka-svabhāvam eva, Pratijñā I.A.7) and all other qualities (a-śiva-guṇas) like pleasure (sukha) and pain (duḥkha), etc., are simply modifications of consciousness under particular circumstances. Moreover, bodha or jñāna is the only svarūpa-upādhi, i.e., a quality that is in or within the svarūpa of the individual ātmā and that is svarūpa-prayukta, eternally conjoined with and invariably present with the ātmā, the eternally self-luminous "I" (aham). These parallels or correspondences make clear that, in developing his essential svarūpa/svabhāva distinction and relation, Yāmuna was building upon ideas that were under development within Pāñcarātra for centuries before the time of Śaṅkara.

Yāmuna's analysis does however represent a definite theoretical advance over the more mythologically oriented scheme of the AhirS and must be viewed as an attempt to revise the Pāñcarātrika theory in response to Śaṅkara's critique of the guṇa-guṇi-tva-kalpanā. Thus, if we may generalize from Yāmuna's theory with regard to the individual ātmā, he would not, in a systematic philosophical context, accept without reinterpretation the AhirS's statements:

svarūpaṃ brahmaṇas tac ca guṇaś ca (II.57ab) and

jñānam eva paraṃ rūpaṃ brahmaṇaḥ paramātmanaḥ (II.62ab).

Yāmuna places the heaviest possible emphasis upon his view that the individual ātmā is not simply consciousness (bodha-mātram, jñāpti-mātram, jñānam eva) but is the possessor of consciousness (jñāna-vān), the independent agent who appears as the "I" in the act of cognition (ātmā tu svatantro jñāta--aham iti).[64] Moreover, he restricts his use of the term svarūpa in the narrowest technical sense so as to designate only the guṇin, the subject or "I" who possesses the guṇa jñāna as its property (dharma), svabhāva or svarūpa-upādhi ("aham" ity eva hi tasya svarūpam/ jñānam api hi tad-dharmatvena tasya--eva prakāśate).[65] While Yāmuna's Extended Discussion on the svarūpa of the Paramātmā (Pratijñā II.A.3) and the Vyūha theory (Pratijñā II.B.4) is no longer extant, it is highly probable that he would have applied his svarūpa/svabhāva distinction in a similar way in order to buttress the Pāñcarātrika Vyūha theory and to overcome Śaṅkara's charge that it confuses the guṇa and the guṇin.

Another reason why the above passage from the AhirS is of interest is that it closes by relating the "Six Qualities" and the Vyūha theory to Chāndogya Upaniṣad 6.2.3, i.e., to the Sad-vidyā again, just as did Śaṅkara when indicating the sort of vyūha theory that was acceptable to him as a Vedāntin.[66] It is therefore interesting to turn now to the passage dealing with the Sad-vidyā in Yāmuna's exceedingly fragmentarily preserved Saṃvit-siddhi (SS). This passage, coming at the beginning of the extant fragment, is significant not only because it deals with this central Vedāntic text but also because it contains three of the most explicit references to the Pañcarātra Āgamas, the Vyūha theory and the Six Qualities that we find in his specifically Vedāntic treatises (i.e., in the Siddhi-traya, treating the AP as a more generally mīmāṃsaka work). Yāmuna begins this section by denying that the Upaniṣadic statement "[Sat is] one only without a second" (ekam eva a-dvitīyam) at ChUp 6.2.1, denies the ultimate reality (sad-bhāva) of anything other than Brahman, as is claimed by the Kevalādvaitins (Absolute Non-dualists) or Māyā-vādins ("Illusionists"), Śaṅkara and his followers. Yāmuna argues that no matter how the compound word "a-dvitīyam" is analyzed it does not imply the negation of the "second" to which Sat is contrasted or opposed but on the contrary presupposes the existence of some other entity or entities.[67] Yāmuna then presents his own understanding of the Upaniṣadic teaching of "non-duality" (a-dvaita):

> Therefore, the reality of the manifest universe (prapañca-sadbhāva) is not contradicted by the Vedic teaching of non-duality (advaita-śruti); rather [its reality], which is established on the basis of our own means of valid knowledge (pramāṇa) [i.e., Perception and Inference], is further confirmed by the Vedic Scriptures. Thus, the meaning of the Scriptural statement "Brahman is without a second (a-dvitīyam)" is as follows:
>
> There never has been, nor is now, nor ever will be, any person fit to be counted a "second" [or one like unto Him] (dvitīya-gaṇanā-yogyo); but the One reckoned to be "without a second" (a-dvitīya) is He of whom there is no equal or superior. Since this universe is merely a small part of an "extension" (vyūha) of His glorious power (vibhava-vyūha-kalā-mātram), how could even that [entire universe of sentient and insentient beings] be understood as the object of the word "a second" [like unto Him]? As the statement "The Coḷa king, the Universal Monarch, is now without a second on the surface of the earth" (coḷa-nṛpas samrāḍ advitīyo 'dya bhūtale) is intended to exclude the possibility of a king equal to him, not to deny the reality of his wife, sons, servants, etc., in just the same way [the statement "Brahman is without a second" does not deny the reality of] these hosts of gods, demons and men within the cosmic egg (brahmāṇḍa) ruled over by Brahmā, who are like drops of water in the ocean of the magnificent manifestations (vibhūti-mahima-samudra) of Viṣṇu, the One of unimaginable glory (a-cintya-vibhava), the One who is the repository of the "Six Qualities,"

Jñāna, etc., (jñānādi-ṣāḍguṇya-nidhi), the Lord of all (akhila-īśitṛ), who is unstained by the consequences of faults and actions. . . . Similarly the statement "there is only one Sun in the sky, not two" does not deny the existence of the rays of the Sun. . . .

Thus, [the Puruṣa Sūkta, Ṛig Veda X.90], declaring that "all beings are but a quarter of Him; the deathless three quarters remain in Heaven," includes the entire universe within His nature (jagat sarvam itthaṃbhāve nyaveśayat). . . .

Other texts also, such as "This entire universe, the cosmic egg, is to Him as an atom is to Mount Meru," intend to reveal that everything is an [infinitesimal] modification of that One (tad-itthaṃbhāva).

But the entire universe of movable and immovable beings is produced by modification (vikāra-jātaṃ) and is merely a phenomenal reality understood according to the conventions of "speech" (vācārambhaṇa-mātra); only Sat, the root cause (mūla-kāraṇam eva) is immutable (kūṭastha).

The effect (kārya) is not other than the cause (an-anyat kāraṇāt) just as the sparks are not different from the fire--this fact is shown by many examples such as clay [and the pot], gold [and golden ornaments], the seed [and the sprout], etc.

Without being nourished by the śakti of that One, fire would not be able to burn grass, water to wet, nor wind to shake.

This whole [universe] should become known through the knowledge of that One Supreme Being (eka-pradhāna-vijñānād). Thus, by these statements of the Vedas and of Āgamas based upon the Vedas (veda-vacana-tan-mūlāpta-āgamair api), it is understood that this manifest universe of sentient and insentient beings achieves its nature or "self" through the "self" of Brahman. Therefore, this Divine Manifestation (brāhmī vibhūtir) is determined to be true (pramīyate); it is not denied. If it were denied reality, then, because of the falseness of everything, all activity, worldly and Vedic, would cease, as would even the knowledge of Brahman.[68]

Yāmuna thus argues that the Sad-vidyā, in teaching that Sat is the material cause (upādāna-kāraṇa) of the universe and that the effect is not different from the cause (sat-kārya-vāda), proposes a realistic theory of modification or manifestation, not an illusionist one--as van Buitenen has shown to indeed be the case.[69] However, the striking aspect of the above passage is that, just as Śaṅkara was willing to associate himself positively with certain aspects of Pāñcarātrika thought and terminology, Yāmuna uses terminology that is distinctively characteristic of Śaṅkara's interpretation of the Sad-vidyā, especially in the verse

vācārambhaṇamātran tu jagat sthāvarajaṅgamam/
vikāra-jātaṃ kūṭasthaṃ mūlakāraṇam eva sat//70

The key word here is -mātra, "merely," which is not in the Chāndogya text vācārambhaṇaṃ vikāro nāmadheyam[71] and is imported by Śaṅkara (vāgālaṃbana-mātraṃ nāma--eva kevalam)[72] to establish his illusionist interpretation. Rāmānuja, in marked contrast to Yāmuna, uses the word -mātra only while presenting the Māyā-vāda Pūrvapakṣa and studiously avoids any such connotation in giving his own interpretation.[73] It would appear that Yāmuna, as a Bhakta and poet, was able to accept this phrasing to heighten the contrast between the real but mutable universe and the immutable root-cause Brahman (kuṭasthaṃ mūlakāraṇam eva sat), while the more prosaically minded Rāmānuja could not.[74]

Another key word is kūṭastha ("immutable"), which leads us back to a consideration of Yāmuna's Pratijñā Siddhānta II.A.3 on the svarūpa of the Paramātmā and its close relation to Pratijñā II.A.2 which represents Śaṅkara's position. I have argued that Yāmuna never uses the word kūṭastha to describe the individual ātmā,[75] which, while being eternal, is subject to change in its svabhāva consciousness;[76] but he clearly applies it to the Paramātmā in this verse from the SS with its Śaṅkaran terminology and overtones. In the same way, in Pratijñā II.A.3, with the words yathā-ukta-svarūpam eva, Yāmuna appears to accept fully the phrase from II.A.2 that clearly represents Śaṅkara's own position on the svarūpa of the Paramātmā:

pratyastamita-miti-māna-matṛ-meya-Īśvara-Īśitavyādi-
bheda-vikalpa-kūṭastha-vijñāna-eka-rasam.77

Apparently Yāmuna had little difficulty accepting Śaṅkara's analysis of those Upaniṣadic texts that describe the absolute non-duality, immutability and lack of difference (a-bheda) or qualification (nirguṇa) within the svarūpa of Brahman itself. However, Yāmuna was unwilling, in what he viewed as an overreaction to the Buddhist critique of everything involved in change or modification as momentary and non-eternal, to follow Śaṅkara--or at least Sankara's followers--into the logical blind alley or cul-de-sac of negating the reality of the universe and of Brahman's relation (saṃbandha) to it (both of which are accepted by many other Upaniṣadic passages) and thereby destroying the basis for the unity and coherence of all human activity and knowledge.

Yāmuna's answer to Śaṅkara in his Siddhānta, Pratijñā II.A.3, was to assert that the only way to integrate or preserve the coherence of all existence is to accept Brahman as a "qualified" being or as upahitam, which word is the precise equivalent, and the source, of the term viśiṣṭa in what later came to be the name of the Śrī Vaiṣṇava school of Vedānta, Viśiṣṭādvaita, "the Non-dualism of that Being who is Qualified." By viewing all of the mutable and everchanging manifest universe (Brahman's qualities such as omniscience, etc.,; the śaktis Māyā and avidyā; all sentient and insentient beings; the "Six Qualities" and the Vyūhas, etc.) as modifications of the self-luminous consciousness (vijñāna) that is the svarūpa-upādhi or svabhāva, the sole "essential quality" in or within--but distinct from--the svarūpa, Yāmuna, in the no longer extant portion of the AtS, would have proposed what, in the context of Vedānta and theistic Bhakti religion, proved to be a powerful integrative model or theory that could preserve both the unity and eternality of Brahman and Brahman's relation to the universe as its Cause (kāraṇa) and Ruling Lord (Īśvara).

Thus, in his Pratijñā Siddhānta III.C.1 on the relation (saṃbandha) between the Paramātmā and the individual ātmā, Yāmuna says that, when both the Upaniṣadic texts declaring Brahman's "essential unity" and lack of difference or qualification (a-dvaita, a-bheda, nir-guṇa) and the texts revealing distinctions (bheda) or qualification (sa-guṇa) are considered, the correct conclusion is that the statements revealing absolute unity are referring to His svarūpa, His essential nature as distinct from everything else (svatas tv aikyam) while those revealing difference refer to His relation to His qualities (upādhito bheda) and that therefore the relation is one of both Difference and Non-difference (bhinna-abhinna-tvam), because Brahman's absolutely unique and distinct svarūpa is qualified by the ātmā, His upādhi (viśiṣṭa-svarūpa-bhāvena). This phrase, viśiṣṭa-svarūpa-bhāvena, makes even clearer the fact that Yāmuna's until now "lost" Siddhāntas, Pratijñās II.A.3 and

III.C.1, are the source for the name Viśiṣṭādvaita, "the non-duality of that Brahman whose svarūpa is qualified (upahita = viśiṣṭa) by His Qualities (upādhis = viśeṣaṇas), the individual ātmās and the manifest universe," an interpretation that is confirmed by Rāmānuja's preferred usage of the terminology viśeṣaṇa-viśeṣya-bhāva in defining this relation.[78]

Yāmuna and Rāmānuja

While I would find it difficult to delineate any major differences of intention between Yāmuna and Rāmānuja, there are some important specific points of difference that have emerged from this study and that probably help explain why Yāmuna's systematic Vedāntic works have been only fragmentarily preserved. According to my reconstruction, Yāmuna uses the term bhinnābhinnatva to describe his system in Pratijñā III.C.1; and, while Rāmānuja's Vedānta was in fact a type of bhedābheda-vāda (in that he explicitly states that both bheda and abheda are to be accepted as ultimately true[79]), he was especially harsh and categorical in his rejection of this terminology, stating that "in all cases bhinnābhinnatva is rejected" (sarvatra bhinnābhinnatvam api nirastam).[80] It appears that in Rāmānuja's Vedāntic context the terms upādhi and bhinnābhinnatvam were too closely tied to the positions of such Bhedābhedavādins as Bhāskara according to which bheda or the distinction between Brahman and the ātmā was only provisionally true (i.e., in the state of bondage) and only a-bheda or non-difference was ultimately or finally real in the state of Release. Rāmānuja was adamant about maintaining the eternal difference between Brahman and His qualities in order to preserve the eternality and purity (a-malatva) of the Godhead.[81]

While Yāmuna also clearly stressed bheda or difference as basic and eternal,[82] the fact that his Vedāntic system might have been somewhat weak and open to question in this regard is probably indicated by the relative ease with which he can accept Śaṅkara's definition of the Paramātmā's svarūpa as being nir-guṇa or absolutely devoid of any qualities or distinctions (pratyastamita-. . .-bheda-vikalpa-kūṭastha-vijñāna-eka-rasam).[83] Rāmānuja's theistic Vedānta lays very heavy emphasis upon sa-guṇa Brahman, a great ocean of auspicious qualities (*kalyāṇa*-*guṇa*-*mahārṇava*) with the term *nir*-*guṇa* being taken to mean only the absence of negative qualities. Yāmuna, in line with his theoretical analysis in terms of the individual *ātmā* and with the *Ahirbudhnya Saṃhitā*'s analysis of the "Six Qualities," would probably reduce all of these auspicious qualities to the one *sole svabhāva jñāna* or *vijñāna* (cf. *kūṭastha*-*vijñāna*-*eka*-*rasa* with *bodha*-*eka*-*svabhāvam eva*).[84] At any rate, Yāmuna's surprising and rather startling tendency to use language evocative of Śaṅkara's, as in the phrase *vācārambhaṇa-mātram* quoted above, must have caused problems for later Viśiṣṭādvaitins in their dispute with Kevalādvaita. Given Yāmuna's own very harsh characterization of Śaṅkara's disciples Sureśvara and Vimuktātman as "Covert Buddhists" (*pracchannās*), we must probably assume that Yāmuna made a distinction between the prestigious Śaṅkara and the later exponents of Kevalādvaita.[85]

Another important difference between Yāmuna and Rāmānuja--and the major one in terms of this study of the integration of Vedānta and Pāñcarātra within the classical Vedic tradition--is that Rāmānuja's Vedānta cannot in any technical sense be termed a system of "Pāñcarātrika Vedānta" as can Yāmuna's. While Rāmānuja defended the Vedic orthodoxy of Pāñcarātra in his Vedāntic commentary and self-consciously formulated a system of Vedānta that was compatible with the theistic devotion and temple ritual of Pāñcarātra, he does not employ such Pāñcarātrika doctrines or concepts as the Vyūha theory or the "Six Qualities" *functionally* within his Vedāntic system, as Yāmuna must have done in his discussion of the Vedāntic disputes about causality (*kāraṇa*-*vāda*) and the manifestation of the universe (*pariṇāma*-*vāda*) in the no longer extant Extended Discussion of Pratijñā Series II.B, if my understanding of the structure of Pratijñā Series II.A-B is correct.[86]

While Rāmānuja often cites the "Six Qualities" in the peculiarly Pāñcarātrika sequence employed by Yāmuna, he generally does so in a devotional context, especially at the beginning of his prose hymn, the *Vaikuṇṭha*-*gadya*, where he is in effect quoting Pratijñā II.B.4.[87] Rāmānuja regularly refers to these "Six Qualities" as the foremost among the *Kalyāṇa*-*guṇas* or "Auspicious Qualities," but carefully distinguishes them from the *five* qualities or properties that *define* the *svarūpa* of Brahman (svarūpa-nirūpaṇa-dharmas), jñāna, ānanda, ananta, satya, and amalatva, all of which he very carefully and specifically derives from the central sacred authorities for Vedānta, the Upaniṣads.[88] In his discussion of the UA Adhik. in the ŚBh, Rāmānuja completely removes the Vyūha theory from its original doctrinal and cosmological context in the Nārāyaṇīya and the jñāna-pādas of the Pañcarātra Āgamas as a theory of the manifestation of the universe, and treats it solely in a devotional context as providing the sacred names of the Godhead to be used in meditation (upāsanā).[89]

In Rāmānuja's treatment of Pāñcarātra, we see the culmination of a long-term and successful process of integrating this Tāntric tradition into the Vedic tradition by stressing its role as an alternate ritual tradition to the Vedic karma-mārga and by adjusting its doctrinal or theological aspects so as to conform to those of Vedānta. However, by Rāmānuja's time, there has been a complete "division of labor" effected in which, as Matsubara has suggested,[90] the Śrī Vaiṣṇava Viśiṣṭādvaita Vedānta has totally preempted the theological role and Pāñcarātra has been restricted to the ritual aspect. Rāmānuja, the cautious Vedic scholar, was probably so successful at completing this process of integration because he maintained this "division of labor" so strictly, thereby providing an unassailable classical Vedāntic theological basis for the popular religious movement, Pāñcarātra.

Yāmuna was not so cautious. He openly accepted as his own the integrative task of the "Miśra" tradition of Pāñcarātrika Vedānta. Drawing upon the dialectial skill, epistemological sophistication and social prestige that he inherited from his grandfather Nāthamuni, he attempted to work out an authentic intellectual synthesis of Vedānta and Pāñcarātra. While he evoked the ire and opposition of many more conservative Brāhmans, his bold venture helped insure the continued vitality of Hindu culture and religion throughout the Medieval period and into the present day.

APPENDIX I

Nāthamuni as Reflected in Yamuna's Works

In this appendix, I will present what we can know or reasonably infer about Nāthamuni, Yāmuna's grandfather and the first Teacher or Ācārya in the Śrī Vaiṣṇava Guru-paramparā, on the basis of Yāmuna's explicit references to him by name.[1] Nāthamuni receives the most direct and proportionally heavy reference in Yamuna's major hymn, the Stotra-ratna (SR).[2] Yamuna both begins and ends this hymn with references to Nāthamuni. In an extraordinary burst of praise and reverence, the first three verses are devoted to the praise of Nāthamuni.

namo 'cintyādbhutākliṣṭajñānavairāgyarāśaye/
nāthāya munaye 'gādhabhagavadbhaktisindhave// 1 //

tasmai namo madhujidaṅghrisarojatattva-
    jñānānurāgamahimātiśayāntasīmne/
nāthāya nāthamunaye 'tra paratra cāpi
    nityaṃ yadīyacaraṇau śaraṇam madiyam// 2 //

bhūyo namo 'parimitācyutabhaktitattva-
    jñānāmṛtābdhiparivāhaśubhair vacobhiḥ/
loke 'vatirṇaparamārthasamagrabhakti-
    yogāya nāthamunaye yamināṃ varāya// 3 //

Homage to the sage (muni) Nātha,
    an unfathomable ocean of devotion (bhakti)
    to the Blessed Lord,
In whom dwells the fullness
    of both knowledge and dispassion (vairāgya),
    beyond imagination, wondrous and unstained.// 1 //

Homage to him who has attained the ultimate
    in the greatness of his love for and knowledge of
    the lotus-feet of Madhujit (Viṣṇu),
To the lord Nāthamuni,
    whose feet are my eternal refuge
    in this world and even in the other.// 2 //

Again I bow to Nāthamuni,
    the best of Yogis (yaminām) in whom
    complete and ultimately true Bhakti-yoga
    has descended among men,
Through words that are as pleasing as
    surging streams from the
    ambrosial ocean of unlimited knowledge of and
    devotion to Acyuta (Viṣṇu).// 3 //

After a verse of praise to Parāśara, the author of the Viṣṇu Purāṇa, and another seemingly dedicated to Nammāḻvār, the exemplar of the Āḻvārs,[3] Yāmuna proceeds to exalt Nārāyaṇa and his heavenly companions, denigrate himself in many ingenious ways and take refuge with the merciful and compassionate Lord. Then in SR 61, he contrasts himself with his ancestors in the following manner:

janitvāham vaṃśe mahati jagati khyātayaśasāṃ
śucīnāṃ yuktānāṃ guṇapuruṣatattvasthitividām/
nisargād eva tvaccaraṇakamalaikāntamanasām
adho 'dhaḥ pāpātmā śaraṇada nimajjāmi tamasi// 61 //

I have been born into a great lineage (vaṃśa)
whose fame is renown throughout the world,
composed of pure and self-disciplined (yukta) knowers
of the true state of the sentient (puruṣa) and
insentient (guṇa) elements of reality,

Whose minds from the very moment of their creation
have been fixed solely on your lotus-feet;

Even so, O Giver of Refuge, I, being evil
in my inner-most being, am sinking lower and lower
into gross darkness.// 61 //

In the next three verses (SR 62-64), Yāmuna details all his evil traits that establish him as the most evil of all (pāpiṣṭhaḥ), gives examples of both Rāma and Kṛṣṇa having had mercy upon such evil ones once they had sought refuge with them, and reminds the Lord of a promise (pratijñā) or vow (vratam) that He made to be merciful to anyone who takes refuge with Him even if only once. Yāmuna then concludes his hymn with a special plea on his own behalf:

akṛtrimatvaccaraṇāravinda-
premaprakarṣāvidhim ātmavantam/
pitāmahaṃ nāthamuniṃ vilokya
prasīda madvṛttam acintayitvā// 65 //

Have mercy, [O Lord] not in accord with
my own activities,
But in consideration of my grand-father, Nāthamuni,
one who is both self-possessed and
possesses the most excellent and genuine love
for your lotus-feet.// 65 //

While it is often difficult to be certain what in such hymns represents simply traditional and stylized piety and what is an original contribution of the composer, Yāmuna's emphasis on his relationship with Nāthamuni is clearly distinctive.

Both the major commentators take note of Yāmuna's unusual and repetitive reference and respect.[4] I have not been able to discover any other hymn devoted primarily to a diety in which a human person or teacher is given as much attention nor in which such heavy explicit emphasis is placed upon one's hereditary biological relationship with one's spiritual master. While there is certainly no mutually exclusive relationship between an hereditary and spiritual relationship, I have not yet discovered a Śrī Vaiṣṇava hymn that puts such primary emphasis upon the former.[5]

Indeed, the Tamil Śrī Vaiṣṇava hymns of the Āḻvārs provide a very marked contrast. For, while the Āḻvārs quite often claim some merit on the basis of the intensity and artistic merit of their devotional outpouring, they place no emphasis upon the worth of their lineage and occasionally explicitly deprecate their family ties.[6] While one finds in the SR the same kind of reveling in one's human failings (that paradoxically makes one most fit for and deserving of the Lord's mercy) as is found in the Āḻvārs' hymns,[7] I also sense a certain conflicting pathos that marks Yāmuna's feeling of loss when he compares himself with his grandfather.

As has been noted before, the traditional Guru-paramparā accounts do record that Yāmuna lost a portion of Nāthamuni's heritage--the Yoga-rahasya or the Secret of the eight-limbed or aṣṭāṅga yoga based upon Patañjali's Yoga-Sūtras.[8] Yāmuna missed the appointment for his initiation into this Secret because he became entranced by one of the Āḻvār's hymns. Traditionally it is because of this lapse on Yāmuna's part that classical Pātañjalian yoga in its full form is no longer practiced among the Śrī Vaiṣṇavas.

Important in this connection is the other reference in Yāmuna's extant works to Nāthamuni by name, since it is there that Yāmuna attests most clearly to Nāthamuni's association with yoga as well as--according to one interpretation--possibly alluding to his connection with the Āḻvārs' Tamil hymns. Yāmuna concludes the AP with the following two verses:

tattatkalpitayuktibhiś śakalaśaḥ kṛtvā
tadīyaṃ mataṃ
yacchiṣyair udamardi sātvatamata-
sparddhāvatām uddhatiḥ/

yaccetas satataṃ mukundacaraṇadvandvāspadaṃ
vartate
jīyān nāthamunis svayogamahima-
pratyakṣatattvatrayaḥ//

ākalpaṃ vilasantu sātvatamatapraspardhi-
duṣpaddhati-
vyāmugdhoddhatadurvidagdhaparisad-
vaidagdhyavidhvaṃsinaḥ/

śrīmannāthamunīndravarddhitadhyiyo
nirdhūtaviśvāśivāḥ
santas santatagadyapadyapadavī-
hṛdyānavadyoktayaḥ//9

May Nāthamuni triumph, he to whom the three elements of ultimate reality are directly perceptible through his own power of yoga, he whose mind eternally dwells at the abode of the two feet of Mukunda (Viṣṇu),

He whose disciples have crushed the arrogance of those who scorn the Sātvata (Pañcarātra) teaching, having slashed their teachings to pieces by turning their own dialectical arguments (yuktis) against them.

Let shine 'till the end of this age those Saints (santas) whose pleasing and faultless uterrances always follow the ways of flowing prose (gadya) or poetry (padya), who have shaken off every inauspicious quality, their intellects nurtured by the Blessed Lord Nāthamuni and his Blessed Lord (śrīman-nāthamuni-indra),

Those good men who have confounded the cunning of the malicious, haughty and confused assemblies of those who follow the evil paths that vie with the good (sātvata) teaching.[10]

The phrase, sva-yoga-mahima-pratyakṣa-tattva-trayaḥ ("he to whom the three elements of ultimate reality are directly perceptible through his own power of yoga"), has become perhaps the single most well-known testimony to Nāthamuni's greatness among the Śrī Vaiṣṇavas.[11] Nāthamuni's powers of transcendental yogic insight are enshrined most centrally in the traditional account of his receiving the hymns of the Āḻvārs through a direct vision of Nammāḻvār.[12] In Yāmuna's writings are testimonies to his high esteem for yoga-ja-pratyakṣa and his recognition of it as a pramāṇa or valid source of knowledge of ultimate reality, a point which he says is accepted without dispute by all debaters (sarvavādi-nirvivādam).[13]

If we may accept the traditional account of the loss of Nāthamuni's yoga-rahasya which is supported implicitly by the entire tone of the SR and explicitly by some of the stanzas,[14]

Yāmuna did not himself practice aṣṭānga-yoga or claim to have attained to yoga-ja-pratyakṣa. Rather he honored it as what gave authority to the teachings of the great sages of the past, such as his grandfather Nāthamuni.[15] As Vedānta Deśika testifies in his commentary on SR 61, Yāmuna is contrasting himself with the family or line of great yogis into which he has been born (mahā-yogi-kula-prasūtatvam, yogi-vaṃśa-), as indicated by the word yuktānāṃ, which derives from the same root yuj as does yoga.[16] In fact, in practically every verse related to Nāthamuni we see words or phrases which can be seen as indicative of his involvement with yoga. The very word muni usually denotes a contemplative ascetic.[17] Also in SR 1, the phrase -akliṣṭa-jñāna-vairāgya- is evocative of Patañjali's terminology.[18] In SR 3, Nāthamuni is called the best of yamis or "those who possess restraint," an integral aspect of yoga with the first of the eight limbs being yama and the second niyama.[19] By the term ātma-vantam, applied to Nāthamuni in SR 65, Yāmuna is clearly contrasting himself, who is not an ātma-vedī (SR 22), with his grandfather, the restrained and dispassionate sage, who has attained his knowledge through his own power of yoga (sva-yoga-mahima). Doubtless this emphasis served the poetic function of establishing Yāmuna's own need of (and worthiness for) divine grace (SR 50). However, it is also in accord with, and perhaps partly the basis for, one aspect of the traditional picture of Nāthamuni.

However, Yāmuna juxtaposes Nāthamuni as the dispassionate and self-restrained yogī with Nāthamuni as the passionate and unrestrained bhakta or devotee at the feet of Viṣṇu--a picture once again in accord with the traditional account of Nāthamuni who on several occasions awoke from his yogic trance to chase after someone he imagined to be Kṛṣṇa or Rāma--doing so in such an unseemly and agitated manner that the result was either his being rebuked by his disciples, his falling into a swoon, or, in the end, his leaving his body for good.[20] Such juxtaposition is seen above in SR 1, 3, 61 and 65, and in the second half of the first verse quoted from the AP. The traditional accounts relate Nāthamuni's strong devotional leanings to his attraction to and recovery of the Āḻvārs' Tamil hymns.[21]

Since this achievement is remembered as Nāthamuni's greatest contribution to the development of the Śrī Vaiṣṇava tradition, one might expect that Yāmuna would eulogize Nāthamuni's association with the Āḻvārs' Tamil hymns. There is a tendency, supported by J. A. B. van Buitenen,[22] to see Yāmuna doing so in the final verse of the AP quoted above. There Yāmuna praises some "good [men] (santas) whose pleasing and faultless utterances always follow the ways of flowing prose or poetry (gadya-padya-padavī) and whose intellects have been nurtured by Śrīman-Nāthamuni-indra," whom van Buitenen takes to be Nāthamuni himself. Even if this reference is exclusively to Nāthamuni and not to Nāthamuni's Lord (in my view, both meanings are intended), it is difficult to see in this verse a specific or exclusive reference to the Āḻvārs' hymns, all of which are in verse form (padya) and not in prose (gadya). Thus, the santas here probably do not refer to the Āḻvārs exclusively, although Yāmuna certainly may have meant to include them within this more general reference.

If I were pressed to find in Yāmuna's references one linking Nāthamuni to the Āḻvārs' hymns, I would suggest SR 3--although I must hasten to add that my suggestion finds no support from the traditional commentaries. In this verse Yāmuna says literally that Nāthamuni "possesses the highest and most complete bhakti-yoga that has descended (avatīrṇa) into the world by means of words (vacobhiḥ) that are as pleasing as . . ."[23] In the traditional account of the way Nāthamuni recovered the lost hymns of the Āḻvārs, he chanted one of the very few hymns that had been preserved--Madhura Kavi's ten stanzas in praise of Nammāḻvār--1200 times before an image of this the greatest Āḻvār. Nammāḻvār was so pleased by this praise that, with the permission of the Goddess Śrī, he manifested himself to Nāthamuni as a "bodiless voice" (a-śarīri-vāṇi), granted him a "divine eye" and revealed to him all the hymns of the Āḻvārs as well as the three sacred mantras (rahasya-traya), the meaning of all darśanas, and the secret of the eight-linked yoga (aṣṭāṅgayoga-rahasya).[24]

In such a context, the "words" (vacobhiḥ) in SR 3 could be taken to refer both to the Āḻvārs' hymns that Nāthamuni chanted to win the favor of Nammāḻvār and to the previously lost hymns and other secrets which Nammāḻvār revealed to Nāthamuni. Thus, the highest and most complete bhakti-yoga would refer to the Divya-prabandham or "Collected Hymns of the Āḻvārs" that descended to earth once again through the words of praise uttered by Nāthamuni. However, as I indicated above, neither Vedānta Deśika[25] nor Periya Vāccān Piḷḷai[26] specifically relate this verse to the Āḻvārs. They take vacobhiḥ in a very general way, although Vedānta Deśika does specifically mention "the Nyāya-tattva, etc."

Thus, we can find no conclusive evidence of Yāmuna's associating Nāthamuni with the Āḻvārs in a specific manner, although the general way in which Nāthamuni is described as a bhakta would indicate that he would be the type of devotee who would be attracted by the Āḻvārs' piety.

As would be expected in a hymn of praise to the Lord, it is Nāthamuni's character as a bhakta at the feet of Viṣṇu that is given predominant emphasis in the SR, being contrasted for poetic and devotional effect with his character as a yogī. There are references to his knowledge (jñāna) about the elements (tattvas) of ultimate reality (guṇa-puruṣa-tattva sthiti);[27] however, such knowledge is ancillary to and derived from his role as either a bhakta or a yogī and does not seem to refer directly to his role as the first important Śrī Vaiṣṇava thinker and author of the Nyāya-tattva. In the first verse quoted above from the conclusion of the more polemically oriented AP, there is reference to Nāthamuni's contribution as a Naiyāyika. However, once again he is primarily and directly characterized by his devotion to the feet of Viṣṇu and by his yogic insight, while his role as an apologetic dialectician or logician is indicated indirectly by the skill of his disciples (yacchiṣyair) at cutting to bits opposed teachings by means of yuktis or logical arguments. According to the traditional accounts, Nāthamuni's heritage was handed on to Yāmuna by the line of disciples that had concentrated on Nāthamuni's śāstra which would have been embodied primarily in his Nyāya-tattva.[28]

Let us summarize what we have gained from these few instances where Yāmuna invokes Nāthamuni by name. We have seen that Nāthamuni was Yāmuna's grandfather (pitāmaham) and the exemplar of a world-renowned, pure, disciplined (yukta), knowledgeable and innately devoted lineage[29] with whom Yāmuna contrasts himself as innately evil (pāpātmā). While this contrast is partly a poetic and devotional device through which Yāmuna establishes himself as the most depraved and therefore paradoxically the one most worthy of the Lord's mercy (SR 50), Yāmuna also establishes Nāthamuni as an eternal intermediary between himself and Viṣṇu (SR 2). Yāmuna's taking refuge (śaraṇam) at Nāthamuni's feet has become the pattern for what the Śrī Vaiṣṇavas call guru-prapatti, a teaching traditionally associated with Yāmuna.[30] However, while Nāthamuni does in the SR play the role of a guru or ācārya to Yāmuna, there is a special intensity to Yāmuna's emphasis that makes it stand out from other Śrī Vaiṣṇava hymns; and this special intensity is related to the emphasis that Yāmuna puts on their hereditary relationship--an emphasis that once again is not typical of Śrī Vaiṣṇava hymns. Yāmuna characterizes Nāthamuni both as a dispassionate yogī or jnānī (muni, yamī, ātmavān, etc.) who has attained much on his own merit and as a bhakta who is passionately attached to and dependent upon Viṣṇu. Nathāmuni is directly (-śubhair vacobhiḥ) or indirectly (-gadya-padya-padavī-hṛdaya-anavadya-uktayaḥ) associated with "pleasing words," probably hymns of praise, that have both established the perfect bhakti-yoga in the world and destroyed other conflicting ways. And, finally, he has established a line of disciples skilled in logical argumentation (nyāya, yukti) who have defeated the opponents of the Sātvata or Pañcaratra teaching at their own game. As we have pointed out, there is a great deal of conformity between the general picture of Nāthamuni and the one preserved in the traditional Guru-paramparas. Of course, this general conformity may be partly explained by the fact that Yāmuna's references would have been instrumental in setting the general tone, though not the details, of the traditional accounts.

APPENDIX II

Correlation of the Extant Text of the Ātma-Siddhi

The following chart presents the correlation between the Summary Śloka concerning the individual ātmā, the extant text of the Extended Discussion, and the corresponding Pratijñā Series, as determined by the argument of Chapter VI:

Summary Śloka	Extended Discussion	Pratijñā Series
Topic (1) The demonstration that the ātmā is that which is other than	AtS, pp. 9.1-74.8 (A, 18.1-123.6)	I.A.
(i) the body (deha),	pp. 9.1-19.6 (A, 18.1-41.7)	1. (Cārvakas)
(ii) the external sense-organs (indriya),	pp. 19.7-20.7 (A, 41.8-43.6)	2.
(iii) the internal sense-organ or mind (manas),	pp. 21.1-27.9 (A, 44.1-54.4)	3.
(iv) the breath or vital force (prāṇa),	pp. 28.1-29.5 (A, 55.1-56.5	4.
(v) and cognition or consciousness (dhī).	pp. 29.6-74.8 (A, 56.6-123.6)	5. (Buddhists and Pracchannas)
Summary Śloka Siddhānta (1)	pp. 72.6-74.8 (A, 120.3-123.6) a preliminary statement of Yāmuna's Siddhānta on the svarūpa of the individual ātmā in opposition to Pratijñā I.A.5.	

Summary Śloka	Extended Discussion	Pratijñā Series
Topic (2) The demonstration that the ātmā is an-anya-sādhanaḥ, "that which is not dependent upon any other means (sādhana, pramāṇa) for its manifestation [in consciousness because it is self-luminous (svayam-jyotiḥ) according to its essential nature (svarūpa)]."	pp. 75.1-150.2 (A, 123.7-222.4)	I.B. and I.A.6-7.
	pp. 75.1-100.11 (A, 123.7-159.8) Presentation and Refutation of Pūrvapakṣas on pramāṇa.	I.B.1-4.
	pp. 75.1-85.6 (A, 123.8-138.8)	I.B.1. (Nyāya-Vaiśeṣikas and Sāṅkhyas)
	pp. 85.7-87.8 (A, 139.1-142.2)	I.B.2. (Śrotriyas)
	pp. 87.9-94.6 (A, 142.3-151.3)	I.B.3. (Bhāṭṭas)
	pp. 94.7-100.11 (A, 151.4-159.8)	I.B.4. (Prābhākaras)

Summary Śloka	Extended Discussion	Pratijñā Series
Summary Śloka Siddhānta (2) *ananyasādhanaḥ*	pp. 100.12-150.2 (A, 160.1-222.4)	Pratijñās I.B.5.a-b. and I.A.6-7.
	pp. 100.12-102.4 (A, 160.1-161.8) explicit statement of Yāmuna's Siddhānta *ananyasādhanaḥ* on the issue of *pramāṇa* and a transition back to the main concern of the *svarūpa*.	I.B.5.a and I.A.7 in a preliminary transitional manner.
	pp. 102.5-110.3 (A, 162.1-171.8) criticism of Yāmuna's view of consciousness and its relation to the *ātmā*.	I.A.6. (Nyāya-Vaiśeṣikas and Neo-Mimamsakas)
	pp. 110.4-149.1 (A, 172.1-221.2) primary statement of Yāmuna's Siddhānta on the *svarūpa* of the individual *ātmā* and its relation to consciousness and cognition.	I.A.7. primarily, and I.B.5.a, secondarily.
	pp. 149.2-150.2 (A, 221.3-222.4) concluding more practically oriented summary of Yāmuna's Siddhānta.	I.B.5.b.

Summary Śloka	Extended Discussion	Pratijñā Series
Topic (3) The demonstration that the _ātmā_ is eternal (_nitya_).	pp. 150.3-151.6 (A, 222.5-224.3) the extant text breaks off shortly after presenting the first Pūrvapakṣa (I.D.1.).	I.D.
Topic (4) The demonstration that the _ātmā_ is pervasive (_vyāpī_).	no longer extant	I.C.
Topic (5) The demonstration that the _ātmā_ is different in each body (_pratiksetram. . . bhinnaḥ_).	no longer extant	I.E.
Topic (6) The demonstration that the _ātmā_ is innately blessed with "happiness" (_svataḥ suhkī_).	no longer extant	I.A.7.a-b.

APPENDIX III

Structure of the Pratijñā Series of the Ātma-Siddhi

The skeletal outline structural analysis presented below is a major interpretative key for decoding the Pratijñā Series and recovering the Siddhāntas of Yāmuna's Vedānta (see Chapters VI and VII).

tadyathā

I. ātma-viṣaye

A. tāvat

1. . . . kecid . . . ācakṣate,

2. . . . anye,

3. " . . . " ity anye,

4. . . . apare,

5. . . . itare,

6. . . . apare,

7. apare tu . . . imam abhidadhati/

a. anye tu . . .,

b. " . . . " ity anye/

B. tathā

"1. . . .,

"2. . . .,

"3. . . .,

"4. . . .,

"5.

a. . . .,

b. idrso 'py . . ."

iti/

C. tathā

"1. . . .,

"2. . . .,

"3. . . .,

"4. svataḥ parimāṇarahito 'pi . . ."

iti/

"a. vyaptir api . . .,

"b. . . .," iti/

I. D. tathā

"1. . . .,

"2. . . .,

"3. . . .,

"4. . . .,

"5. . . .,

"6. . . .,"

iti/

E.

"1. . . .,

"2. . . .,"

iti ca tathātathā pratipadyante

II. tathā paramātmaviṣaye 'pi

A.

1. kecit . . .,

2. . . . eke . . .,

3. apare tu . . . imam abhidadhati,

B. tathā

1. anye . . . ādriyante,

2. anupahitam api . . . apare pratipedire,

3. apariṇāminam api . . . itare rocayante,

4. anye tu . . . ātiṣṭhante

C. tathā tadviśeṣe 'pi

1. . . . vivadante,

2. mūrtiviśeṣaviṣayāś ca . . . -vitarkāḥ prādurbhavanti,

3. parijanasthānādigocarāśca

D. tathā pramāṇato 'pi

"1. . . ." -ity eke,

"2. . . . ca" -ity anye,

"3. . . . ca" -ity apare

III. tathā ātmaparamātmanoḥ saṃbandhe 'pi

"A. . . ." iti kecit,

"B. . . ." iti anye,

"C.

1. svatas tv . . . itare,

2. . . ." iti ca nānāvidhā vādāḥ

IV. tathā . . . brahmaprāptilakṣaṇamokṣe 'pi

"A. . . .,

"B. . . .,

"C. . . .,

"D. . . .,

"E. . . .,

"F. . . .,

"G. . . .,

"H. . . .,"

iti tathā tathā vivadante

V. tatsādhanato 'pi

"A. . . .,

"B. . . .,

"C. . . .,

"D. . . .,

"E. . . .,"

iti

APPENDIX IV

Concordance of the Editions of the Āgama-prāmāṇya

The following gives a concordance of my text of primary reference for the Āgama-prāmāṇya, The Pandit edition (AP), with the published version of the critical edition [AP(CE 1976)] by M. Narasimhachary and with the translation [AP(tr)] by J. A. B. van Buitenen. The references in the notes to AP(CE) are to the unpublished version of 1966 (see Chapter I, n. 34).

AP	AP(CE 1976)	AP(tr)
p. 1.1 ff	p. 1.1 ff	#1 ff
2.1	2.11	#4
3.1	4.15	#6
4.1	6.5	#8
5.1	7.12	#10
6.1	9.7	#11
7.1	11.2	#13
8.1	13.4	#15
9.1	15.3	#16
10.1	17.3	#16
11.1	19.6	#17
12.1	23.8	#19
13.1	25.6	#22
14.1	27.2	#23
15.1	28.9	#25
16.1	30.8	#27
17.1	33.1	#28
18.1	36.4	#30
19.1	38.7	#32
20.1	40.8	#35
21.1	42.3	#36
22.1	44.2	#39
23.1	46.4	#42
24.1	48.13	#43
25.1	50.12	#45

AP	AP(CE 1976)	AP(tr)
p. 26.1 ff	p. 53.1 ff	#47
27.1	55.14	#49
28.1	57.7	#49
29.1	58.12	#52
	Yamuna's Siddhānta	
p. 29.10 ff	p. 59.2 ff	#53 ff
30.1	60.4	#55
31.1	61.14	#57
32.1	63.7	#58
33.1	65.5	#60
34.1	67.3	#61
35.1	69.4	#63
36.1	72.1	#66
37.1	74.3	#68
38.1	76.14	#71
39.1	79.4	#73
40.1	80.9	#75
41.1	82.2	#77
42.1	84.1	#78
43.1	86.8	#79
44.1	87.14	#79
45.1	89.14	#81
46.1	91.7	#83
47.1	94.6	#83
48.1	97.1	#85
49.1	98.13	#86
50.1	100.7	#86
51.1	102.3	#89
52.1	104.6	#90
53.1	105.11	#92
54.1	107.9	#94
55.1	111.1	#95
56.1	113.10	#97
57.1	116.6	#98
58.1	118.2	#101
59.1	118.7	#101
60.1	120.9	#103
61.1	122.8	#107

AP	AP(CE 1976)	AP(tr)
p. 62.1 ff	p. 124.8 ff	#109
63.1	126.1	#112
64.1	127.13	#114
65.1	131.3	#115
66.1	132.11	#115
67.1	135.4	#116
68.1	137.3	#117
69.1	139.3	#118
70.1	141.8	#121
71.1	142.14	#122
72.1	144.5	#125
73.1	146.1	#125
74.1	147.11	#126
75.1	149.4	#127
76.1	151.3	#129
77.1	154.3	#131
78.1	156.3	#132
79.1	158.4	#134
80.1	160.6	#134
81.1	161.14	#135
82.1	163.8	#135
83.1	165.3	#135
84.1	167.3	#136
85.1	169.3	#138
86.1	170.8	#138
87.1	170.12	#139

NOTES

CHAPTER I

1. On the early Śrī Vaiṣṇava Ācāryas and Yāmuna's relation to Rāmānuja, see John B. Carman, *The Theology of Rāmānuja: An Essay in Interreligious Understanding* (New Haven: Yale Univ. Press, 1974), pp. 24-48 *passim*; J. A. B. van Buitenen, "On the Archaism of the *Bhāgavata Purāṇa*," in *Krishna: Myths, Rites and Attitudes*, ed., by Milton Singer (Honolulu: East-West Center Press, 1966), pp. 26-40; and his Introductions to his *Rāmānuja on the Bhagavadgītā* (R on BhG) ('S-Gravenhage: H. L. Smits, 1953), pp. 5-12; *Rāmānuja's Vedārthasaṃgraha* (VAS) (Poona: Deccan College, 1956), pp. 43-48; and *Yāmuna's Āgama Prāmāṇya* [AP(tr)] (Madras: Ramanuja Research Society, 1971), pp. 1-6; M. Narasimhachary, *Contribution of Yāmuna to Viśiṣṭādvaita* (Madras: Prof. M. Rangacharya Memorial Trust, 1971), pp. 1-11, 308-312; Surendranath Dasgupta, *A History of Indian Philosophy* (HIP) (Cambridge: University Press, 1961), Vol. III, pp. 94-164; R. Ramanujachari, "Nathamuni, His Life and Times," *Journal of the Annamalai University*, IX (1940), pp. 267-77; "Yāmunācārya," *Proceedings and Transactions of the All-India Oriental Conference*, First Session, 1955, pp. 397ff; Gerhard Oberhammer, *Yāmunamunis Interpretation von Brahmasūtram 2, 2, 42-45, Eine Untersuchung zur Pāñcarātra-Tradition der Rāmānuja-schule* (YIB) (Wien, 1971), pp. 5-8; Roque Mesquita, "Yāmunamuni: Leben, Datierung und Werke," *Weiner Zeitschrift für die Kunde Südasiens* (WZKS), XVII (1973), pp. 177-93; "Recent Research on Yāmuna," WZKS, XVIII (1974), pp. 183-208; A. Govindacharya, *The Life of Rāmānuja* (Madras: S. Murthy and Co., 1906); C. R. Srinivasa Aiyengar, *The Life and Teachings of Sri Ramanujacharya* (Madras: R. Venkateshwar and Co., n.d.); T. A. Gopinatha Rao, *Sir Subrahmanya Ayyar Lectures on the History of Śrī Vaiṣṇavas* (Madras: Univ. of Madras, 1923).

2. It is exceedingly difficult to document concretely and specifically the influence of the growing presence of Islam upon the development of the Śrī Vaiṣṇava sect since our sources are essentially silent on this matter. However, it is clear that Islam, with its egalitarian emphasis and its social and political cohesiveness and power, made increasingly substantial inroads among the Hindu populace and that its monotheistic piety exerted a long-term and pervasive general influence upon the development of Hindu theistic Bhakti religion. Thus, even when we cannot document the process precisely, the growing influence of Islam must be acknowledged as an overarching cultural and religious factor in the growing openness of such Vedic leaders as the Śrī Vaiṣṇava Brāhmans to popular theistic religious movements such as that of the Tamil Āḻvārs. With the Śrī Vaiṣṇavas we see the first instance of a Hindu sectarian pattern that, with its own more egalitarian emphasis, social cohesiveness and popularly oriented theistic devotional piety, could

compete with Islam on its own terms while remaining faithful to and in continuity with the ancient classical Sanskritic Vedic heritage of India. See Tara Chand, Influence of Islam on Indian Culture (Allahabad: Indian Press, 1954), pp. 29-48, 84-129; Ishtiaq Husain Qureshi, The Muslim Community of the Indo-Pakistan Subcontinent (610-1947) ('S-Gravenhage: Mouton, 1962), pp. 11-33.

3. On the Āḻvārs, see K. C. Varadachari, Āḻvārs of South India, Bhavan's Book University 143 (Bombay: Bharatiya Vidya Bhavan, 1966); A. Gōvindāchārya, The Holy Lives of the Āzhvārs or The Drāvida Saints (Mysore, 1902).

4. For the best theological interpretation of Viśiṣṭādvaita, see John B. Carman, The Theology of Rāmānuja.

5. The popular Bhakti of the Tamil hymns of the Āḻvārs still awaits an adequate interpreter.

6. "On the Archaism of the Bhāgavata Purāṇa," in Krishna: Myths, Rites and Attitudes, ed. by Milton Singer (Honolulu: East-West Center Press, 1966), p. 35. On M. N. Srinivas' theory of "Sanskritization," see his Religion and Society among the Coorgs of South India (London and New York: Oxford Univ. Press, 1952) and "A Note on Sanskritization and Westernization," in his Caste in Modern India and Other Essays (Bombay: Asia Pub. House, 1962), pp. 42-62. On the need to bring both textual and contextual studies to bear on this process, see Milton Singer, When A Great Tradition Modernizes (New York: Praeger, 1972), pp. 39-52.

7. "On the Archaism," pp. 33-40.

8. Ibid., pp. 34-35, n. 47.

9. See the Āgama-prāmāṇya (AP), p. 26.10-11 (CE, p. 158; tr, #48) (see n. 34 below), at which Yāmuna's Smārta opponents draw a hard and fast distinction between vaidika and tāntrika, concluding that Pañcarātra is excluded from the Vedic way because it is included within the Tāntric ("vaidikaṃ tāntrikaṃ ca--iti vibhāga-karaṇād api/ gamyate pañcaratrasya veda-bāhyatva-niścayaḥ//"). Yāmuna's task, therefore, in defending the Vedic orthodoxy of Pañcarātra is to overcome this absolute distinction and to integrate the two categories.

10. van Buitenen, "On the Archaism," n. 42, p. 217; Thomas J. Hopkins, The Hindu Religious Tradition (Encino: Dickenson, 1971), pp. 95-96, 112-17, 119-21.

11. Hopkins, The Hindu Religious Tradition, pp. 112-17, 126-30.

12. See Ch. II, n. 35.

13. H. Daniel Smith, "The 'Three Gems' of the Pāñcarātra Canon--a Critical Appraisal," in Ex Orbe Religionum, Studia Geo Widengren, ed. by C. J. Bleeker (Leiden: Brill, 1972), pp. 42-43. On the Pañcarātra Āgama(s) and the Pāñcarātra Tāntric tradition (see n. 22 below), see F. Otto Schrader, Introduction to the Pāñcarātra and the Ahirbudhnya Saṃhitā (Madras: Adyar Library, 1916); Jan Gonda, Viṣṇuism and Śivaism, A Comparison (London: Athlone Press, 1970), pp. 26, 49ff, 55-61, 93ff, passim; Mitsunori Matsubara, "The Early Pāñcarātra with Special Reference to the Ahirbudhnya Saṃhitā," (Unpublished Ph.D. dissertation, Harvard University, 1972); S. R. Bhatt, The Philosophy of Pancharatra (Advaitic Approach) (Madras: Ganesh & Co., 1968); D. L. De, "A Historical Survey of Pāncarātra Religion," (Unpublished Ph.D. thesis, Univ. of London, 1931); Sanjukta Gupta, "The Caturvyūha and the Viśākha-yūpa in Pāñcarātra,"

Adyar Library Bulletin (ALB), XXXV (1971), 189-204; Śrī Pāñcarātrarakṣā of Śrī Vedānta Deśika, ed. by M. Duraiswami Aiyangar and T. Venugopalacharya (Madras: Adyar Library, 1967); see also n. 18 below.

The study of the Pañcarātra Āgamas will reach a new plateau with the full publication and utilization of the following group effort initiated and directed by Prof. H. Daniel Smith and assisted by such Indian scholars as Dr. V. Raghavan, Dr. M. Narasimhachary and Dr. K. K. A. Venkatachari: H. Daniel Smith, A Descriptive Bibliography of the Printed Texts of the Pāñcarātrāgama, Gaekwad's Oriental Series (Baroda: Oriental Institute); Vol. I, containing a chapter by chapter description of the contents of the printed Āgamas, was published as No. 158 in 1975; Vol. II, an invaluable index of the contents along with an introduction by Dr. V. Raghavan, is still awaited.

14. Schrader, Introduction to the Pāñcarātra, pp. 22-23; Bhatt, Philosophy of Pancharatra, pp. 7-8.

15. See Chs. II and VIII especially.

16. Smith, "Three Gems," pp. 44-45; Schrader, Introduction to the Pāñcarātra, pp. 22-23.

17. Matsubara, "Early Pāñcarātra," pp. 41-43.

18. Schrader, Introduction to the Pāñcarātra, pp. 24-26; J. A. B. van Buitenen, "The Name 'Pancaratra'," History of Religions (HR) I (1962), 291-99; Introduction to Yāmuna's Āgama Prāmāṇya [AP(tr), see n. 34 below], pp. 6-16; V. Raghavan, "The Name Pāñcarātra: with an Analysis of the Sanatkumāra-Saṃhitā in Manuscript," Journal of the American Oriental Society (JAOS), Vol. 85 (1965), 73-79; Matsubara, "Early Pāñcarātra" (1972), pp. 3-11, 114ff; 142, n. 19; H. Daniel Smith, "A Typological Survey of Definitions: The Name 'Pāñcarātra'," Journal of Oriental Research (Madras) (JOR), XXIV-XXV (1973), 102-17.

19. "Early Pāñcarātra," pp. 5-11.

20. "The Name 'Pañcarātra'," pp. 291-96; Introduction to AP(tr), pp. 7-13.

21. "Early Pāñcarātra," p. 9.

22. In the Āgama-prāmāṇya, Yāmuna invariably uses the form "Pañcarātra" in referring in the singular or the plural to the Tantra(s), Āgama(s), etc. The only derivative he uses is "Pāñcarātrika" for those who follow the Pañcarātra Tantra. In addition to establishing the conventions of using "Pañcarātra" for the revelation or the scripture(s) and "Pāñcarātra" for the system or tradition, I will use "Pāñcarātrika" as a general adjective and "Pāñcarātrin" for the adherents.

23. See Schrader, Introduction to the Pāñcarātra, pp. 24-26; Smith, "Typological Survey," pp. 103ff.

24. Matsubara, "Early Pāñcarātra," pp. 15ff, 129, places the Nārāyaṇīya after the Bhagavad Gītā (which is a sacred basis for Pāñcarātra but can not be called Pāñcarātrika itself) and before the earliest Saṃhitas; therefore approximately in the second or third centuries C. E.

25. The Mahābhārata, critically edited by Vishnu S. Sukthankar and S. K. Belvalkar (Poona: Bhandarkar Oriental Research Institute, 1954), Vol. 16, p. 1864.

26. Ibid., pp. 1815-64.

27. Ibid., p. 1853; see also 12.326.28-31,
jagatpratiṣṭhā devarṣe pṛthivy apsu pralīyate/
jyotiṣy āpaḥ pralīyante jyotir vāyau pralīyate//

khe vāyuḥ pralayaṃ yāti manasy ākāśam eva ca/
mano hi paramaṃ bhūtaṃ tad avyakte pralīyate//
avyaktaṃ puruṣe brahmanniṣkriye saṃpralīyate/
nāsti tasmāt parataraṃ puruṣād vai sanātanāt//
nityaṃ hi nāsti jagati bhūtaṃ sthāvarajaṅgamam/
ṛte tam ekaṃ puruṣaṃ vāsudevaṃ sanātanam/
sarvabhūtātmabhūto hi vāsudevo mahābalaḥ//.

28. Ibid, 12.326.66, p. 1858,
eṣo hi vyaktim āgamya tiṣṭhāmi divi śāśvataḥ/
tato yugasahasrānte saṃhariṣye jagat punaḥ/
kṛtvātmasthāni bhūtāni sthāvarāṇi carāṇi ca//;
and 12.326.70cd-71ab, pp. 1858-59,
etāṃ sṛṣṭiṃ vijānīhi kalpādiṣu punaḥ punaḥ//
yathā sūryasya gaganād udayāstamayāv iha/.

29. Ibid., 12.326.62cd-63, p. 1858,
ahaṃ dattvā varān prīto nivṛtti-paramo 'bhavam//
nirvāṇaṃ sarvadharmāṇāṃ nivṛttiḥ paramā smṛtā/
tasmān nivṛttim āpannaś caret sarvāṅganirvṛttaḥ//.

30. Ibid., 12.326.64-65,
vidyāsahāyavantaṃ māṃ ādityasthaṃ sanātanam/
kapilaṃ prāhur ācāryāḥ sāṃkhya-niścitaniścayāḥ//
hiraṇyagarbho bhagavān eṣo chandasi suṣṭutaḥ/
so 'haṃ yoga-gatir brahman yogaśāstreṣu śabditaḥ//
When these verses are related to the phrases "mahopaniṣadaṃ caturvedasamanvitam sāṃkhyayogakṛtaṃ" that precede "pañcarātra-anuśabditam" in 12.326.100, then it becomes clear beyond doubt that the name "pañcarātra" is derived from the content of this passage, i.e., 12.326.62-71, and that the word rātra or "night" in the name is to be taken as a symbolic image for pralaya or nirvāṇa (see nn. 27-28 above).

31. Ibid., 12.326.74,
ekākī vidyayā sārdhaṃ vihariṣye dvijottama/
tato bhūyo jagatsarvaṃ kariṣyāmīha vidyayā//

32. As H. Daniel Smith, "A Typological Survey," p. 116, points out, while Pāñcarātrika sectarian interpretations have been etymologically untenable, outsiders' etymological interpretations have usually been "quite beside the point" since they have had "little or nothing to do with the way the term is understood and used today by Pāñcarātrins." My suggestion may be able to satisfy both groups.

33. See Ch. II, nn. 47-50, and Ch. IV, n. 6.

34. My primary reference for the Āgama-prāmāṇya will be to the Āgamaprāmāṇyam (AP) by Śrī Yāmunāchārya Swāmin, edited by Rāma Miśra Śāstrī (Varanasi: The Pandit, 1900 [reprinted 1937]). However, parallel references will also be made to the two following works that, through the generosity of their authors, I was able to utilize in manuscript form prior to their publication and that have been essential aids to my understanding of this text:

(1) The Āgamaprāmāṇya of Śrī Yāmunāchārya [AP(CE)], critically edited by M. Narasimhachary, unpublished manuscript presented to the Univ. of Madras as partial fulfillment of requirements for the Ph. D. in Sanskrit, 1966. This critical edition has since been published as Āgamaprāmāṇya of Yāmunācārya [AP(CE 1976)], Gaekwad's Oriental Series, No. 160 (Baroda: Oriental Institute, 1976). Unfortunately, the references to AP(CE) generally in this work are to the unpublished version since I did not receive the published edition in time for the

preparation of the notes. However, I have prepared as Appendix IV a concordance of my text of primary reference (AP) with AP (CE 1976) and with the following work, AP(tr).

(2) Yāmuna's Āgama Prāmāṇyam [AP(tr)], Sanskrit Text and English Translation by J. A. B. van Buitenen (Madras: Ramanuja Research Society, 1971). Reference to this work is by paragraph number (except for the Introduction, which is by page number) and generally primarily to the translation, since the Sanskrit text is based upon The Pandit edition (AP) and occasionally its division into paragraphs does not conform to that of the translation.

35. My primary reference for the Ātma-siddhi (AtS) will be to the Siddhitraya by Yāmunācārya (ST), edited with English translation and notes by R. Ramanujachari and K. Srinivasacharya, Annamalai University Philosophy Series, No. 4 (Annamalainagar, 1943); this edition, which is the closest we have to a critical edition, has recently been reissued with a new introduction by Prof. Ramanujachari as Sri Yamunacharya's Siddhi Trayam, with an Introduction in English by R. Ramanujachari and Translation in English by R. Ramanujachari and K. Srinivasacharya (ca. 1972) [to be referred to as AtS(2), ST(2), etc.]. A slightly revised version of the English translation together with the new introduction has also been published as the second part of Sri Yamunacharya's Siddhi Trayam with a Sanskrit Commentary (Gooda Prakasa), by Sri U. Ve. Abhinava Desika Uttamur T. Viraraghavacharya, with an Introduction in English by R. Ramanujachari and Translation in English by R. Ramanujachari and K. Srinivasacharya, (Madras: Ubhaya Vedanta Granthamala Book Trust, 1972) [to be referred to as AtS(1972), ST(1972), GPrak(1972)]. I will also give parallel references in parentheses to another frequently cited edition, the Siddhi-trayam, edited with the commentary Siddhāñjana-Vyākhyā by P. B. Annaṅgarācārya, (Bombay: Nirnaya Sagar Press, 1954) [to be referred to as AtS(A), ST(A), SVy]. Occasional references will also be made to the following very helpful edition and brief commentary: the Siddhitrayam, edited with the commentary Gūḍha-prakāśa by Uttamūr T. Vīrarāghavācārya, (Tirupati: Śrīvāṇī Press, 1942) [to be referred to as AtS(V), ST(V), GPrak]; a revised edition of this work has been issued in 1972 (see this note above) and will be referred to as AtS(1972), ST(1972) and GPrak(1972).

36. Yāmuna's other extant works will be drawn upon on occasion. His other, very fragmentarily preserved systematic works are the Īśvara-siddhi (IśS) and the Saṃvit-siddhi (SS) which are included with the AtS in the Siddhi-traya (see n. 35 above). Three other brief but significant works have been totally preserved. The Gītārthasaṃgraha (GAS) is a thirty-two verse summary of the Bhagavad Gītā that provides the basic structure for Rāmānuja's commentary on this sacred text (see van Buitenen, Introduction to R on BhG, pp. 5-12). Yāmuna's two devotional hymns, the Stotra-ratna (SR) and the Catuś-ślokī (CŚl) or Śrī-stuti, have actually had the greatest continuing influence within the Śrī Vaiṣṇava tradition and are important both for a picture of his piety and for his relation to the Āḻvārs' hymns (see Appendix I).

37. On śiṣṭās and śiṣṭācāra, see van Buitenen, "On the Archaism," p. 37 and n. 48; and Ch. III, n. 30 below.

38. See Ch. V, nn. 77-78.

39. Satyavrata Singh, *Vedānta Deśika: His Life, Works and Philosophy* (Varanasi, 1958).
40. See Ch. V, n. 23.
41. Carman, *The Theology of Rāmānuja*, pp. 16-17, 24-48.
42. *Ibid.*, pp. 16-17, 34-35, 41-42.
43. Introduction to AP(tr), pp. 5-6.
44. See Ch. II, especially n. 34.
45. T. A. Gopinātha Rao, *Sir Subrahmanya Ayyar Lectures*, p. 31.
46. *Ibid.*
47. *Ibid.*, pp. 29-30.
48. For a convincing argument that Rāmānuja probably lived until at least 1156 A.D., see T. N. Subramaniam, "A Note on the Date of Ramanuja," in *South Indian Temple Inscriptions*, Vol. III, Pt. 2, Madras Government Oriental Series, No. 157 (Madras, 1957), pp. 147-160.
49. See *Karandi Plates of Rājendra Coḷa*, eighth year [ca. 1020 A.D.], v. 19. I owe this reference to the kindness of Dr. K. G. Krishnan of the Government Epigraphist Office, Mysore, who granted me access to his unpublished edition of the copper-plate inscription.
50. K. A. Nilakanta Sastri, *The Coḷas* (Madras: Univ. of Madras, 1955), pp. 12-13, 677-78.
51. *Ibid.*, pp. 204-10,227, 234-35.
52. R. Ramanujachari, "Yamunacharya," *Proceedings and Transactions of the All-India Oriental Conference*, 1955, p. 397. See Ch. V, nn. 31-38.
53. John B. Carman, *The Theology of Rāmānuja*, pp. 29-30; A. Govindacharya, *The Life of Rāmānujāchārya*, pp. 45-57; C. R. Srinivasa Aiyengar, *The Life and Teachings of Sri Ramanujacharya*, pp. 42-43, 65-81.
54. Carman, *The Theology of Rāmānuja*, p. 30.

NOTES

CHAPTER II

1. For Yāmuna's statement of the major figures in his Vedāntic milieu, see AtS, p. 8.4-8 (A, pp. 15.4-17.2).

2. See Ch. III for this polemic.

3. J. A. B. van Buitenen, "On the Archaism of the Bhāgavata Purāṇa," pp. 29-34; Introduction to AP (tr), pp. 1-6.

4. V. S. Ghate, The Vedānta (Poona: Bhandarkar Oriental Research Institute, 1960), pp. 80-82; S. Radhakrishnan, The Brahma Sūtra (London: George Allen & Unwin Ltd., 1960), pp. 393-96.

5. Introduction to AP (tr), pp. 16-22. While this commentatorial tradition is not unanimous since the later (ca. 13th century) commentators Nimbārka and Madhva maintain that Bādarāyaṇa is here rejecting the Śākta Tantra, not Pāñcarātra (see Ghate, The Vedānta, pp. 80-82), the agreement of Śaṅkara, Bhāskara, Yāmuna and Rāmānuja that Pāñcarātra is at issue here shows that Nimbārka's and Madhva's interpretation is a late tactical development meant to remove any lingering suspicion about Pāñcarātra's orthodoxy. B. N. K. Sharma's championing of Madhva on this point is not convincing in light of the unanimity of the earlier traditions (The Brahmasūtras and their Principal Commentaries [Bombay: Bharatiya Vidya Bhavan, 1974], Vol. II, pp. x-xi, 104ff.).

6. Śaṅkara, The Brahma-Sūtra-Śāṅkara-Bhāṣyam [hereafter BSBh(K)], The Kāśī Sanskrit Series, No. 71 (Benares: The Chowkhamba Sanskrit Series Office, 1929), Vol. I, pp. 572-76; Bhāskara, Brahmasūtra-Bhāṣyam (hereafter BBh), The Chowkhamba Sanskrit Series, No. 20 (Benares, 1915), pp. 128-29. As D. H. H. Ingalls notes [PhilEW, XVII (1967), 61], the Chowkhamba edition of Bhāskara's BBh is rife with errors and J. A. B. van Buitenen is preparing a critical edition to appear in the Harvard Oriental Series. Through Prof. van Buitenen's generosity, I have had early access to his translation and critical emendations of Bhāskara's commentary on the UA Adhik. in his Introduction to AP(tr), pp. 26-28 and notes thereon.

7. On the general significance of agreement and disagreement between Śaṅkara and Bhāskara, see D. H. H. Ingalls, "The Study of Śaṁkarācārya," Annals of the Bhandarkar Oriental Research Institute (hereafter ABORI), XXXIII (1952), 9-10. On the significance for this specific problem and a response to Ingalls' theory, see van Buitenen, Introduction to AP(tr), pp. 17-18.

8. Yāmunamunis Interpretation von Brahmasūtram 2, 2, 42-45 (hereafter YIB), Eine Untersuchung zur Pāñcarātra-Tradition Der Rāmānuja-Schule (Wien: Hermann Böhlaus Nachf., 1971).

9. Ibid., p. 114.

10. Ibid., pp. 41-100. See Ch. IV.A below for further discussion of Oberhammer's analysis and these sources.

11. While Oberhammer at several points notes the conditional nature of Śaṅkara's refutation--i.e., that only certain parts, not the whole system, are to be rejected--the course of his argument leads him to see Śaṅkara's conditions as being derived from another source and of merely theoretical significance to Śaṅkara's own position and therefore to exaggerate the negativity of Śaṅkara's attitude toward Pāñcarātra; see YIB, pp. 19-20; 104-105, n. 253; p. 116.

12. "Relations of Early Advaitins to Vaiṣṇavism," Wiener Zeitschrift für die Kunde Süd- und Ostasiens (hereafter WZKSO), IX (1965), pp. 151-52.

13. Jan Gonda, Viṣṇuism and Śivaism: A Comparison, Jordan Lectures, 1969 (London: The Athlone Press, 1969), pp. 48-61. For other references on the Vyūha theory, see n. 17 below.

14. BSBh(K) II.ii.42, Vol. I, p. 573.9-12, tatra yat tāvad ucyate -- yo 'sau nārāyaṇaḥ paro 'vyaktāt prasiddhaḥ paramātmā sarvātmā sa ātmanā--ātmānam anekadhā vyūha-avasthita iti, tan na nirākriyate, 'sa ekadhā bhavati tridhā bhavati' (Chām. 7/26/2) ity ādi-śrutibyaḥ paramātmano 'nekadhā bhāvasyādhigatatvāt.

15. Ibid., II.ii.44, Vol. I, p. 575.14, . . . brahmādi-stambaparyantasya samastasyaiva jagato bhagavad-vyūhatva-avagamāt.

16. For a full discussion of Śaṅkara's comments on the Vyūha theory, see Ch. VIII.

17. BSBh(K) II.ii.44, Vol. I, p. 574.13; and II.ii.45, Vol. I, p. 575.17. On the Vyūha theory and the "Six Qualities," see F. Otto Schrader, Introduction to the Pāñcarātra and the Ahirbudhnya Saṃhitā (Madras: Adyar Library, 1916), pp. 29-42, 50-53, 143-45, passim; J. Gonda, Viṣṇuism and Śivaism, pp. 48-61; Mitsunori Matsubara, "The Early Pāñcarātra with Special Reference to the Ahirbudhnya Saṃhitā" (unpublished Ph. D. dissertation, Harvard Univ., 1972), pp. 18, 25, 39ff, 66, 73, 107-114, passim; S. R. Bhatt, The Philosophy of Pancharatra (Advaitic Approach) (Madras: Ganesh & Co., 1968), pp. 28, 35, 59-63; John B. Carman, The Theology of Rāmānuja, pp. 62, 92, 162-63; and Ch. VIII below.

18. Bhagavad-Gītā with the Commentary of Śrī Śaṅkarācārya (hereafter BhGBh), ed. by Dinkar Vishnu Gokhale (Poona: Oriental Book Agency, 1950), p. 2.5.

19. Śaṅkara, the Vedāntin, would probably have argued that his primary source for the above phrase was the acceptably Vedic smṛti, the Viṣṇu Purāṇa, in which, at 6.5.79, the term Bhagavān is defined in terms of these six qualities. However, in the Viṣṇu Purāṇa they are not given in the characteristically Pāñcarātrika sequence. While the slight variation in sequence may merely be caused by metrical requirements, nevertheless, Śaṅkara must have had some source other than the Viṣṇu Purāṇa for the sequence he used, perhaps some Pañcarātra Āgama or perhaps simply Vedāntic commentatorial tradition on the UA Adhik. Regardless of Śaṅkara's source, my main point--based merely on his own usage of the six guṇas--is that Śaṅkara did not consider the Pāñcarātrika overtones to be damning but rather was able to accept and utilize this characterisically Pāñcarātrika phrasing.

20. Introduction to AP(tr), p. 22. I am assuming that "last sutras" is a misprint for "last sūtra" since only in II.ii.45 is the charge of veda-vipratiṣedha made.

21. Śaṅkara, BSBh(K) II.ii.45, Vol. I, pp. 575.15-576.1. The Chowkhamba edition of Bhāskara's BBh lacks this sūtra, but van Buitenen's critical edition (see n. 6 above) has recovered it; see Introduction to AP(tr), p. 41, n. 42, "read tathāpy utpattyasaṃbhavaḥ pratipāditaḥ/ VIPRATIṢEDHĀC CA/ for tathāpy utpattyasaṃbhavaḥ/ pratipāditavipratiṣedhāc ca, and thus restore the submerged sūtra."

22. Oberhammer, YIB, p. 20.

23. S. K. Belvalkar, ed. and trans., The Brahma-sūtras of Bādarāyaṇa, with the Comment of Śaṅkarāchārya (hereafter BSBCŚ) (Poona: Bilvakunja Publishing House, 1931), notes, p. 206; emphasis and translations in brackets are my own.

24. Śaṅkara, BSBh(K) II.ii.45, Vol.I, pp. 575.18-576.1, veda-vipratiṣedhaś ca bhavati, caturṣu vedeṣu paraṃ śreyo 'labdhvā śāṇḍilya idaṃ śāstram adhigatavān ity-ādi-veda-nindā-darśanāt. As van Buitenen notes [Introduction to AP(tr), p. 41, n. 43], all MSS of Bhāskara's BBh have the idiosyncratic reading " . . . idaṃ śāstram śāṇḍilyaś cakāra . . .," which is puzzling since according to Pāñcarātra Vāsudeva himself "composed this śāstra."

25. AP, p. 56.18-20 (CE, pp. 235-36; tr, #98), yat paraṃ vipratiṣedhāt iti caturṣu vedeṣu iti śruti-vipratiṣedhāt tantrāṇāṃ parasparavipratiṣadhād vā apramāṇam iti/ tatra śruti-vipratiṣedhas tu prāg eva pratyuktaḥ.

26. AP, p. 10.6-11 (CE, pp. 111-12; tr, #17).

27. Ibid., pp. 51.15-52.16 (CE, pp. 218-21; tr, ##90-91).

28. BSBh(K) II.ii.37, Vol. I, pp. 566.11-567.4. See specifically on Sāṅkhya-Yoga, II.ii.10 (vipratiṣedhāc cāsmañjasam), also I.i.5, I.i.18, I.iv.28; on Vaiśesika, II.ii.17 (aparigrahāc cātyantam anapekṣā); on Śaivas, II.ii.37-38.

29. Bhāskara, BBh, p. 128.15-16, vāsudeva eva--upādāna-kāraṇaṃ jagato nimitta-kāraṇaṃ ceti te manyante. Cf. Śaṅkara, BSBh(K) II.ii.42, Vol. I, p. 572.14-19. See also Ghate, The Vedānta, p. 80, "Śaṅkara commences by remarking that the Bhāgavata doctrine deserves our acceptance, so far as it holds that Īśvara is both the efficient and material cause of the Universe."

30. The Vedānta, p. 82. Indeed, if one accepts that the doctrine of Brahman's being both nimitta- and upādāna-kāraṇa is the single most important distinguishing or defining characteristic of Vedānta--as it often seems to be in the context of the VS in which a major concern is with showing that neither the Sāṅkhya pradhāna nor any other insentient entity can be the material cause (see VS I.iv, especially sūtras 23-27; II.ii.1-17, 34-41; etc.)--then one would almost seem justified in asserting that Pāñcarātra is here being treated as if it were a parochial or sectarian (eka-deśa) form of Vedānta. While I doubt that either Śaṅkara or Bhāskara would have agreed with the assertion, I do feel that their treatment of Pāñcarātra would have afforded Pāñcarātrins a firm basis for claiming the status of eka-deśin Vedāntins vis-à-vis Śaṅkara and Bhāskara.

31. Oberhammer, YIB, p. 120.

32. Ibid., pp. 71-100. See Ch. IV.A below.

33. Ibid., pp. 95-100.

34. See Nakamura Hajime, "Upaniṣadic Tradition and the Early School of Vedānta as Noticed in Buddhist Scripture." Harvard Journal of Asiatic Studies (HJAS), XVIII (1955), 103, "The term vedāntavāda appears for the first time in the works of

Bhavya (c. 490-570), an eminent philosopher of the Mādhyamika school. . . . Here Vedānta as a school is clearly criticized in the gross for the first time . . . . there is no doubt that the school of Vedānta became influential in the fifth century A.D." See also his "The Vedānta as Noticed in Mediaeval Jain Literature," Indological Studies in Honor of W. Norman Brown, American Oriental Series (AOS), #47, 1962, pp. 188, 193-94; and V. V. Gokhale, "The Vedānta-Philosophy Described by Bhavya in His Madhyamakahṛdaya," Indo-Iranian Journal (IIJ), II (1958), 165-80.

35. Jan Gonda, Die Religionen Indiens, II. pp. 26-52. M. Matsubara, "Early Pāñcarātra," pp. 15-35, places the earliest extant Pañcarātra Saṃhitās (Pauṣkara, Jayākhya and Sāttvata) in the fifth century, A.D.

36. Van Buitenen, Introduction to VAS, pp. 19-23; S. K. Belvalkar, "Jaimini's Sārīraka-Sūtra," Aus Indiens Kultur, Festgabe Richard von Garbe, ed. by J. von Negelein (Erlangen, 1927), pp. 165-70.

37. Louis Renou, The Destiny of the Veda in India (Delhi: Motilal Banarsidass, 1965), ##3-5, pp. 4-7; ##36-39, pp. 35-40. Thomas J. Hopkins, The Hindu Religious Tradition (Encino: Dickenson Publishing Co., 1971), pp. 108-30.

38. See for example the distinction Śaṅkara draws between pravṛtti-lakṣaṇam dharmaṃ and nivṛtti-lakṣaṇam dharmaṃ, BhGBh, Introduction (pp. 1-3) and II.10 (pp. 10-14). See also Ghate, The Vedānta, pp. 21-24; Paul Deussen, The System of Vedānta (New York: Dover Publications, 1973), pp. 401-17.

39. Gonda, Die Religionen Indiens, II, pp. 28-30; P. C. Bagchi, "Evolution of the Tantras," The Cultural Heritage of India, ed. by H. Bhattacharyya (Calcutta: The Ramakrishna Mission, Second ed., 1956), Vol. IV, 211-14; Renou, Destiny of the Veda, #5, pp. 6-7.

40. Gonda, Die Religionen Indiens, II, pp. 27, 35-42, 120-21, 196-97; Renou, Destiny of Veda, #3, pp. 4-5; Hopkins, The Hindu Religious Tradition, pp. 95-99, 112-18, 126-30.

41. Yāmuna, in refuting the charge of "scorn for the Vedas" (veda-nindā), cites as an example of the manifold "praise for the Vedas" (veda-praśaṃśā) found in Pañcarātra the statement "vedāntair idam evoktaṃ tattva-jñānopapādakaiḥ" [AP, p. 52.8-9 (CE, p. 221; tr, #90)]. He frequently refers to Pañcarātra by such phrases as vedānta-sāra-sarva-svam [AP, p. 54.13-14 (CE, p. 227; tr, #94); see also pp. 51.10-11 (CE, p. 218; tr, #89), 53.20-21 (CE, p. 224; tr, #94); etc.]. This special relationship between Pañcarātra and the jñāna-kāṇḍa of the Vedas should not, however, be taken to indicate hostility toward and rejection of all aspects of the karma-kāṇḍa, for the Pāñcarātrins were anxious to establish positive links with the Vedas at every point at which they could consistently do so. As has often been noted, Pāñcarātrika doctrine has at several points developed positive relations with the Saṃhitā and Brāhmaṇa portions of the karma-kāṇḍa, e.g., the Puruṣa-sūkta of RV X.90 and the Pañcarātra-sattra of ŚBrāh XIII.6.1 (see Schrader, Introduction to Pāñcarātra, pp. 25-26, 143-45; Gonda, Viṣṇuism and Śivaism, pp. 57-58; Matsubara, "Early Pāñcarātra," pp. 90, 107-108; Sanjukta Gupta, "The Caturvyūha and the Viśākha-yūpa in the Pāñcarātra," Adyar Library Bulletin (ALB), XXXV [1971], 189-204). See also S. L. De, "Pāñcarātra and the Upaniṣads," Indian Historical Quarterly, IX (1933), pp. 645-62. For some

brief comments on the relation of Pāñcarātrika doctrine to the Vedānta darśana, see Matsubara, "Early Pāñcarātra," pp. 39-43, who argues for the consistency of the Jñāna sections of the early Saṃhitās with later Viśiṣṭādvaita Vedānta and for the hypothesis that the Jñāna sections were lost or became less significant because Śrī Vaiṣṇava Vedāntins took over the doctrinal aspect of Pāñcarātra. Matsubara's argument is much stronger historically than that of Bhatt, The Philosophy of Pancharatra, p. vii, passim, who maintains that the dominant trend of Pāñcarātrika thought is in line with Śaṅkara's Kevalādvaita rather than Viśiṣṭādvaita.

42. Jayanta Bhaṭṭa (fl. ca. 900 C.E.), a cosmopolitan and open-minded Brāhmaṇa, dramatizes the difference of attitude between these two types of Brāhmans in his play, Āgama-ḍambara (The Clash of the Āgamas). In the opening dialogue of the fourth act (in which Pāñcarātra is defended against its critics), Jayanta satirizes a ritualist (Ṛtvik) who complains to a teacher (Upādhyāya) that his livelihood (vṛtti) from performing Vedic rituals is being threatened by those Pāñcarātrins who perform Tāntric temple ritual. The teacher, with whom Jayanta obviously identifies himself, is unthreatened by the Pāñcarātrins and tries to convince the anxious ritualist to adopt a live-and-let-live attitude. See The Āgama-ḍambara, otherwise called Ṣaṇmatanāṭaka of Jayanta Bhaṭṭa, ed. by V. Raghavan and Anantalāl Thakur, Mithila Institute Series, Ancient Text No. 7 (Darbhanga: Mithila Institute, 1964 [actually appeared in 1969]), pp. 74-76. (I am grateful to Dr. Raghavan for allowing me to read the page proofs of the Āgama-ḍambara with him before its publication.) See also AP, pp. 77.10-78.3 (CE, pp. 285-88; tr, #132), where Yāmuna, in a less satirical vein, makes the point that a Bhāgavata Brāhmaṇa who performs pūjā for his livelihood (vṛtty-artham) is no different from a Vedic priest who performs the Jyotiṣṭoma for a "gift" (dakṣiṇā).

43. See all commentators ad VS I.i.1, athāto brahma-jijñāsā. See also Ghate, The Vedānta, p. 53, "All [commentators] agree in the explanation of the word 'therefore' (ataḥ), i.e., 'for the reason that karman and its fruits are known to be perishable and limited and that it is the knowledge of Brahman alone which can lead to eternal bliss.'"

44. BSBCŚ, notes, p. 205; cf. VS II.ii.10, "vipratiṣedhāc cāsamañjasam;" II.ii.17, "aparigrahāc cātyantam anapekṣā;" and II.ii.32, "sarvathānupapatteśca."

45. On the principle of Vikalpa or "Option," see Ganganatha Jha, Pūrva-Mīmāṃsā in its Sources (hereafter PM Sources), (Varanasi: Banaras Hindu Univ. Press, second ed., 1964), pp. 311-15. See also AP, pp. 85.1-86.1 (CE, pp. 302-304; tr, #138), and Ch. III, n. 24.

46. See AP, p. 85.14-15 (CE, pp. 303-304; tr, #138), where Yāmuna calls the Vedic karma "svarga-putrādi-viṣaya-upabhoga-sādhana-," and p. 45.20-21 (CE, p. 203; tr, #82), where he disparages "the sensuous happiness" (vaiṣayika-sukha) of such goals as heaven and sons, which are always mixed with suffering (duḥkha).

47. AP, p. 52.15-16 (CE, p. 221; tr, #91).

48. Ibid., p. 45.20-25 (CE, p. 203; tr, #82).

49. ĀtS, p. 7.1 (A, p. 13.5); see Ch. VII, Pratijñā Ser. IV.

50. AP, p. 85.15-17 (CE, p. 304; tr, #138).

51. "On the Archaism," p. 30.

NOTES

CHAPTER III

1. AP, p. 87.1-8 (CE, p. 304; tr, #139); see Appendix I for the text and translation of these verses. See also Ch. V for further analysis of the significance of these verses.

2. AP, p. 87.1-2 (CE, p. 304, tr, #139). See J. A. B. van Buitenen, "On the Archaism," n. 25, p. 216, on Sātvata as a name for Kṛṣṇa, Krishnaite Bhāgavatas, and Pāñcarātrins.

3. "On the Archaism," pp. 26ff.

4. AP, pp. 7.3-10.3 (CE, pp. 102-111; tr, ##14-16). On the Vaiśya-vrātyas, see Narasimhachary, Contribution, pp. 134-35, n. 540; van Buitenen, "On the Archaism," pp. 27-29.

5. AP, p. 75.4-21 (CE, pp. 278-80; tr, #128).

6. AP, p. 75.14-18 (CE, p. 280; tr, #129).

7. AP, pp. 75.22-76.6 (CE, pp. 280-81; tr, #129). On the Pāñcakālikā daily ritual, which Yāmuna here treats as the defining characteristic of Pāñcarātra as a distinct tradition or sect, see K. Rangachari, The Sri Vaishnava Brahmans, (Madras, 1931), pp. 48-98. For references to these rituals in the Pañcarātra Āgamas, see H. Daniel Smith, A Descriptive Bibliography of the Printed Texts of the Pāñcarātrāgama, Vol. II, Index, s.v., pañcakāla (forthcoming in Gaekwad's Oriental Series; Vol. I appeared in 1975 as No. 158).

8. On the arcakas as a distinct class of Śrī Vaiṣṇava Brāhman, see K. Rangachari, The Sri Vaishnava Brahmans, pp. 99-101; N. Jagadeesan, "History of Śrī Vaishnavism," p. 411. On different classes of temple priests in general, see K. A. Nilakanta Sastri, Development of Religion in South India, pp. 112-16.

9. AP, pp. 8.18-10.3 (CE, pp. 107-11; tr, #16). See van Buitenen, "On the Archaism," pp. 27ff, especially n. 32, on the Devalakas or "godlingers."

10. AP, pp. 8.27-9.3 (CE, pp. 107-108; tr, #16),
tathā ca parama-saṃhitāyāṃ teṣām eva vacaḥ/
āpadyapi ca kaṣṭāyāṃ bhīto vā durgato 'pi vā/
pūjayennaiva vṛttyartham devadevaṃ kadācana// iti.
See Parama Saṃhitā, Gaekwad's Oriental Series, No. LXXXVI (Baroda, 1940), Ch. 28, vv. 33cd-34ab, pp. 182-83; see also 30.7, p. 191.

11. AP, p. 77.12-13 (CE, p. 285; tr, #132).

12. AP, pp. 77.14-78.3 (CE, pp. 285-288; tr, #132); see Ch. II, n. 42.

13. AP, p. 78.4-26 (CE, pp. 288-89; tr, #133).

14. AP, pp. 85.1-86.1 (CE, pp. 302-303; tr, #138); see n. 24 below.

15. AP, pp. 8.18-10.3 (CE, pp. 107-111; tr, #16).

16. AP, pp. 4.16-5.21 (CE, pp. 95-98; tr, #10); 50.19-51.14 (CE, pp. 216-18; tr, #89).

17. See Ch. II, n. 45.

18. AP, p. 50.24-25 (CE, p. 217; tr, #89).
19. G. Jha, PM Sources, Ch. XXI, pp. 187-224.
20. Van Buitenen, AP(tr), #12, note 18 on p. 124.
21. AP, p. 5.9-10 (CE, p. 97; tr, #10).
22. AP, pp. 5.11-6.9 (CE, pp. 97-99; tr, ##10-11).
23. Cf. AP, p. 45.20-21 (CE, p. 203, tr, #82), svarga-putrādi-vaiṣayika-sukham.
24. AP, pp. 85.1-86.1 (CE, pp. 302-304; tr, #138), yad apy uktaṃ garbhādhāna-ādi-dāha-anta-saṃskāra-antara-sevanād bhāgavatānām a-brāhmaṇyam iti tatrāpy ajñānam eva--aparādhyati, na punar āyuṣmato doṣaḥ, yad ete vaṃśa-paramparayā vājasaneya-śakhām adhīyānāḥ kātyāyanādi-gṛhyokta-mārgeṇa garbhādhānādi-saṃskārān kurvate/ ye punaḥ sāvitry-anuvacana-prabhṛti-trayī-dharma-tyāgena ekāyana-śruti-vihitān eva cattvāriṃśat saṃskārān kurvate, te 'pi sva-śākhā-gṛhyoktam arthaṃ yathāvad anutiṣṭhamānāḥ na śākhā-antarīya-karma-ananuṣṭhānād brāhmaṇyāt pracyavante, anyeṣām api para-śākhā-vihita-karma-ananuṣṭhāna-nimitta-abrāhmaṇya-prasaṅgāt/ sarvatra hi jāti-caraṇa-gotra-adhikārādi-vyavasthitā eva samācārā upalabhyante/ yady api "sarva-śākhā-pratyayam ekaṃ karma", tathā 'pi na paraspara-vilakṣaṇa-adhikāri-sambaddhā dharmāḥ kvacit samuccīyante/

vilakṣaṇāś ca trayī-vihita-svarga-putrādi-viṣaya-upabhoga-sādhana-aindra-āgneyādi-karma-adhikāribhyo dvijebhyas trayy-anta-ekāyana-śruti-vihita-vijñāna-abhigamana-upādāna-ijyā-prabhṛti-bhagavat-prāpty-eka-upāya-karma-adhikāriṇo mumukṣavo brāhmaṇā, iti na--ubhayeṣām apy anyonya-śākhā-vihita-karma-ananuṣṭhānam abrāhmaṇyam āpādayati/ yathā ca--ekāyana-śākhāyā a-pauruṣeyatvaṃ tathā kāśmīra-āgama-prāmāṇya eva prapañcitam iti na--iha prastūyate.

On the Ekāyana-śākhā or śruti and the Kāśmīra-āgama-prāmāṇya, see Narasimhachary, Contribution, pp. 2-3, 12-13, 136-137. While noting that the authorship of the Kāśmīra-āgama-prāmāṇya is open to doubt, Narasimhachary accepts this as another lost work of Yāmuna (Contribution, pp. 2-3, 12-13) because it is mentioned in a similar manner to that of the Puruṣa-nirṇaya (see n. 105 below). However, the latter work is traditionally ascribed to Yāmuna while the former is not; and as R. Ramanujachari has shown [Introduction to ST(1972), pp. 7-8], the form of reference is also similar to that used for many works not Yāmuna's own. Therefore, I tend to view Yāmuna's reference as being to the work of some previous authority. See Ch. V, n. 79, on the significance of the North Indian associations suggested by this reference.

25. See Ch. II, nn. 47-50, and Ch. VII, Pratijñā Series IV.
26. AP, pp. 69.3-10 (CE, pp. 265-66; tr, #119) and 86.1-3 (CE, p. 304; tr, #138).
27. AP, p. 86.1-3 (CE, p. 304; tr, #138), prakṛtānāṃ tu bhāgavatānāṃ sāvitry-anuvacanādi-trayī-dharma-saṃbandhasya sphuṭataram upalabdher na tat-tyāga-nimitta-vrāttyatvādi-saṃdehaṃ sahata iti.
28. AP, p. 87.1-8 (CE, p. 304; tr, #139). See Ch. V on Nāthamuni's śiṣṭa family of Bhāgavatas, the coṭṭai kulam.
29. AP, p. 6.10-23 (CE, pp. 100f; tr, #12).
30. Jha, PM Sources, pp. 208-211; P. V. Kane, History of Dharmaśāstra, Vol. III, Ch. XXXII, pp. 825ff.
31. AP, p. 69.3-10 (CE, pp. 265-66; tr, #119), uktaś ca vaidika-samasta-āstika-pravara-bhṛgu-bharadvāja-dvaipāyana-prabhṛti-maharṣi-jana-parigrahaḥ/ adyatve 'pi hi pañcarātra-

tantra-vihita-mārgeṇa prāsādakaraṇa-pratimāpratiṣṭhāpana-praṇāma-pradakṣiṇa-utsava-ādīni pratyakṣa-śruti-vihita-agnihotrādivat śreyas-karatara-buddhyā--anutiṣṭhataḥ śiṣṭān paśyāmaḥ/ na caitad ācaraṇaṃ nirmūlam iti yuktaṃ, sandhyāvandana-aṣṭakā-ācaraṇāder api nirmūlatva-prasaṅgāt/ uktaṃ ca śiṣṭācārasya prāmāṇyam 'api vā kāraṇāgrahaṇe prayuktāni pratiyerann' iti. See also pp. 6.24-7.2 (CE, p. 101; tr, #13).

32. On the relation of Bhāsarvajña (tenth century A.D.) to the Śaiva Pāśupatas, see Minoru Hara, "Materials for the Study of Pāśupata Śaivism" (Unpublished Ph D. dissertation, Harvard Univ., 1967), pp. 137ff; "Nakulīśa-Pāśupata-Darśanam," IIJ, II (1958), 10-11; Friedrich A. Schultz, Die Philosophisch-theologischen Lehren des Pāśupata-Systems nach den Pañcārthabhāṣya und der Ratnatīkā, Beiträge zur Sprach- und Kulturgeschichte des Orients, Heft 10 (Walldorf-Hessen, 1958), pp. 8-9; Surendranath Dasgupta, A History of Indian Philosophy (HIP) (Cambridge: University Press, 1962), Vol. V, 11-14, 143-48.

33. AP, pp. 6.10-11.11 (CE, pp. 100-17; tr, ##12-17); 26.7-28.21 (CE, pp. 157-63; tr, ##48-51).

34. AP, pp. 67.3-86.3 (CE, pp. 261-304; tr, ##117-138).

35. E.g., AP, pp. 2.25-4.12 (CE, pp. 91-94; tr, ##6-8); 14.9-19.6 (CE, pp. 124-138; tr, ##24-33); 20.15-26.6 (CE, pp. 141-57; tr, ##36-47).

36. AP, pp. 1.1-29.9 (CE, pp. 86-163; tr, ##1-52); see also M. Narasimhachary, Contribution, pp. 97-120.

37. AP, pp. 1.13-2.3 (CE, pp. 88-89; tr, #4).

38. AP, pp. 2.3-11.11 (CE, pp. 89-117; tr, ##4-17)

39. AP, pp. 2.8-4.12 (CE, pp. 90-94; tr, ##4-8); 14.9-18.6 (CE, pp. 124-36; tr, ##24-30).

40. AP, pp. 11.22-14.8 (CE, pp. 118-23; tr, ##18-23).

41. AP, pp. 12.2-42.3 (CE, pp. 119-95; tr, ##20-78). For the details of the argument, see Narasimhachary, Contribution, pp. 102-17, and Roque Mesquita, "Das Problem der Gotteserkenntnis bei Yāmunamuni" (Unpublished Doctoral Dissertation, Universität Wien, 1971), Chs. I-II, pp. 14-121.

42. AP, pp. 12.2-13.22 (CE, pp. 119-123; tr, ##20-23).

43. AP, pp. 14.9-18.6 (CE, pp. 124-36; tr, ##24-30).

44. Translation by van Buitenen, AP(tr), #24, p. 24 (AP, p. 16.20-21; CE, p. 130).

45. AP, p. 17.5-17 (CE, pp. 131-33; tr, #29).

46. AP, pp. 18.7-19.6 (CE, pp. 136-38; tr, ##31-33).

47. Narasimhachary, Contribution, pp. 112-13, assumes that the speaker at this point is still the Pāñcarātrika Naiyāyika and not Yāmuna. Van Buitenen [AP(tr), n. 62 to #34, p. 128], on the other hand, maintains that "This is Yāmuna's objection, which states the extent to which he concurs in the preceeding Mīmāṃsā argument against Nyāya." Since Yāmuna repeats portions of this section verbatim in his Siddhānta, I follow van Buitenen in ascribing this objection and the following section to Yāmuna himself; cf. AP, p. 19.6-26 (CE, pp. 139-40; tr, #35) with pp. 39.24-40.7 (CE, p. 190; tr, #75). Roque Mesquita, "Yāmunamuni: Leben, Datierung und Werke," Wiener Zeitschrift für die Kunde Südasiens (WZKS), XVII (1973), 189, suggests that this objection is based upon the position of Yāmuna's now lost Puruṣa-nirṇaya which thus would have been the source for the identically worded passages; see n. 105 below.

48. AP(tr), #34, p. 28. (AP, p. 19.7-12; CE, pp. 138-39): nanu ca kevala-tarka-balād ayaṃ yadi siṣādhayiṣāpadam īśvaraḥ/

bhavatu nāma tathāsati dūṣaṇaṃ śruti-śiraḥ-pramito hi maheśvaraḥ// yadā tu sakala-bhuvana-nirmāṇa-kṣama-sarvajña-sarveśvara-paramapuruṣa-pratipādakāni nitya-āgama-vacanāny eva bahulam upalabhyante, kathaṃ tadā tad-anubhava-mūla-smaraṇa-prāmāṇya-anaṅgīkaraṇam.

49. AP(tr), n. 62 to #34, p. 128 (see n. 47 above). For van Buitenen's fuller statement of his understanding of the text, see n. 52 to #24, p. 127: "Yāmuna concurs in the Mīmāṃsaka's refutation of the Naiyāyika's views, to the extent that he too rejects that the existence of God can be proved by reason; but he will counter the Mīmāṃsā assertion that God cannot be proved at all, ... For Yāmuna, God has all the characteristics He has for the Naiyāyika, but he proves them from Scripture, not reason." Van Buitenen later qualifies his initial interpretation (see n. 50 below).

50. AP, p. 20.7-9 (CE, p. 141; tr, #35), itthañ ca śruti-śata-samadhigata-vividha-bodha-aiśvaryādi-vaibhave bhagavati sāmānya-darśana-avasita-asārvajñya-vigrahavattādayo doṣā na--avakāśam aśnuvate [my own translation]. Van Buitenen's note [AP(tr), n. 67 to #35, p. 129] also confirms my interpretation: "This sums up the conclusion of the refutations of both the Naiyāyika's and Mīmāṃsaka's views: the defects consequent on the Nyāya proofs of God are avoided on the basis of scriptural examination, since Scripture can indeed validly pronounce on God."

51. The most direct testimony of Yāmuna on this matter is given in the introduction to the AtS where he summarizes the various views on the pramāṇas with regard to the Paramātman in such a way as to indicate clearly that he believes the Paramātman is known by means of Scripture (ānuśravika) and Inference (ānumānikaś ca) and Yogic Perception (viśiṣṭa-pratyakṣa-samadhigamyaś ca) [AtS, p. 6.2-3 (A, p. 12.3-5)]. See Ch. VII, Pratijñā Series II.D. Neither van Buitenen nor Narasimhachary discuss this summary statement which conflicts so sharply with their understanding of Yāmuna's position in the AP. Narasimhachary (Contribution, p. 301), in his brief chapter summarizing Yāmuna's philosophy primarily on the basis of the introductory section of the AtS, unaccountably ignores this explicit statement and infers Yāmuna's position on the basis of another statement in the AtS that demonstrably does not even represent Yāmuna's own viewpoint; see Ch. VII, notes on Pratijñās I.B.2 and II.D.3. Roque Mesquita, who also agrees with van Buitenen's and Narasimhachary's interpretation of Yāmuna's position in the AP, does take note of Yāmuna's conflicting statement in the AtS and attempts to resolve the conflict by means of the hypothesis that Yāmuna changed his position between the writing of the AtS, one of his earlier works, and the composition of the AP, which according to Mesquita was Yāmuna's last work; see Mesquita, "Das Problem der Gotteserkenntnis bei Yāmunamuni," pp. 5-11, 98-133; and "Yāmunamuni," WZKS, XVII (1973), 188-89, 191-92. While there are some ambiguous statements in the AP that might be taken so as to support Mesquita's hypothesis, I feel that it is also possible to resolve these ambiguities in terms of my own hypothesis. Yāmuna twice in the course of the AP repeats in precisely the same words a statement that on its face would seem to indicate that he felt Scripture and Scripture alone was a pramāṇa with regard to the Bhagavān. The passage reads: atha vilakṣaṇa-agnihotrādi-

viṣaya-kāryasya--asambhāvita-mānāntaratayā tatpratipādayad vacaḥ pramāṇam, hanta tarhi niratiśaya-avabodha-aiśvarya-mahānanda-sandoha-vapuṣi bhagavati na mānāntara-gandha-sambandha iti sarvam samānam anyatra--abhiniveśāt/ AP, p. 19.22-26 and p. 40.4-7 (CE, pp. 140 and 190; tr, ##35 and 75).

While this strong statement would seem to challenge my hypothesis, I believe that it can be interpreted in terms of my general understanding of the course of the argument. First of all it must be noted that this statement comes in the middle of a passage devoted to showing the absurdity of the very view that he appears to be accepting in the statement. Thus, the most reasonable way of interpreting the statement is to assume that Yāmuna is here employing the common polemical device of granting the opponents' position for the sake of argument and then showing that even on their own terms their argument is unsound. However, there is a further subtlety to Yāmuna's statement. Immediately preceeding this statement, Yāmuna had stated that certain Vedic *kāryas* are known by means of other *pramāṇas* and that therefore the criterion *mānāntarāpūrva* was invalid with regard to them. He then says

> Now [if you mean that only a Vedic] statement that sets forth a *kārya* about an absolutely unique ritual such as the Agnihotra, etc., is a *pramāṇa* because such a unique act could not conceivably be the object of any other *pramāṇa*--come then, there is not even any association with the smell of another *pramāṇa* in the case of the Bhagavān whose form is a mass of unsurpassed Knowledge, Lordliness and Supreme Bliss.

Now if my understanding of Yāmuna is correct, he does *not* mean to say that there is no other *pramāṇa* that can give *some* form of valid knowledge about the Bhagavān (e.g., that He exists), but rather that there is no other *pramāṇa* that can give valid knowledge about the precise nature of Bhagavān *as qualified by niratiśaya-avabodha-aiśvarya-mahānanda*; qualities that establish the Bhagavān as the unique Spureme Person totally removed from the faults that inhere in all other persons.

52. Van Buitenen, Introduction to VAS, p. 51.

53. AP, p. 19.12-15 (CE, p. 139; tr, #35); p. 39.15-23 (CE, p. 189; tr, #74).

54. AP, pp. 20.13-22.24 (CE, pp. 141-47; tr, ##36-41). In his translation, van Buitenen takes the śloka at p. 20.13-14 with #35. In his CE, Narasimhachary, correctly in my opinion, sees this verse as the beginning of the Prābhākara attack on Yāmuna.

55. AP, p. 29.12-13 (CE, p. 164; tr, #53). Narasimhachary [AP (CE), p. 164] notes that two MSS read *nirdoṣajñāna-janyatvāj*. Since this reading would give the unambiguous interpretation, "because it is produced by faultless knowledge," it should probably be rejected as the *lectio facilior*.

56. The formal steps in the Inference (*anumāna*) are Thesis (*pratijñā* or *pakṣa*): "vivādādhyāsitam tantram pramāṇam"; Reason (*hetu* or *sādhana*): "nirdosajñānajanmatvāt"; Example (*dṛṣṭānta* or *udāharaṇa*): "jyotiṣṭomādivākyavat."

57. *Contribution*, p. 120, "At the very outset [of his Siddhānta], Yāmuna makes the following inferential statement: 'The Pāñcarātra *tantra* is authoritative like the Vedic sentences ordaining *jyotiṣṭoma*, etc., on the ground that it is, like the Vedic sentences, based upon knowledge which is free

from all defects.'" [See also AP (CE 1976), p. 33].

58. Van Buitenen, AP(tr), #53, p. 43, ". . . we now submit that the Tantra in question must be accepted as valid, because it produces faultless knowledge, like the scriptural statements on Vedic sacrifices like jyotiṣṭoma, etc."; and Oberhammer, YIB, p. 95, n. 231, "Es muss angenommen werden, dass das zur Diskussion stehende Tantram Autorität ist, weil es eine fehlerfreie Erkenntnis hervorbringt wie die Aussagen über das Jyotiṣṭoma usw."

59. AP, pp. 29.14-32.26 (CE, pp. 164-70; tr, ##54-59). Pp. 29.16-32.6 (CE, pp. 164-69; tr, ##54-58) are devoted to demonstrating the absence of any Fallacies of the Thesis (pratijñā- or pakṣa-ābhāsās); pp. 32.7-26 (CE, pp. 169-70; tr, #59) the absence of Fallacies of the Reason (hetu-ābhāsās). Van Buitenen, in his translation of this section, makes an error that is quite confusing, as his n. 119 on #56 reflects. At p. 29.24-25 (#55), an objector tries to show that the Thesis of Yāmuna's original anumāna suffers from the fallacy of anumāna-viruddhaḥ, i.e., being contradicted by another anumāna. Yāmuna then embarks on a long disucrsus (pp. 30.1-31.14; ##55-57), showing that the objector's anumāna is invalid because it suffers from a number of fallacies. Van Buitenen takes the charge of the fallacy āgama-viruddha at 30.11 as being directed against Yāmuna's original anumāna when in fact it is Yāmuna's charge against his opponent's counter anumāna. Yāmuna deals with the implied charge of āgama-viruddha against his own anumāna at p. 31.15-17 (#58).

60. Y. V. Athalye, ed., Tarka-saṁgraha of Annambhaṭṭa (TS), Bombay Sanskrit Series No. LV (Bombay, 1930), p. 307.

61. AP, pp. 32.27-42.3 (CE, pp. 171-95; tr, ##60-78).

62. -avāptakāma-, "whose desires are completely attained [and who therefore has nothing to gain from deceiving us by composing false Tantras]."

63. Yāmuna's statement of the principle of svataḥ prāmāṇya as an axiom accepted by both his opponents and himself reveals quite definitely the essentially Mīmāmsaka character of the AP, since this principle, together with the related one of extrinsic invalidity or non-authoritativeness (parataḥ aprāmāṇya), is perhaps the most important distinguishing epistemological characteristic of Mīmāṃsā. "According to the Mīmāṃsakas all knowledge is intrinsically right knowledge, it is reliable by itself qua knowledge [prāmāṇyam svataḥ], since it is knowledge, not error. It can be erroneous only in the way of an exception, in two cases, either when it is counterbalanced by another and stronger cognition [bādhaka-jñāna] or when its origin is proved to be deficient [kārana-doṣa], as for instance when a daltonist perceives wrong colors. The principle is laid down that knowledge is right by itself, its deficiency can be only established by a subsequent operation of the mind [prāmāṇyam svataḥ, aprāmāṇyam parataḥ]." (Th. Stcherbatsky, Buddhist Logic [BL], two vols. [New York: Dover Publications, 1962], I, 66.). While this principle forms "the very key-stone of Mīmāṃsā" primarily because it supports the authoritativeness of the Vedas, to many Mīmāmsakas, Kumārila and Yāmuna among them, it is also an essential basis for all forms of human understanding, communication and activity; see Ganganatha Jha, Pūrva-Mīmāṃsā in its Sources (PM Sources) (Varanasi: The Banaras Hindu University, second ed., 1964), p. 71; Govardhan P. Bhatt,

Epistemology of the Bhaṭṭa School of Pūrva Mīmāṃsā, The Chowkhamba Sanskrit Studies, Vol. XVII (Varanasi: Chowkhamba Sanskrit Series Office, 1962), pp. 424-25.

64. On this absurd statement, see G. A. Jacob, A Third Handful of Popular Maxims (Bombay, 1911, second revised edition), pp. 4-5.

65. AP, p. 32.27-33.13 (CE, p. 171; tr, #60), [Pūrva Mīmāṃsaka:] "nanu kathaṃ pauruṣeyatva-sāmānyād āpatantī doṣa-saṃbhāvanā apanīyate pañcarātratantrāṇām/" [Yāmuna:] "kathaṃ vākya-sāmānyād āpatantī vedeṣu sā vāryate/ apauruṣeyatvād iti cet, tad ihāpi sarvajña-avāptakāma-parama-puruṣa-praṇītatayā--ity avagamya śāmyatu bhāvan/
etad uktam bhavati

naiva śabde svato doṣāḥ prāmāṇyaparipanthinaḥ/
santi kin tu svatas tasya pramāṇatvam iti sthitiḥ//
vaktur āśaya-doṣeṇa keṣu cit tad apodyate/
aṅgulyagre 'sti mātaṅga-yūtham ity evam ādiṣu//
prastuta-grantha-saṃdarbhe vaktur āśaya-gāminīm/
doṣa-śaṅkāṃ trayī-mūrddha-dhvanir evāpamārṣṭi naḥ//
vadanti khalu vedāntāḥ sarvajñaṃ jagataḥ patim/
mahākāruṇikaṃ tasmin vipralambhādayaḥ katham//"

66. AP, p. 33.14-16 (CE, p. 172; tr, #61).

67. AP, p. 33.17-34.6 (CE, p. 172; tr, #61). See especially pp. 33.17-18 and 34.5-6.

68. AP, p. 34.18-22 (CE, p. 174; tr, #62).

69. AP, pp. 34.23-35.16 (CE, pp. 175-77; tr, ##63-64). See especially p. 35.1-5.

70. A. B. Keith, The Karma-Mīmāṃsā, The Heritage of India Series (London: Oxford Univ. Press, 1921), pp. 41-43.

71. AP, pp. 35.17-38.4 (CE, pp. 178-85; tr, ##65-71).

72. AP, p. 38.3-4 (CE, p. 185; tr, #71): ata eva yathāyathaṃ laukika-śabdebhyas tat-siddhārtha-gocarā buddhayo jāyante.

73. AP, p. 38.5-16 (CE, pp. 185-87; tr, #72).

74. Narasimhachary, Contribution, p. 121, n. 521. See also Stcherbatsky, BL, I, 66.

75. See n. 63 above.

76. AP, p. 38.17-19 (CE, p. 187; tr, #73).

77. AP, p. 38.23-24 (CE, p. 188; tr, #73), ato vidita-pada-padārtha-saṅgateḥ śrotus sahasaiva śabdo 'rtham avabodhayati, mūla-jñānaṃ na pratīkṣate.

78. Cf. AP, pp. 61.18-63.14 (CE, pp. 247-51; tr, ##109-112) for a discussion of the relation between svataḥ prāmāṇyam and knowledge of faults or lack of faults in the source. See also n. 63 above and Oberhammer, YIB, p. 80ff.

79. AP, p. 39.1-14 (CE, p. 188; tr, #73). See also n. 63 above.

80. AP, p. 39.15-16 (CE, p. 189; tr, #74).

81. AP, p. 39.20-23 (CE, p. 189; tr, #74), tataś ca yāny etāni vilakṣaṇa-puruṣa-pratipādikāni vedānta-vacāṃsi "sa eṣa sarvādhipatiḥ sarvasyeśānaḥ sarvam idaṃ praśāsti," "tasyādhyakṣam idaṃ sarvam" ity ādīni tāny api tatra pramāṇaṃ tad-viṣaya-asandigdha-aviparyaya-vijñāna-hetuvāt.

82. AP, p. 40.12-13 (CE, p. 191; tr, #75), tasmāt parinișṭhitānuṣṭeyādi-bheda-śūnyam asandigdha-aviparyasta-vijñānaṃ pramāṇam eṣṭavyam.

83. See AP, p. 23.1-16 (CE, pp. 148-50; tr, #42) for the statement of this objection.

84. AP, p. 40.14-17 (CE, p. 191; tr, #76).

85. See Ch. VI, n.174.
86. AP, p. 40.18-20 (CE, pp. 191f; tr, #76).
87. AP, pp. 40.21-41.9 (CE, pp. 192f; tr, #77).
88. AP, p. 41.10-25 (CE, pp. 193-94; tr, ##77-78).
89. AP, p. 42.1-3 (CE, p. 195; tr, #78), tad evam udīrita-śruti-śata-samadhigata-avitatha-sahaja-sarva-sākṣātkāra-kāruṇyādi-kalyāṇa-guṇa-eka-rāśau bhagavati sidhyati, sidhyaty eva tad-anubhava-mūlatayā tantra-prāmāṇyam.
90. See n. 58 above. The passages in the AP that are of relevance to a contextual word-study of nirdoṣa-jñāna-janmatvāt are

(I) AP, p. 29.12-13 (CE, p. 164; tr, #53);
(II) p. 32.10-13 (p. 169; #59);
(III) pp. 32.27-33.13 (p. 171; #60);
(IV) pp. 38.14-39.14 (pp.187f; ##72-73);
(V) p. 39.20-23 (p. 189; #74);
(VI) p. 40.12-13 (p. 191; tr, #75);
(VII) p. 42.1-3 (p. 195; #78);
(VIII) p. 42.14 (p. 197; #79);
(IX) p. 44.4-5 (p. 200; #79);
(X) p. 45.17-25 (p. 203; ##81-82);
(XI) p. 50.5-14 (p. 215; ##86-87);
(XII) p. 51.4-14 (pp.217f; #89);
(XIII) p. 55.23-26 (p. 233; #96);
(XIV) pp. 59.17-60.2 (pp. 241f; #103);
(XV) p. 60.5-6 (p. 242; #104);
(XVI) p. 60.19-24 (p. 244; #106);
(XVII) pp. 60.25-61.9 (pp. 244f; #107);
(XVIII) pp. 61.18-63.14 (pp. 247-51; ##109-12);
(XIX) pp. 63.23-64.19 (pp. 251-54; #114);
(XX) p. 68.5-9 (p. 263; #118), and
(XXI) p. 69.1-2 (p. 265; #118).

91. AP, p. 39.20-23 (CE, p. 189; tr, #74). See n. 81 above for this text.
92. B. Jhaḷakīkar, Nyāya-kośa, Bombay Sanskrit Series No. XLIX (Bombay: Government Central Book Depot, 1893), s.v., pramāṇa, meanings 1. and 2. See also Sukhlalji Sanghvī, Advanced Studies in Indian Logic and Metaphysics (ILM), ed. and trans. by K. K. Dixit (Calcutta, 1961), pp. 34-38.
93. See n. 58 above.
94. See the use of pramāṇaṃ in the sentence quoted in n. 81 above.
95. See the definition of pramāṇaṃ in the passage quoted in n. 82 above.
96. See n. 82 above. Cf. also the passage quoted in n. 81 in which the phrase "-asandigdha-aviparyaya-vijñāna-" is used for the result or fruit of a pramāṇa, now being employed in the sense of the means or cause. Cf. AP, p. 61.3 (CE, p. 245; tr, #107), where vijñāna is defined as "viśiṣṭaṃ jñānam asambhavat-skhalanam."
97. Sanghvi, "The Logical Tradition (Tārkika Paramparā) of Defining Pramāṇa (Pramāṇa-lakṣaṇa)," ILM, pp. 34-38.
98. See above ns. 63, 65, 78, 81, 89, and 90 (Passages X, XII, XIV, XVI, XVII, XVIII, XIX, and XXI). Sanghvi, ILM, pp. 34-36, notes that from the earliest times this concern for the purity of the cause (kāraṇa) of cognition was a central one in the attempts to define pramāṇa. He also shows how attention was often focused primarily upon the effect, i.e., cognition

itself, with a consequent lessening of explicit emphasis upon the purity of the cause. According to Sanghvi, it was among the Bhāṭṭa school of Pūrva Mīmāṃsā (Yāmuna's main opponents in the AP) that the criterion of "originating from a non-defective cause" (aduṣṭa-kāraṇa-ārabdha) continued to be an essential element of the definition of pramāṇa.

99. AP, p. 50.8-10 (CE, p. 215; tr, #87), svataḥpramāṇaṃ vijñānaṃ bhavatāṃ nanu darśane// satyaṃ tad eva vijñāna-prāmāṇyam apanīyate/ bādha-kāraṇa-doṣābhyām, tāv api dvāv iha sphuṭau// See Stcherbatsky, BL, I, 66 (quoted in n. 63 above), on bādhaka-jñāna and kāraṇa-doṣa; also Sanghvi, ILM, p. 35, n. 26.

100. When he demonstrated the absence of all possible faults (doṣā) or logical fallacies from his initial Inference, especially while showing that its Thesis, tantraṃ pramāṇam, is not vitiated by being contradicted (viruddhaḥ) by the pramāṇas Perception, Inference or Scripture nor by any inherent contradiction within its own language. See AP, p. 29.14-15 (CE, p. 164; tr, #54); pp. 29.22-32.6 (CE, pp. 164-69; tr, ##54-58). See n. 59 above.

101. AP, p. 30.5-7 (CE, p. 165; tr, #55).

102. Cf. AP, p. 30.1-10 (CE, p. 165; tr, #55) where Yāmuna gives a three-fold definition of aprāmāṇya: jñāna-anutpatti-lakṣaṇa, saṃśaya-lakṣaṇa and viparyaya-lakṣaṇa. The first of these simply refers to cases where no meaningful or coherent knowledge or cognition is produced.

103. See ns. 81 and 96 above.

104. AP, pp. 42.4-45.25 (CE, pp. 195-203; tr, ##79-82).

105. AP, p. 45.15-16 (CE, p. 202; tr, #81), sarvam caitat puruṣa-nirṇaye nipuṇataram upapaditam iti neha prapañcyate. On the Puruṣa-nirṇaya, see Narasimhachary, Contribution, pp. 12-16; and Mesquita, "Yāmunamuni," WZKS, XVII (1973), 183, 187-92.

106. AP, pp. 46.1-50.14 (CE, pp. 203-15; tr, ##83-87). See n. 99 above.

107. AP, pp. 26.17-28.8 (CE, pp. 159-62, tr, #49).

108. AP, pp. 53.2-67.2 (CE, pp. 223-60; tr, ##94-116).

NOTES

CHAPTER IV

1. AP, pp. 10.6-11, 10.25-11.2, 26.17-28.8 (CE, pp. 111-112, 114, 159-62; tr, ##17, 49) (see Ch. I, n. 34).

2. AP, pp. 53.12-67.2 (CE, pp. 223-60; tr, ##94-116).

3. AP, p. 51.15-19 (CE, pp. 218-19; tr, #90), na hi nindā nindyaṃ ninditum pravartate, api tu ninditāt itarat praśaṃsitum.

4. AP, pp. 51.19-52.6 (CE, pp. 219-20; tr, #90).

5. AP, p. 52.7-9 (CE, p. 221; tr, #90).

6. AP, p. 52.10-16 (CE, p. 221; tr. #91), api ca caturṣu vedeṣu iti na--ayam arthaḥ vedeṣu puruṣārtho na--astīti, kiṅ tu yas teṣu puruṣārthas tam alabhamāna iti/ . . . ato vedesu yaḥ puruṣārthas tam alabhamānaḥ tad-abhilāṣī pañcarātra-śāstram adhītavān iti pañcarātra-śrutyor aikārthyam eva pratīyate/.

7. AP, pp. 53.12-54.14 (CE, pp. 223-27; tr, #94). Apparently Vācaspati Miśra is the earliest definitely identified writer and Vedāntin to ascribe the VS to Vyāsa (in the dedicatory verse of his Bhāmatī); see Sengaku Mayeda, "The Authenticity of the Bhagavadgītābhāṣya Ascribed to Śaṅkara," WZKSO, IX (1965), p. 187. However, Yāmuna's Bhāsyakāra or at least the tradition stemming from him apparently also made the identification; see below, nn. 46 40.

8. AP, p. 53.20 (CE, p. 224; tr, #94).

9. AP, p. 54.13-14 (CE, p. 227; tr, #94).

10. See Ch. II, n. 8.

11. Only a very brief section of Oberhammer's study is devoted to presenting Yāmuna's own position; and even there the primary purpose is to enable him to distinguish more precisely the character of one of Yāmuna's sources, not to arrive at an adequate understanding of Yāmuna (see YIB, pp. 93-100).

]2. YIB, pp. 73; 93-94; 97, n. 240; 99-100.

13. Source-critical and form-critical analysis are useful tools in the hermeneutical task of interpreting literary documents. However, there are very real dangers involved when such analysis becomes an end in itself. When isolated fragments are abstracted from the wholeness of their literary context, it is usually very difficult to recover their original contexts to any degree of completeness. The fragmented sources must then be interpreted in what is nearly a contextual vacuum, leaving great scope for purely speculative reconstruction based upon what seems "logical" to the interpreter.

14. YIB, pp. 99-100.

15. Ibid., pp. 5-6, n. 2. He also justifies his relative neglect of Yāmuna himself by citing the difficulties of assessing his contribution because it is only partially preserved and because we know so little of his predecessors and immediate followers. While there are certainly great difficulties facing any attempt to understand and evaluate Yāmuna's position and

achievement, how much greater are the obstacles to understanding Yāmuna's infinitely more fragmented sources! If Oberhammer can derive as much information about these fragmented sources as he does, then surely it is possible to do much more than he has done in understanding and appreciating the nature and significance of Yāmuna's own achievement. See Ch. III above for my illustration of this fact through a criticism of Oberhammer's understanding of Yāmuna's Siddhānta and a more adequate exposition of it.

16. As indicated by Yāmuna's statement of purpose in the introduction of the AtS; see AtS, p. 8 (A, pp. 14-17) and Ch. VII.

17. YIB, p. 114.

18. Ibid., pp. 42-54.

19. Oberhammer, YIB, pp. 27-30, 42-54, 125-26 (lines 1-60); AP, pp. 54.15-57.3 (CE, pp. 227-36; tr, ##95-98).

20. YIB, pp. 43f, 47-50, 54. Oberhammer's reconstruction of a "single" Source I is the most questionable portion of his analysis. It seems much more likely that Yāmuna's refutation of the pūrvapakṣa was, as would seem natural, a compilation of arguments against the orthodox Vedāntic opposition's position from various of Yāmuna's sources, including perhaps among them the one isolated by Oberhammer. However, Oberhammer's hypotheses with regard to Yāmuna's other sources, which give positive interpretations of these sūtras, seem much more well founded.

21. YIB, pp. 30-31, 55-61, 126-27 (lines 61-98); AP, pp. 57.3-59.16 (CE, pp. 237-41; tr, ##99-102).

22. YIB, pp. 56-61.

23. Ibid., pp. 32, 62-71, 127 (lines 99-114); AP, pp. 59.17-60.6 (CE, pp. 241f; tr, ##103-104).

24. YIB, pp. 62, 120.

25. Oberhammer fails to stress the point that this shift brings the discussion of the UA Adhik. into line with Yāmuna's general concern in the AP. See Ch. V below for a discussion of the possible significance of this point.

26. See Ch. V for a further discussion of this point.

27. My basic point in criticism of Oberhammer's attempt to isolate this source is that, when dealing with such a brief fragment, an attempt to consider it in isolation may lead us off into murky waters and obscure what can be said with relative clarity about the meaning of the fragment as it is presented to us in the context of the redactor's composition. See also n. 13 above.

28. YIB, pp. 32-39, 71-100, 128-31 (lines 115-274); AP, pp. 60.7-66.20 (CE, pp. 243-59; tr, ##105-115).

29. Even according to Oberhammer's analysis, Yāmuna does not attempt to modify the position of this source, but rather states its position faithfully and consistently, integrating it into his own viewpoint by means of brief introductory and concluding remarks (YIB, p. 72). For the introductory remarks, see AP, p. 60.7-8 (CE, p. 243; tr, #105; YIB, p. 123, lines 115-116), yad vā sūtrāṇāṃ nyāya-pradarśana-paratvāt pañcarātra-śrutyor asantam api virodhaṃ kṛtvā--atra cintyate tathā hi. . . (CE reads cintyate, not cityante). For the concluding passage, see AP, p. 66.19-20 (CE, p. 259; tr, #115; YIB, p. 131, lines 274-75), virodhe 'pi vikalpaḥ syād bhagavac-chāstra-vedayoḥ/ virodha eva nāstīti prāg eva pratyapādayan//.

30. YIB, pp. 72-73, 77-88. See AP, p. 61.1-2 (CE, pp. 244-45; tr, #107; YIB, p. 128, lines 134-135), viruddhārtham api vikalpena pramāṇam ity arthaḥ, asambhavad-vibhrama-vipralambha-bhagavad-anubhava-mūlatvād; and AP, p. 64.18-20 (CE, p. 254; tr, #114; YIB, p. 130, lines 222-24), tena nirdoṣa-vijñāna-kāraṇatvād dvayor api/ nirviśaṅkaṃ pramāṇatvam bhagavacchāstra-vedayor// tataś ca tulya-śiṣṭatvād vikalpena pramāṇatā/.

31. YIB, pp. 72-73, 77-78, 90-91, 93-100.

32. Ibid., pp. 72-73, 77-78, 93-100.

33. While Oberhammer's argument for this position's being from some other source and not Yāmuna's own composition is not conclusive as it stands, there are additional factors which lead me to accept his hypothesis. The major weakness in Oberhammer's argument is his failure to see that much of the difference between this source and Yāmuna's overall viewpoint in the AP can be accounted for by the very simple contextual consideration given in the following text above. While this consideration weakens Oberhammer's argument in one sense, it may strengthen it in another. That is, the section that Oberhammer isolates as Source IV appears originally to have been composed fully in accord with the context of the Tarka-pāda and as a commentary upon VS II.ii.42-45. It has then clearly been "stitched" into the context of the AP by means of an introductory sentence and a concluding verse that deny that the posited or assumed contradiction between Pañcarātra and the Veda exists at all (see n. 29 above). While it is possible that Yāmuna himself could have composed this section in isolation and then integrated it into the AP in such a manner, it seems more likely that the section was extracted from a commentary upon the VS. Yāmuna himself did not compose such a commentary. Thus, when we learn--as we shall below--that there is strong evidence for linking this lengthy section with the words of Śrīvatsāṅka Miśra who composed an extensive commentary on the VS, it seems to me that Oberhammer's hypothesis is confirmed. Moreover, even allowing for the difference in context, it does seem that Source IV is more willing to accept conflict between Pañcarātra and the Veda than Yāmuna would be (see n. 40 below).

34. G. Jha, PM Sources, pp. 311-15.

35. AP, p. 63.10 (CE, p. 251; tr, #112; YIB, p. 129, line 188).

36. Jha, PM Sources, p. 315.

37. See n. 6 above.

38. See n. 30 above.

39. AP, p. 61.6-9 (CE, p. 245; tr, #107; YIB, p. 128, lines 139-42), bhagavatas tu svābhāvika-niraṅkuśa-aiśvaryasya śruti-śata-samadhigata-avitatha-sahaja-samasta-dharmādharmādi-sākṣātkāraṃ jñānam iti vijñānam ity uktaṃ, tādṛśasya tasya--ādibhāve mūlatve sati tad-apratiṣedhaḥ pramāṇam eveti/. See YIB, p. 97, where Oberhammer in effect admits that this statement contravenes the rigid theoretical distinction which he develops between Source IV and Yāmuna.

40. See especially AP, p. 64.17 (CE, p. 254; tr, #114; YIB, p. 130, line 221) where Source IV defends Pañcarātra by showing that even the Veda is not immune to criticism since some "wise men dispute the eternality of the Veda" (kin tu vedasya nityatve vivadante vipaścitaḥ). See also AP, p. 60.19-21 (CE, p. 244; tr, #106; YIB, p. 128, lines 127-29); p. 62.25-27 (CE, p. 249; tr, #111; YIB, p. 129, lines 179-81); p. 63.23-26

(CE, pp. 251-52; tr, #114; YIB, p. 130, lines 200-203); p. 65.6-17 (CE, p. 256; tr, #115; YIB, p. 235, lines 237-46). See n. 33 above.

41. Oberhammer, YIB, p. 117, dates Source IV in the early ninth century.

42. See Ch. II.

43. YIB, pp. 40, 100-13, 132 (ll. 275-79); AP, pp. 66.21-67.2 (CE, p. 260; tr, #116).

44. In the Devatā-adhikaraṇa, Pūrva Mīmāṃsā Sūtra IX.i.9. See van Buitenen, VAS, p. 282, n. 675.

45. AP, pp. 66.21-67.2 (CE, p. 260; tr, #116). nanv atra bhavatāṃ bhāṣyakārāṇāṃ viruddhāṃśāprāmāṇyābhidhānaṃ katham iva/ yady api virodhaḥ kṛtvā cintayā parihṛtas, tad api gambhīra-nyāya-sāgaram avagāṭhum aparibṛḍhānāṃ komalamanasāṃ vedānādaro mā bhūd ity evaṃparam; yathaiva hi bhagavato jaimineḥ karmaphalopanyāsaḥ karmaśraddhāsaṃvarddhanāyeti/.

46. Such is the clear and reasonable statement of this position according to Rāmānuja: nanu ca, "sāṅkhyaṃ yogaḥ pañcarātraṃ vedaḥ pāśupataṃ tathā/ kim etāny ekaniṣṭhāni pṛthaṅniṣṭhāni vā mune//" (MBh 12.337.1-2) ityādinā sāṃkhyādīnām apy ādaraṇīyatā -- ucyate/ śārīrake tu sāṃkhyādīni pratiṣidhyante/ ata idam api tantraṃ tattulyam/ [ŚBh(K) II.ii.42, Vol. II, pp. 702-703; ŚBh with Śruta-Prakāśikā, Vol. II, p. 328.14-16]. Strangely, Oberhammer completely ignores this evidence from the ŚBh, perhaps because it conflicts with the more convoluted explanation found in the Śruta-Prakāśikā and calls seriously into question his hypothesis that Yāmuna's Bhāṣyakāra, Rāmānuja's "others" and Sudarśanasūri's "some" are all one and the same written source. See n. 48 on this conflict and its implications.

47. YIB, pp. 102-113.

48. The major piece of evidence in this regard is the fact that this position as presented by Sudarśanasūri conflicts sharply with Rāmānuja's presentation on the one point that the latter dealt with in any detail (see n. 46 above). According to Rāmānuja, these "others" are saying that since Bādarāyaṇa in the MBh praised Sāṃkhya, Yoga and Pāśupata alongside of Pañcarātra and then in the preceding adhikaraṇas of the Tarka-pāda refuted certain aspects of the former three, it follows that in the concluding adhikaraṇa dealing with Pañcarātra he also intended to refute certain aspects of this system. Such an interpretation of this position is clear, reasonable and in accord with the general commentatorial understanding of the structure of the Tarka-pāda. On the other hand, the position as presented by Sudarśanasūri (Śruta-Prakāśika, Vol. II, p. 337.20-27) conflicts both with Rāmānuja's statement and with the usual understanding of the Tarka-pāda. According to this version, the UA Adhik. is not devoted to Pañcarātra alone but rather to all four of the orthodoxly acceptable (śiṣṭa-parigṛhītāḥ) Āgamas with Pañcarātra being singled out simply for the purpose of exemplifying (pradarśanārtham) the class (see Oberhammer, YIB, p. 103, n. 249). In contrast to Rāmānuja's straightforward version, this convoluted account, according to the usual understanding of the Tarka-pāda, would involve the fault of redundancy since the other three Āgamas would already have been considered in previous adhikaraṇas.

Thus, while Rāmānuja may have been referring directly to Yāmuna's Bhāṣyakāra's position, it would seem likely that

Sudarśanasūri was drawing upon some later exposition of this position. Indeed, if, as Oberhammer suggests, Yāmuna's Bhāṣyakāra's were the ancient authority Dramiḍa-bhāṣyakāra, it would be surprising for such a late author as Sudarśanasūri to be able to produce such a large number of quotations or close paraphrases from a work by an authority who is known to much earlier authors only by means of a few scattered fragments. Hence, while I cannot accept Oberhammer's claim that Sudarśanasūri's citations stem directly from the commentary of Yāmuna's Bhāṣyakāra, he has nevertheless performed a great service in pointing out our only source for a full understanding of the position that is based upon that commentary.

49. Kapila in the case of Sāṃkhya, Hiraṇya-garbha for Yoga, Paśupati for Pāśupata and Nārāyaṇa for Pañcarātra; see Rāmānuja, ŚBh(K) II.ii.42, Vol. II, p. 703.

50. YIB, pp. 103-104.

51. YIB, pp. 115-16; 118-19.

52. AtS, p. 8 (A, pp. 15-16) ". . . bhagavatā bādarāyaṇena--idamarthāny eva sūtrāṇi praṇītāni, vivṛtāni ca tāni parimita-gambhīra-bhāṣiṇā bhāṣyakṛtā, vistṛtāni ca tāni gambhīra-nyāya-sāgara-bhāṣiṇā bhagavatā śrivatsāṅkamiśreṇa--api . . ." See Ch. VII, for the text and its translation in its full context.

53. YIB, pp. 115-16.

54. See n. 45 above for the full text.

55. YIB, pp. 40, 115; AP(tr), #116.

56. See AP, p. 28.21 (CE, p. 163; tr, #51); p. 33.4 (CE, p. 171; tr, #60); p. 50.8 (CE, p. 215; tr, #87); p. 79.11 (CE, p. 290; tr, #134); etc. On the related use of the vocative particle bhos, see p. 55.24 (CE, p. 253; tr, #96).

57. AP, p. 50.8 (CE, p. 215; tr, #87).

58. R. Mesquita, "Recent Research on Yāmuna," WZKS, XVIII (1974), p. 204, interprets the phrase "bhavatām bhāṣyakārāṇām" correctly and also notes that it strengthens Oberhammer's hypothesis.

59. YIB, p. 115.

60. While this edition lacks a critical apparatus, I have been personally assured by Professor R. Ramanujachari, the translator and co-editor, that all of the manuscripts available in the major manuscript collections in South India were consulted in establishing the text; see also ST (1972), "Preface" to English translation, p. l.

61. Introduction to VAS, pp. 19-29.

62. Van Buitenen's argument rests upon the assumption that, since Rāmānuja and Yāmuna come from a "common milieu," it would be strange for Yāmuna not to mention the vṛtti-kāra in whom Rāmānuja sets such great store (Introduction to VAS, p. 24). My entire thesis challenges this assumption that, in terms of their Vedānta sources, Yāmuna and Rāmānuja come from a "common milieu." Rather, in my view, the little known Śrīvatsāṅka Miśra held the place in Yāmuna's Vedāntic milieu that Bodhāyana held in Rāmānuja's; and Rāmānuja's innovation was precisely the integration of Bodhāyana into Yāmuna's tradition of Vedānta. As U. T. Vīrarāghavācārya attests (Gūḍha-Prakāśa, p. 10, n. 1), Yāmuna's failure to mention Bodhāyana conforms to the traditional view that he had never seen this vṛtti and that Rāmānuja and his chief disciple Kureśa (who is also known as Śrīvatsāṅka Miśra) had to travel to Kaśmīr in order to see it.

63. The fact that for the later Śrī Vaiṣṇava tradition the most famous and authoritative "Bhāṣyakāra," before Rāmānuja became the pre-eminent recipient of this title, was Dramiḍācārya cuts both ways. On the one hand, as van Buitenen would maintain, after the true identity of Yāmuna's Bhāṣyakṛt had been forgotten, it could have led to a confusion between this figure and the Dramiḍa-bhāṣyakāra that produced the corrupted variant reading dramiḍa-bhāṣyakṛtā. On the other hand, it is also possible that Yāmuna's prestigious, pre-Rāmānuja Bhāṣyakāra was in fact the same as the prestigious pre-Rāmānuja Bhāṣyakāra of the later Śrī Vaiṣṇava tradition and that the variant reading was produced, after Rāmānuja became the Bhāṣyakāra, as a legitimate attempt to designate Yāmuna's Bhāṣyakāra more accurately and explicitly. Van Buitenen's strongest argument against identifying the Bhāṣyakṛt of the AtS with the Dramiḍa-bhāṣyakāra is that all other evidence seems to establish the latter to have been a commentator on the Chāndogya Upaniṣad, not on the VS (Introduction to VAS, p. 28). However, the strength of this argument is weakened when van Buitenen himself points out later on the same page that "Belvalkar on plausible grounds goes so far as to contend that the original [Vedānta] Sūtras were Chāndogya Sūtras." Thus strong positive proof linking the Dramiḍa-bhāṣyakāra with the Chāndogya Upaniṣad is not effective in establishing his lack of relation to the VS.

64. Van Buitenen, Introduction to VAS, pp. 25-30. However, if my interpetation of the phrase "bhavatāṃ bhāṣyakārāṇāṃ" is correct, Yāmuna's Bhāṣyakāra may be presumed to have had a closer relationship to Yāmuna's tradition than to that of his opponents. Similarly, Dramiḍācārya is cited more often in Śrī Vaiṣṇava works than in those of other traditions (van Buitenen, VAS, Appendix, pp. 302-311; S. Kuppuswami Sastri, "Bodhāyana and Dramiḍācārya, Two Old Vedāntins Presupposed by Rāmānuja," Proceedings and Transactions of the Third Oriental Conference, Madras, 1924, pp. 468-72); and, as van Buitenen maintains, his preserved quotations on the whole "are more favourable to Rāmānuja's than to Śaṅkara's system of Vedānta." (Introduction to VAS, p. 30).

65. The former's position as presented by Rāmānuja and Sudarśanasūri is integrally linked with the MBh, and the same two authors stress that the latter relies on a text from the BhG at a place where one would expect a śruti text. (ŚBh with Śruta-Prakāśika, Vol. I, p. 64).

66. S. Kuppuswami Sastri, "Bodhāyana and Dramiḍācārya," p. 470.

67. Draviḍācārya is simply a common variant of Dramiḍācārya; see Ibid., p. 470, and van Buitenen, Introduction to VAS, p. 27, n. 76.

68. YIB, pp. 118-19.

69. See n. 52 above.

70. See n. 45 above.

71. AP, p. 60.7-8 (CE, p. 243; tr, #105).

72. See n. 52 above.

73. ŚBh(K), Vol. I, p. 2.

74. See Vāsudeva's comparing of Bhāsarvajña's greatest work, the Nyāya-Bhūṣaṇa, to an ocean while explaining why he has written a commentary on Bhāsarvajña's brief Nyāya-sāra: nyāyabhūṣaṇa-mahāmbudhau budhā ye 'lam āvicarituṃ na jānate/

tatkṛte kṛtir iyaṃ mayā kṛtā nyāyasārapada-pañcikābhidhā// (Nyāyasāra of Ācārya Bhāsarvajña with the Nyāyasārapada-pañcikā of Vāsudeva of Kashmir, Poona, 1922, p. 98.)

75. Tattva-ṭīkā, Śrī Vaiṣṇava-Siddhānta Granthamālā, No. 2 (Madras, 1938), pp. 38-45.

76. Ibid., p. 45.2-3.

77. VAS, #93.

78. AtS, p. 8 (A, p. 16); see Ch. VII.

79. Tattva-ṭīkā, p. 45.4-5.

80. Ibid., p. 42.10ff.

81. See Ch. VII, n. 2.

82. VAS, #2.

83. Tattva-ṭīkā, p. 42.11-14.

84. Ibid., p. 42.13-14.

85. See Ch. V, n. 37. Traditionally the content of this oral instruction is preserved in summary form in Yāmuna's Gītārthasaṃgraha (GAS); see n. 88 below. Another full study of the integration of the Classical and the Popular in the Śrī Vaiṣṇava tradition could be done on the basis of the BhG, the GAS, Rāmānuja's Gītā-bhāṣya, Vedānta Deśika's commentaries on Yāmuna's and Rāmānuja's works, and other later Śrī Vaiṣṇava works on or about the BhG.

86. See Ch. V for a fuller analysis of this traditional account.

87. Tattva-ṭīkā, p. 45.6-7, sūtrāṇāṃ bahvartha-sūcaka-alpākṣaratayā.

88. See Vedānta Deśika's Gītārtha-saṃgraha-rakṣā ad GAS, śl. 32, where the "noble Rāma" (rāma-ārya) that revealed the meaning of the BhG to Yāmuna in accord with the command of Nāthamuni is called Rāma Miśra: itham eva sattva niṣṭha-saṃpradāya-paraṃparagatas samīcīno gītārthaḥ/ napunaḥ kudṛṣṭibhir unnītaḥ/ sacaiṣa svayoga-mahima-cuḷakita-parama-puruṣa-vibhūti-yugaḷa-bhagavan-nāthamuni-niyogānuvarti śrīmad-rāma-miśra-sakāśad bahuśāstravidbhir asmābhir bahuśaḥ śrutasya bhagavad-gītārtha-prapañcasya saṅgraha iti. (GAS with GAS Rakṣā [Conjeeveram, 1901], p. 34).

89. See Ch. V, nn. 44-55 and accompanying text on the possible significance of this name "Miśra."

90. Oberhammer (YIB, pp. 118-19, n. 271), with his emphasis upon the differences between Yāmuna and his sources, seems to be led to the opposite conclusion that Yāmuna is without a Vedāntic tradition behind him and must invent a tradition by naming Vedānta Sūtra commentators of other schools. While there are of course differences between Yāmuna and his sources, I have shown that there were also major and central points in common.

91. Introduction to VAS, p. 29. While van Buitenen does not accept the identification of Yāmuna's Bhāṣyakāra with Dramiḍ-ācārya, he does stress the latter's acceptance of popular devotional and theistic religion; see pp. 30, 302-311 (especially Fragments II.a, VII and XV).

92. YIB, p. 117.

NOTES

CHAPTER V

1. See Appendix I for an analysis of Yāmuna's explicit references to Nāthamuni. On Nāthamuni as the initiator of the Śrī Vaiṣṇava Darśana, see Vedānta Deśika, Tattvamuktākalāpaḥ, Adravya-sara, V. 136 cd, nātha-upajñaṃ pravṛttaṃ, bahubhir upacitaṃ yāmuneya-prabandhais, trātaṃ samyag yatīndrair idam akhilatamaḥ-karśanaṃ darśanaṃ naḥ// (p. 321). See also R. Ramanujachari, "Nathamuni, His Life and Times," Journal of the Annamalai University, IX (1940), pp. 267-77.

2. Stotra-ratna (SR), vv. 1-3, 61 and 65. See Appendix I for my analysis of these verses.

3. See below nn. 77-79 and accompanying text on the coṭṭai kulam; see also Ch. III on Bhāgavata Class IV.

4. AP, p. 87.1-8 (CE, p. 304; tr, #139). See Appendix I for my translation and analysis of these verses; see also Ch. III.

5. For information on the nature of the NyT from fragments and references found in later Śrī Vaiṣṇava works, see R. Ramanujachari, "Fragments from Nyāya-Tattva," in Professor K. V. Rangaswami Aiyangar Commemoration Volume (Madras, 1940), pp. 555-71; V. Varadachari, "Nyayatattva of Nathamuni," Indian Philosophy and Culture, VI (1961), pp. 484-89; M. Narasimhachary, Contribution, pp. 6-8, 313-18. These collections of fragments are by no means exhaustive of the direct quotations from and references to the NyT in the works of Vedānta Deśika. See n. 12 below for Yāmuna's references to the NyT in the AtS.

6. YIB, pp. 119-20, n. 273.

7. Ibid., p. 62.

8. See Ch. IV, n. 25, on Source III.

9. Vedānta Deśika, Nyāya-Pariśuddhi (Chow.), p. 13; N. B. that Oberhammer (YIB, pp. 67f) likens the position of Source III to that of the Nyāya-Bhūṣaṇam of Bhāsarvajña, a Naiyāyika who also proposed an alternative system and who is traditionally associated with the Śaiva Pāśupata Tantra. Cf. Ch. III, n. 32.

10. Nyāya-mañjarī, Vol. I, pp. 3.16-23; 4.27-5.7.

11. AP (CE), p. 242 (pp. 59.25-60.2; tr, #103), "yas sākṣāt kurute sadā sahajayā buddhyā samastaṃ jagat/ . . ." According to Vedānta Deśika (Tattva-ṭīkā, p. 52; Gadya-traya-bhāṣya on Śaraṇāgati Gadya, p. 111), the first line of a verse from the NyT reads "yo vetti yugapat sarvaṃ pratyakṣaṃ sadā svataḥ/". According to Narasimhachary (Contribution, p. 7) and U. T. Vīrarāghavācārya (Gūḍha-Prakāśa, p. 2), this is the first line of an introductory stanza that concludes "taṃ praṇamya hariṃ śāstraṃ nyāyatattvam pracakṣmahe"; however, neither author cites an authority for this additional line. See also n. 15 below.

12. Yāmuna refers to the NyT by name and quotes from it at AtS, p. 140.2-4 (A, p. 208.7-9); see Ch. VI, n. 161, for the

text. In addition, there are at least seven other points in the extant portion of the text at which Yāmuna is probably referring to it: pp. 34.4-5, 90.1-3, 94.8, 122.8, 127.7, 132.1-2 and 135.3-6 (A, pp. 65.2-4, 145.4-6, 151.7-8, 188.1, 194.2-3, 199.5-6 and 202.7-203.2).

13. Sarvārthasiddhi ad Tattvamuktākalāpa IV.56, pp. 221-22.

14. See AtS, pp. 94.8, 122.8, 127.7, 132.1-2, 135.3-6 and 140.2-4 (A, pp. 151.7-8, 188.1, 194.2-3, 199.5-6, 202.7-203.2 and 208.7-9.

15. Cf. the summary of Source III in Ch. IV above with the statement of Yāmuna's Siddhānta in Ch. III. Yāmuna concludes his most explicit statement of his own Siddhānta with the verse "vadanti khalu vedāntāḥ sarvajñaṃ jagataḥ patim/ mahākāruṇikaṃ tasmin vipralambhādayaḥ katham//" (see Ch. III, n. 65). Cf. the striking similarity of the verses that conclude the statement of Source III's position: "yas sākṣāt kurute sadā sahajayā buddhyā samastaṃ jagat/ yaḥ puṃsām abhivāñcchitāni diśati dhyānaikasaṃtarpitaḥ// nityāvāptasamastakāma iti yaṃ prahus trayīpāragāḥ/ tasmin vibhrama-vipralambhana-mukhā doṣā bhaveyuḥ katham//" (AP, pp. 59.25-60.2). See n. 11 above for the similarity of these verses to one from the NyT.

16. Oberhammer himself admits that such an interpretation of the words of Source III is not impossible: "Es ist zwar möglich, dass das besondere Hervorheben des Wortes vijñānam im Kommentar zu Br. sū. 2,2,44 so zu verstehen ist, dass damit die Lehre der Mīmāṃsā vom svataḥprāmāṇyam angedeuted wird und dadurch das in das Wort ādi hineininterpretierte āptoktatvam wie etwa bei Kumārila den Zweck hat, das Nicht-Erkenntnismittel-Sein, das durch die Fehler des Sprechers verursacht wird, auszuschliessen." (YIB, p. 68).

17. YIB, pp. 69-70; see Ch. III.

18. AP, p. 87.1-4 (CE, p. 304; tr, #139). See Appendix I for the Sanskrit text and my full translation.

19. See below nn. 23ff on this figure and the traditional Guru-paramparās.

20. Satyavrata Singh, Vedānta Deśika: His Life, Works and Philosophy, Chowkhamba Sanskrit Series Studies, Vol. V (Varanasi, 1958), pp. 116-17.

21. Vedānta Deśika, Śata-dūṣaṇī (Conjeeveram, 1901), Vol. I, vāda 7, p. 132, kiñca svāniṣṭaṃ prasañjakaṃ parāniṣṭaṃ prasañjanīyam iti tu tarkatattva-vyavasthā/ uktañ ca śrīpuṇḍarīkākṣācāryaiḥ "prasañjakan tu svāniṣṭaṃ parāniṣṭaṃ prasajyate/ viparyaye parābhīṣṭaṃ svābhīṣṭe paryavasyati// prasañjake tu svābhīṣṭe svāniṣṭe paryavasyati/ svābhīṣṭasya tv asiddhis syāt pareṣṭasya prasañjana//" iti/.

22. We can probably see these two traditions and their merging reflected in various statements of Vedānta Deśika. In n. 1 above, Vedānta Deśika traces "our darśana" from Nāthamuni through Yāmuna to Rāmānuja (Yatīndra). In the verse quoted in Ch. IV (n. 84), he refers to a tradition protected by Rāma Miśra and Yāmuna. In the statement from the GAS Rakṣā (Ch. IV, n. 88), Rāma Miśra is said to have revealed the meaning of the BhG to Yāmuna at the command of Nāthamuni.

23. For my sources on the traditional biographies or hagiographies of the early Ācāryas, I will depend primarily upon the two Maṇi-pravāḷam (Sanskritized Tamil) Guruparamparās, which are probably the earliest full accounts and the texts that are basic for, and most representative of, the two major tradition-

al versions: (1) the Teṅgalai Ārāyirappaḍi Guru-paramparā-prabhāvam (6000 GPP) of Pinbaḷagiya Perumāḷ Jīyar (mid-thirteenth century), ed. by C. Krishṇamācārya (Triplicane, Madras, 1927); and (2) the Vaḍagalai Mūvvāyirappaḍi Guru-paramparā-prabhāvam (3000 GPP) of Brahmatantra Svatantra Svāmi (mid-fourteenth century), ed. by K. Anandācārya (Triplicane, Madras, 1913). For much of my understanding of these texts I am indebted to K. K. A. Venkatachari of Madras with whom I read them. Many aspects of the following reconstruction of early Śrī Vaiṣṇava history have also been developed in conjunction with Prof. John B. Carman of Harvard Univ.; see his The Theology of Rāmānuja, Ch. 2,"Rāmānuja's Life."

24. 3000 GPP, pp. 41ff.

25. 6000 GPP, pp. 98ff.

26. Puṇḍarīkākṣa was born at Tiruveḷḷarai, less than ten miles north of Śrī Rangam; and Rāma Miśra, as his Tamil name Maṇakkāl Nambi indicates, at Maṇakkāl, approximately seven miles east (see Āḷkoṇḍvilli Govindācārya, The Holy Lives of the Āzhvārs or the Drāvida Saints (Mysore, 1902), Appendix, "The Table . . . of Saints and Sages . . ."). Tiruveḷḷarai is the home of one of the most important and wealthy of the five sub-temples associated with the Śrī Rangam temple (see Census of India 1961, Vol. IX, Madras, Part XI.D.ii, Temples of Madras State: Tiruchirapalli and South Arcot, pp. 196-97). It was also the birthplace of Eṅgeḷāḻvān (Viṣṇu-citta), one of the Teachers of the post-Rāmānuja period and, like Puṇḍarīkākṣa, reputed to have been a Pūrvaśikhī or Coḷiya Brāhmaṇa (see below n. 40). See 6000 GPP, pp. 98-107; 3000 GPP, pp. 32-42.

27. 3000 GPP, pp. 38-39.

28. 6000 GPP, p. 106; 3000 GPP, p. 41.

29. 6000 GPP, pp. 108f; 3000 GPP, p. 42.

30. 6000 GPP, pp. 110-15; 3000 GPP, pp. 44-47. See Ch. IV, nn. 85 and 88.

31. 6000 GPP, pp. 111-13; 3000 GPP, pp. 44-46.

32. 6000 GPP, p. 113; 3000 GPP, p. 46.

33. Ibid.

34. R. Ramanujachari, "Yamunacharya," Proc. and Trans. of the All-India Oriental Conference, 1955, p. 397.

35. 6000 GPP, pp. 113-14; 3000 GPP, pp. 46-47.

36. 6000 GPP, p. 114; 3000 GPP, pp. 46-47.

37. 6000 GPP, p. 114; 3000 GPP, p. 47. See also Ch. IV, nn. 85 and 88.

38. 6000 GPP, pp. 114-15; 3000 GPP, pp. 47-48.

39. 3000 GPP, pp. 38-39.

40. For the best treatment to date of these Coḷiya Brāhmaṇas and their major and, in the pre-Rāmānuja period, clearly dominant role in the integration of classical and popular elements that resulted in the Śrī Vaiṣṇava tradition, see N. Jagadeesan, "History of Śrī Vaishnavism in the Tamil Country (Post Rāmānuja)" (unpublished doctoral thesis, University of Madras, 1967), pp. 411-12. See also N. Subrahmanian, "The Brahmin in the Tamil Country (in ancient and medieval times) (unpublished manuscript, 1968), pp. 40-42, 47; J. F. Staal, "notes on some Brahmin Communities of South India," Journal of the Royal India, Pakistan and Ceylon Society, XXXII, p. 2.

41. Thus Uyyakkoṇḍār means "he who took (the cold rice) to save," i.e., to save Nāthamuni the embarrassment and opprobrium that would have followed had his disciple refused to accept

the rice in a gracious manner. See 3000 GPP, p. 39.

42. 6000 GPP, pp. 113-14; 3000 GPP, p. 46.

43. For example, another Śrīvatsāṅka Miśra, i.e., Kūreśa, Rāmānuja's major disciple and scribe; another Rāma Miśra, according to some tradition a son of Śrīvatsāṅka Miśra (Kūreśa); Varada Viṣṇu Miśra, a learned but, according to Vedānta Deśika, somewhat unorthodox thinker; see S. Singh, Vedānta Deśika, pp. 118-19, 122-23.

44. Jogendra Nath Bhattacharya, Hindu Castes and Sects (Calcutta: Editions Indic, 2nd ed., 1968 [1st ed., 1896]), pp. 24-50 [33-64].

45. A. Subrahmanya Sastri, ed., Prakaraṇa Pañcikā of Śrī Śalikanātha Miśra, Banaras Hindu University Darśana Series No. 4 (Banaras, 1961), p. vii.

46. On the wide-spread and long-term practice of South Indian kings' encouraging Northern Brahmaṇas to immigrate for such purposes by offering them village and land grants called agrahāras, brahmadeyas or caturvedimaṅgalams, see C. Minaksi, Administration and Social Life Under the Pallavas (Madras: Univ. of Madras, 1938), pp. 136, 186ff; A. Appadorai, Economic Conditions in Southern India (1000-1500 AD), 2 vols., Madras University Historical Series No. 12 (Madras, 1936), I, 72ff, 111ff, 140ff; Basudeva Upadhyay, "Migration of Brāhmaṇas from Madhyadesha," J. of Bihar R. S., XXXXV (1959), pp. 308-12; D. D. Kosambi, An Introduction to the Study of Indian History (Bombay, 1956, pp. 291-305); George W. Spencer, "Royal Leadership and Imperial Conquest in Medieval South India: The Naval Expedition of Rajendra Chola I, c. 1025 A. D.," unpublished Ph. D. thesis, Univ. of California--Berkeley, 1967, pp. 14-16, 21-33, 59ff.

47. F. Otto Schrader, Introduction to the Pāñcarātra, pp. 16-19.

48. Allen W. Thrasher, "The Advaita of Maṇḍana Miśra's Brahma-Siddhi," unpublished Ph. D. thesis, Harvard Univ., 1972, pp. 197-99.

49. V. S. Apte, The Practical Sanskrit-English Dictionary (Poona, 1957), Part II, s.v. miśra.

50. See Ch. IV, n. 84.

51. Bhattacharya, Hindu Castes, pp. 36, 470.

52. I owe this suggestion to my former fellow student, Dr. Allen W. Thrasher, who wrote his Ph. D. thesis on Maṇḍana Miśra; see n. 48 above. Cf. the classic story about Vācaspati Miśra who became so engrossed in his studies that he ignored his wife and attempted to make amends by naming his great Vedāntic commentary, the Bhāmatī, after her.

53. Umesha Miśra, History of Indian Philosophy, (Allahabad: Tirubhukti Pub., 1966), Vol. II, pp. 99-100.

54. The Prapannāmṛta by Anantācārya, IV. 7, XXXVII.4 and XXXVIII.1.

55. "vaidikas tāntriko miśra iti me trividho makhaḥ/ trayāṇām īpsitena--eva vidhinā māṃ samarcayet//" BhP XI.27.7, cf. vv. 26 and 49); see A. Gail, Bhakti im Bhāgavata Purāṇa (Wiesbaden, 1969), p. 7, n. 21. See also the Sanatkumāra Saṃhitā, Ṛṣi-rātra, 5.37, "vaidikaṃ tāntrikaṃ caiva tathā vaidika-tāntrikam/ mantra-trayam . . ."; and Bhatt, Philosophy of Pāñcarātra, pp. 11-13; p. 19, nn. 36-37.

56. Kōil Oḷugu, The Chronicle of the Sri Rangam Temple, ed. and tr. by V. N. Hari Rao (Madras, [1961]), pp. 33-37.

57. 6000 GPP, pp. 98-107; 3000 GPP, pp. 32-43.

58. See nn. 25-26 above.

59. 6000 GPP, p. 116-17, ummaippōlē oru darśana-pravarttaka-raiyum uṇḍākkiyaruḷik kōyile viḍādeyirum. The Śrī Rangam temple is known simply as Kōyil, "The Temple," among Śrī Vaiṣṇavas.

60. See AP, p. 87.4 (CE, p. 304; tr, #139) and Appendix I.

61. Narasimhachary, Contribution, p. 6; Vedānta Deśika, Srimad Rahasyatrayasara of Srī Vedantadesika, tr. by M. R. Rajagopala Ayyangar (Kumbakonam, [1956]), p. 5.

62. 6000 GPP, pp. 106, 116-18; 3000 GPP, pp. 48-50.

63. See Appendix I.

64. See n. 62 above; see also J. B. Carman, Theology of Rāmānuja, pp. 25-26.

65. See P. B. Annangaracharya Swami, The Glory of the Tamil Prabandha (The Background of Ramanuja's System), English adaptation by M. V. V. K. Rangachari (Kakinada, 1955), pp. 116-20, for the fullest analysis of the many points in common between Yāmuna's SR and the Āḻvārs' hymns.

66. 6000 GPP, pp. 101-103; 3000 GPP, pp. 34-36.

67. See Appendix I for these arguments.

68. Further doubt is thrown upon the traditional account, according to which the institutionalizing of the Āḻvārs' hymns in the ritual at Śrī Rangam is made possible by Nāthamuni's efforts, by the fact that the earlier figure Tirumaṅgai Āḻvār is also made responsible for instituting the practice of reciting Nammāḻvār's hymns during the Adhyayana-utsava at Śrī Raṉgam; see Govindāchārya, Holy Lives of the Āzhvārs, p. 186.

69. Jagadeesan, "History of Śrī Vaishnavism in the Tamil Country," p. 412.

70. Prince Ilangō Adigal, Shilappadikaram (The Ankle Bracelet), tr. by Alain Daniélou (New York: New Directions Books, 1965), Canto XIII (vv. 38-40), p. 87. On music as a non-Vedic profession, see Manu 4.2.10 and Subrahmanian, "The Brahmin in Tamil Country," p. 24.

71. K. C. Varadachari, Āḻvārs of South India, Bhavan's Book University 143 (Bombay: Bharatiya Vidya Bhavan, 1966), p. 126.

72. Govindāchārya, Holy Lives of the Āzhvārs, pp. 24-30.

73. Ibid., pp. 25-26.

74. Ibid., pp. 26-28.

75. It is quite possible that some of these Pūrva-śikhī Bhāgavatas at one time were arcakas but gave up the practice under the pressure of orthodox criticism; cf. the Śaiva Dīkṣitars of the Cidambaram temple who wear the top knot of hair in the front (see K. A. Nilakanta Sastri, Development of Religion in South India, pp. 113-14).

76. See Ch. III on Bhāgavata Class III, especially n. 24.

77. 3000 GPP, p. 49, "nam-kaṇṇan coṭṭaik-kulattut teyvam;" see also 6000 GPP, pp. 117-18.

78. On coṭṭai, see Tamil Lexicon (Madras: Univ. of Madras, 1928), Vol. 3, s.v. This straight-forward explanation has perhaps been resisted because many of the meanings of the Tamil coṭṭai are derogatory. For my photograph of Mannanār with Nāthamuni and Yāṃuna, see the frontispiece of the original form of my doctoral dissertaion, "Yāmuna's Pāñcarātrika Vedānta," Harvard University, 1974.

79. 6000 GPP, pp. 98-99, 106; 3000 GPP, pp. 33, 41. Even more strongly than in the case of the Miśras, the evidence suggests that the coṭṭai kulam immigrated to the South at a relatively late date, thus deriving much of their status from their close association with the sacred places of the North. In addition to the evidence derived from this northern pilgrimage and their nearly settling on the banks of the Yamunā, see Yāmuna's reference to a Kāśmīra-āgama-prāmāṇya at AP, pp. 85.19-86.1 (CE, p. 304; tr, #138). See Ch. III, n. 24, on Yāmuna's reputed authorship of this work.

80. See John B. Carman, The Theology of Rāmānuja, pp. 26-48.

NOTES

CHAPTER VI

1. AtS, p. 1 (A, pp. 1, 4). See Ch. VII for the text and translation of the introductory portions of the extant text.

2. AtS, pp. 2-8 (A, pp. 4.3-17.4). For a preliminary analysis of the significance of this introductory section, see van Buitenen, Introduction to VAS, pp. 43-48.

3. AtS, p. 2.1-4 (A, pp. 4.3-5.4).

4. AtS, p. 2.4 (A, p. 5.5-6).

5. AtS, pp. 2.4-4.3 (A, pp. 5.6-9.1); see Ch. VII, Pratijñā Series I.

6. AtS, pp. 4.4-6.3 (A, pp. 9.2-12.5); see Ch. VII, Pratijñā Series II.

7. AtS, p. 6.4-8 (A, pp. 12.6-13.4); see Ch. VII, Pratijñā Series III.

8. AtS, p. 7.1-5 (A, pp. 13.5-14.4); see Ch. VII, Pratijñā Series IV.

9. AtS, p. 7.6-7 (A, p. 14.5-7); see Ch. VII, Pratijñā Series V.

10. AtS, p. 8.1-3 (A, pp. 14.8-15.2); see Ch. VII, n. 10.

11. See Ghate, Vedānta, p. 42, for the definition of a sūtra as "without doubt" (a-saṃdigdha).

12. For my interpretation of this phrase which is crucial for an understanding of Yāmuna's relationship to the following list of Vedāntins, see Ch. VII, n. 83.

13. On these Vedāntins whose works Yāmuna considered to be flawed with error to varying degrees and therefore relatively untrustworthy and confusing in comparison with those of the preceding three authorities, see Ch. VII, nn. 84-89; see also van Buitenen, Introduction to VAS, pp. 24-30.

14. AtS, p. 8.4-8 (A, pp. 15.4-17.2).

15. As Oberhammer has done: "Denn Yāmunamuni scheint...gar kein Vedāntin gewesen zu sein, sondern ein Pāñcarātrin. Dies geht zum Beispiel daraus hervor, ...dass er sich zur Vyūha-Theologie des Pāñcarātra bekennt und selbst ein ganzes Werk, das Āgamaprāmāṇyam, dem Versuch gewidmet hat, die Autorität des Pāñcarātra zu beweisen." (YIB, p. 6).

16. J. A. B. van Buitenen, in a public lecture delivered at Madras ("Lectures on Vedānta: Bhāskara, Yāmuna and Rāmānuja," Prof. M. Rangacharya Memorial Lectures, Madras, March 25-27, 1968), raised the question of whether or not we should consider Yāmuna a Vedāntin and answered it by saying that he was more of a Vedāntin than anything else [significantly basing his argument (contra Oberhammer, see n. 15) upon the AP in which Yāmuna argues as a Vedāntin or Uttara Mīmāṃsaka vis-à-vis his Pūrva Mīmāṃsā opponents, especially the Prābhākaras (see Ch. III above).

17. Ch. V, n. 12; for the text of the explicit reference to the NyT, see n. 161 below.

18. Vedānta Deśika, Nyāya-siddhāñjana (Madras, 1934), p. 274. According to U. T. Vīrarāghavācārya, the Siddhitrayam with Gūḍha-prakāśa, pp. 2-3 [GPrak (1972), p. 1], Vedānta Deśika's statement indicates that the AtS is a discussion of only one portion of Nāthamuni's śāstra, i.e., the pramātṛ-pāda.

19. See Ch. V.

20. AtS, p. 8.10-11 (A, p. 17.3-4, śl. 3).

21. Introduction to VAS, p. 43.

22. The Siddhitrayam with Gūḍha-prakāśa, p. 145 (n. to p. 7.1) [GPrak (1972), p. 6.20-21], sarvatra siddhānti-pakṣasya--eva--ante kīrtanād iha--apy evam; see Ch. VII, n. 38.

23. Introduction to VAS, p. 45, n. 125.

24. See Ch. VII, Pratijñā Series III.

25. Personal conversation, University of Madras, 1967. In the Preface to the 1972 edition of the translation (see Ch. I, n. 35), Prof. Ramanujachari states that they also consulted two other traditional Pandits, Nyaya Vedantakesari Madhurantakam Sri Viraraghavachariar and Panditaraja D. T. Tatachariar [ST (1972), p. 1 of prefactory material to English translation].

26. In the Journal of Annamalai University, Vols. IV-XII (1935-43). It was issued as Vol. 4 of the Annamalai University Philosophy Series in 1943 and reissued in ca. 1972 (see Ch. I, n. 35).

27. Siddhitrayam, ed. with Gūḍhaprakāśa-ākhya-ṭippaṇādi (GPrak) (Tirupati: Srīvāṇī Press, 1942). A revised edition was published in 1972 (see Ch. I, n. 35).

28. Introduction to VAS, pp. 43-48.

29. Siddhitrayam, ed. with Siddhāñjana-vyākhyā (SVy) (Bombay: Nirnaya Sagar Press, 1954).

30. "Contribution of Śrī Yāmunācārya to Viśiṣṭādvaita" (Doctoral thesis, Univ. of Madras, 1966). This thesis has since been published under the title Contribution of Yāmuna to Viśiṣṭādvaita (Madras: Prof. M. Rangacharya Memorial Trust, 1971).

31. Personal conversation, Madras, 1967.

32. Aṇṇaṅgarācārya's edition [ST(A), AtS(A), SVy] has also been used as the text of reference in two other more specialized studies of Yāmuna's works: Oberhammer's YIB and R. Mesquita's "Das Problem der Gotteserkenntnis bei Yāmunamuni." Therefore, I will give parallel references, first to the Annamalai edition and translation (1943) and then to Aṇṇaṅgarācārya's, e.g., AtS, p. 2.4-6 (A, p. 5.6-9), referring to page 2, lines 4-6, etc., of the Sanskrit text.

33. Madras, June-July, 1968.

34. GPrak, pp. 5-6 [GPrak(1972), p. 5]; SVy, p. 6. Ramanujachari in his translation also follows this interpretation; see AtS, p. 3, n. 10.

35. Introduction to VAS, p. 43, n. 115.

36. AtS, p. 3.3-6 (A, p. 7.1-5); see Ch. VII, Pratijñā Series I.B. and Appendix III.

37. AtS, p. 3.7-8 (A, p. 8.1-3); see Ch. VII, Pratijñā Series I.C. and Appendix III.

38. AtS, p. 4.1-2 (A, p. 8.2-4); see Ch. VII, Pratijñā Series I.D. and Appendix III.

39. AtS, p. 4.3 (A, p. 8.4-9.1); see Ch. VII, Pratijñā Series I.E. and Appendix III.

40. GPrak, p. 7.21 [GPrak(1972), p. 6.28], tathātathety anena svatassukhitva-tad-abhāva-grahaṇam/. Aṇṇaṅgarācārya,

SVy, p. 9, says--in a more general way and with less syntactical plausibility--"ca-kāro 'nukta-vipratipatti-samuccāyakaḥ/." I take the *tathātathā* as simply summing up what has been said in association with the governing verb, *pratipadyante*.

41. The closest parallel to the AtS in both structure and subject matter that I have been able to find is the *Tattvāloka* (TA), the eighth *prakaraṇa* of the *Prakaraṇa-pañcikā* by the Prābhākara Śālikanātha Miśra (Banaras Hindu Univ. Darśana Series, No. 4). There, the introduction (pp. 315-16) is identical in structure but exceedingly brief.

42. AtS, p. 90.1-3 (A, p. 145.4-6) and p. 143.4 (A, p. 213.4-5). These references establish that Yāmuna did not deal with this topic simply in the course of discussing the first topic as might be maintained by one who wished to resist my suggestion that Pratijñā I.A.7 is Yāmuna's Siddhānta.

43. Since a few lines of the discussion of the *ātmā*'s eternality (*nityatva*) are extant, it is certain that in the Extended Discussion he followed the order of Summary Śloka and not that of Pratijñā Series on this topic; see AtS, pp. 150.3-151.6 (A, pp. 222.5-224.3).

44. See AtS, p. 7.4 (A, p. 14.3), tad-guṇa-anubhava-janita-niratiśaya-sukha-. See also Ch. VII, Pratijñā IV.I, and J. A. B. van Buitenen, "The Śubhāśraya Prakaraṇa (Viṣṇu Purāṇa 6, 7) and the Meaning of Bhāvanā," ALB, XIX (1955), 3-19.

45. See preceding note.

46. Paul Hacker, "Śaṅkara der Yogin und Śaṅkara der Advaitin, einige Beobachtungen," WZKSO, XII/XIII (1968-69), 127-35.

47. AtS, p. 9.1-2 (A, p. 18.1-2), ahaṃ jānāmi--iti jñātā hy ātmā aham iti cakāsti/

48. Aṇṇaṅgarācārya, SVy, p. 5; Narasimhachary, *Contribution*, pp. 143-49.

49. For the corresponding Extended Discussion, see AtS, pp. 9.1-19.6 (A, pp. 18.1-41.7).

50. For Extended Discussion, see AtS, pp. 19.7-20.7 (A, pp. 41.8-43.6).

51. For Extended Discussion, see AtS, pp. 21.1-27.9 (A, pp. 44.1-54.4).

52. For Extended Discussion, see AtS, pp. 28.1-29.5 (A, pp. 55.1-56.5).

53. See AtS, p. 28.4 (A, p. 55.5) where the proponent of this Pratijñā refers to *śruti* or rather presumption based thereon (*śruty-arthāpatti*) as a *pramāṇa*. See also E. H. Johnston, *Early Sāṁkhya* (London: Royal Asiatic Society, 1937), pp. 18-19, on *prāṇa* as the ultimate principle in the Upaniṣads.

54. For the rejection of Pratijñā I.A.1, see AtS, pp. 12.7-19.6 (A, pp. 27.1-41.7); of I.A.2, p. 20.1-7 (A, pp. 42.4-43.6); of I.A.3, pp. 21.5-27.9 (A, pp. 44.6-54.4); of I.A.4, pp. 28.5-29.5 (A, pp. 55.6-56.5).

55. For the corresponding Extended Discussion, see AtS, pp. 29.6-74.8 (A, pp. 56.6-123.6). See also Narasimhachary, *Contribution*, pp. 149-63.

56. AtS, p. 33.4 (A, p. 63.4-5).

57. AtS, p. 33.4-6 (A, p. 63.6-7), yathāhuḥ prakaṭāḥ/ avibhāgo 'pi buddhy-ātmā viparyāsitadarśanaiḥ/ grāhya-grāhaka-saṃvitti-bhedavān iti lakṣyate// On the source of this oft-quoted verse by Dharmakīrti, see D. H. H. Ingalls, "Śaṁkara's Arguments Against the Buddhists," PhilEW, III (1953-54), 300, n. 15.

58. See Narasimhachary, Contribution, pp. 151-54, on Yāmuna's Kevalādvaitin opponents. Sureśvara is the authority quoted by name [AtS, pp. 36.6-37.2 (A, p. 69.2-5) and 52.5-7 (A, 93.7-9), but Yāmuna responds most directly and systematically to the first verse and introductory discussion of Vimuktātman's Iṣṭa-siddhi [AtS, pp. 36.5ff (A, pp. 69.1ff); see also M. Hiriyanna, ed., Iṣṭa-siddhi of Vimuktātman, Gaekwad's Oriental Series No. LXV (Baroda, 1933), p. xii].

59. AtS, p. 57.4-5 (A, p. 100.3-4), tasmāj jñātṛtayā siddhyann aham-artha eva pratyag-ātmā, na jñāpti-mātram/; p. 60.1-2 (A, p. 104.1-2), aham ity eva hi tasya svarūpam/ jñānam api hi tad-dharmatvena tasyaiva prakāśate; pp. 72.7-73.7 (A, pp. 120.4-122.4), ātmā tu prakāśa-svabhāva eva/ na ca tāvatā jñānatvam, svatantratvāt/ paratantram āgantu yāvad-artha-indriya-sannikarṣādi-kāraṇa-sannidhānam avatiṣṭhamānam artha-avacchinna-rūpaṃ jñānam iti prāg evāvocāma/ ātmā tu svatantro jñātā--aham iti pratyātmaṃ prathate/ . . . tathā "katama ātmā" iti praśnapūrvakam idam eva lakṣaṇam āmananti vājasaneyinaḥ "yo 'yam vijñānamayaḥ prāṇeṣu hṛdy antar-jyotiḥ puruṣaḥ" iti [Bṛhadāraṇyaka Up. IV.iii.7]/ atra hi yo 'yam sarvaloka-anubhava-siddho vividha-viṣaya-vedana-pracuraḥ prāṇeṣu prerakatayā sthito hṛdayāyatane antar-jyotir aham iti pratyaktvena prakāśate/; p. 74.7 (A, p. 123.6), tat siddhaṃ jñātā--eva--ayam ātmā--iti/.

60. AtS, p. 75.1 (A, p. 123.7-8).

61. See above n. 43.

62. AtS, p. 102.5-6 (A, p. 162.1-2).

63. AtS, p. 2.6 (A, p. 6.1-2).

64. See Ch. VII, n. 23 for an identical progression in the TA of Śālikanātha Miśra's Prakaraṇa-pañcikā.

65. For the Extended Discussion, see AtS, pp. 75.1-85.6 (A, pp. 123.8-138.8). On Yāmuna's view of the relation between Sāṅkhya and the Prachannas, see AtS, p. 85.2-3 (A, p. 138.2-4), na ca dṛśi-mātra-ātma-vādināṃ sāṅkhyānāṃ tad-upajīvināñ ca pracchannānāṃ draṣṭṛtvaṃ vāstavam asti/.

66. For the Extended Discussion, see AtS, pp. 85.7-87.8 (A, pp. 139.1-142.2).

67. AtS, pp. 87.9-94.6 (A, pp. 142.3-151.3).

68. AtS, pp. 94.7-100.11 (A, pp. 151.4-159.8).

69. AtS, pp. 100.12ff (A, pp. 160.1ff). The only exception being the last paragraph, pp. 150.3-151.6 (A, pp. 222.5-224.3), which initiates the discussion of Summary Śloka Topic (3), nityo.

70. AtS, pp. 100.12-102.4 (A, pp. 160.1-161.8).

71. Especially AtS, pp. 100.12-101.8 (A, p. 160.1-12), beginning with the verse sajātīya-svasādhyārtha-nirapekṣa-ātma-siddhayaḥ/ sarve padārthās tena--ātmā nirapekṣa-svasiddhikaḥ// and ending with "ity an-anya-apekṣā hy ātma-svarūpa-siddhiḥ." Yāmuna's use of ātmā-siddhayaḥ and ātma-svarūpa-siddhiḥ here indicates that, as is often the case with Yāmuna, he intends the title of his work Ātma-siddhi to be taken in a double sense: 1) "the conclusive determination of the true nature of the ātmā and the Paramātmā" in which the term siddhi represents a genre of literature and "stands for conclusive ascertainment as a result of careful investigation" [S. Kuppuswami Sastri, ed., Brahmasiddhi by Ācārya Maṇḍanamiśra, Madras Government Oriental Manuscripts Series No. 4 (Madras, 1937), pp. xxi-xxii] and 2) "the manifestation [in cognition of the svarūpa] of the

ātmā" [cf. AtS, p. 93.7 (A, p. 150.4); 94.6 (A, p. 151.4), and 95.2-3 (A, p. 152.1-2)]. Doubtless, this second meaning of siddhi should also be applied to the Paramātmā. Cf. "ātma-svarūpa-siddhiḥ" with the phrase "anuditānastamita-svarūpa-prakāśaḥ" which appears in both Pratijñā I.B.5.a and I.A.7, stamping them both as Yāmuna's Siddhāntas.

72. Especially AtS, p. 101.9-102.4 (A, p. 161.1-8), tad evam cit-svabhāvasya puṃsaḥ svābhāvikī citiḥ/ nānā-padārtha-saṃsargāt tat-tad-vittitvam aśnute// yathaiva khalu sūrya-ālokas tena tenārthabhedena saṃsargāt tat-tat-prakāśo bhavati ghaṭa-prakāśaḥ paṭa-prakāśa iti, evam ātmanaḥ prakāra-bhūtam caitanyaṃ artha-viśeṣa-saṃsargāt ghaṭa-saṃvit paṭa-saṃvid ityādi-prakhyā-upākhye pratipadyate/ te ca caitanyasya daśā-viśeṣāś cetayitur ātmano dharma-viśeṣatvād eva tasya--aparokṣā bhavanti, kādācitka-bodha-vādinām iva bodhasya viṣaya-bheda-avacchedādayaḥ/ All of the rest of Yāmuna's extended systematic argumentation for his Siddhānta is in effect a discussion of this brief passage and the issues it raises as to the relation of the ātmā, consciousness, and the cognition of objects; thus Yāmuna concludes his formal theoretical argument with the words: tat siddhaṃ caitanya-svabhāva eva--ayam ātmā ātmānaṃ vidann eva--āste/ anyat tu nimitta-bheda-anusāreṇa jānāti na jānāti ceti/ [AtS, pp. 148.7-149.1 (A, pp. 220.5-221.2)].

73. AtS, pp. 102.5-110.3 (A, pp. 162.1-171.8), nanu ātmanaś caitanyam āgantukam iti nyāya-vaiśeṣikās tanmata-upajīvinaś ca--abhinava-mīmāṃsakāḥ . . . .

74. AtS, pp. 110.4-149.1 (A, pp. 172.1-221.2), atrāhur ātma-tattva-jñāḥ . . .

75. Cf. Pratijñā I.A.7, . . . bodha-eka-svabhāvam eva . . . anuditānastamita-svarūpa-prakāśaṃ svayaṃjyotiṣam imam [AtS, pp. 2.8-3.1 (A, p. 6.3-6)], with Pratijñā I.B.5.a, jñāna-svabhāvatayā--anuditānastamita-svarūpa-prakāśaḥ svayaṃjyotiḥ [AtS, p. 3.4 (A, p. 7.2-3)].

76. AtS, pp. 149.2-150.2 (A, 221.3-222.4).

77. On the significance of this usage of the term ahaṃkāra, see Ch. VII, notes to Pratijñā I.A.6.

78. AtS, p. 2.7 (A, p. 6.2), āgantuka-bodha-sukha-duḥkhādy-asādhāraṇa-guṇa-ādhāram. See also Ch. VII, Pratijñā I.A.6.

79. AtS, pp. 100.4-101.8 (A, pp. 159.1-160.12), beginning with the kārikā with which he concludes his refutation of the Prābhākaras: sarvasyārthasya tad-vitteḥ sākṣi sarvatra sammataḥ/ ātmaivāstu svataḥsiddhaḥ kim anekais tathāvidhaiḥ// See also above nn. 59 and 71, and Narasimhachary, Contribution, pp. 177-79.

80. AtS, pp. 75.1-77.4 (A, 123.7-127.2); see also Narasimhachary, Contribution, pp. 163-64.

81. AtS, pp. 87.9-88.2 (A, p. 142.3-7). See also Narasimhachary, Contribution, pp. 173-74, and Ch. VII, note to Pratijñā I.B.3.

82. AtS, p. 94.6 (A, p. 151.4), astu tarhi grāhakatayaiva sarvārtha-grahaṇa-samayeṣv ātma-siddhiḥ/ See above n. 71 on this sense of ātma-siddhi.

83. AtS, pp. 94.6-95.3 (A, pp. 151.4-152.2), abhyupagantavyā hi saṃvidaḥ svataḥsiddhiḥ . . ./ ataḥ kḷptārthāntara-sādhano-bhāvayā tayā--eva--ātmano 'pi siddhir abhyupagantuṃ nyāyyā/ See also Narasimhachary, Contribution, pp. 174-77.

84. Stcherbatsky, BL, I, 51.

85. AtS, p. 2.6 (A, 6.2). See Ch. VII, Pratijñā I.A.6 and notes thereto.

86. AtS, p. 2, "like ether and the like, it has a non-intelligent nature."

87. See Ch. VII, notes to Pratijñā I.A.6.

88. AtS, pp. 103.8-9, 131.6, 135.8 (A, pp. 163.5-164.1, 198.11, 203.5); see also Saṃvit-siddhi (SS), p. 191.3 (A, p. 299, śl. 91cd).

89. AtS, pp. 95.6-97.7 and 102.5-110.3 (A, pp. 152.6-155.5 and 162.1-171.8).

90. AtS, p. 97.6 (A, p.155.4-5), ato nāsty apavarga-daśāyāṃ jñānam/.

91. AtS, p. 110.9-10 (A, p. 173.1-2), buddhi-sukha-duḥkha-ādi-niśśeṣa-vaiśeṣika-ātma-guṇa-atyantika-uparama-lakṣaṇo hi mokṣaḥ kaṇabhakṣa-akṣacara-mate/. At AP, p. 47.17-19 (CE, p. 210; tr, #84), this view of mokṣa is ascribed to the Pāśupatas and the Śaivas: ātyantikā duḥkha-nivṛttir duḥkhānta-śabdenoktā, tām eva niśśeṣa-vaiśeṣika-ātma-guṇa-uccheda-lakṣaṇāṃ muktiṃ manyante/. See also Ch. VII, Pratijñā IV.C. It is relatively clear that the Śaiva Bhakti and Tāntric movements developed a close relationship on the theoretical side with Nyāya-Vaiśeṣika just as the Vaiṣṇava did with Vedānta. What is intriguing and suggestive is the association of the Neo-Mīmāṃsaka with this view of mokṣa. It may well be that the acceptance of such a view of mokṣa and of the idea that the ātmā is a-cit-svabhāva by the dominant schools of Pūrva Mīmāṃsā was one of the major factors in the rather late assertion of Vedānta or Uttara Mīmāṃsā as a distinct darśana (see Ch. II).

92. AtS, pp. 110.8-111.4 (A, pp. 172.5-173.7). See below, n. 136.

93. AtS, pp. 35.6-65.2 (A, pp. 67.3-110.4).

94. AtS, p. 36.4-5 (A, p. 68.7-8), ato nirdhūta-nikhila-bheda-vikalpā nirdharma-prakāśa-mātra-eka-rasā kūṭastha-nityā saṃvid eva--ātmā paramātmā ca/.

95. AtS, p. 59.9-10 (A, p. 103.8-10), yat tu muktāv aham-artho nānuvartata iti tad vārtam, yatas tathā sati vaināśika-darśana iva ātma-nāśa eva--apavargaḥ prakārāntareṇa pratijñātaḥ syāt/.

96. Translation by R. Ramanujachari, AtS, p. 60 [AtS(1972), p. 53]. The text reads: anyac ca yaḥ sāṃsārika-duḥkhair duḥkhitvena--ātmānaṃ tattvato bhrāntyā vā pratyeti duḥkhy aham iti, sa sarvam idam aniṣṭajātaṃ katham aham apunarudayam apanudya avyākulaṃ svastho bhūyāsam iti saṃjāta-mumukṣaḥ tat-sādhane pravartate/ sa yadi sādhana-anuṣṭhānād aham eva na bhaviṣyāmīty avagacchati, apagacched asau mokṣa-kathā-prasaṅgād api/ tataś ca--asaṃbhavad-adhikāritayā sarva eva vedānta-vidhayaḥ sarvāṇi ca mokṣa-śāstrāṇi prāmāṇyād eva pracyaveran/ [AtS, p. 60.4-9 (A, p. 104.4-10)].

97. Aṇṇaṅgarācārya, SVy, p. 7, tattad-vādy-ukteṣu yāvad upapannam, tāvad ākāravattvaṃ cātmanaḥ saṃmatam eva hi siddhānte/.

98. See above n. 34.

99. See above n. 35.

100. See above n. 71.

101. See above n. 59 and below p. 137.

102. See below pp. 142ff.

103. See below pp. 130ff.

104. See below pp. 141ff.

105. See below pp. 127ff.
106. See below pp. 129-30.
107. Ramanujachari, tr., AtS, p. 2, "Others again say that it is of the nature of pure consciousness itself . . ."; see also Annaṅgarācārya, SVy, p. 6, sāṅkhya-matam āha "apare" iti/ bodhaikasvabhāvam eva--bodhaś caitanyam, tad eva svo bhāvaḥ svarūpaṃ yasya tam, jñāna-svarūpam eva/. On dṛśi-mātra-ātma-vādināṃ sāṅkhyānāṃ, see AtS, p. 85.2 (A, p. 138.3).
108. See John B. Carman, The Theology of Rāmānuja: An Essay in Interreligious Understanding (New Haven: Yale University Press, 1974), Ch. VI, "Svarūpa and Svabhāva: Two Kinds of Divine Essence," pp. 88-97, and Ch. VII, "The Five Defining Attributes of God's Essential Nature," pp. 98-113; see also van Buitenen, VAS, pp. 184-85, n. 20, "svarūpa- 'proper form' (where 'form' is the principle of individuality, cf. nāma-rūpa-), free from adventitious adjuncts but (for R.) possessed of essential properties; svabhāva- 'this essential form in the process of being and becoming with and through its essential qualities.'"
109. G. P. Bhatt, Epistemology of Bhāṭṭa School, pp. 11-21.
110. AtS, p. 113.5-6 (A, p. 176.1-2), nanv evam artha-siddhi-vyavasthāpakatayā abhyupagataṃ jñānam āgantukaṃ kriyā-rūpam iti kathaṃ tad ātma-svabhāvaḥ/.
111. AtS, pp. 114.1-115.4 (A, pp. 176.6-177.8).
112. See AtS, p. 128.7ff (A, pp. 195.6ff), especially pp. 131.4-132.5 (A, pp. 198.9-199.11), anyac ca arthasya prakāśakaṃ jñānam bhavatām/ sarvaṃ ca prakāśya-vastu-sannikṛṣṭam eva prakāśakaṃ dṛṣṭaṃ dīpa-prabhādi/ atas tad api tatheti yuktam āśrayitum/ vyomavad amūrtasya na kriyā-vat-tvam iti cet, keyaṃ mūrtir nāma yad-virahiṇaḥ kriyā-ayogaḥ/ yadi paribhāṣikī dravyatve sati kvācitkatā--iti, iṣyata eva sā caitanye/ na hi tat-sarvagataṃ dravyaṃ, tathā sati yugapat sarvārtha-siddhi-prasaṅgāt/ . . . niratiśaya-vegaṃ ca tat, yugapad iva--atiśighram aneka-indriya-adhiṣṭhāna-darśanāt/ ato yathoditaṃ mūrtatvaṃ siddham/ sparśavattā mūrtiḥ, tad-virahān niṣkriyatvam iti cet . . ./ sparśa-rahitasya--api manaindriyasya kriyā-vat-tvaṃ padārtha-vākyārtha-vidām ubhayeṣām api sammatam eva/ and pp. 134.6-135.7 (A, pp. 202.2-203.3), ata indriyādi-dvāreṇa caitanyam api tad-artha-abhimukhaṃ nirgacchati--iti nyāyyam/ . . . yat tu guṇaś caitanyaṃ guṇinam apahāya katham anyato yātīti, tad ayuktam prahāṇa-anubhyupagamāt/ a-prahāya--eva--ātmānam itas tataś cetanā indriyādi-dvārā niścarati/ vicchinnāyāś ca tasyāḥ saṃdhāna-abhāvaś śāstra eva--uktaḥ/ dṛśyante ca guṇā api śabda-gandha-sūryāloka- ratnaprabhādayo gatimanto dharmy-ativartinaś ca/; (see also Narasimhachary, Contribution, pp. 199-204). In this section of a text in which the "guṇa" caitanyam is also accepted as a dravya possessing limited dimension (kvācitkatā) and form (mūrtatvam) and thus being able to possess activity (kriyā-vat-tvam) and to go out (nirgacchati) with exceedingly great speed (niratiśaya-vegam) by means of the sense-organs and make contact with objects, Yāmuna is probably following Nāthamuni's Nyāya-tattva, as indicated by the reference to śāstra (śāstra eva--uktaḥ) and by the use of the term niratiśaya-vegam which is reminiscent of Nāthamuni's definition of jñāna as preserved by Vedānta Deśika: nyāya-tattve tu prathamādhikaraṇe lakṣaṇāntarāṇi bahūni dūṣayitvā "atyanta-vegita-atyanta-saukṣmyaṃ nirbharatā tathā/ svasattākālabhāvyāptir jñāne

lakṣmacatuṣṭayam//" iti svoktalakṣaṇopasaṃhārah kṛtaḥ/ [*Nyāya-siddhāñjanam* (Madras), p. 249]. For other evidence on Nāthamuni's NyT as the source of this view of *jñāna* as both a *dharma* or *guṇa* and a *dravya* which has developed into the distinctive Viśiṣṭādvaita tenet of *dharma-bhūta-jñāna*, see. R. Ramanujachari, "Fragments from Nyāyatattva," pp. 559, 561; and "Nathamuni: His Life and Times," p. 276. See also immediately below for some of the ambiguities with regard to the terms *dharma* and *guṇa* which contributed to such a modification of the traditional Nyāya-Vaiśeṣika categories.

113. See AtS, p. 113.6-9 (A, p. 176.2-6), where Yāmuna's opponent maintains this point.

114. AtS, p. 115.4-6 (A, pp. 177.8-178.2), ato yaṃ pratyasādhāraṇo yathodita-dharmaḥ tadīya-asādhāraṇa-dharma-nimitta ity etāvat/ sa ceṣyata evātmanaś caitanyaṃ raver iva tejasvitvam/.

115. B. Jhaḷakīkar, *Nyāya-kośa* (NyK), s.v. *asādhāraṇa-dharmaḥ*: lakṣyatā-avacchedaka-samaniyato dharmaḥ.

116. See Śrīdhara, *Nyāya-kandalī* (Varanasi, 1963), p. 5.10-12, on the meaning of the title of Praśastapāda's *Padārtha-dharma-saṅgraha*: padārthā dravyādayaḥ ṣaṭ, teṣāṃ dharmāḥ sādhāraṇa-asādhāraṇa-svabhāvāḥ saṃgṛhyante . . . aneneti padārthadharmasaṅgrahaḥ/.

117. Athalye, ed., TS, p. 96.

118. *Ibid.*, pp. 96-97; D. N. Shastri, *Critique of Indian Realism* (Agra: Agra Univ., 1964), pp. 138-40.

119. Bhatt, *Epistemology of Bhāṭṭa School*, pp. 15-19.

120. *Ibid.*

121. See n. 112 above.

122. AtS, pp. 102.5-7 and 115.7-8 (A, pp. 162.1-4 and 178.2-3).

123. AtS, p. 115.8-9 (A, p. 178.5-6); cf. p. 106.1 (A, p. 167.1), avikṛta-prakāśa-hetu-kiraṇa-saṃhatāv apy ahimamahasi . . . .

124. AtS, p. 116.1-3 (A, pp. 178.6-179.2), svārasikatve 'py āditya-prakāśasya prakāśya-deśa-sambandha-kādācitkatayā avaccheda-pratītir upapadyata iti cet, ihāpi tarhi--indriyādi-pratyāsatti-samāsādita-yogya-bhāvo 'nubhāvya-bhedaḥ svābhāvikam ātmanaś caitanya-guṇam avacchinatti.

125. AtS, p. 116.5-6 (A, p. 179.5-6), kathaṃ punar atra nirṇayaḥ dyumaṇi-maṇi-prakāśāder iva--aupādhiko 'yaṃ bhedaḥ, na tu gamana-pacanāder iva svābhāvika iti.

126. AtS, p. 116.6-9 (A, 179.6-180.4).

127. AtS, (1), p. 59.3-4 (A, p. 102.8); (2), p. 61.5-6 (A, p. 106.1-2); (3), p. 72.7 (A, p. 120.4); (4), p. 101.9 (A, p. 161.1); (5), p. 118.4 (A, p. 182.2); (6) p. 119.8 (A, p. 183.6-7); (7), p. 123.3 (A, p. 188.6); (8), p. 145.7 (A, p. 217.1); (9), p. 146.8 (A, p. 218.6); (10), p. 148.2 (A, p. 219.2); (11), p. 148.7 (A, pp. 220.5-221.1); (12), p. 149.2 (A, p. 221.3).

128. AtS, pp. 142.8-146.2 (A, pp. 212.5-217.3); see below p. 141.

129. See above n. 125. See also AtS, p. 135.6 (A, p. 203.2), śabda-gandha-sūryāloka-ratna-prabhādayo; and p. 147.3 (A, p. 218.9-10), "yathā na kriyate jyotsnā malaprakṣālanān maṇeḥ/ doṣaprahāṇān na jñānam ātmanaḥ kriyate tathā//" [Viṣṇudharmottara 104.55].

130. AtS, p. 143.3-6 (A, p. 213.3-214.1), sukha-duḥkhe ca na--ātma-dharmau, indriya-sauṣṭhava-nāśayor eva tad-bhāva-upapādanāt/ . . . rāga-dveṣādayo 'pi manovasthā-viśeṣāḥ na sākṣād-ātma-guṇāḥ/. See also pp. 89.5-91.4 (A, pp. 144.3-146.4).

131. AtS, p. 90.1-3 (A, p. 145.4-7) and p. 143.4 (A, p. 213.4-5).

132. AtS, p. 110.4-5 (A, p. 172.1-2).

133. GPrak, pp. 78-79, n.4 [GPrak (1972), pp. 68-69, n.6], svarūpam upādhiḥ prayojakaṃ yasya dharmasya, tat-tvāt; yad vā svarūpasya--upādhir nirūpako vyavacchedako dharmas tat-tvād iti/.

134. AtS, pp. 110 (1972, p. 96).

135. AtS, pp. 143.1-3, 144.5-146.2 (A, pp. 213.1-3, 215.3-217.4). See also p. 106.4-5 (A, p. 167.5-6) and below p. 141.

136. AtS, pp. 110.6-111.5 (A, pp. 172.3-173.7), caitanyāśrayatāṃ muktvā svarūpaṃ nānyad ātmanaḥ/ yad dhi caitanyarahitaṃ na tad ātmā ghaṭādivat// citiśaktyā na cātmatvaṃ muktau nāśaprasaṅgataḥ/ buddhi-sukha-duḥkhādi-niśśeṣa-vaiśeṣika-ātma-guṇa-ātyantika-uparama-lakṣaṇo hi mokṣaḥ kaṇabhakṣa-akṣacaraṇa-mate/ na ca--atyanta-lupta-kāryaṃ vastu tat-kārya-janana-śaktam ity atra kin cit pramāṇam kramate/ dehādy-viśiṣṭa-sambandhitayā dṛśyamāna-sukha-duḥkha-jñānādi-kāryaṃ viśiṣṭa-vartinīm eva--ātma-utpāda-śaktim kalpayati, dhūma iva--ārdrendhana-sambandhini dhūmadhvaje sva-utpādana-sāmarthyam, vrīhy-aṅkura iva ca sa-tuṣa-taṇḍule/ api ca bodhe saty eva--ātmano 'nātma-vyavacchede sambhavati kṛtaṃ tac-chakty-āśrayaṇena/.

137. Daniel H. H. Ingalls, Materials for the Study of Navya-Nyāya Logic, Harvard Oriental Series, Vol. 40 (Cambridge: Harvard Univ. Press, 1951), pp. 40-43.

138. Śrīdhara, Nyāya-kandalī (Varanasi, 1963), p. 35, dravyatvādiṣu sāmānya-śabdo mukhyaḥ, anuvṛtti-hetutvasya sāmānya-lakṣaṇasya sambhavāt, viśeṣa-śabdaś ca bhāktaḥ, svāśrayo viśiṣyate sarvato vyavacchidyate yena sa viśeṣa iti; cf. n. 136, ". . . ātmano 'nātma-vyavacchede . . ." See also Athalye, TS, pp. 89-91, and A. B. Keith, Indian Logic and Atomism (ILA) (New York: Greenwood Press, 1968), pp. 192-95.

139. Athalye, TS, pp. 91-93; G. Jhā, tr., The Padārtha-dharmasangraha, p. 31, nn. 3-5; Keith, ILA, pp. 194-95.

140. See the early (ca. tenth or eleventh century) standard syncretistic Nyāya-Vaiśeṣika manual, the Saptapadārthī of Śivāditya (Calcutta Sanskrit Series, No. VIII), #41, p. 37.1-2, sāmānyaṃ jāti-rūpam upādhi-rūpaṃ ca/ jāti[rūpaṃ] sattā-dravya-guṇa-karmatvādi/ upādhi-rūpaṃ pācakatvādi// (also ##48 and 145). See also the Kiraṇāvalī of Udayana (tenth-eleventh centuries), pp. 25.12-14 and 32.10-34.5 (Vaiśeṣikadarśanam, Benares Sanskrit Series).

141. Athalye, TS, pp. 91-93; Keith, ILA, p. 194.

142. Ingalls, Materials, pp. 40-42; Bimal Krishna Matilal, The Navya-Nyāya Doctrine of Negation, Harvard Oriental Series, Vol. 46 (Cambridge: Harvard Univ. Press, 1968), pp. 33, 41-42.

143. Athalye, TS, pp. 91-92.

144. Matilal, The Navya-Nyāya Doctrine of Negation, pp. 40-42.

145. Ibid., p. 40.

146. Ibid., pp. 40-41.

147. Ibid., pp. 41-42.

148. Ibid., p. 40.

149. Ingalls, Materials, pp. 39-42; Matilal, Navya-Nyāya, pp. 44, 142, 11.

150. Ingalls, Materials, p. 40.

151. Ibid., pp. 40-41; Matilal, Navya-Nyāya, pp. 18, 69.

152. Matilal, Navya-Nyāya, p. 69.

153. Ingalls, Materials, p. 38; Matilal, Navya-Nyāya, pp. 42-43.

154. Matilal, Navya-Nyāya, p. 44.

155. Nyāya-pariśuddhi, Chowkhamba Sanskrit Series, Vol. 51, p. 13.8-9, bhagavan-nāthamunibhir nyāyatattva-samāhvayā/ avadhīrayākṣapādīn nyabandhi nyāyapaddhatiḥ//.

156. Ibid., p. 25.6-8, yat punar arvāgbhir akṣacaraṇa-pañcādhyāyyāṃ kuśakāśāvalambanena kaṇacaraṇa-kathāṃ niveśya naigamikyaḥ padavyo nirudhyante/.

157. Matilal, Navya-Nyāya, pp. 68-69.

158. Ibid., pp. 42-43.

159. AtS, pp. 141.8-142.2 (A, p. 211.1-4), nairantarya-pada-paryāyam atyanta-sāmīpya-mātraṃ ca saṃyogaḥ/ sa eva paratantrāśritaḥ samavāya-pada-paribhāṣā-bhūmir vaiśeṣikānām iti na--arthāntaratvam ūrīkṛtya vikalpas sambhavati/ yathā ca saṃyoga-antarbhāvaḥ samavāyasya tathā saṃbandha-vimarśe darśayiṣyāmaḥ/ [cf. pp. 137.9-138.2 (A, pp. 206.3-207.1)]. On the NyT as the basis of this view, see Vedānta Deśika, Nyāya-siddhāñjana (Madras), p. 361, who quotes from the NyT as follows: atyanta-sāmīpyaṃ saṃyogaḥ, dūratvaṃ viyogaḥ (cf. pp. 267-68); see also Ramanujachari, "Fragments from Nyāya-tattva," pp. 563, 564-65; and Narasimhachary, Contribution, p. 210. See above n. 112 for another example of the way in which Nāthamuni and Yāmuna modified the Nyāya-Vaiśeṣika categories.

160. See above Ch. V, n. 12 and Ch. VI, nn. 112 and 159.

161. AtS, p. 140.1-4 (A, p. 208.6-10) yady evaṃ kas tarhi prakāśate-padārthaḥ . . ./ ucyate--nūnaṃ bhavān aśrutapūrvī prathamādhikaraṇasya nyāya-tattve/ abhihitaṃ hi tatra--idaṃ anubhave smṛtim upapādayabhir anubhava-adūratvaṃ smṛti-nimittam iti/ etad uktaṃ bhavati--saṃvidadūratvaṃ prakāśa iti/; see also Vedānta Deśika, Nyāya-siddhāñjana (Madras), p. 252.

162. See above, n. 136.

163. AtS, p. 60.1-2 (A, p. 104.1-3); see also above n. 59.

164. Matilal, Navya-Nyāya, pp. 49-50; on "occurrence-exacting" and "non-occurrence-exacting" relations, see pp. 49-51 and Ingalls, Materials, pp. 44, 73 and 56 (##19, 44 and 55).

165. van Buitenen, Introduction to R. on BhG, p. 1, n. 1; V. Varadachari, "Antiquity of the Term Viśiṣṭādvaita," ALB, XXVI (1962), p. 177.

166. See n. 149 above.

167. See AtS, pp. 137.9-138.4 (A, pp. 206.3-207.3), [Objection:] nanv evaṃ caitanya-saṃyogaḥ saṃyoga-jo vā kaś cit prakāśaḥ prāptaḥ/ ubhyam api tan na caitanye sambhavati, bheda-apekṣatvāt saṃbandhasya/ ātmano 'pi na caitanyena saṃyogaḥ, tad-dharmitvāt/ na hi dharma-dharmiṇoḥ saṃbandhaḥ saṃyogaḥ/ samavāyo hi saḥ; ayuta-siddha-saṃbandhatvāt/ saṃyogas tu pṛthak-siddhayor dravyayoḥ kriyā-nimittā prāptiḥ a-kārya-kāraṇayor vā tayoḥ nirantara-sthitiḥ/ caitanya-saṃyoga-samavāyayor anyatarasya saṃbandha-mātrasya vā prakāśatve jñātṛ-jñāna-jñeya-śarīra-indriyeṣv avyāpty-ativyāptī yathāyogam ādarśayitavye/ and pp. 141.8-142.2 (A, p. 211.1-4), [Yāmuna's reply:] nairantarya-pada-paryāyam atyanta-sāmīpya-mātraṃ ca saṃyogaḥ/ sa eva paratantrāśritaḥ samavāya-pada-paribhāṣā-

bhūmir vaiśeṣikānām iti na--arthāntaratvam ūrīkṛtya vikalpas sambhavati/ yathā ca saṃyoga-antarbhāvaḥ samavāyasya tathā saṃbandha-vimarśe darśayiṣyāmaḥ/; see also Narasimhachary, Contribution, pp. 207-11; above nn. 112 and 159; and below Ch. VII, Pratijñā Series III.

168. See Ch. VII, Pratijñā Series III.

169. See above n. 136.

170. See AtS, pp. 103.9 (A, 164.1-2); 135.3 (A, 202.7); and 138.1 (A, 206.5-6).

171. AtS, p. 49.1-2 (A, p. 89.4-6), tad evam anubhava-viśiṣṭam asmad-artham avabhāsayann ayam ahaṃ-pratyayaḥ katham iva viśeṣaṇa-bhūta-anubhūti-mātra-avalambanaḥ pratijñāyeta daṇḍa-mātra iva daṇḍī devadatta iti pratyayaḥ; p. 102.2 (A, p. 161.4-5), ātmanaḥ prakāra-bhūtam caitanyam . . .. On viśeṣaṇa (qualifier) and prakāra (chief qualifier) in Navya-Nyāya, see Ingalls, Materials, pp. 42-43.

172. ŚBh(K) III.ii.28, Vol. III, pp. 828.10-13, jīva-vat pṛthak-siddhy-anarha-viśeṣaṇatvena--acid-vastuno brahmāṃśatvam/ viśiṣṭa-vastu-ekadeśatvena--abheda-vyavahāro mukhyaḥ/ viśeṣaṇa-viśeṣyayo svarūpa-svabhāva-bhedena bheda-vyavahāro 'pi mukhyaḥ/ brahmaṇo nirdoṣatvaṃ ca rakṣitam/ tad evaṃ prakāśa-jāti-guṇa-śarīrāṇāṃ maṇi-vyakti-guṇy-ātmanaḥ pṛthak-siddhy-anarha-viśeṣaṇatayā yathāṃśatvaṃ tatheha jīvasya--acidvastunaś ca brahma pratyaṃśstvam/ [cf. III.ii.29, Vol. III, p. 829.4]. From this statement we can derive the chart:

svarūpa = viśeṣya	/	svabhāva = viśeṣaṇa
maṇi	- - - - - - - - - - - - - -	prakāśa
vyakti	- - - - - - - - - - - - -	jāti
guṇin	- - - - - - - - - - - - -	guṇa
ātmā	- - - - - - - - - - - - - -	śarīra
brahman	- - - - - - - - - - - -	jīva and acid-vastu.

173. Matilal, Navya-Nyāya, p. 69.

174. No doubt a major reason for Yāmuna's attraction to the specific term svabhāva was its Upaniṣadic associations and overtones; see svābhāvikī jñāna-bala-kriyā (Śvetāśvatara Up. 3.19) quoted at AP, p. 40.17 (CE, p. 191; tr, #76). However, there were also precedents for Yāmuna's use of the term within other darśana traditions; see Richard H. Robinson, "Classical Indian Philosophy" in Chapters in Indian Civilization, Vol. I, Classical and Medieval India, ed., by Joseph W. Elder (Dubuque: Kendall/Hunt, 1970), pp. 203-204, "Own-being (svabhāva) is a cover-term for the ultimate substances posited by the various schools--Brahman-Ātman in the Upaniṣads, prakṛti (world-substance) and puruṣa (soul) in Sāṅkhya, the nine substances in Vaiśeṣika, and the dharmas (elemental force-factors) in Abhidharma. The term svabhāva seems originally to have been introduced by the Materialists. For them it meant the inherent powers of the four elements. The Abhidharmists use the word to mean the own-mark, the inalienable class-property, of each dharma, and also the substratum of the own-mark, the thing marked, that persists through the transition from future to present to past, 'Own-being always exists, a being is not termed permanent, and the being is not other than the own-being.' [Abhidharmakośa, v. 58]." This Buddhist use of svabhāva as "own-mark" (svalakṣaṇam), "the inalienable class-property, of each dharma" would seem to provide a striking precedent for Yāmuna's use of it as a svarūpa-upādhi. However, unlike the Buddhists, Yāmuna needed to provide some eternal

unchanging basis for the svabhāva that is engaged in change and modification; hence the svarūpa/svabhāva distinction. There would also seem to be other Brāhmanic precedents tending toward Yāmuna's formulation of this distinction. Śrīdhara in his Nyāya-kandalī uses svabhāva for dharmas in the most general sense (see n. 116 above) and defends the eternality of the ātmā by maintaining that production and destruction occur only with regard to the guṇas (= dharma = svabhāva) but not with regard to the svarūpa (p. 207.1-2, nityasya hi svarūpa-vināśaḥ svarūpāntaropādaś ca vikāro neṣyate, guṇa-nivṛttir guṇāntara-utpādaś ca--aviruddha eva). However, Śrīdhara does not develop the term svabhāva in a specialized technical manner as does Yāmuna.

175. See above n. 125.

176. AtS, p. 62.8 (A, p. 107.2-3); SS, p. 185.10-186.5 (A, pp. 288-89, vv. 59-62); 202.1-2 (A, 316, v. 152).

177. AtS (A), p. 213.1-2 (V, p. 101.4-5, śl. 42 [(1972), p. 83]). In construing this śloka I am following Aṇṇaṅgarācārya and Vīrarāghavācārya who are in turn probably depending upon Raṅgarāmānuja's interpretation of the verse as quoted in Vedānta Deśika's Nyāya-siddhāñjana: naivaṃ sukhāditi--sukhādi tu naivam, svarūpopādhi na bhavatīty arthaḥ/ bodhopādhir iti--jñānam ātmatva upādhiḥ prayojokam ity arthaḥ/ [Vyākhyā on Nyāya-siddhāñjana (Madras), p. 273.5-6]. This interpretation seems to be more in accord with the following phrase than is that of Ramanujachari and Śrīnivasacharya: naivam sukhādhibodhas tu . . ., "but the knowledge of pleasure and pain is not . . ." (AtS, p. 143 [(1972), p. 126]).

178. AtS, p. 143.3 (A, p. 213.3); see above n. 177.

179. AtS, pp. 144.5-145.6 (A, pp. 215.3-216.5), . . .tasyāḥ svābhāvikatvasya tasyām eva śrutau śrūyamāṇatvāt/ śrūyate hi "na vijñātur vijñāter viparilopo vidyate" [Bṛh. Up. IV.iii.30] iti "na hi draṣṭur dṛṣṭer viparilopo vidyate avināśitvāt" [Bṛh. Up. IV.iii.23] iti ca/ jñātur avināśitvād eva jñānasya--avināśam upapādayantīyaṃ śrutir jñātuḥ svarūpa-prayuktaṃ jñānam iti darśayati/.

180. AtS, p. 145.6-7 (A, p. 216.5-6).

181. See above, n. 135.

182. See above, nn. 71, 72 and 75.

183. AtS, (1) p. 61.5-6 (A, p. 106.1-2); (2) p. 67.3 (A, p. 113.4-5); (3) p. 101.8 (A, p. 160.12); (4) p. 120.1-2 (A, p. 184.3-4); (5) p. 123.2-3 (A, p. 188.6); (6) p. 124.3 (A, p. 189.9); (7) p. 124.5 (A, p. 190.1); (8) p. 145.7-146.2 (A, p. 217.1-3); (9) p. 146.3-8 (A, pp. 217.6-218.6).

184. Bṛhadāraṇyaka Up. IV.iii.9.

185. See also above n. 59 for another significant reference to this same section of the Bṛhadāraṇyaka Up.

186. See Ch. VII, Pratijñā Series II.A-B on the Paramātmā and Series III on the relation (saṃbandha) between the ātmā and the Paramātmā; see also Pratijñā Series I.C.

187. See above n. 75.

188. See above n. 126.

189. Sadananda Bhaduri, Studies in Nyāya-Vaiśeṣika Metaphysics (Poona: Bhandarkar Oriental Research Inst., 1947), pp. 131-32.

190. See above n. 136.

191. See above n. 136.

192. For a possible Pāñcarātrika Tāntric precedent for this view that the śakti to be a kāraṇa and to produce a kārya exists only in an ātmā that is jñāna-vān, see Ahirbudhnya-saṃhitā, ed. by M. D. Ramanujacharya, The Adyar Library Series, Vol. 4, (Adyar, Madras, Second Revised Ed., 1966), VI.3, naiva śaktyā vinā kaś cic chaktimān asti kāraṇam/ na ca śaktimatā śaktir vinaikā vyavatiṣṭhate//.

193. See above n. 136.

194. AtS, pp. 117.8-124.6 (A, pp. 181.5-190.2).

195. AtS, pp. 149.2-151.2 (A, pp. 221.3-222.4). tad evaṃ caitanya-svabhāvaḥ parisphurann apy ayam ātmā gambhīra-jalāśaya-cara-mīna-vaj jala-saṃsṛṣṭa-kṣīra-vac ca na vivicya sphuṭaṃ cakāsti--iti tad-upapādana-nyāya-anugatāḥ pūrvānumānabhedā vacanāni ca ādriyante/ tair apy aparituṣyanto yama-niyamādi-yogāṅga-anuṣṭhāna-kṣapita-aśuddhy-āvaraṇa-malā nirodha-abhyāsa-puṭapāka-nirdhūta-rajas-tamaḥ kaḷaṅka-sattva-udreka-samuttha-svetara-sakala-viṣaya-vailakṣaṇya-aparokṣa-jñānāya prayatante/ bhāvanā-prakarṣa-paryante ca--aparokṣa-jñānam udayata iti sarvavādi-nirvivādam iti na tad-upapādanāyādya prayatyate/ evam ātmā svatassiddhyann āgamenānumānataḥ/ yogābhyāsabhuvā spaṣṭaṃ pratyakṣeṇa prakāśyate//.

196. See Ch. V and Appendix I.

197. AtS, pp. 83.8-9 (A, p. 136.5-6); 109.4-5 (A, p. 171. 2-3); 122.6-9 (A, pp. 187.9-188.3).

198. See Ch. V and Appendix I.

199. Personal conversation, Harvard University.

200. The rather formal way in which he acknowledges the universal acceptance of such a perception without expanding would seem to support such a view. Note also that the way of aṣṭāṅga yoga is only for those who are not satisfied by āgama and anumāna and who wish to "strive or exert themselves" for aparokṣa-jñāna, i.e., it is probably only for the exceptional few.

201. AP, p. 87.4 (CE, p. 304; tr, #139).

NOTES

CHAPTER VII

1. For a full presentation of the traditional Śrī Vaiṣṇava interpretations of Yāmuna's views on the śakti or Consort Śrī as expressed in his four verses in praise of Śrī (Śrī-stuti or Catuś-ślokī [CŚl]) and in his longer hymn the Stotra-ratna (SR), see Narasimhachary, Contribution, pp. 16-62, 66-67, and 73. See nn. 49 and 51 below.

2. See Rāmānuja's dedicatory verse to the Śrī Bhāṣya:

akhilabhuvana-janma-sthema-bhaṅgādilīle
    vinata-vividha-bhūta-vrāta-rakṣaikadīkṣe/
śrutiśirasi vidīpte brahmaṇi śrīnivāse
    bhavatu mama parasmin śemuṣī bhaktirūpā//
[ŚBh(K), Vol. I, p. 1.1-4]

As Narasimhachary (Contribution, p. 308) points out, Rāmānuja's verse was obviously patterned after Yāmuna's, even to being written in the same mālinī metre. It is probably significant that the ŚBh does not have a dedicatory verse to Yāmuna as do three of Rāmānuja's other works, VAS, Gītā-bhāṣya (GBh), and the Vaikuṇṭha-gadya. In the ŚBh, Rāmānuja's debt to Yāmuna, while clearly implicit at many points, is never made explicit. Although Rāmānuja quotes a number of verses from the ĀtS, he does not explicitly acknowledge their source [e.g., ŚBh(K), I.i.1, Vol. I, pp. 71.12-13, 72.6-7, 73.5]--the same is true of some verses which he quotes and which Sudarśana Sūri ascribes to Nāthamuni's NyT [ŚBh(K) I.i.1, Vol. I, pp. 125-126; ŚBh with Śrutaprakāśikā, Vol. I, p. 257.9-11]. Apparently, while many of Nāthamuni's and Yāmuna's ideas were of significance, their names were not ones to be reckoned with in Rāmānuja's wider Vedāntic milieu (see Ch. IV, n. 62). This situation in the ŚBh is in striking contrast to that in the more sectarian VAS, which is not only explicitly dedicated to Yāmuna but in which he is quoted in the most explicit and reverential terms; see VAS, #91.

3. See Ch. VI, n. 71, on the double meaning of ātma-siddhi.

4. See the introductory verse to the Tattvāloka (TA), the eighth prakaraṇa of the Prakaraṇa-pañcikā (PrakP) by Śālikanātha Miśra (ca. ninth century), the classical exponent of the Prābhākara school of Pūrva Mīmāṃsā:

ātmatattve bahuvidhā vivādās santi vādinām/
vayaṃ prābhākarās tattva-nirṇayāya yatāmahe//

(Banaras Hindu Univ. Darśana Series No. 4, p. 315.1-2). Among the śāstric literature with which I am familiar, it is this prakaraṇa that offers the closest parallel in structure to the ĀtS, which Yāmuna also calls a prakaraṇa. In both cases the structure is:

(I) An introductory verse giving as its purpose the authoritative determiniation of the true nature of the ātmā in the face of many conflicting opinions (TA, p. 315.1-2);

(II) A presentation of the various conflicting teachings (vipratipattis) to be considered, arranged in series according to topics (vādāḥ) with the author's own position or Siddhānta given last in each series (TA, pp. 315.3-316.2);

(III) A summary verse (saṃgraha-śloka) giving a capsulized statement of all the Siddhāntās to be established by the extended argumentation (TA, p. 316.3-5);

(IV) An extended systematic discussion in which all of the opposition viewpoints are presented and refuted and the Siddhāntas defended and established (TA, pp. 317-46).

The main difference in structure between the two prakaraṇas is that the TA proposes to deal only with the individual ātmā (since Śālikanātha does not accept the existence of a paramātmā) while the AtS undertakes to deal not only with the paramātmā but also with all other Vedāntic topics. The TA is thus one of the most valuable aids we possess for understanding the structure and argumentation of the AtS (see below nn. 10, 12 and 23).

5. Śvetāśvatara Up. I.6.

6. Bṛhadāraṇyaka Up. 4.4.12.

7. Chāndogya Up. 7.1.3.

8. Taittirīya Up. 2.1.1.

9. By proceeding to demonstrate this confusing and misleading welter of vipratipattis, Yāmuna is establishing the necessity of and justification for the AtS, an essential first step in all śāstric compositions.

10. As indicated in Ch. VI.A, Yāmuna, immediately after presenting these Pratijñā Series (see below), will summarize his task as defining both the ātmā and the Paramātmā in terms of five major concerns or topics: (l) svarūpataḥ, (ii) pramāṇataḥ, (iii) saṃbandhataḥ, (iv) prāptitaḥ, (v) tat-sādhanataś ca. Thus with regard to both ātmās, the first Series of Pratijñās (I.A and II.A) is concerned with determining their unique essential natures as opposed to all things other than themselves. A. Subrahmanya Sastri, the editor of the PrakP (see n. 4 above) calls the corresponding series in the TA dravya-bheda-vivādān, "the disputes on the different substances or entities [that are called ātmā]" (PrakP, TA, p. 315, n. 4). Pratijñā Series I.B and II.D seem to correspond to (ii) pramāṇataḥ; Series III to (iii) saṃbandhataḥ; Series IV to (iv) prāptitaḥ; and Series V to (v) tat-sādhanataś ca. The remaining Series (I.C-E and II. B-C) should probably be correlated with (i) svarūpataḥ, i.e., as meant to clarify other issues related to defining the distinctive nature of the ātmā or the Paramātmā.

11. For references to the extant Extended Discussion of the first four Pratijñās (I.A.1-4), which probably represent gradations of the Cārvāka or "Materialist" position, see Ch. VI, nn. 48-54.

12. See Ch. VI, nn. 55-58, for references on this cleverly worded Pratijñā representing the position of both "the professed or honest Buddhists and the covert or deceitful ones" (saugatāḥ prakaṭāḥ pracchannāś ca). While this Pratijñā is thus explicitly labelled a Buddhist position, there can be no doubt that his main concern is with refuting the Pracchannas, his fellow Vedāntins like Sureśvara and Vimuktātman who follow the interpretation of Śaṅkara. However, he feels that he can best refute them by refusing to accord them the dignity of an

independent position and showing that their supposedly Vedic interpretation is actually dependent upon a non-Vedic heretical (veda-bāhya) teaching. It is interesting to note that in the TA Śālikanātha Miśra, who probably lived in the ninth or early tenth century (before Vācaspati Miśra), i.e., a century or two before Yāmuna, presents the position "buddhir eva--ātmā" as an exclusively Vijñāna-vāda Buddhist position (PrakP, pp. 317.1-319.3), quoting the same verse of Dharmakīrti's as does Yāmuna (cf. PrakP, p. 317.6-7, with Ch. VI, n. 57). On the other hand Rāmānuja in the eleventh-twelfth centuries--while basing much of his Mahāpūrvapakṣa and Mahāsiddhānta within ŚBh I.i.1 [for the most obvious example, cf. ŚBh(K) I.i.1, Vol. I, pp. 71-82, with AtS, pp. 52.8-65.2 (A, pp. 94.1-110.4)] upon Yāmuna's treatment of this Pratijñā--completely reverses the emphasis, practically ignoring the Buddhists [see ŚBh(K) I.i.1, p. 61.11-13 for the sole vague reference] and putting forth the Kevalādvaitins as the main opponent. In the change of the treatment of this position from Śālikanātha Miśra to Yāmuna to Rāmānuja, we are witnessing one of the many ramifications of the gradual decline of the Buddhists as the dominant Indian philosophers and of the manner in which controversies initiated by them were continued after their demise (see Ch. VI).

13. On this Pratijñā representing the position of Nyāya-Vaiśeṣikas and Neo-Mīmāṃsakas of both the Bhāṭṭa and the Prābhākara schools, see Ch. VI, nn. 62-68, 73.

14. On the significance of the fact that Yāmuna begins this Pratijñā with a phrase that is the equivalent of his Summary Śloka Siddhānta (1), see Ch. VI, nn. 63-64 and accompanying text; see also n. 23 below.

15. Ramanujachari (AtS, p. 2) and Aṇṇaṅgarācārya (SVy, p. 6) take this term ākāśa-ādi-vad with the following acitsvabhāvam, i.e., "that, like [the mahābhūtas or material elements] ākāśa, etc., is insentient in nature." However, whenever ākāśa (vyoman, nabhas) is considered in the Extended Discussion it is used as an example of entities that are amūrta and vibhu and therefore not able to become involved in activity or movement; see Ch. VI, n. 88. For the correct interpretation of this term, see the Praśastapāda-bhāṣya with the Commentary Nyāya-kandalī (Ganganātha Jhā Granthamāla, Vol. I), pp. 58-59, ākāśa-kāla-dig-ātmanāṃ sarva-gatatvaṃ parama-mahattvaṃ sarva-saṃyogi-samāna-deśa-tvañ ca/ (see also pp. 153 and 213).

16. On this view of the ātmā as that entity which is manifest in the cognition "I," see Ch. VI, text accompanying nn. 59, 77-96. This view is essential both for Yāmuna and for his Nyāya-Vaiśeṣika and Neo-Mīmāṃsaka opponents; indeed it must be accepted in some sense by all Vedic thinkers [see Paul Hacker, "Śaṅkara der Yogin und Śaṅkara der Advaitin," WZKSO, XII/XIII (1968-69), 133, 137 and 138]. For a classical Nyāya-Vaiśeṣika expression of ahaṃkāra in this sense, see Śrīdhara, Nyāya-kandalī, p. 204.3-4, "ahaṃkārena--aham iti pratyayena . . . eka-adhikaraṇatvam . . ." J. A. B. van Buitenen's comments on the early meaning and development of the term ahaṃkāra as a Sāṅkhya evolute are of interest here ("Studies in Sāṃkhya (II)," JAOS, 77 (1957), 15-25). He maintains that the earliest, most grammatically plausible, and more widely applicable and significant meaning of the term is "the cry, uttering or ejaculation [or, in Yāmuna's context, cognition]: Aham!" (p. 17). However, the context is now quite different from the mythological

cosmogonic one that van Buitenen considers. The term developed within the "philosophical" śāstric context not only toward the classical Sāṅkhyan conception but also in another direction that was both more in line with its etymological meaning and much more significant than the Sāṅkhyan usage--at least while the Buddhists were still a dominating influence among the Indian darśanas. For the main function of the ahaṃ-[kāra-]pratyaya, the cognition "I," and the "recognition" (pratyabhijñā) of its continuity over time in different cognitions, was to maintain the unity and eternality of the ātmā in opposition to the Buddhist view that the "ātmā" or essential nature of man is a series of discrete, discontinuous and momentary events of cognition. For the arguments, see Pūrva Mīmāṃsā supercommentaries on Śābara-bhāṣya on Mīmāṃsā Sūtra I.1.5, especially Kumārila Bhaṭṭa's (probably the most forceful and influential propounder for this argument against the Buddhist) Śloka-vārtika, ātmā-vāda, vv. 107-139; and Vedānta commentaries on VS II.ii.18-32 (ŚBh II.ii.17-30), especially on sūtra 25.

17. See Ch. VI for my argument that Pratijñā I.A.7 is Yāmuna's Siddhānta.

18. See Ch. VI, nn.184-85, on the Upaniṣadic overtones Yāmuna is invoking by this phrase.

19. For my understanding of the sub-series Pratijñās I.A.7.a-b, see Ch. VI, text accompanying nn. 34-46. See also Pratijñās IV.H and IV.I, which parallel I.A.7.a and I.A.7.b.

20. While the previous opponents (Pratijñās I.A.1-6) were non-Vedāntins--with the exception of the heretical Pracchanna Kevalādvaitins, the phrase jñāna-ānanda-svabhāvam, with its Upaniṣadic overtones [especially Bṛhadāraṇyaka Up. 3.9.28.7, (vijñānam ānandaṃ brahma) and 4.3.32; Taittirīya Up. II, the ānanda-valli] probably indicates a shift to an intra-Vedānta dispute, with the opponents being eka-deśinaḥ, i.e., "parochial" or sectarian, Vedāntins with whom Yāmuna would disagree on specific points but would accept as being within the orthodox Vedāntic tradition. Indeed, as Vīrarāghavācārya [GPrak, p. 6.17-18; (1972), p. 5.17-18] attests, the way I.A.7.a is stated suggests that all following "bodhaikasvabhāvam eva" in I.A.7 should be repeated for I.A.7.a (although according to Vīrarāghavācārya the latter is an Advaita modification of the Sāṅkhya I.A.7). Aṇṇaṅgarācārya (SVy, p. 6) says of this Pratijñā "[anye] mīmāṃsaka-eka-deśinaḥ siddhānty-eka-deśino vā"--without, however, indicating any awareness of the significance of the latter alternative for Pratijñā I.A.7, which he also considers to be Sāṅkhya. In line with the possibility that I.A.7.a represents a siddhānty-eka-deśin, it is interesting to note that Rāmānuja frequently uses both jñāna and ānanda in this context (e.g., VAS #5, " . . . jñāna-ānanda-eka-guṇaṃ") although his interpretation of what ānanda means seems generally in line with Pratijñā I.A.7.b [see VAS #142; ŚBh(K) II.iii.29, Vol. III, pp. 731-32]. For Vedāntic discussion of ānanda, see VS I.i.12-19 (ŚBh I.i.13-20), the ānanda-maya-adhikaraṇa, concerning Taittirīya Up. II; Maṇḍana Miśra, Brahma-siddhi, pp. 1.16-6.6; Vimuktātman, Iṣṭa-siddhi, pp. 25ff.

21. See Ch. VI for my argument; see also Pratijñā IV.I.

22. On the structure of Pratijñā Series I.B-E, see Ch. VI, text accompanying nn. 36-40, and Appendix III.

23. See Ch. VI, text accompanying nn. 60-76, for my interpretation of Pratijñā Series I.B and the manner in which it is

related to and integrated into Series I.A in the Extended Discussion. The corresponding series of Pratijñās in Śālikanātha Miśra's TA in the PrakP (see n. 4 above) helps to buttress my argument in Ch. VI and to clarify the structure of the AtS. After giving the three Pratijñās proposing buddhi, indriyāṇi, and deha as ātmā, Śālikanātha Miśra does not continue to give an independent series on the svarūpa of the ātmā but rather proceeds (exactly as Yāmuna does in the Extended Discussion of the AtS) to consider the question of pramāṇa: tathā--(1) eke buddhīndriya-śarīra-vyatirekiṇam anumeyam āhuḥ, (2) ke cit tu mānasa-pratyakṣa-gamyam, (3) svayamprakāśañ ca ke cit, (4) sakala-pratīti-siddhaṃ tv anye manyante/ (PrakP, p. 315.4-6). In the Extended Discussion as well, Śālikanātha Miśra proceeds to discuss the svarūpa of the ātmā in terms of how it is known.

24. See Ch. VI, n. 65.

25. See Ch. VI, n. 66, and below nn. 65 and 67.

26. See Ch. VI, nn. 67 and 81. Pūrva Mīmāṃsakas, although primarily concerned with the interpretation of scriptural statements (vākya), do not base their valid cognition of the ātmā upon the pramāṇa āgama. Rather, the basic Mīmāṃsā position is that the individual ātmā is known through a direct, immediate cognition, i.e., the aham-pratyaya (see n. 16 above), that is based upon some form of the pramāṇa pratyakṣa--the dispute being how "perception" is to be understood in this case and especially through what mechanism it takes place. While there may be a number of factors involved, I feel that this basic Mīmāṃsā position with its emphasis upon the direct "perception" of the ātmā as the "I" derives primarily from the debate with the Buddhists over whether or not there is an eternal knower or cognizer separate from the momentary cognition itself. Since āgama is excluded as a pramāṇa in this debate between those of different āgamas, the discussion is carried on on the basis of pratyakṣa and anumāna. Both admit that there is an immediate experiential cognition (anubhava) of a distinct "I" or cognizer. But the Buddhists maintain on the basis of anumāna that this cognition of a cognizer distinct from cognition is an erroneous one--as is the perception of two moons by a person with astigmatism--and that in reality there is only cognition itself. However, the Mīmāṃsakas feel that their argument is a strong one because even the Buddhists admit that pratyakṣa is a stronger pramāṇa than anumāna, the validity of the latter being based upon the former. Therefore, the validity of the Buddhists' anumāna must be demonstrated beyond all doubt and must be based upon some sound pratyakṣa before it is competent to disprove the validity of the aham-pratyaya. Thus, by showing that the Buddhists' anumāna is fallacious, and that no valid cognition based upon pratyakṣa contradicts the distinctness, unity and continuity of the aham-pratyaya, the Mīmāṃsakas feel that they have defeated the Buddhist an-ātma-vāda on its own terms and have maintained the ātma-vāda upon which the Vedic tradition depends for its validity. (See Kumārila Bhaṭṭa, Śloka Vārtika, nirālambana-vāda, śūnya-vāda and ātma-vāda; especially ātma-vāda, vv. 107-136.)

27. See Ch. VI, nn. 68, 82-84.

28. See Ch. VI for my argument that I.B.5.a-b are Yāmuna's.

29. See Ch. VI, text accompanying nn. 69-88 and 185-93.

30. See Ch. VI, text accompanying nn. 76, 194-201.

31. Pratijñā Series I.C corresponds to Summary Śloka Topic (4) *vyāpī* ("pervasive") and is closely linked with the concerns of *Series* I.D. and Summary Śloka Topic (3) *nityo* (eternal), the issues of the dimension and mode of pervasion of the *ātmā* having become crucial in dealing with the questions of its relation to change and modification and its eternality (see Vedānta Deśika, *Nyāya-Siddhāñjana*, *jīva-pariccheda*, pp. 129.2-134.5; and n. 15 above). Hence Yāmuna's position in this Series is of great importance in terms of understanding how as a Vedāntin he dealt with the traditional Vedāntic charge against Pāñcarātra that it teaches *jīvotpatti*, i.e., that its views of the *jīva* or *ātmā* involves it in production (*utpatti*) and modification (*vikāra*) and therefore in the fault of non-eternality (*a-nityatva*) (see Chs. II and VIII).

Within Vedāntic and śāstric discussion in general this fault is generally typified as "the fault of the Jainas" (*arhata-doṣa*), who teach that the *ātmā* expands and contracts in pervading and assuming the dimension of whatever body it inhabits (*śarīra-parimāṇa*, see Pratijñā I.C.3), and is therefore subject to modification (*vikāra*) and is therefore non-eternal [see VS II.ii.33-36 (ŚBh, 31-34)]. It seems highly significant that in this present Series the Jaina position comes just before the statement of Yāmuna's Siddhānta (Pratijñā I.C.4) and is obviously closer to Yāmuna's own viewpoint than are the views usually accepted by orthodox Brāhmanic thinkers, which are rejected in the first two Pratijñās (I.C.1-2). Apparently Yāmuna was willing to associate himself to some degree with unorthodox viewpoints rather than accept orthodox but extreme positions that he considered sterile and destructive (see Ch. VI for some aspects of Yāmuna's criticism of these orthodox extremes). Unfortunately, the text for the Extended Discussion of this Series is no longer extant, although there are some references to it or related concerns; see AtS, pp. 29.3-5 (A, 52.3-5), 103.8-106.7 (A, 163.5-168.1), 125.9-126.2 (A, 191.9-192.4), 131.6-137.8 (A, 198.11-206.2) and 142.3-5 (A, 211.4-212.2); see also AP, pp. 3.24-4.7 (CE, pp. 93-94, tr, #8). For Vedāntic discussions of this topic, see commentaries on VS II.ii.19-32 (ŚBh, II.ii.20-32) and Ghate, *The Vedānta*, pp. 86-90.

32. The view of the Nyāya-Vaiśeṣikas and Neo-Mīmāṃsakas, corresponding to the phrase *ākāśādivad* in Pratijñā I.A.6; see n. 15 above, especially on *Praśastapāda-bhāṣya*, p. 58, "sarvagatatvaṃ parama-mahattvam." The corresponding series in the TA reads "aṇu-parimāṇaḥ, śarīra-parimāṇaḥ, sarva-gata ityādi vādino vivadante/" (PrakP, p. 316.1), with Śālikanātha Miśra indicating his Siddhānta by *vibhur* (p. 316.4). Yāmuna's comments in the extant portion of the text (see n. 31 above) seem primarily concerned with distinguishing his view from this one [AtS, p. 29.3 (A, p. 52.3), "a-vibhutvena--asya--ātmanaḥ . . ."; p. 131.7-8 (A, p. 199.2-3), "na hi tat-sarvagataṃ dravyam"] which makes the *ātmā* a substance that cannot possess activity (*krīya*) as is required by certain Vedāntic texts (see VS II.iii. 20) and for the *ātmā* to engage in the process of cognition as an active knower (see Ch. VI, nn. 110-14).

33. Aṇṇaṅgarācārya, SVy, p. 8, and Narasimhachary, *Contribution*, p. 299, maintain that this second Pratijñā is Yāmuna's Siddhānta, probably because this is Rāmānuja's viewpoint [ŚBh (K) II.iii.20, Vol. III, p. 727] as well as, apparently, Bādarāyaṇa's (VS II.iii.19-28) and most other Vedāntins' except

Śaṅkara (see Ghate, The Vedānta, pp. 86-90). Vīrarāghavācārya [GPrak, pp. 6-7, (1972, pp. 5-6)] recognizes that such cannot be the case and devotes considerable attention to the question of why Yāmuna differs from the Śrī Vaiṣṇava Siddhānta on this point (see n. 35 below). While Yāmuna does not affirm that the ātmā is aṇu, he is at one with the intention of the Vedāntins who do, i.e., to prove that the ātmā is an active agent (jñātṛ, jña), not insentient or pure knowledge (jñāna); see Ch. VI.

34. Position usually ascribed to Jainas or Arhatas; see n. 31 above. Cf. Śaṅkara, BSBh(K) II.ii.34, Vol. I, p. 563; and Bhāskara, BBh II.ii.34, p. 126. For references to Jainas or Jaina positions in Yāmuna's extant works, see AtS, p. 104.2-10 (A, pp. 164.4-165.4); SS, pp. 181.5-183.11 (A, pp. 280.4-285.4, vv. 37-50); AP, p. 68.3-4 (CE, p. 263; tr, #117).

35. As Vīrarāghavācārya [GPrak, pp. 6-7; (1972), pp. 5-6] and van Buitenen (Introduction to VAS, p. 44) accept, Pratijñā I.C.4 is Yāmuna's Siddhānta, corresponding to Summary Śloka Siddhānta (4) vyāpī. As noted above (n. 33), M. Narasimhachary maintains that vyāpī should be interpreted to mean aṇu, saying,

> Another important thing, according to Yāmuna, as according to Rāmānuja, is that the individual self is aṇu or atomic in size. Although the text relating to the topic is not available, this is to be taken as his view, from his statement that the ātman is 'vyāpī', which, according to Rāmānuja, means 'aṇu'. (Contribution, p. 299)

This statement, as well as a number of other conclusions in his work, reveal Narasimhachary's assumption that we can fill in the gaps in Yāmuna's system by accepting what Rāmānuja said as what Yāmuna intended. While such is always a dubious procedure in a task of historical reconstruction, it is wholly inappropriate in this case since Rāmānuja, in explicitly glossing Yāmuna's vyāpī, does not tell us that it means aṇu.

In conclusion of that section of the Mahāsiddhānta of ŚBh I.i.1 that is based upon the AtS (see nn. 2 and 12 above), Rāmānuja quotes Yāmuna's Summary Śloka on the individual ātmā, glossing the two terms that he feels are ambiguous as follows:

> 'ananyasādhanaḥ' svaprakāśaḥ/ 'vyāpī' atisūkṣmatayā sarva-acetana-antaḥpraveśa-svabhāvaḥ/ [ŚBh(K) I.i.1, Vol. I, p. 82.3]

As both Sudarśana Sūri (ŚBh with Śruta-prakāśikā, I.i.1, Vol. I, p. 174.1-6) and Vedānta Deśika (Tattva-ṭīkā, p. 422.14-17) tell us, the first term is glossed because sādhana is usually used of production (utpādana), in which sense the term nitya would be redundant; and the second is explained to avoid its being taken in the sense of vibhu or sarva-vyāpī. Now it is doubtless true that Rāmānuja himself would have interpreted atisūkṣmatā as aṇutva (see above n. 33); however, what he explicitly does state corresponds very well with Pratijñā I.C.4, with which Rāmānuja was obviously familiar and which explicitly distinguishes itself from Pratijñā I.C.2, aṇu-parimāṇaḥ. Thus, Rāmānuja definitely does not tell us that "vyāpī . . . means aṇu," although he quite correctly warns us against confusing vyāpī with vibhu, the viewpoint to which Yāmuna is most opposed (see n. 32 above).

My translation of this Pratijñā is based upon a suggestion of Vīrarāghavācārya [GPrak, p. 7; (1972), p. 6]. After giving two unsatisfactory explanations of how Yāmuna could make this statement while still adhering to the Śrī Vaiṣṇava Siddhānta of aṇu-paramāṇa, he proposes a third possibility:

yadvā siddhānte naiyāyikādimata iva parimāṇa-rūpa-guṇa-antara-asvīkārasya nyāya-tattva-anusāri-nyāya-siddhāñjana-uktatvāt parimāṇa-anāsthayā tathoktir iti/

There is considerable evidence that Nāthamuni and Yāmuna (as well as other innovative thinkers like Bhāsarvajña and Raghunātha Śiromaṇi) were hostile to the traditional Nyāya-Vaiśeṣika Padārthas and the consequences that follow their acceptance (see Ch. VI, nn. 112, 155-59). Therefore, Yāmuna's rejection of the term parimāṇa as applicable to the svarūpa of the ātmā may indicate his opinion that all the traditional options on this matter are inadequate and that the basic categories must be rethought. (See Ramanujachari, "Fragments from Nyāyatattva," pp. 568-70, on Nāthamuni's view of parimāṇa as included within the category saṅkhyā which in turn is to be included within saṃyoga; see also Ch. VI, n. 159).

As noted above (see n. 31), Yāmuna's Siddhānta seems to be closer to the Jaina position than to any other, i.e., the ātmā in some sense conforms to the dimension of the body pervaded. Indeed, the Eka-deśin Śrī Vaiṣṇava Varadaviṣṇu Miśra gave Yāmuna's vyāpī an interpretation that Vedānta Deśika criticized as being tainted by the Jaina or Arhata conception (see n. 38 below). Such is of course not to say that Yāmuna self-consciously aligned himself with the heretical Jainas--wherever Yāmuna mentions the Jainas he does so in a manner that makes clear his opposition to them (see n. 34 above). Only one of the three references is extensive and complete enough to be of any assistance in distinguishing Yāmuna's position from that of the Jainas. In the section of the Extended Discussion of the AtS that corresponds to Pratijñā I.A.6 in which the Nyāya-Vaiśeṣikas and Neo-Mīmāṃsakas attempt to refute Yāmuna's view that consciousness is innate and eternal (svābhāvikī citiḥ) by showing it to be adventitious or occasional (āgantuka), Yāmuna attempts to counter this criticism by saying that the occasional character of cognition depends upon the occasional nature of its contact with different objects at different times by means of the same sense organs [AtS, p. 103.5-7 (A, p. 163.1-4); this position is clearly Yāmuna's own and based upon Nāthamuni's NyT--see AtS, pp. 128.7-135.5 (A, 195.6-203.4) and Ch. VI, n. 112]. It is then necessary to show how consciousness can go out by means of the indriyas and make contact with the objects, and Yāmuna proposes four alternative ways in which this would be possible--the first being patterned after the Jaina teaching of the ātmā and the last being Yāmuna's own view, stated in such a way as to self-consciously distinguish it from the Jaina.

The Jaina view is stated as follows:

athocyeta dvedhā khalv ayaṃ pratyagartho 'vastiṣṭhate bahalo viralaś ca/ tatra bahalaḥ pratyak-cetana-kṣetrajñādi-pada-paryāya ātmā/ viralas tu caitanya-jñānādi-padābhidheyaḥ pratyagartha-tantratayā guṇa ity upacaryate tejovat, yathā bahalaṃ tejaḥ pradīpo 'gnir iti, viralaṃ tu prabhā jyotir iti/ ato viralātma-pradeśatayā caitanyasya--ālokasya--iva gamanaṃ saṃyogādikam upapadyata iti/ [AtS, p. 104.2-6 (A, p. 164.4-9)].

This view of the ātmā (pratyag-artha) as being two-fold

(dvedhā) is criticized scathingly by Yāmuna's opponents and dismissed as an ātmā-vāda flawed or tainted by its imitation of the Jaina teaching ("alam anena--arhata-mata-anukāra-dūṣitena--ātma-vādena"). The Nyāya-Vaiśeṣikas and Neo-Mīmāṃsakas say that such a view is fine if one is prepared to accept an ātmā that is composed of parts, has a form, is non-eternal, bound, etc. ("sāvayavatva-mūrtatva-anityatva-saṃsargitvādikam").

Several paragraphs later Yāmuna gives his own view of the matter which is obviously meant to remove the weaknesses inherent in the Jaina approach:

> athocyeta dvidhā hi jñānam ātmanaḥ svasminn anyatra ca/ tatra--ādyam udayāstamaya-rahitam ātma-svarūpa-prayuktam anavaratam anuvartate, itarat tu tattad-artha-sambandhi-indriyādy-āgantuka-hetu-bheda-āyatta-ātma-lābhaṃ tad-bhāva-abhāva-anuvidhāyi tattad-artha-prakāśatayā--udīyate līyate ca/ tad-apekṣayaiva svāpa-jāgarādy-avasthāpi saṅgaṃsyata iti. [AtS, p. 106.4-7 (A, pp. 167.5-168.1)]

This significant passage has not previously been recognized as representing Yāmuna's own Siddhānta. That it does is shown not only by its identity of terminology and content with Yāmuna's Siddhānta [cf. "udaya-astamaya-rahitam ātma-svarūpa-prayuktam" with "anudita-anastamita-svarūpa-prakāśa" and "svarūpa-prayukta," etc.] but also by the course of the argument, for Yāmuna's opponents admit that such a position would be acceptable if it could be established that jñāna is nitya in the ātmā [AtS, p. 106.7-8 (A, p. 168.1-3)] and of course Yāmuna devotes all of the following pages to establishing precisely that fact [see Ch. III for an identical progression in the AP]. Thus, in distinguishing himself from the Jainas, Yāmuna says that it is not the ātmā itself but rather its dharma, guṇa or svabhāva, jñāna, that is two-fold, the first being eternal uninterrupted self-consciousness ("aham ity eva hi tasya svarūpam") that is ātma-svarūpa-prayuktam and the second being the rising and falling cognition of objects that is dependent upon āgantuka-hetu-bhedas. [See AtS, pp. 101.9-102.4 (A, p. 161.1-8) on the distinction between "svābhāvikī citiḥ" (="ātmanaḥ prakāra-bhūtaṃ caitanyaṃ") and "ghaṭa-saṃvit paṭa-saṃvit" for further proof that this passage corresponds to Yāmuna's Siddhānta.] Of course, in preserving the ātmā's nityatva by confining all change or modification to its guṇas, Yāmuna is following a well-established pattern adhered to by his Nyāya-Vaiśeṣika opponents; see Ch. VI, n. 174, on Śrīdhara.

36. According to syntactical structure, Pratijñās I.C.4.a-b are formally a new series in parallel with Series I.B-E and governed by the "tathātathā pratipadyante" coming after Series I.E (see Appendix III); however, in terms of its content it is a sub-series on a related topic raised by the words vyāpya-vastu-, in Pratijñā I.C.4. See VS II.ii.23-28 (ŚBh, 24-28) where, after the ātmā is shown to be aṇu in the preceding sūtras, the discussion turns to the issue of how an aṇu entity can pervade the entire body (Ghate, Vedānta, pp. 86-90). The term vyāpin(-tva) is used frequently there (see Śaṅkara and Bhāskara on VS II.iii.23, 24, 25, 27 and 28); and Yāmuna's use of vyāpī in his Summary Śloka probably derives from that context.

37. The most likely assumption is that this Pratijñā refers to the position expressed by VS II.iii.25 (ŚBh, 26), "guṇād vā

ālokavat," "or [the aṇu ātmā pervades the body] through his quality (guṇa) [consciousness] as [the sun pervades space through its quality] light (āloka)." Since Rāmānuja, as well as all Vedāntins other than Śaṅkara and his followers, considers this sūtra to express Bādarāyaṇa's Siddhānta, there has been a tremendous pressure among Śrī Vaiṣṇavas at least since the time of Sudarśana Sūri (ŚBh with Śruta-prakāśika, I.i.1, Vol. I, p. 174) to ascribe this viewpoint to Yāmuna--indeed, I myself have difficulty understanding why Yāmuna would not agree with it. However, the structure of this sub-series indicates that Pratijñā I.C.4.b is his Siddhānta--the issues involved will be fully discussed in note 38.

While Pratijñā I.C.4.a is probably directed primarily against the above view, given Yāmuna's tendency to group his opponents together within ambiguously worded Pratijñās (see Pratijñās I.A.5 and 6) and given the fact that there is only one Pūrvapakṣa in this Series, I wonder if "caitanya-mātreṇa" should not also be taken as "by virtue of the ātmā being nothing but conscious ("caitanya-mātra," cf. "bodha-mātra" of Pratijñā I.A.5) [that is all-pervasive (vibhu)]." Thus in a secondary manner this Pratijñā would also represent the viewpoint of the Pracchannas, which Śaṅkara expresses ad VS II.ii. 29, as Bādarāyaṇa's Siddhānta. If such is the case, then Yāmuna intends his Siddhānta I.C.4.b to somehow distinguish itself from the two major Vedāntic options: that of those who hold the ātmā to be aṇu and that of those who consider it to be vibhu.

38. Van Buitenen has accepted this Pratijñā as Yāmuna's, translating the combined Siddhāntas of I.C.4 and I.C.4.b as "Although the ātman is in itself without magnitude, it is localized by the magnitude of the corporeal mass which it pervades in its totality, not merely by knowledge or consciousness" (Introduction to VAS, p. 44). Śrī Vaiṣṇavas have great difficulty accepting this conclusion, however, because the most natural interpretations of the word "svarūpeṇa" imply either (1) that the ātmā is all-pervasive (vibhu) or (2) that the svarūpa of the ātmā undergoes modification in some sense as it pervades bodies of different magnitude. Since Yāmuna explicitly denies the former (see n. 32 above), the latter would seem to be suggested. Indeed, it would appear that something very like this Jaina-like interpretation of Yāmuna's "vyāpī" was suggested by the sectarian but prestigious Varadaviṣṇu Miśra who in his now lost Māna-yathātmya-nirṇaya maintains "jīvasyāpi saṅkoca-vikāśa-yogitvam" [Vedānta Deśika, Nyāya-siddhāñjana (Madras), p. 133.1-8; Varadaviṣṇu Miśra apparently agrees with Bhāskara that ātmā is aṇu in state of samsāra but sarvavyāpī in mokṣa; see Bhāskara, BBh II.iii.29]. Varadaviṣṇu Miśra thus accepts that both the svarūpa of the ātmā and its attribute jñāna undergo contraction and expansion against the Śrī Vaiṣṇava Siddhānta that only jñāna undergoes such variations (Nyāya-siddhāñjana, pp. 133-34). Vedānta Deśika maintains Yāmuna does hold the svarūpa of the ātmā to be aṇu but can only point to places in the Ātma-siddhi (see n. 32 above) where he denies vibhutva but does not affirm aṇutva (Nyāya-siddhāñjana, p. 132).

Faced with these difficulties in the interpretation of Series I.C, Aṇṇaṅgarācārya (SVy, p. 8), with Narasimhachary following him, maintains that Yāmuna simply did not give his

Siddhānta last in this series and sub-series and that Pratijñās I.C.2 and I.C.4.a represent his viewpoint. It is greatly to Vīrarāghavācārya's credit that he does not accept this way out, noting

sarvatra siddhānti-pakṣasya--eva--ante kīrtanād iha--apy evam/ [GPrak, p. 145, note to p. 7, line 1 (1972, p. 6.20-21)]

Because in every case only the position of the siddhāntin is recited at the (end of the series), here also it must be so.

Thus, Vīrarāghavācārya accepts Pratijñā I.C.4 as Yāmuna's Siddhānta, although arguing ingeniously that it is consistent with I.C.2. However, with regard to the sub-series I.C.4.a-b, he follows another tack, noting that Sudarśana Sūri, in commenting upon Rāmānuja's gloss of Yāmuna's "vyāpī" (see n. 35 above), gives what appears to be a variant reading for this text:

jīvasya dharma-bhūta-jñānena vyāptir ātma-siddhāv eva--ucyate, "vyāptir api caitanya-mātreṇa--eva; na svarūpeṇa" iti/ (SBh with Śruta-prakāśikā, Vol. I, p. 174)

By accepting this reading, Vīrarāghavācārya can maintain that Pratijñās I.C.4.a-b are not another Series or sub-series but rather [like I.B.5.b and III.C.2 (see below)] an additional sentence meant to clarify some aspect of the Siddhānta I.C.4. He also claims that if I.C.4.a-b were a two-membered series, there would necessarily have to be a "vā" ("or") after the second position.

While Vīrarāghavācārya's argument is an appealing one, it is not totally convincing. His latter point can be dismissed because Pratijñā Series I.E below is clearly a two-membered series but Yāmuna does not employ a "vā." Also, his argument that Pratijñās I.C.4.a-b do not form a separate sub-series is implausible in light of the over-all structure of Series I.B-E (see n. 36 above and Appendix III). Pratijñā Series I.C.1-4 and Pratijñā sub-series I.C.4.a-b are each enclosed by a separate "iti", indicating that each is a series of conflicting theses. Therefore, I feel that Pratijñā I.C.4.b "svarūpeṇa" probably represents Yāmuna's Siddhānta, although I am not certain exactly how the phrase should be interpreted.

39. Corresponds to Summary Śloka Topic (3) nityo; see Appendix II. See also n. 31 above.

40. The extant text of the AtS breaks off after beginning to present this Buddhist Pūrvapakṣa; see Appendix II.

41. Aṇṇaṅgarācārya, SVy, pp. 8-9, ascribes to the Audulomi of VS I.iv.21. Could also be Bhāskara; see BBh IV.iv.4, p. 243.10-11.

42. All other interpreters take kūṭa-stho along with the following nitya as Yāmuna's Siddhānta. However, Yāmuna states his Siddhānta simply as nityo in the Summary Śloka and I assume that the same solitary term is his Siddhānta here in this series of otherwise one term Pratijñās. While Yāmuna uses kūṭastha with reference to the Paramātmā [SS, p. 180.3 (A, p. 277.1, v. 29)], I know of no instance of his applying it to the individual ātmā. The only instance of his use of the term in the case of the individual ātmā comes in his presentation of the Pracchanna Kevalādvaitins' position; see AtS, p. 36.4 (A, p. 68.8) "kūṭastha-nityā saṃvid evātmā paramātmā ca." My assumption is that Yāmuna is here distinguishing his own position from his various orthodox opponents (the Pracchannas and

Sāṅkhyas, the Nyāya-Vaiśeṣikas and Neo-Mīmāṃsakas) who, in reaction to the Buddhists, have made the ātmā absolutely immutable and passive; see nn. 31-35 above and Ch. VI.

43. Yāmuna's Siddhānta here is stated exactly as Summary Śloka Siddhānta (3) nityo without any expansion. While Yāmuna of course maintains that the individual ātmā is eternal, his position would obviously be open to the same criticisms as lodged against Pāñcarātra and the Jainas since he is not willing to follow his orthodox opponents to the extreme of reducing the ātmā to an absolutely immutable and passive entity in order to avoid the essentially Buddhistically inspired critique of all things involved in activity, change and modification as non-eternal (a-nitya). To Yāmuna, such an extreme reaction is every bit as negative and nihilistic as the Buddhist viewpoint in that it destroys both the theoretical epistemological and the practical emotional basis for an individual's involvement in both transcendental religious and normal human activities and concerns (see Ch. VI). Thus, rather than surrender the view of the ātmā as an involved individual conscious agent (jñātṛ), Yāmuna is willing to leave his position theoretically open to the charges of jīva-utpatti and a-nitya-tva, while attempting to construct a more viable systematic approach to the issues involved. See above nn. 31, 35 and 42 and Ch. VIII below.

44. This series corresponds to Summary Śloka Topic (5); see Appendix II. See also SS, pp. 200.13-201.12 (A, pp. 314.3-316.3, vv. 146-51) for a discussion of this topic.

45. For Yāmuna's refutation of the Kevalādvaitin position, see passage in SS cited in n. 44 above.

46. This Pratijñā corresponds to Yāmuna's Summary Śloka Siddhānta (5), "pratikṣetram ātmā bhinnaḥ"; see SS, p. 201.9-12 (A, pp. 315.3-316.3, vv. 150-51).

47. Pratijñā II.A.1 represents primarily the position of Yāmuna's Neo-Mīmāṃsaka opponents in the AP and the IśS; see Ch. III. Yāmuna would certainly affirm of Īśvara the qualities here denied; see AP, pp. 13.13-14.8 (CE, pp. 122-23; tr, #23); 61.6-7 (CE, p. 245; tr, #107); etc.

48. Pratijñā II.A.2 clearly represents the position of the Pracchanna Kevalādvaitins following Śaṅkara and probably was intended to represent Śaṅkara himself; see BSBh(K) I.iii.19, Vol. I, p. 338.10-15, eka eva parameśvaraḥ kūṭastha-nityo vijñāna-dhātur avidyayā māyayā māyāvi-vad anekadhā vibhāvyate, na--anyo vijñāna-dhātur astīti/ . . . tatrāyam abhiprāyaḥ -- nitya-śuddha-buddha-mukta-svabhāve kūṭastha-nitye ekasminn asaṅge paramātmani tad-viparītaṃ jaivaṃ rūpaṃ vyomnīva talamal-ādi parikalpitam; and II.i.14, pp. 470.1-472.19, especially pp. 470.17ff, nanu kūṭastha-brahma-ātma-vādina ekatvaikāntyād īśitṛ-īśitavya-abhāve īśvara-kāraṇa-pratijñā- virodha iti cet/ na/ avidyā-ātmaka-nāma-rūpa-bīja-vyākaraṇāpekṣatvāt sarvajña-tvasya . . . nitya-śuddha-buddha-mukta-svarūpāt sarvajñāt sarva-śakter īśvarāj jagaj-jani-sthiti-pralayāḥ, na--acetanāt pradhānād anyasmād vā--ity eṣo 'rthaḥ pratijñātaḥ 'janmādy asya yataḥ' (Br. Sū. 1.1.4) iti/ . . . tad evam avidyā-ātmaka-upādhi-paricchedāpekṣam eva--īśvarasya--īśvaratvaṃ sarvajñatvaṃ sarvaśaktitvaṃ ca, na paramārthato, vidyayāpāsta-sarva-upādhi-svarūpe ātmani--īśitṛ-īśitavya-sarvajñatvādi-vyavahāra upapadyate. Pratijñā II.B.3 also represents Śāṅkara-advaita; and the failure to see that Series II.A.1-3 and Series II.B.1-4 are

two series and not one has previously made it impossible to understand the logical sequence of these very important Pratijñās: see Vīrarāghavācārya, GPrak, pp. 7.22-8.26 (1972, p. 7.12-26); Aṇṇaṅgarācārya, SVy, pp. 9-11; van Buitenen, Introduction to VĀS, p. 42.

49. N.B. that Pratijñā II.A.3, which according to my analysis is Yāmuna's Siddhānta (see n. 51 below), accepts fully this Kevalādvaita description of the svarūpa of the Paramātmā, differing with it only on the status of the Paramātmā's manifestation as an Īśvara or "qualified" (upahitam) personal Lord (see n. 52 below).

50. On the appropriateness of Yāmuna's ascribing to Śaṅkara the use of these "Six Qualities," see Ch. II, especially nn. 17-19, where I have shown that Śaṅkara, at least in the context of his Bhagavad Gītā commentary, does use these "Six Qualities" in their Pāñcarātrika sequence. See Ch. VIII for further discussion on these Qualities and Śaṅkara's relation to the Vyūha theory.

51. One of the most intriguing and potentially significant results of my attempt to decode Yāmuna's Siddhāntas from among these Pratijñā Series is my hypothesis that Pratijñā II.A.3 represents Yāmuna's Siddhānta on the svarūpa of the Paramātmā. The factors that have led me to accept this hypothesis are:

(1) Yāmuna begins and ends Pratijñā II.A.3 with precisely the same phrases that he used in Pratijñā I.A.7, which in Ch. VI has been established as his Siddhānta; both Pratijñās are framed as follows: "apare tu . . . imam abhidadhati" (see Appendix III). The particle tu of course is employed to indicate some change or contrast; and I will argue that, with only one exception (I.A.7.a), tu is used by Yāmuna to indicate his own Siddhānta (see I.A.7, II.A.3, II.B.4, III.C.1 and Appendix III).

(2) The Pratijñā following Pratijñā II.A.3 begins with the word tathā. At every other place in the Pratijñā Series where tathā is used in this way, it introduces a new topic or Series (see Pratijñā Series I.B, I.C, I.D, II, II.C, II.D, III and IV; see Appendix III). I believe that tathā does the same here and that the four Pratijñās following II.A.3 are not a continuation of the same Series but--as was the case with Pratijñās I.A.7. a-b--form a new Series (II.B.1-4) on a closely related topic (see n. 55 below). Therefore, Pratijñā Series II.A concludes with II.A.3, Yāmuna's Siddhānta.

(3) The most distinctive point made by Pratijñā II.A.3 is that the Paramātmā as Īśvara is upahitam. As our discussion of Yāmuna's use of the related terms upādhi and svarūpa-upādhi in Ch. VI has shown, such terminology is not necessarily alien to or incompatible with Yāmuna's general theoretical perspective. I believe that, in light of the analysis of Ch. VI, upahitam here can be quite reasonably and coherently interpreted as "qualified or distinguished by certain properties (upādhis, dharmas, guṇas, viśeṣaṇas) of which He is the possessor." When the term upahitam ("qualified") is correlated on the one hand with Yāmuna's svarūpa-upādhi and svarūpa/svabhāva distinction and on the other with Pratijñā III.C.1 (which I argue is Yāmuna's Siddhānta on the relation between the ātmā and the

Paramātmā and in which appear the terms "upādhito bheda" and "viśiṣṭa-svarūpa-bhāvena"), then we have recovered a clear view of the manner in which Yāmuna's interpretation of Vedānta was the basis for what later came to be called Viśiṣṭādvaita, "the non-dualism of that which is qualified."

I believe that this Pratijñā can also be interpreted in accord with the point made in Ch. VI that the śakti or power to produce effects can exist only in a qualified entity (viśiṣṭa-vartinīm eva); see Ch. VI, nn. 136, 171-72, 177. Thus, in Pratijñā II.A.3, the Paramātmā is māyā-upahita and thus able to produce the manifold universe. In Yāmuna's hymn the Catuśśloki (CŚl) devoted to the Goddess Śrī, she is called Māyā (see n. 53 below); and Māyā's role here as the active and productive śakti of the Lord reflects the Pāñcarātra Tāntric background of Yāmuna's Vedāntic Siddhānta--see for example the verse from the Ahirbudhnya Saṃhitā quoted in n. 192, Ch. VI. On avidyā as one of the śaktis of God (tirobhāva-śakti or nigraha) in the Pāñcarātra Āgamas, see n. 54 below.

52. Yāmuna thus fully accepts the phrase "pratyastamita-miti-māna-mātṛ-meya-īśvara-īśitavyādi-bheda-vikalpa-kūṭastha-vijñāna-eka-rasam" from II.A.2, a phrase which he himself must intend to represent the position of the usually despised Pracchannas, Śaṅkara or his followers, on the svarūpa of the Paramātmā; van Buitenen indeed (Introduction to VAS, p. 42) takes this Pratijñā to be "an important description of the advaita doctrine of God (= impersonal brahman)." See in this regard the section of the SS [pp. 175-178 (A, pp. 267-280, vv. 1-36)] dealing with the Sadvidyā in which Yāmuna refutes the Kevalādvaita interpretation and affirms the reality (sadbhāva) of the universe, but then proceeds, in terms starkly similar to Śaṅkara's own, to establish the radical insignificance of the universe when compared with Sat or Brahman [e.g., vācārambhanamātram tu jagat . . . kūṭastham mūlakāraṇam eva sat, SS, p. 180.2-3 (A, pp. 276.4-277.1, v. 29)]. Thus, the issue between Yāmuna and Śaṅkara is not over the svarūpa of the Paramātmā but over the ultimate reality of Brahman's manifestations, forms or "qualities" (Yāmuna's svarūpa-upādhis or svabhāvas) as Īśvara, the individual ātmā and the physical universe; see Ch. VIII for further discussion of this point.

53. See CŚl, v. 1, in which Yāmuna uses the term māyā for the beloved of the Highest Person who is rightly named Śrī: "kāntas te puruṣottamaḥ . . . yavanikā māyā jagan-mohinī/ . . . śrīr ity eva ca nāma te . . . ." See n. 1 above.

54. The phrase "avidyā-upadhānena tad-guṇa-sāratayā" is hard to interpret lacking Yāmuna's Extended Discussion. My suggestion that avidyā = karma is based upon Viṣṇu Purāṇa 6.7.61, "avidyā karma-saṃjñā--anyā tṛtīyā śaktir iṣyate," that is cited by Rāmānuja (VAS, #43) who regularly interprets avidyā ("ignorance") as karma (see VAS, #4, n. 25; #43; #91, n. 438; etc.), the power of past deeds which acts to expand or contract the consciousness that is the essential property of the self (ātma-dharma-bhūtasya caitanyasya svābhāvikasyāpi karmaṇā pāramārthikaṃ saṃkocaṃ vikāsaṃ ca, VAS, #43). See also Yāmuna's similar use of the term upadhāna in his Siddhānta I.A.7.

On avidyā (also called māyā) as one of the five śaktis of the Godhead (tirobhāva-śakti or nigraha, the obscuring or punishing power) in the Pañcarātra Āgamas, see Matsubara, "Early Pāñcarātra," p. 69, who cites Ahirbudhnya Saṃhitā 14.17, 14-28;

38.13; 45.3-4; Lakṣmî Tantra 3.16-19, 33; 12.15-20; 13.38; 14.55-56; Parama Saṃhitā 1.82; Pauskara Samhitā 43.121; Jayākhyā Samhitā 3.17; 4.10, 51; see also Viṣṇu Purāṇa 6.7.63; 1.20.11; 1.22.73, 77; 5.17.15; 5.30.15; 2.7.30; 2.61.2.

55. According to my understanding of the progression between Series II.A and II.B, the topic of Series II.B is suggested by the phrase in Pratijñā II.A.3, svādhîna-vicitra-vivarta-svabhāva-māyā-upahitatayā. In II.B.1-3, others propose alternate views of how the Paramātmā manifests and is related to the universe; and then Yāmuna restates his position in II.B.4. The structure is in accord with the central Vedāntic issue of how Brahman, the ultimate source (janma) or cause, can be both the efficient (nimitta-kāraṇa) and the material (upādāna) cause of the universe (see Ch. II, nn. 29-30). See the quote from Śaṅkara in n. 48 above that sets the discussion of this issue in the context of VS I.i.4, "janmādy asya yataḥ."

56. Sāṅkhya-yoga dualism, in the context of the VS the main opponent of Upaniṣadic non-dualism (a-dvaita), teaching that the physical universe comes forth from the insentient pradhāna or prakṛti, not from Brahman (see Ch. II, n.30). See Vyāsa, Yoga-Sūtra-Bhāṣya I.24.

57. A typification of a rather primitive type of pariṇāma-vāda which asserts, in opposition to Sāṅkhya-Yoga dualism, that Brahman is both the efficient (nimitta) and the material (upādāna) cause (kāraṇa), such as is generally recognized to have been the view of Bādarāyaṇa in the VS (see van Buitenen, Introduction to VAS, p. 15, n. 41, and Ghate, The Vedānta, p. 162). Such a view, however, especially in the context of a Buddhist critique, would seem to implicate Brahman in change and the fault of non-eternality (a-nitya-tva). Pratijñās II.B.3 and II.B.4 represent respectively Śaṅkara's and Yāmuna's attempts to avoid these implications and to preserve the eternality (nityatva) of the Paramātmā while still accepting the basic Vedāntic axiom that Brahman is the material cause of the universe.

58. The pratibimba-vāda or vivarta-vāda of Śāṅkara-advaita according to which the manifold universe is simply an illusory "reflection" or "appearance" and not ultimately real; see n. 48 above to Pratijñā II.A.2. See also Paul Hacker, Vivarta (Wiesbaden, 1953). On Viśva, Taijasa and Prājña, see Māṇḍukya Up. Kārikās of Gauḍapāda, kārikā 3, and Śaṅkara's commentary thereon.

59. Pratijñā II.B.4 is universally accepted as Yāmuna's and is exceedingly significant (see n. 62 below). In it Yāmuna is clearly asserting that the only way in which to maintain both the eternality of the svarūpa of the Paramātmā or Brahman (i.e., the kuṭastha-vijñāna proposed by Śaṅkara in II.A.2 and accepted by Yāmuna in II.A.3) and His relation to the universe as its sole (a-dvaita) Cause (kāraṇa) and Lord (îśvara) is to accept Him as a "qualified" (upahitam) personal being (puruṣa-viśeṣam). Only in this manner can modification (pariṇāma) or change be excluded from His svarūpa, i.e., by restricting the pariṇāma to His "essential qualities" ("svābhāvika- . . . -guṇa-") or properties. In the now lost Extended Discussion of this Pratijñā, Yāmuna would doubtlessly have developed this position in terms of his svarūpa-upādhi and the svarūpa/svabhāva distinction just as we have seen him do in the case of the individual ātmā; see nn. 16-17, 26, 28-38, 48-49, 51-52, 55-58 above; Ch.

VI, passim, especially nn. 108-127 and 132-85 and accompanying text; and Ch. VIII. For the manner in which Rāmānuja has developed Yāmuna's svarūpa/svabhāva distinction in just such a way with regard to the Paramātmā, see references in n. 108 of Ch. VI.

60. See Yoga Sūtras I.24; Yāmuna would seem to be invoking overtones of Patañjali's identical phrase and perhaps of Nāthamuni's Yoga-rahasya.

61. The phrase "sakala-kalyāṇa-guṇa-mahārṇava" becomes one of Rāmānuja's favorites; see J. B. Carman, Theology of Rāmānuja, Chs. 4, 6, 7, passim.

62. It is the use of the "Six Qualities" (ṣaḍ-guṇas) in this particular sequence in this Pratijñā, one that is universally accepted as one of Yāmuna's Vedāntic Siddhāntas, that most explicitly indicates that his is a system of "Pāñcarātrika Vedānta," since he is here self-consciously integrating the peculiarly Pāñcarātrika Vyūha theory into his Upaniṣadic or Vedāntic Siddhānta on the Paramātmā as the source or cause of the physical universe and employing the Vyūha theory to explain in what manner Brahman is the material cause (upādāna-kāraṇa). See Ch. VIII below and Ch. II above, especially nn. 13-19.

63. The trividha-cetana-acetana probably refers to the categories referred to in the dedicatory verse to the AtS; see above. The three insentient (a-cetana) would be 1) the unmanifest (a-vyakta) Prakṛti, 2) the manifest (vyakta) and 3) time (kāla). The three sentient (cetana) are 1) the bound (baddha) selves (puruṣas), 2) the released (muktas) and 3) the eternally released (nitya-siddhas).

64. Strictly according to the syntactical structure, II.C and II.D should be major headings in parallel with Series I, II.A-B, III, IV, and V (see Appendix III). However, treating them as sub-headings of Series II seems to accord better with both the structure of Series I on the individual ātmā and the five categories given in the concluding paragraph of the introduction.

65. Pratijñā II.D.1 clearly corresponds to Pratijñā I.B.2 (āgama-eka-vedyaḥ) which in the extant Extended Discussion is presented and rejected by Yāmuna as the position of unthinking Śrotriyas or Scripturalists. See AtS, pp. 85.7-87.8 (A, pp. 139.1-142.2). Contemporary Śrī Vaiṣṇava scholars, in order to bring Yāmuna's position on the pramāṇas into line with the latter traditional Siddhānta and to refute Dasgupta's somewhat rash and poorly balanced interpretation of Yāmuna as a Naiyayika on this matter (HIP, III, 152-55), have tried to identify Yāmuna with these Śrotriyas and thus with Pratijñā II.D.1; see Narasimhachary, Contribution, p. 301. This argument is clearly fallacious and does no honor to a highly critical thinker like Yāmuna (see Ch. III, n. 51).

66. As Aṇṇaṅgarācārya, SVy, p. 12, accepts, the ca in this Pratijñā indicates that the preceding position is also to be accepted here. Cf. Vyāsa, Yoga-sūtra bhāṣya I.25, "sāmānya-mātra-upasaṃhare ca kṛta-upakṣayam anumānam, na viśeṣa-pratipattau samartham iti/ tasya saṃjñādi-viśeṣa-pratipattir āgamataḥ paryanveṣyā."

67. Aṇṇaṅgarācārya, SVy, p. 12, accepts this interpretation of this Pratijñā as Yāmuna's Siddhānta:

> śruto mataś ca śrutito 'nuamānataś ca prema-pūrva-
> anudhyāna-saṃskṛta-mano-grāhyaśca--iti tu siddhāntinaḥ//

The ca's in II.D.2 and II.D.3 thus indicates that all three pramāṇas are accepted by Yāmuna, as was the case in Pratijñā I.B.5.b. Rāmānujāchāri's translation [AtS, p. 6 (1972, p. 5)] of this series is therefore incorrect; see n. 65 above. See Vyāsa, Yoga-sūtra-bhāṣya I. 48-49, for what seems to be a very close parallel to Yāmuna's position, e.g., "āgamena-anumānena dhyāna-abhyāsarasena ca."

68. The structure of this series is of critical importance and is ambiguous and much disputed. The series ends ". . . iti ca nānāvidhā vādāḥ." This phrase is similar to the one, "iti ca tathātathā pratipadyante," that concludes the section I. B-E, which is comprised of four series and one sub-series, each clearly concluded and marked off by an "iti" (see Appendix III). On the basis of this parallel, one would expect that each of the Pratijñās in Series III would be concluded by an "iti." However, in this series, Yāmuna seems to have combined this manner of division with another which he uses frequently, that of indefinite pronominal forms in the nominative plural (ke cit, anye, etc.) employed to indicate the different speakers. Thus, at the end of the first Pratijñā we find "iti ke cit." While it would be possible to take "ke cit" with what follows, in the other instances where Yāmuna uses "ke cit" (Pratijñās I.A.1 and II.A.1), it indicates only the first Pratijñā of a series; therefore, it seems likely that "iti ke cit" goes with the first Pratijñā here also. Now, when Yāmuna uses such pronominal forms in a series, his usual pattern is to have one such form for each Pratijñā (cf. Pratijñās I.A, II.A, and II.D). Thus, when Series III begins with the pattern ". . . iti ke cit, . . .ity anye," we are led to expect a structure like that of Series II.D (. . . ity eke, . . . ity anye, . . . ity apare"). Unfortunately, this pattern seems first to merge with and then change over to the pattern of using "iti" alone to mark off the Pratijñās. The final pattern of "iti's" and pronouns is " . . . iti ke cit, . . . ity anye, . . . iti . . . itare . . . iti ca nāvāvidhā vādāḥ" (see Appendix III). Vīrarāghavācārya [GPrak, p. 9.5-11 (1972, p. 8.5-9)] and van Buitenen (VAS, p. 45, n. 125) both suggest that there are four Pratijñās, the first three being marked off by the pronouns and the last by "iti ca" ("A." iti ke cit; "B." ity anye; C. itare; "D." iti ca) with the last being Yāmuna's Siddhānta.

My own reconstruction of this series accepts Vīrarāghavācārya's and van Buitenen's division of it into four units and also accepts the fourth as Yāmuna's own. However, I feel that, precisely as was the case with the Pratijñās I.B.5.a and I.B. 5.b, the third unit (III.C.1. "svatas tv aikyam upādhito bheda iti viśiṣṭa-svarūpa-bhāvena bhinnābhinnatvam itare") is Yāmuna's Siddhānta, while the fourth unit (III.C.2. "nānātve saty eva abheda nāmānvayaḥ . . . bhṛtyasvāmi-lakṣaṇa") is an addendum dealing with an issue raised by the statement of his Siddhānta, i.e., how precisely to understand "the relation called abheda" (see also Pratijñās I.A.7.a-b and Series II.B). According to my interpretation, the final "iti ca" encloses both Pratijñā III.C.1 and III.C.2 (see Appendix III).

69. Corresponds with the position of Pratijñās II.A.2 and II.B.3, i.e., Śāṅkara-advaita and Śaṅkara himself; see nn. 48-49 above.

70. Probably a typification of a primitive form of bheda-abheda-vāda or dvaita-advaita-vāda corresponding to the posi-

tion of Pratijñā II.B.2 and responding to the absolute kevala-advaita of III.A. Pratijñā III.C then gives Yāmuna's more sophisticated form of bhedābheda.

71. If my interpretation of Pratijñā III.C.1 as Yāmuna's Siddhānta is correct, then we probably see here in the phrase viśiṣṭa-svarūpa-bhāvena the earliest known source of the name viśiṣṭa-advaita which came in later centuries to represent the Śrī Vaiṣṇava Siddhānta on the saṃbandha, i.e., viśeṣaṇa-viśeṣya-bhāva or dharma-dharmi-bhāva; see nn. 49, 51 and 59 above and Ch. VI, nn. 136, 149-172 and accompanying text. It may be that Śrī Vaiṣṇava scholars would resist this conclusion since such terms as upādhi and bhinnābhinnatvam have come to be closely associated with such Bhedābhedavādins as Bhāskara who were soundly condemned and utterly rejected by Rāmānuja [ŚBh(K) I.i.1, Vol. I, p. 48, "ata eva sarvatra bhinnābhinnatvam api nirastam"]. However, according to my understanding, the obstacles to Śrī Vaiṣṇava acceptance of Pratijñā III.C.1 are more terminological than substantive. It would appear that in Yāmuna's Vedāntic milieu the terms upādhi and bhinnābhinnatvam were acceptable, somewhat neutral ones that could be utilized and defined as one wished. We have established in Ch. VI that Yāmuna used upādhi in a sense compatible with my understanding of Pratijñā III.C.1, although he felt it necessary to qualify it (as svarūpa-upādhi) and redefine it (as svabhāva) when applying it to a property (dharma) or quality (guṇa) that is eternally related to its possessor (svarūpa-prayukta). Moreover, in the extant fragment of the SS, Yāmuna would appear to defend bhedābheda against Kevalādvaita; see SS, pp. 185.7-188.3 (A, pp. 288.2-294.2, vv. 58-74), especially p. 187.2-3 (A, pp. 291.3-292.1, v. 67) that gives his definitions of abheda and bheda which seem totally in accord with Pratijñā III.C.1: "abhedo bheda-mardîti svāśrayībhūta-vastunoḥ/ bheda parasparaānātmyaṃ bhāvānām."

The phrase "svatas tv aikyam, upādhito bheda" also relates this Pratijñā to Pratijñā II.A.3, which I also argue is Yāmuna's Siddhānta and which says that Īśvara is upahitam or "qualified" by Māyā, the jīva-bhedas, avidyā, etc. Moreover, the logical sequence between II.A.2 (Śaṅkara) and II.A.3 (Yāmuna) is precisely the same as between III.A and III.C.1 here, i.e., Yāmuna first grants or accepts Śaṅkara's statement about the essential unity and immutability of the svarūpa of the Paramātmā ("kuṭastha-vijñāna-eka-rasa", "svatas tv aikyam"), but then asserts that this eternal One is "qualified."

72. According to my understanding, Pratijñā III.C.2, which Vīrarāghavācārya and van Buitenen take as the full statement of Yāmuna's Siddhānta, is a supplementary statement further defining the sense in which bhinnābhinnatvam is to be understood (see n. 68 above). This phrase, "nānātve saty eva," is a comment upon bhinnatva and reveals the degree to which Yāmuna agrees with Rāmānuja's criticisms of those Bhedābhedavādins such as Bhāskara for whom bheda is only conditionally real and ultimately dissolved in abheda (see VAS, ## 54-64, 84-85). For Yāmuna and Rāmānuja, bheda must be accepted as an ultimately real given--on the one hand so that the valid evidence of perception is not contradicted and on the other hand so that Brahman does not become implicated in the imperfections that afflict the individual ātmā. Thus, accepting bheda as a given, the task is to define the relation termed "abheda", as Yāmuna

proceeds to do in the remainder of III.C.2. See van Buitenen, Introduction to VAS, pp. 44-48.

73. See ŚBh(K) III.ii.29, Vol. III, p. 829, where Rāmānuja says the *aṃśāṃśibhāva* can be understood only in terms of *viśeṣaṇa-viśeṣyatva*.

74. See Ch. VI, nn. 159 and 167 for Yāmuna's brief indication of his definition of *samavāya* as a type of *saṃyoga*.

75. See AtS, p. 82.5-6 (A, p. 124.3-4), for Yāmuna's definition of the *śeṣa-śeṣī* relation. See J. B. Carman, *Theology of Rāmānuja*, pp. 147-57, *passim*, on the *śeṣa-śeṣi-bhāva-sambandha* as a central category for Rāmānuja.

76. See SR, vv. 51, 53-55, 60.

77. See Ch. VI, n. 91.

78. Cf. with Pratijñā I.A.7.a.

79. For passages in Yāmuna's extant works related to this Siddhānta, see AP p. 1.1 (CE, p. 86; tr, #1), p. 41.22 (CE, p. 194; tr, #78), 47.22 (CE, p. 210; tr, #84), 62.11-12 (CE, p. 248; tr, #109); SS, p. 188.1-3 (A, pp. 213.4-214.1, v. 74); SR, vv. 43, 46, 54, 55, 57, 60, 62, 63; GAS, 29-32. See also Pratijñā I.A.7.b.

80. See GAS, 23-26. This Siddhānta is quoted by Rāmānuja, VAS, #92.

81. Some MSS apparently have the variant reading "dramiḍa-bhāṣyakṛtā," which is given by AtS(A), p. 15.5, and AtS(V), p. 10.12 (1972, p. 9.8), and tentatively utilized by Oberhammer, YIB, pp. 115f, n. 269. See Ch. IV for a discussion of Yāmuna's "Commentator," especially nn. 59-66 and accompanying text.

82. See Chs. IV and V on this shadowy but crucially important figure.

83. "-sita-asita-vividha-nibandhana-", lit. "various compositions that are white and black, good and evil." In the preceding sentence, Yāmuna has used the word *an-ava-sita*, "unascertained", "undetermined", "ambiguous." Therefore, I think that Yāmuna intends *sitāsita* to be taken also in the sense of "bound and unbound", "reasoned and unreasoned", "coherent and incoherent", "correct and incorrect." Rāmānujāchāri (AtS, p. 8) and Aṇṇaṅgarācārya (SVy, p. 16) interpret *sitāsita* in the sense that certain of the books and authors listed are acceptable to Yāmuna while others are not, in order to explain how certain teachers, such as Ācārya-ṭaṅka and, presumably, another Śrīvatsāṅka, who are accepted by Rāmānuja and the later Śrī Vaiṣṇava tradition could be included in this list. Van Buitenen (Introduction to VAS, pp. 24-29), on the other hand, takes this as "a series of adversaries" and then strives to "understand why Ṭaṅka was excluded by Yāmuna and included by Rāmānuja."

My interpretation provides a middle ground that may help resolve the difficulty. Cf. the phrase *sitāsita-guṇa*, "having black and white yarn alternately for warp and woof" (Apte, s.v., *sita*). Thus Yāmuna's image implies not that the works are *all* bad--or some all bad and others all good--but that they are ambiguously interwoven with good and bad ideas in varying proportions and are therefore confusing to those who cannot distinguish between the two. Therefore, Ācārya-ṭaṅka's inclusion in this list does not necessarily indicate his complete rejection by Yāmuna (as Vīrarāghavācārya, GPrak, p. 147, suggests, the use of *ācārya* indicates a degree of praise), although it does indicate at the very least that Yāmuna feels his words are ambiguous and need to be clarified. Indeed, this view of Ṭaṅka would seem to be historically correct since his words have been interpreted to support Śaṅkara, Bhāskara, and Rāmānuja.

84. On Ācārya-ṭaṅka, see M. Hiriyanna, "Fragments from Brahma-nandin," pp. 151-58, K. B. Pathak Commemorative Volume, Poona, 1934; J. A. B. van Buitenen, Introduction to VAS, pp. 24-29; Dasgupta, HIP, III, pp. 106-108; P. V. Kane, Proceedings and Transactions, Fifth Indian Oriental Conference, 1928, Vol. II, pp. 942-44.

85. M. Hiriyanna, "Bhartṛ-prapañca: an Old Vedāntin," Indian Antiquary, LIII (1924), 77-86; "Fragments of Bhartṛ-prapañca," Proceedings and Transactions, Third Oriental Conference, Madras, 1924, pp. 439-50; P. N. Srinivasachari, The Philosophy of Bhedābheda, Adyar Library Series No. 74 (Madras, 1950), pp. 152-54.

86. M. Hiriyanna, "Brahma-datta: an Old Vedāntin," Journal of Oriental Research, Madras, 1928, pp. 1ff.

87. This unreliable Vedāntin Śrīvatsāṅka is obviously not to be confused with the Bhagavān Śrīvatsāṅka Miśra whom Yāmuna immediately before has acknowledged as the source for his fullest, most profound and closely reasoned interpretation of the VS.

88. Srinivasachari, The Philosophy of Bhedābheda, pp. 3-139; D. H. H. Ingalls, "Bhāskara the Vedāntin," PhilEW, XVII (1967), 61-67; V. Raghavan, "Bhaskara's Gītābhāṣya " WZKSO XII/XIII (1968/69), 281-94.

89. P. V. Kane, "Vedānta Commentators before Śaṅkarācārya," Proceedings and Transactions, Fifth Indian Oriental Conference, Lahore, 1928, Vol. II, pp. 937-53.

NOTES

CHAPTER VIII

1. See Ch. II.
2. See Ch. VI, n. 15.
3. See Ch. II, nn. 14-15, 18-19; and Ch. VII, n. 50 to Pratijñā II.A.2.
4. AP, pp. 54.21-55.8 (CE, pp. 228-31; tr, #95); 56.1-17 (CE, pp. 233-35; tr, #97); 57.23-59.5 (CE, pp. 239-40; tr, #101).
5. See Ch. VII, Pratijñā II.B.4, especially nn. 59 and 62.
6. F. Otto Schrader, Introduction to Pāñcarātra, pp. 32ff; Jan Gonda, Viṣṇuism and Śivaism, pp. 55-57; Ahirbudhnya Saṃhitā V. 16ff. See also Ch. II, n. 17.
7. See below and R. Mesquita, "Recent Research on Yāmuna," WZKS XVIII (1974), 192, n. 41.
8. See Ch. VII, nn. 49, 51, 52, 55-63, especially n. 62.
9. Oberhammer, YIB, pp. 21-22, n. 24.
10. Śaṅkara, BSBh (K) II.ii.42, Vol. I, p. 573.2-7, 14-16.
11. Ibid., p. 573.14-15.
12. Ibid., pp. 573.15-574.4; Bhāskara, BBh, p. 128.24-28. See Ch. VII, nn. 31-43, for some aspects of Yāmuna's response to this charge, which is more generally termed the "fault of the Jainas."
13. Schrader, Introduction to the Pāñcarātra, pp. 27-93; Matsubara, "Early Pāñcarātra," pp. 18ff, 107ff, 114.
14. See van Buitenen, Introduction to AP (tr), pp. 19-21, for a discussion of this sūtra and a suggestion that it might have been intended to accept this version of the Vyūha theory, although the fourth sūtra would have been concluded again with a general rejection of Pāñcarātra.
15. Bhāskara, BBh, p. 129.4-14; see van Buitenen, Introduction to AP (tr), pp. 27-28 for a translation and for critical emendations of the text.
16. Śaṅkara, BSBh(K) II.ii.44, Vol. I, pp. 574.11-575.14.
17. Ibid., p. 575.14; see Ch. II, n. 15 for text.
18. See Ch. II, especially nn. 18-19.
19. BSBh(K) II.ii.44, p. 574.12, na caite saṃkarṣaṇādayo jīvādi-bhāvena--abhipreyante.
20. Ibid., p. 574.13-14.
21. nir-adhiṣṭhānā nir-upādānā ata eva nir-avadyā a-nitya-tvādi-doṣarahitāḥ, Bhāmatī, p. 751.2, in Śaṅkara, Śārīraka-mīmāṃsā-bhāṣyam with three commentaries, ed. by K. Veṅkaṭācala-śāstri and Śrīchoṭūpatiśāstrī (1835 Śaka).
22. Śaṅkara, BŚBh(K) II.ii.44, Vol. I, p. 575.1.
23. Ibid., p. 575.1-3.
24. Ibid., p. 575.3-5, paraspara-bhinnā eva--ete vāsudevādayaś catvāra īśvarās tulya-dharmāṇo na--eṣām eka-ātmakatvam astīti.

25. *Ibid.*, p. 575.7, ekasya--eva bhagavata ete catvāro vyūhās tulya-dharmāṇaḥ.

26. *Ibid.*, p. 575.5-6.

27. *Ibid.*, p. 575.8-14, na hi vāsudevāt saṃkarṣaṇasya--utpattiḥ saṃbhavati, saṃkarṣaṇāc ca pradyumnasya, pradyumnāc ca--aniruddhasya, atiśaya-abhāvāt/ bhavitavyaṃ hi kārya-kāraṇayor atiśayena yathā mṛd-ghaṭayoḥ/ na hy asaty atiśaye kāryaṃ kāraṇam ity avakalpate/ na ca pañcarātra-siddhāntibhir vāsudevādiṣv eka-ekasmin sarveṣu vā jñāna-aiśvarya-ādi-tāratamya-kṛtaḥ kaścid bhedo 'bhyupagamyate vāsudevā eva hi sarve vyūhā nir-viśeṣā iṣyante/ na ca--ete bhagavad-vyūhāś catuḥ-saṃkhyāyām eva--avatiṣṭheran, brahma-ādi-stamba-paryantasya samastasya--eva jagato bhagavad-vyūhatva-avagamāt.

28. *Ibid.*, II.ii.42, p. 573.1-14.

29. See Ch. II, nn. 14-15.

30. Supply *pravibhajya* as at p. 573.3; see *Ahirbudhnya Saṃhitā* V. 30, *vibhajaty ātmanātmānam*.

31. Śaṅkara, BSBh(K) II.ii.42, Vol. I, p. 573.9-12; see Ch. II, n. 14 for text.

32. See van Buitenen, Introduction to VAS, pp. 1-18.

33. Śaṅkara, *ChUp Bhāṣya* 6.2.3-4, pp. 249-51, in *Ten Principal Upanishads with Śaṅkarabhāṣya*, Works of Śaṅkarācārya, Vol. I (Delhi: Motilal Banarsidass, 1964).

34. *Ibid.*, 6.3.2, pp. 252.21-253.9; 6.8.6, pp. 264.23-265.22; 6.15.1, p. 274.4-7.

35. *Ibid.*, 6.3.3-4, p. 253.10-26.

36. *Ibid.*, 6.3.2-4, pp. 252.8-253.9.

37. *Ibid.*, 6.3.2, p. 253.4-5, sarvaṃ ca nāmarūpādi sad-ātmanā--eva satyaṃ vikāra-jātaṃ, svatas tv anṛtameva; 7.17.1, p. 293.8-22.

38. *Ibid.*, 6.1.4, p. 245.14-17, vācāraṃbhaṇaṃ vāgāraṃbhaṇaṃ vāgālaṃbanam ity etat/ vāgālaṃbano-mātraṃ nāma--eva kevalaṃ na vikāro nāma vastv asti; 6.2.2, p. 249.10-11; 6.3.2, p. 253.4-9; 6.8.4, p. 263.25-28.

39. *Ibid.*, 6.8.4, p. 263.25-28.

40. *Ibid.*, 6.16.3, p. 275.20-27; 6.2.1, p. 246.12-29; 6.2.2, p. 249.12-17; 7.24.1, p. 295.14-25.

41. *Ibid.*, 7.24.1, p. 295.14-25.

42. Śaṅkara, BSBh(K), II.i.14, Vol. I, p. 470.4ff. See Ch. VII, n. 48 for the text.

43. Ghate, *The Vedānta*, pp. 162, 74; van Buitenen, Introduction to VAS, p. 15.

44. van Buitenen, Introduction to VAS, p. 15. See Ch. VII, Pratijñā II.B.2, n. 57.

45. Śaṅkara, BSBh(K) II.i.14, Vol. I, pp. 469.13-472.19. See Ch. VII, Pratijñā II.B.3 that begins *a-pariṇāminam api*.

46. See Ch. II, n. 30.

47. See Paul Hacker, *Vivarta, Studien zur Geschichte der illusionistischen Kosmologie und Erkenntnistheorie der Inder*, Abhandlungen der Geistes- und Sozialwissenschaftlichen Klasse, 1953, Nr. 5 (Mainz, 1953) pp. 208-13.

48. Paul Hacker, "Eigentümlichkeiten der Lehre und Terminologie Śaṅkaras: Avidyā, Nāmarūpa, Māyā, Īśvara," *Zeitschrift der Deutschen Morgenländischen Gesellschaft*, 100 (1950), pp. 261-64.

49. See Ch. VII, Pratijñā Series II.A-B, especially nn. 57-59.

50. See Ch. II, n. 30.

51. See Ch. VII, Pratijñās II.A.3, II.B.4, III.C.1-2, nn. 57, 59, 71-76.
52. "The Study of Śaṃkarācārya", ABORI, XXXIII (1952), 9-11.
53. Bhāskara, BBh, p. 129.10-14; van Buitenen, Introduction to AP(tr), p. 28.
54. BSBh(K) II.ii.45, Vol. I, p. 575.16-18.
55. Bhāmatī ad VS II.ii.45, p. 752.6-7, guṇibhyaḥ khalv ātmabhyo jñānādīn guṇān bhedena--uktvā punar abhedaṃ brūte.
56. Ghate, The Vedānta, pp. 165-70.
57. Matsubara, "Early Pāñcarātra", p. 35.
58. Ahirbudhnya-saṃhitā of the Pāñcarātrāgama (AhirS), edited by M. D. Ramanujacharya, Adyar Library Series, Vol. IV, (Madras: Adyar Library and Research Centre, second ed., 1966), Vol. I, p. 18, II.53, sarva-dvandva-nirmuktaṃ sarva-upādhi-varjitam/ ṣāḍguṇyaṃ tat paraṃ brahma sarva-kāraṇa-kāraṇam//
59 Ibid., II.54cd, kathaṃ ca guṇahīnaṃ tat ṣāḍguṇyaṃ parigīyate.
60. Ibid., II.55.
61. See n. 13 above.
62. AhirS, II.55cd-62, pp. 19-20, śṛṇu nārada ṣāḍguṇyaṃ kathyamānaṃ mayānagha// ajaḍaṃ svātmasaṃbodhi nityaṃ sarvāvagāhanam/ jñānaṃ nāma guṇaṃ prāhuḥ prathamaṃ guṇacintakāḥ// svarūpaṃ brahmaṇas tac ca guṇaś ca parigīyate/ jagatprakṛtibhāvo yaḥ sā śaktiḥ parikīrtitā// kartṛtvaṃ nāma yat tasya svātantryaparibṛṃhitaṃ/ aiśvaryaṃ nāma tat proktaṃ guṇatattvārthacintakaiḥ// śramahānis tu yā tasya satataṃ kurvato jagat/ balaṃ nāma guṇas tasya kathito guṇacintakaiḥ// tasya--upādāna-bhāve 'pi vikāra-viraho hi yaḥ/ vīryaṃ nāma guṇaḥ so 'yam acyutatvāparāhvayam// sahakāryanapekṣā yā tat tejaḥ samudāhṛtam/ ete śaktyādayaḥ pañca guṇā jñānasya kīrtitāḥ// jñānam eva paraṃ rūpaṃ brahmaṇaḥ paramātmanaḥ/ ṣāḍguṇyaṃ tat paraṃbrahma svaśaktiparibṛṃhitam/ bahu syām iti saṃkalpaṃ bhajate tat sudarśanam//
63. See also the Jayākhya-saṃhitā (IV.38ff) for a distinction between types of jñāna that are different (bhinna) from Brahman and that which is brahma-abhinna (IV.50-51).
64. See Ch. VI, n. 59.
65. See Ch. VI, n. 59.
66. See above n. 31 and Ch. II, n. 14.
67. SS, pp. 175.2-177.8 (A, pp. 238-72, śls. 2-15).
68. SS, pp. 177.9-180.13 (A, pp. 272-279, śls. 16-34), tasmāt prapañca-sadbhāvo na--advaita-śruti-bādhitaḥ/ sva-pramāṇa-balāt siddhaś śrutyā cāpy anumoditaḥ// tena--"advitīyaṃ brahma"--iti śruter artho 'yam ucyate/:

dvitīya-gaṇanāyogyo nāsīd asti bhaviṣyati// samo vābhyadhikāro vāsya yo 'dvitīyas tu gaṇyate/ yato 'sya vibhava-vyūha-kalā-mātram idaṃ jagat// dvitīyavāgāspadatāṃ pratipadyeta tat katham/ yathā coḷa-nṛpas samrāḍ advitīyo 'dya bhūtale// iti tat-tulya-nṛpati-nivāraṇa-paraṃ vacaḥ/ na tu tad-bhṛtya-tat-putra-kaḷatrādi-niṣedhakam// tathā surāsuranara-brahma-brahmāṇḍa-koṭayaḥ/ kleśa-karma-vipākādyair aspṛṣṭasya--akhila-īśituḥ// jñāna-ādi-ṣāḍguṇya-nidher acintya-vibhavasya tāḥ/ viṣṇor vibhūti-mahima-samudra-drapsa-vipruṣaḥ// . . . yathā--eka eva savitā na dvitīyo nabhastale/ ity uktyā na hi sāvitrā niṣidhyante 'tra raśmayaḥ// . . .
tathā,

pādo 'sya viśvā bhūtāni tripādasyāmṛtaṃ divi/
iti bruvan jagat sarvam itthaṃbhāve nyaveśayat//

tathā, . . .

meror ivāṇur yasyedaṃ brahmāṇḍam akhilaṃ jagat// ityādikās samastasya tad-itthaṃbhāva-tat-parāḥ/ vācārambhaṇa-mātran tu jagat sthāvara-jaṅgamam// vikāra-jātaṃ kūṭasthaṃ mūlakāraṇam eva sat/ an-anyat kāraṇāt kāryaṃ pāvakād visphuliṅgavat// mṛttikā-loha-bījādi-nānādṛṣṭānta-vistaraiḥ/ nāśakad dagdhum analas tṛṇaṃ majjayituṃ jalam// na vāyuś calituṃ śaktas tacchaktyāpyāyanād ṛte/ eka-pradhāna-vijñānād vijñātam akhilaṃ bhavet// ityādi-veda-vacana-tan-mūla-āpta-āgamair api/ brahmātmanātmalābho 'yaṃ prapañcaś cidacinmayaḥ// iti pramīyate brāhmī vibhūtir na niṣidhyate/ tan-niṣedhe samastasya mithyātvāl loka-vedayoḥ// vyavahārās tu lupyeraṃs tathā syād brahma-dhīr api/

69. Introduction to VAS, pp. 11ff.
70. SS, p. 180.2-3 (A, pp. 276-77, śl. 29).
71. ChUp 6.1.4, etc.
72. See n. 38 above.
73. VAS, #31.
74. See Carman, The Theology of Rāmānuja, pp. 210-11, for another example of this contrast between the poet Yāmuna and the strict systematizer Rāmānuja.
75. See Ch. VII, Pratijñās I.D.5-6, nn. 42-43.
76. See Ch. VII, Pratijñā Series I.C, nn. 31-38.
77. See Ch. VII, Pratijñās II.A.2-3, nn. 48-52; cf. Pratijñās III.C.1 and III.C.2, n. 71.
78. ŚBh(K) III.ii.28-29, Vol. III, pp. 828-29; see Ch. VI, n. 172, and Ch. VII, n. 73.
79. See VAS, ##60, 83-85.
80. ŚBh(K) I.i.1, Vol. I, p. 48; see Ch. VII, n. 71. See also VAS, #59.
81. On Rāmānuja's distinctive emphasis on Brahman's "purity" or a-malatva, see Carman, The Theology of Rāmānuja, pp. 103ff.
82. See Ch. VII, Pratijñā III.C.2, n. 72.
83. See Ch. VII, Pratijñās II.A.2-3, nn. 49 and 52. See also Yāmuna's own phrase "apagata-sakala-karaṇa-kalāpa-sva-mahima-pratiṣṭha-brahmaṇaḥ," AP, p. 55.20 (CE, p. 232; tr, #96).
84. N.B. that Rāmānuja (VAS, #5) uses the phrase "jñāna-ānanda-eka-guṇa" which corresponds to Pratijñā I.A.7.a, "jñāna-ānanda-svabhāvam," which Yāmuna rejects in I.A.7.b, reaffirming bodha-eka-svabhāvam eva.
85. See Ch. VI, nn. 56-58.
86. See Ch. VII, Pratijñā Series II.A-B, nn. 55-63.
87. The Gadya-traya of Sri Ramanujacharya, ed. and trans. by M. R. Rajagopala Ayyangar (Madras, n.d.), p. 8.3-5, #2.
88. Carman, The Theology of Rāmānuja, Chs. 6-7.
89. ŚBh(K) II.ii.41, Vol. I, pp. 696-98.
90. See Ch. I, n. 17.

NOTES

APPENDIX I

1. For general references on Nāthamuni and on his *Nyāyatattva*, see Ch. V, nn. 1, 5, 12, 14, 15, 21; Ch. VI, nn. 112, 159, *passim*.

2. Svāmī Ādidevānanda, ed. and tr., *Stotraratna or the Hymn-jewel of Śrī Yāmunācārya* (SR) (Mylapore, Madras: Sri Ramakrishna Math, 1951).

3. SR 5, mātā pitā yuvatayas tanayā vibhūtis sarvaṃ yad eva niyamena madanvayānām/ ādyasya naḥ kulapater bakulābhirāmaṃ śrīmattadaṅghriyugaḷaṃ praṇamāmi mūrdhnā// 5 // According to a strong tradition, this verse is dedicated to Nammāḻvār who at *Tiruvāimoḻi* 4.10.11 refers to himself as one "whose breast shines with a garland of *mahir* [= *v(b)akula*] blossom" and who is traditionally identified with the feet of the Lord; see P. B. Annangaracharya Swami, *The Glory of Tamil Prabandha*, pp. 116-17.

4. Vedānta Deśika, *Stotraratna-bhāṣya*, Vedānta-granthamalā, Vol. I (Madras: R. Venkateswar and Co., n.d.), pp. 18.5, "ādarātiśayāt punar namasyati;" 18.30, "audārya-viśiṣṭam;" see also Periya Vāccān Piḷḷai, *Stotraratna-vyākyānam*, pp. 4-9.

5. See Śrī Kāñcī Prativādibhayaṅkara Aṇṇangarācāryaḥ, ed., *Stotramālā* (Kāñcīpuram: Granthamālā Kāryālaya, 1958), for a collection of Sanskrit hymns by the major early Ācāryas.

6. See K. C. Varadachari, *Āḻvārs of South India*, pp. 93-99 (Tiru-mālai, vv. 25-43), for the attitude of the Coḻiya Brāhmaṇa āḻvār, Vipranārāyaṇa (Toṇḍaraḍippoḍi); and J. S. M. Hooper, tr., *Hymns of the Āḻvārs*, (London: Oxford Univ. Press, 1929), pp. 44-45, for that of the royal āḻvār, Kulaśekhara.

7. Cf. SR 47-51 with Varadachari, *Āḻvārs*, pp. 95-97 (Tiru-mālai, vv. 29-37).

8. See Ch. V, nn. 61-64.

9. AP, p. 87.1-8 (CE, p. 304; tr, #139); see Ch. V on the significance of the reference to Nāthamuni and his disciples in the first of these verses.

10. Van Buitenen's translation of this last verse [AP(tr), #139] is incorrect in that he takes "-uktayaḥ" ("sayings") as the subject instead of "santas" ("saints," "good men"); "santas" would have to be "satyas" (nom. f. pl.) if it were modifying -uktayaḥ.

11. See Vedānta Deśika, *Stotraratna-bhāṣyam*, p. 18.5-6, "tasmai 'svayogamahimapratyakṣatattvatraya' iti suprasiddhāya"; and *Śrī Pāñcarātra-rakṣā*, Adyar Library Series, Vol. 36 (Adyar, Madras, 1967), p. 59.2-4.

12. See Ch. V, n. 66.

13. See Ch. VI, nn. 195-200.

14. See SR 61 quoted above; see also SR 22, "na cātma-vedī"; 62, "cala-matir."

15. See Ch. VI, nn. 199-200.

16. Vedānta Deśika, Stotraratna-bhāṣyam, p. 88.18ff.
17. Śrīdhara, Nyāya-kandalī, pp. 3.12-4.2, "munim iti śuddhātmajñāna-pradīpa-kṣapita-tamasam atyugratapasaṃ sākṣād-aśeṣa-tattvāvabodhayuktaṃ puruṣaviśeṣam."
18. See Yoga-sūtras 1.15, 2.3ff.
19. See Ch. VI, n. 195.
20. 6000 GPP, pp. 105-107.
21. 6000 GPP, pp. 101-103; 3000 GPP, pp. 34-36.
22. AP(tr), #139, n. 304; see n. 10 above.
23. See above in this Appendix for the full text and translation.
24. 6000 GPP, p. 102.
25. Stotraratna-bhāṣyam, p.19.12-14.
26. Stotraratna-vyākhyānam, pp. 8-9.
27. See SR 1, 2, 3, and 61.
28. See Ch. V.
29. See Ch. V on the coṭṭai kulam.
30. 6000 GPP, pp. 133-37.

BIBLIOGRAPHY

I. Yāmuna's Extant Works: texts, translations, and commentaries

Āgama-prāmāṇyam (AP). Edited by Rāma Miśra Śāstrī. Vārāṇasī: The Pandit, 1900 (reprinted 1937). My basic text, utilized in conjunction with the following two editions, to which parallel references have been made.

The Āgamaprāmāṇya of Śrī Yāmunāchārya [AP(CE)]. Critically edited by M. Narasimhachary. Unpublished manuscript presented to the Univ. of Madras as partial fulfillment of the requirements for the Ph. D. in Sanskrit, 1966. Since published as Āgamaprāmāṇya of Yāmunācārya [AP(CE 1976)]. Gaekwad's Oriental Series, No. 160. Baroda: Oriental Institute, 1976. The published version reached me too late for the preparation of the notes. Therefore, the references to AP(CE) are generally to the unpublished version. However, I have prepared (see Appendix IV) a concordance of my text of primary reference (AP) with AP(CE 1976) and the following edition and translation AP(tr) (see Chapter I, note 34).

Yāmuna's Āgama Prāmāṇyam or Treatise on the Validity of Pañcarātra [AP(tr)]. Sanskrit text and English translation by J. A. B. van Buitenen. Madras: Ramanuja Research Society, 1971.

Siddhi-traya by Yāmunācārya (ST). Edited with English translation and notes by R. Ramanujachari and K. Srinivasacharya. Annamalai University Philosophical Series, No. 4. Annamalainagar, 1943. Originally published serially between 1935-43 in the Journal of Annamalai University. My basic text of reference. [Parallel references have also been given to the following edition, ST(A).] This edition, which is the closest we have to a critical edition, has recently been reissued with a new introduction by Prof. Ramanujachari as Sri Yamunacharya's Siddhi Trayam, with an Introduction in English by R. Ramanujachari and Translation in English by R. Ramanujachari and K. Srinivasacharya (ca. 1972). A slightly revised version of the English translation together with the new introduction has also been published as the second part of Sri Yamunacharya's Siddhi Trayam with a Sanskrit Commentary (Gooda Prakasa), by Sri U. Ve. Abhinava Desika Uttamur T. Viraraghavacharya (see below).

Siddhi-trayam [ST(A)]. Edited with Siddhāñjana-vyākhyā (SVy) by P. B. Aṇṇaṅgarācārya. Bombay: Nirnaya Sagar Press, 1954.

Siddhi-trayam [ST(V)]. Edited with Gūḍha-prakāśa-ākhya-ṭippaṇa (GPrak) by U. T. Vīrarāghavācārya. Tirupati: Śrīvāṇī Press, 1942. A revised edition of this valuable modern Sanskrit commentary together with a slightly revised version of the above cited English translation has been issued as Sri Yamunacharya's Siddhi Trayam with a Sanskrit Commentary (Gooda Prakasa) [ST(1972), GPrak(1972)]. Edited by Sri U. Ve. Abhinava Desika Uttamur T. Viraraghavacharya, with an Introduction in English by R. Ramanujachari and Translation in English by R. Ramanujachari and K. Srinivasacharya. Madras: Ubhaya Vedanta Granthamala Book Trust, 1972.

Siddhi-traya [ST(Chow)]. Edited by Rāma Miśra Śāstrī. Chowkhamba Sanskrit Series, No. 10. Benares, 1900.

Siddhi-traya. Partial German translation by Rudolf Otto. Appeared in sections in Logos, 1928; Zeitschrift für Religionspsychologie, 1929, and Zeitschrift für Theologie und Kirche, 1929.

Gītārtha-saṃgraha. Edited with English translation by J. A. B. van Buitenen in his Rāmānuja on the Bhagavad-gītā. 'S-Gravenhage, 1953, pp. 177-82.

--------. Text with English translation and notes by M. R. Sampatkumaran in his tr., The Gitabhashya of Ramanuja. Madras, 1969, pp. 535-45.

--------. Edited by P. B. Ananthachariar, with the Gītārtha-saṃgraha-rakṣā by Vedānta Deśika. Śāstra-mutkāvalī, No. 10. Conjeeveram: Sri Sudarsana Press, 1901.

--------. Edited with Sanskrit text and English Commentary by V. K. Ramanujachariar. Madras: Sri Ranganatha Paduka, 1971.

Stotra-ratna and Catuś-ślokī. Text in the Stotra-māla, edited by Śrīkāñcī P. B. Aṇṇaṅgarācārya. Kāñcīpuram, 1958.

--------, with the commentaries of Vedānta Deśika. Edited by K. T. I. V. Śrīnivāsācārya and A. V. Nṛsiṃhācārya. Vedāntagrantharatnamāla, No. 1. Madras, n. d.

--------. Sanskrit texts with the Maṇipravāḷam commentaries by Periyavāccān Piḷḷai. Edited by K. Śrīnivāsa Ayyangār. Tiruccirāpalli, n. d.

Stotraratna or The Hymn-jewel of Śrī Yāmunācārya (SR). English translation by Svami Ādidevānanda. Madras: Sri Ramakrishna Math, 1950.

The Stotra-ratna of Śrī Yāmunācārya. English translation by M. R. Rajagopala Ayyangar. Madras, n. d.

Catuś-ślokī. German translation by Rudolf Otto in his Vischnu-Nārāyana, text zur Indischen Gottesmystik. Jena: Eugen Diederichs, 1923, pp. 158-59.

Catuś-ślokī. English translation by K. Rangachari in his The Sri Vaishnava Brahmans. Madras, 1931.

II. Other Texts and Secondary Works

Adigal, Prince Ilangō. Shilappadikaram (The Ankle Bracelet). Translated by Alain Daniélou. New York: New Directions Books, 1965.

Ahirbudhnya-saṃhitā. Edited by M. D. Ramanujacharya. Adyar Library Series, Vol. 4. 2 Parts. Adyar, Madras, 1966.

Anantācārya, Prapannāmṛtam. Edited by Śrīnivāsanṛsiṃhācārya. Śaka, 1829.

Aṇṇaṅgarācāryaḥ, Śrī Kañci Prativādibhayankara. The Glory of the Tamil Prabandha (The Background of Ramanuja's System). English adaptation by M. V. V. K. Rangachari. Kakinda, 1955.

--------, editor. Stotramāla. Kañcīpuram: Granthamālā Kāryālaya, 1958.

Appadorai, A. Economic Conditions in Southern India (1000-1500 A.D.). Two vols. Madras University Historical Series No. 12. Madras, 1936.

Athalye, Yashwant Vasudev, ed. Tarka-saṅgraha of Annambhaṭṭa. Translated by Mahadev Rajaram Bodas. Bombay Sanskrit Series No. LV. Bombay: Bhandakar Oriental Institute Press, 1930.

P. C. Bagchi. "Evolution of the Tantras." The Cultural Heritage of India. Volume IV. Edited by H. Bhattacharyya. Calcutta: The Ramakrishna Mission, second ed., 1956.

Belvalkar, S. K., ed. and trans. The Brahma-Sūtras of Bādarāyaṇa, with the Comment of Śaṅkarāchārya. Chapter II, Quarter I & II. Poona: Bilvakunja Publishing House, 1931 (1924).

--------. "Jaimini's Sārīraka-Sūtra." Aus Indiens Kultur, festgabe Richard von Garbe. Edited by J. von Negelein. Erlangen, 1927.

Bhaduri, Sadananda. Studies in Nyāya-Vaiśeṣika Metaphysics. Poona: Bhandarkar Oriental Research Institute, 1947.

Bhāsarvajña. Nyāyasāra of Ācārya Bhāsarvajña with the Nyāyasārapada pañcika of Vasudeva of Kashmir. Poona, 1922.

Bhāskara. Brahma-sūtra-bhāṣyam. Edited by V. P. Dvivedin. Chowkhamba Sanskrit Series, Vol. 20. Benares, 1903-1915.

Bhatt, Govardhan P. Epistemology of the Bhaṭṭa School of Pūrva Mīmāṃsā. The Chowkhamba Sanskrit Series, Vol. XVII. Varanasi: Chowkhamba Sanskrit Series Office, 1962.

Bhatt, S. R. The Philosophy of Pancharatra (Advaitic Approach). Madras: Ganesh & Co., 1968.

Bhattacharya, Jogendra Nath. Hindu Castes and Sects. Calcutta: Editions Indic, Second edition, 1968. [First edition, 1896].

Brahmatantra Svatantra Svāmi. Mūvvāyirappaḍi Guru-paramparā-prabhāvam. Edited by K. Anandācārya. Triplicane, Madras: 1913.

Carman, John B. The Theology of Rāmānuja: An Essay in Inter-religious Understanding. New Haven: Yale University Press, 1974.

Census of India 1961, Vol. IX, Madras. Part XI.D.ii, Temples of Madras State: Tiruchirapalli and South Arcot. Madras, 1966.

Chand, Tara. Influence of Islam on Indian Culture. Allahabad: Indian Press, 1954.

Dasgupta, Surendranath. A History of Indian Philosophy. Five volumes. Cambridge: Cambridge University Press, 1940.

De, Dhirendra Lal. "A Historical Survey of Pāñcarātra Religion." Unpublished Ph. D. thesis, University of London, 1931.

Deussen, Paul. The System of Vedānta. New York: Dover, 1973.

Gail, Adalbert. Bhakti im Bhāgavatapurāṇa, Religionsgeschichtliche Studie zur Idee der Gottesliebe in Kult und Mystik des Viṣṇuismus. Wiesbaden: Harrassowitz, 1969.

Ghate, V. S. The Vedānta: A Study of the Brahma-sūtras with the Bhāṣyas of Śaṁkara, Rāmānuja, Nimbārka, Madhva and Vallabha. Poona: Bhandarkar Oriental Research Institute, 1960.

Gokhale, V. V. "The Vedānta-Philosophy Described by Bhavya in His Madhyamakahṛdaya." Indo-Iranian Journal, II (1958), 165-80.

Gonda, Jan. Die Religionen Indiens, II Der jüngere Hinduismus. Stuttgart: W. Kohlhammer Verlag, 1963.

--------. Viṣṇuism and Śivaism: A Comparison. (Jordan Lectures, 1969). London: The Athlone Press, 1970.

Gopinatha Rao, T. A. Sir Subrahmanya Ayyar Lectures on the History of Śrî Vaiṣṇavas. Madras: Government Press, 1923.

Gōvindāchārya, A. The Holy Lives of the Āzhvārs or The Drāvida Saints. Mysore, 1902.

--------. The Life of Rāmānujāchārya. Madras: S. Murthy and Co., 1906.

Gupta, Sanjukta. "The Caturvyūha and the Viśākha-yūpa in the Pāñcarātra." Adyar Library Bulletin, XXXV (1971), 189-204.

--------, translator. Lakṣmî Tantra, A Pāñcarātra Text. Leiden: E. J. Brill, 1972.

Hacker, Paul. "Relations of Early Advaitins to Vaiṣṇavism." Wiener Zeitschrift für die Kunde Süd- und Ostasiens, IX (1965), 147-154.

--------. "Śaṅkara der Yogin und Śaṅkara der Advaitin, einige Beobachtungen." Weiner Zeitschrift für die Kunde Süd- und Ostasiens, XII/XIII (1968-69), 127-35.

Hacker, Paul. Vivarta, Studien zur Geschichte der illusionistischen Kosmologie und Erkenntnistheorie der Inder. Abhandlungen der Geistes- und Sozialwissenschaftlichen klasse Jahrgang 1953, Nr. 5. Wiesbaden: Akademie der Wissenschaften und der Literatur, 1953.

Hara, Minoru. "Materials for the Study of Pāśupata Śaivism." Unpublished Ph. D. dissertation, Harvard University, 1967.

--------. "Nākulīśa-Pāśupata-Darśanam." Indo-Iranian Journal, II (1958), 8-32.

Hiriyanna, M., editor. Iṣṭa-siddhi of Vimuktātman. Gaekwad's Oriental Series, No. LXV. Baroda, 1933.

Hopkins, Thomas J. The Hindu Religious Tradition. Encino, California: Dickenson Publishing Company, Inc., 1971.

Hari Rao, V. N., ed. and trans. Kōil Oḻugu, The Chronicle of the Sri Rangam Temple. Madras: Rochouse and Sons Private Ltd., 1961.

Hooper, J. S. M., trans. Hymns of the Aḻvars. London: Oxford University Press, 1929.

Ingalls, Daniel Henry Holmes. Materials for the Study of Navya-Nyāya Logic. Harvard Oriental Series, Vol. 40. Cambridge: Harvard University Press, 1951.

--------. "Śaṁkara's Arguments Against the Buddhists." Philosophy East and West, III (1953-54), 291-306.

--------. "The Study of Śaṁkarācarya." Annals of the Bhandarkar Oriental Research Institute, XXXIII (1952), 1-14.

Iśvara-saṃhitā. Śāstramuktāvalī, No. 45. Kāñcipuram, 1923.

Jacob, G. A. A Third Handful of Popular Maxims. Bombay, 1911, second revised edition.

Jagadeesan, N. "History of Śrī Vaishnavism in the Tamil Country (Post Rāmānuja)." Unpublished doctoral thesis, University of Madras, 1967.

Jayākhyasaṁhitā of Pāñcarātra Āgama. Edited by Embar Krishnamacharya. Gaekwad's Oriental Series, No. 54. Baroda: Oriental Institute, 1967.

Jayanta Bhaṭṭa. Āgamaḍambara, otherwise called Ṣanmatanāṭaka of Jayanta Bhaṭṭa. Edited by V. Raghavan and Anantlal Thakur. Mithila Institute Series, Ancient Texts, No. VII. Darbhanga, 1964.

--------. Nyāyamañjarī. Kashi Sanskrit Series, No. 106. Two parts. Benares, 1936.

Jha, Ganganath, trans. The Padārthadharmasangraha of Praśastapāda with the Nyāyakandalī of Śrīdhara. Benares: Pandit Reprint, 1916.

--------. Pūrva-Mīmāṁsā in its Sources. Varanasi: The Banaras Hindu University Press, second edition, 1964. [With a critical bibliography by V. Mishra.]

Jhaḷakīkar, Bhīmāchārya. Nyāyakośa. Bombay Sanskrit Series No. XLIX. Bombay: Government Central Book Depot, 1893.

Johnston, E. H. Early Sāṁkhya. London: Royal Asiatic Society, 1937.

Kane, Pandurang Vaman. History of Dharmaśāstra (Ancient and Medieval Religious and Civil Law). Government Oriental Series Class B, No. 6. Vol. III. Poona: Bhandarkar Oriental Research Institute, 1946.

Keith, A. Berriedale. The Karma-Mīmāṁsā. The Heritage of India Series. London: Oxford University Press, 1921.

--------. Indian Logic and Atomism. New York: Greenwood Press, 1968.

Kosambi, D. D. An Introduction to the Study of Indian History. Bombay, 1956.

Lakṣmī-tantra: A Pāñcarātra Āgama. Edited by V. Krishnamacharya. Adyar Library Series, Vol. 87. Adyar, 1959.

Matilal, Bimal Krishna. The Navya-Nyāya Doctrine of Negation. Harvard Oriental Series, Vol. 46. Cambridge: Harvard University Press, 1968.

Matsubara, Mitsunori. "The Early Pāñcarātra with Special Reference to the Ahirbudhnya Saṃhitā." Unpublished Ph. D. dissertation, Harvard University, 1972.

Mayeda, Sengaku. "The Authenticity of the Bhagavadgītā-bhāṣya Ascribed to Śaṅkara." Wiener Zeitschrift für die Kunde Süd- und Ostasiens, IX (1965), 155-197.

Mesquita, Roque. "Das Problem der Gotteserkenntnis bei Yāmunamuni." Unpublished doctoral dissertation, Universität Wien, 1971.

--------. "Yāmunamuni: Leben, Datierung und Werke." Wiener Zeitschrift für die Kunde Südasiens, XVII (1973), 177-193.

--------. "Recent Research on Yāmuna." Wiener Zeitschrift für die Kunde Südasiens, XVIII (1974), 183-208.

Minaksi, C. Administration and Social Life Under the Pallavas. Madras: University of Madras, 1938.

Mishra, Umesha. History of Indian Philosophy. Vol. II. Allahabad: Tirabhukti Pub., 1966.

Nakamura, Hajime. "Upaniṣadic Tradition and the Early School of Vedānta as Noticed in Buddhist Scripture." Harvard Journal of Asiatic Studies, 18 (1955), 74-104.

--------. "The Vedānta as Noticed in Mediaeval Jain Literature." Indological Studies in Honor of W. Norman Brown. American Oriental Series, XLVII, 1962.

Narasimhachary, M. Contribution of Yāmuna to Viśiṣṭādvaita. Madras: Professor M. Rangacharya Memorial Trust, 1971.

Nilakanta Sastri, K. A. The Cōḷas. Madras: University of Madras, 1955.

--------. Development of Religion in South India. Bombay: Orient Longmans, 1963.

Oberhammer, Gerhard. Yāmunamunis Interpretation von Brahmasūtra 2, 2, 42-45. Untersuchung zur Pāñcarātra-Tradition der Rāmānuja-Schule. Wien: Hermann Böhlaus Nachf., 1971.

Paramasaṃhitā. Edited and translated by S. Krishnaswami Aiyangar. Gaekwad's Oriental Series, Volume 86. Baroda: Oriental Institute, 1940.

Pārameśvara-saṃhitā. Edited by Śrī Govindācārya. Śrīraṅgam, 1953.

Pauṣkara-saṃhitā. Edited by Y. S. Ramanuja Muni. Bangalore, 1934.

Periya Vāccān Piḷḷai. Stotraratna-vyākyānam. Periyan Vāccān Piḷḷai Śrīsūktimālā, No. 2. Tiruchirapalli, n. d.

Pinbaṛagiya Perumāḷ Jīyar. Ārāyirappaḍi Guru-paramparā-prabhāvam. Edited by C. Krishṇamācārya. Triplicane, Madras, 1927.

Qureshi, Ishtiaq Husain. The Muslim Community of the Indo-Pakistan Subcontinent (610-1947). 'S-Gravenhage: Mouton, 1962.

Radhakrishnan, S. The Brahma Sūtra: The Philosophy of Spiritual Life. London: George Allen and Unwin Ltd., 1960.

Raghavan, V. "The Name Pāñcarātra." Journal of the American Oriental Society. Volume 85, Number 1 (January-March, 1965), 73-79.

Rāmānuja. Brahmasūtra-Śrībhāṣya with Śrutaprakāśika of Sudarśanasūri. Edited by U. T. Vīrarāghavācārya. Two volumes. New Delhi: Government of India, 1967.

--------. The Gadya-traya of Sri Ramanujacharya. Edited and translated by M. R. Rajagopala Ayyangar. Madras, n. d.

--------. Śrī Bhagavad-Rāmānuja-Granthamālā (Collected Works). Edited by Śrī Kāñci P. B. Aṇṇaṅgarācārya Svami. Kāñcipuram, 1956.

--------. Śrībhāṣya of Rāmānuja. Edited and translated by R. D. Karmarkar. University of Poona Sanskrit and Prakrit Series, Volume I, three parts. Poona, 1959-64.

Ramanujachari, R. "Fragments from the Nyāya-Tattva." Professor K. V. Rangaswami Aiyangar Commemoration Volume. Madras, 1940.

--------. "Nathamuni, His Life and Time." Journal of the Annamalai University, IX (1940), pp. 267-77.

--------. "Yāmunācārya." Proceedings and Transactions of the All-India Oriental Conference. First session, 1955, pp. 397ff.

Rangachari, K. The Sri Vaishnava Brahmans. Bulletin of the Madras Government Museum. Madras, 1931.

Renou, Louis. The Destiny of the Veda in India. Edited by Dev Raj Chanana. Delhi: Motilal Banarsidass, 1965.

Śālikanātha Miśra. Prakaraṇa Pañcikā with Nyāya-siddhi. Edited by A. Subrahmanya Sastri. Banaras Hindu University Darśana Series, No. 4. Banaras, 1961.

Sanatkumāra-saṃhitā of the Pāñcarātrāgama. Edited by V. Krishnamacharya. Adyar Library Series, Volume 95. Adyar, 1969.

Sanghvi, Sukhlalji. Advanced Studies in Indian Logic and Metaphysics. Edited and translated by Krishna Kumar Dixit. Indian Studies Past and Present reprint. Calcutta, 1961.

Śaṅkara. Bhagavad Gītā with the Commentary of Śrī Śankarācārya. Edited by Dinkar Vishnu Gokhale. Poona: Oriental Book Agency, 1950.

--------. The Brahma-sūtra-Śankara-bhāṣya, with the Ratna-prabhā Commentary by Govindānanda and Purnānandī Commentary on Ratnaprabhā by Purnānanda. Edited by Dhundirāj Sāstri. Kāśi Sanskrit Series, No. 71, Parts I and II. Benares: The Chowkhamba Sanskrit Series Office, 1929.

--------. Śārīraka-mīmāṃsā-bhāṣyam with three commentaries, the Ratnaprabhā by Govindānanda, the Bhāmatī by Vācaspati Miśra and the Nyāyanirṇaya by Ānandagiri. Edited by K. Veṅkatācalaśāstrī and Śrīchoṭūpatiśāstrī. Śaka 1835.

--------. Ten Principal Upanishads with Śaṅkarabhāṣya. Works of Śaṅkarācārya, Vol. I. Delhi: Motilal Banarsidass, 1964.

Sastri, S. Kuppuswami. "Bodhāyana and Dramiḍācārya, Two Old Vedāntins Presupposed by Rāmānuja." Proceedings and Transactions of the Third Oriental Conference. Madras, 1924, pp. 468-72.

--------, editor. Brahmasiddhi by Ācārya Maṇḍanamiśra. Madras Government Oriental Manuscript Series, No. 4. Madras, 1937.

Schrader, F. Otto. Introduction to the Pāñcarātra and the Ahirbudhnya Saṃhitā. Madras: Adyar Library, 1916.

Schultz, Friedrich A. Die Philosophisch-theologischen Lehren des Pāśupata-Systems nach den Pañcārthabhāṣya und der Ratnaṭīkā. Beiträge zur Spach- und Kulturgeschichte des Orients, Heft 10. Walldorf-Hessen, 1958.

Sharma, B. N. K. The Brahmasūtras and Their Principal Commentaries (A Critical Exposition). Vol. II. Bombay: Bharatiya Vidya Bhavan, 1974.

Shastri, D. N. Critique of Indian Realism. Agra: Agra University, 1964.

Singer, Milton, editor. Krishna: Myths, Rites and Attitudes. Honolulu: East-West Center Press, 1966.

--------. When a Great Tradition Modernizes, An Anthropological Approach to Indian Civilization. New York: Praeger, 1972.

Singh, Satyavrata. Vedānta Deśika: His Life, Works and Philosophy. Chowkhamba Sanskrit Series Studies, Volume V. Varanasi, 1958.

Śivāditya. Saptapadārthī. Calcutta Sanskrit Series, No. VIII. Calcutta, 1934.

Smith, H. Daniel. A Descriptive Bibliography of the Printed Texts of the Pāñcarātrāgama. Two Volumes. Gaekwad's Oriental Series. Baroda: Oriental Institute. No. 158, Vol. I, 1975; Vol. II, Index, forthcoming.

Smith, H. Daniel. "The 'Three Gems' of the Pāñcarātra Canon--a Critical Appraisal." Ex Orbe Religionum, Studia Geo Widengren. C. J. Bleeker, editor. Leiden: Brill, 1972. pp. 42-51.

--------. "A Typological Survey of Definitions: The Name 'Pāñcarātra.'" The Journal of Oriental Research (Madras). XXXIV-XXXV (1973), 102-17.

Spencer, George W. "Royal Leadership and Imperial Conquest in Medieval South India: the Naval Expedition of Rajendra Chola I, c. 1025 A.D." Unpublished Ph. D. thesis, Univ. of California-Berkeley, 1967.

Śrīdhara. Nyāyakandalī in Praśastapādabhāṣya with commentary Nyāyakandalī of Śrīdharabhaṭṭa. Gaṅgānātha-Jhā-Granthamālā, Volume I. Varanasi, 1963.

Srinivas, Mysore N. Caste in Modern India and Other Essays. Bombay: Asia Publishing House, 1962.

--------. Religion and Society Among the Coorgs of South India. London and New York: Oxford University Press, 1952.

Srinivasa Aiyengar, C. R. The Life and Teachings of Sri Ramanujacharya. Madras: R. Venkateshwar and Co., n. d.

Srinivasachari, P. N. The Philosophy of Bhedābheda. Adyar, Madras: The Adyar Library, 1950.

--------. The Philosophy of Viśiṣṭādvaita. Adyar, Madras: The Adyar Library, 1946.

Staal, J. F. "Notes on some Brahmin Communities of South India." Journal of the Royal India, Pakistan and Ceylon Society, XXXII, pp. 1-7.

Stcherbatsky, Theodore. Buddhist Logic. Two volumes. New York: Dover Publications, 1962.

Subrahmanian, N. "The Brahmin in the Tamil Country (in ancient and medieval times)." Unpublished manuscript, 1968.

Sukthankar, Vishnu S., and S. K. Belvalkar, editors. The Mahābhārata. Vol. 16. Poona: Bhandarkar Oriental Research Institute, 1954.

Tamil Lexicon. Madras: University of Madras, 1928.

Thrasher, Allen W. "The Advaita of Maṇḍana Miśra's Brahma-Siddhi." Unpublished Ph. D. thesis, Harvard University, 1972.

Udayana. Kiraṇāvalī. Vaiśeṣikadarśanam. Benares Sanskrit Series. Benares, 1919.

Upadyay, Basudeva. "Migration of Brāhmaṇas from Madhyadesha." Journal of Bihar Research Society, XXXXV (1959), pp. 308-12.

van Buitenen, J. A. B. "On the Archaism of the Bhāgavata Purāṇa." Krishna: Myths, Rites and Attitudes. Edited by Milton Singer. Honolulu: East-West Center Press, 1966.

--------. "The Name 'Pañcarātra.'" History of Religions, I (1962), 291-99.

van Buitenen, J. A. B. Rāmānuja on the Bhagavadgītā, a condensed rendering of his Gītābhāṣya with Copious Notes and an Introduction. 'S-Gravenhage: H. L. Smits, 1953.

--------, editor and translator. Rāmānuja's Vedārthasaṃgraha. Deccan College Monograph Series, No. 16. Poona, 1956.

--------. "The Śubhāśraya Prakaraṇa (Viṣṇu Purāṇa 6, 7) and the Meaning of Bhāvanā." Adyar Library Bulletin, XIV (1955), 3-19.

Varadachari, K. C. Āḻvārs of South India. Bhavan's Book University 143. Bombay: Bharatiya Vidya Bhavan, 1966.

--------. Viśiṣṭādvaita and its Development. Tirupati: Chakravarthy Publications, 1969.

Varadachari, V. "Antiquity of the Term Viśiṣṭādvaita." Adyar Library Bulletin, XXVI (1962), 177-81.

--------. "Nyayatattva of Nathamuni." Indian Philosophy and Culture, VI (1961), 484-89.

Vedānta Deśika. Gadya-traya-bhāṣya. Śrīmad-Vedānta-Deśika-Granthamālā, Vyākhyānavibhāga. Part I. Conjeevaram, 1940.

--------. Nyāya-Pariśuddhi. Chowkhamba Sanskrit Series, No. 51. Benares, 1923.

--------. Nyāyasiddhāñjana with commentary of Raṅgarāmānuja in Śrī Vedānta Deśika's Works. Volume I. Madras, 1934.

--------. Śata-dūṣaṇī. Four volumes. Conjeevaram, 1901.

--------. Srimad Rahasyatrayasara of Śrī Vedāntadeśika. Translated by M. R. Rajagopala Ayyangar. Kumbakonam, [1956].

--------. Śrī Pāñcarātra-rakṣā. Adyar Library Series, Volume 36. Adyar, Madras, 1967.

--------. Stotraratna-bhāṣya. Vedānta-granthamālā, Volume I. Madras: R. Venkateswar and Co., n. d.

--------. Tattvamuktākalāpaḥ with Sarvārthasiddhi. Śrīmad-Vedānta-Deśika-Granthamālā, Vedāntavibhāga. Part III. Conjeevaram, 1941.

--------. Tattva-ṭīkā. Śrī-Vaiṣṇava-Siddhānta Granthamālā, No. 2. Madras, 1938. Pp. 38-45.

HARVARD DISSERTATIONS IN RELIGION

published under the aegis of the

HARVARD THEOLOGICAL REVIEW

by

THE SCHOLARS PRESS

Harvard Dissertations in Religion **publishes outstanding dissertations in the study of religion submitted to Harvard University for the Ph.D. or Th.D. degree. Nomination of dissertations for the series is normally by the departments or thesis committees to which they have been submitted. Volumes are reproduced directly from typescript provided by the authors.**

Harvard Dissertations in Religion
Series Price: $6.00 ($4.00)

020101	*A Historical and Semantic Study of the Term "Islam"* Jane I. Smith
020102	*Jesus' Death as Saving Event* Sam K. Williams
020103	*Transformations of the War Oracle in Old Testament Prophecy* Duane L. Christensen
020104	*The Nature of Theological Argument: A Study of Paul Tillich* Robert William Schrader
020105	*Population Growth and Justice: An Examination of Moral Issues Raised by Rapid Population Growth* Ronald M. Green
020106	*The Pre-Existence of Christ in the Writings of Justin Martyr: An Exegetical Study with Reference to the Humiliation and Exaltation Christology* Demetrius C. Trakatellis
020107	*The Presentation of Biblical History in the Antiquitates Judaicae of Flavius Josephus* Harold W. Attridge
020108	*Value-Freedom in Science and Technology* Robert M. Veatch
020109	*The Combat Myth in the Book of Revelation* Adela Yarbro Collins

Harvard Dissertations in Religion publishes outstanding dissertations in the study of religion submitted to Harvard University for the Ph.D. or Th.D. degree. The goal of the HDR is to make the work of promising scholars available expeditiously and inexpensively. The HDR is published under the aegis of the *Harvard Theological Review*.

Nomination of dissertations for the HDR is normally by the departments or thesis committees to which they have been submitted, although nominations from individual faculty members will also be considered.

Volumes in the HDR are reproduced directly from the typescript provided by the authors. Responsibility therefore rests with the individual author for the accuracy and consistency of style and typography.

Caroline Bynum
George Rupp
Editors